To our genesis —
Love, Kathy

The teacher who ate her pet

The teacher
who ate her pet ...

and other true stories
by 32 people like you

Edited by Nancy Seubert

TALK PRETTY PRESS
MONROE, MICHIGAN

Although the authors, editor, and publisher have researched all sources to ensure the accuracy and completeness of the information contained in this book, we assume no responsibility for errors, inaccuracies, omissions, or any inconsistency herein.

Library of Congress Catalog Number: 2005907362

The teacher who ate her pet and other true stories by 32 people like you / edited and introduced by Nancy Seubert.
        ISBN 0-9771824-0-1

This book is printed on recycled paper.

First Talk Pretty Press USA Edition: 2006

ATTENTION CORPORATIONS, UNIVERSITIES, COLLEGES, AND PROFESSIONAL ORGANIZATIONS: Quantity discounts are available on bulk purchases of this book for educational purposes, fund-raising, or gift-giving. For information, please contact Talk Pretty Press, 102 Sheridan Drive, Monroe, MI 48162, 517.775.2636, nancyseubert@aol.com.

Acknowledgment

This book reflects the efforts of its thirty-two authors, as well as our families, in crafting and editing the stories, assembling the manuscript, working out the publication details, and designing publicity for its release. Among us, we have had varying degrees of time and energy to apply to our book, but all have given generously as we moved from an idea to a wish to a finished product.

The book is proof of our belief in each other.

I'd like to thank David Olds, the director of photography for the democratic caucus of the Michigan House of Representatives, who took photos of all but five of the authors. Based in East Lansing, Michigan, Dave has spent the last three decades covering news and sports for numerous publications and organizations, including Time Magazine, USA Today, the Associated Press, and United Press International.

The graphic artist, Susan Bamford, delivered a fine design for our cover and book interior – elegant, playful, and without revealing the identity of the pet in our title story. Thank you.

I extend my gratitude to Margaret McGinley, IHM, who applied the skills of forty-two years of teaching to our book. Although the book had been through eight screens before she read it, Margaret found the slippery grammatical errors and typos that had escaped detection.

My thanks go also to Maxine Kollasch for copy editing our book. Max has been a writer and an editor for twenty-five years. A member of the religious congregation, the Sisters, Servants of the Immaculate Heart of Mary, Max has won several writing awards and is currently a freelance writer and editor. The week she accepted this project, the book that she spent the last two years writing – *A Vision, A Voice, A Presence: The First Forty Years of the Michigan Catholic Conference* – went to press. After she finished work on this book, she began writing her own memoirs. She warns anyone who reads *The Teacher Who Ate Her Pet* to watch out – memoir-writing is contagious!

Also by Talk Pretty Press

Something that Happened at Night: A Workbook to Begin Your
Memoirs or End Writer's Block, by Nancy Seubert, 2006.
   The workbook is filled with 106 exercises, each with six writing
   prompts, chosen from the best of the author's memoir-writing
   class.

Foreword

All writing is deeply introspective. Writing about one's own life, however, is an especially intimate process and a personal product. It is a process of transformation – from a web of events and emotion into a work of art.

Some art is made to be displayed – crafted with the intent of sharing it widely. But other art, like many memoirs, is designed for an intimate audience of close friends, family – and sometimes just the artist.

We are especially lucky that the authors of this volume came together to share their stories, their past, and their art with us. In them we find laughter, inspiration, triumph, and tragedy – elements of their lives that you will find, as I did, reflected in your own.

You will also find in this book a uniquely Michigan collaboration and perspective. These are tales by people whose lives have been shaped by Michigan. And they are truly a pleasure to read.

JENNIFER M. GRANHOLM
GOVERNOR OF MICHIGAN

July 22, 2005
Lansing

Contents

Introduction

In the fall of 1995, I put together a community education class called "Life Stories: Writing Your Memoirs," which I have offered in Lansing, Michigan every fall, winter, and spring for the past ten years. All of the writers represented in this book have been through at least one eight-week session – and some have been through quite a few. Rayl Conyers, who enrolled in that first class in October, 1995, has attended every session since then. He is now ninety.

Most of the writers who have passed through our classroom have not yet achieved Rayl's seniority. About half are in our seventies and eighties and about half are in our fifties and sixties. We are farmers, psychologists, psychotherapists, educators, housewives, social workers, police officers, business people, entertainers, missionaries, and nurses. A number of writers are emigrants from other countries. In *The Teacher Who Ate Her Pet*, we have stories from Cuba, Italy, Germany, Puerto Rico, Korea, and the Philippines. Some of us are flaming liberals and some of us are dyed-in-the-wool conservatives. We are evangelicals and atheists, able-bodied and living with disabilities, widowed, divorced, married, and single.

The rich diversity of experiences reflects quite different, often opposing, viewpoints and patterns of thinking. In some social situations, that can be a problem. But when you are writing memoirs, you don't introduce yourself with a label, a title, or a philosophical position. You begin with a story. Story is the great builder of bridges. Story-telling benefits from diversity and makes the most of diversity.

Although the Life Stories class is designed for non-professional writers, many talented writers have been through the class, some with a yearning to publish. In 2004, I invited all of the writers to publish a book of our favorite memoirs. I proposed that we divide among us the expense, the page space, the work of putting the book together, the printed books, and the profits from any sales. If ten people said they were interested, I said I would guide the boat to shore.

Thirty-two people were willing to risk $500 upfront. *The Teacher Who Ate Her Pet and Other True Stories by 32 People Like You* is the compilation of our favorite memoirs.

Occasionally, a writer brings to class a work of fiction. Fiction is not technically memoir-writing, but some writers believe that we reveal ourselves more honestly through fiction than through memoir, as we tend to present what we think is our best selves in memoir. We decided to allow submissions of anything that had emerged from or been brought to the class, including poetry and opinion pieces that are not attached to a narrative. You will probably heighten your enjoyment of the stories if you use this broader definition of memoir.

All of us have a story to tell because all of us have done things and had things happen to us. That something happens at all is a kind of first order experience. But that is not enough. We tell someone else some of the things we have done and some of the things that have happened to us. As we relate what happened, we are shaping a story.

Stories are selective; they don't tell everything that happened, but just enough to convey the experience. There is a difference between watching a movie and reading a story. In a movie, there can be visual stimuli that don't detract from the story. In fact, developed scenes enhance the movie. But when you tell a story, the only way to get into the scene a woman walking down the sidewalk who has nothing to do with the plot is to go out of your way as a writer to place her there. You have to have a good reason to do so – even if she really was there in your experience. When you write a memoir, you have to choose some aspects of an event and let others go.

Now here is the tricky part. When you select and discard, you are editing for your listener. You are not presenting "the truth, the whole truth, and nothing but the truth." As I write these words, a ceiling fan hums and rotates above me, stalks of garlic dry on a garden cart on my patio about ten feet away, and a light smell of gasoline from my neighbor's car wafts through the screen door – and I have not begun to mention everything that is part of this writing experience. It would take a book to describe it all, without ever getting to a plot.

So you have the first order experience. Then you edit and shape the experience and tell someone the story. As you tell the story, you relive the experience and, at the same time, transform it. Now what happened has become a second order experience.

Stories are built for response, and your listener complies. You have told the story to elicit an endorsement of some kind and you have probably gotten one. But maybe not. Maybe there was something in the way your listener affirmed you, a hesitation or the shadow of a doubt. Or maybe your listener wanted to know more. In the exchange, the story is further shaped, this time through the influence of the listener: a third order experience.

Time passes, years pass, or you might be quickly drawn to write down the experience. What you write is not the same as what you told your friend. It would be much too boring to read that. So again you are shaping and editing, this time privately and quietly, like a spider fashioning a web. By the time you are actually writing your memoirs, you are probably in a fourth order experience.

If you take your story to a writing group or a memoir-writing class, you'll read your story to others. The writers will question you about your story content, comment about the writing techniques you used, offer suggestions for other things you might try. This feedback is not about your first order experience; it's about your fourth order experience. The interaction takes the experience to the fifth order.

A week later, or maybe five years later, maybe longer, you go back to your story and now it is the story itself that speaks to you, hinting at a pattern, attracting another memory, inviting you back for another look. You might feel like rewriting the story, placing the event in a new context. Allowing story to inform you is a sixth order experience.

Writing your memoirs is not a static event. You are changed by it. Story is not fixed and unchanging, but dynamic and interactive. If you understand this, you will not be disillusioned if a writer tells you he could have told the story another way or she merged two things that did not occupy the same time frame in her life.

I urge you to turn the page and begin reading the book. You will meet fascinating people here who share openly what is most important to them. We are like you and we are different, too.

The Teacher Who Ate Her Pet reflects the wide range of experiences of it diverse authors. It also demonstrates a variety of writing styles. One writer has the gift of dialogue, another has the ability to build tension, another offers a sense of humor, another can describe a situation so that you feel like you are there. You may find that you resonate with one author more than another, or with one of an author's stories more than another story. Our book is part of a spiraling process of self-discovery and integration. The authors and the particular stories are in different places in that process.

Each of the thirty-two authors has included a tip based on her or his experience writing memoirs. When you are finished reading the book, it is our hope that you will begin writing your own memoirs.

Nancy Seubert

Judy Rohm

I am a retired educator and lifelong writer. I attribute my love of storytelling to my witty, articulate father and the dynamic Southern Baptist evangelists who preached at my church when I was a child. They were my role models. They made me laugh, made me cry, made me seek salvation on my knees. I live in Mason, Michigan with my dog, Bugsy Malone, and three cats: Figgy, Ollie, and Razzle-Taz.

Listen to the Dialogue of Your Characters

Memoirs are powerful mirrors. Writing a memoir is kind of what we do when we dream. The characters and dialogue are all projections of the dreamer, or in the case of a memoir, the author. It's revealing and a little scary.

Some of my writing comes from my long term memory, but some of it is prompted by everyday events. This was the case with The Wrong Prescription. The details, dialogue and characterizations were easy to remember and record because the episode I wrote about was so recent. The story is truthful, with few embellishments. What I witnessed and experienced with my mother at the nursing home that day was incredible, yet on another level quite ordinary.

I got the idea for writing "The Dark Side of the Picture" from *The World Below* by Sue Miller. I thought about the hidden parts of my own world. This brought up my sister, Susan, who died shortly after birth, when I was seven years old. Although the event was significant, it was rarely talked about within our family. Sometimes I even forgot I ever had a sister. After a discussion with my book club, I wanted to find evidence of her birth and death. The search revealed a photograph of my mother when she was pregnant with Susan. I studied the old picture and the story began to unfold.

The Dark Side was harder to recreate than The Wrong Prescription because I had to pull the details and dialogue from my long term memory. I did not immediately go to the computer to write. Instead, I made lists of details I wanted to include. This particular list included the following: my mother's bathing suit; her large pregnant belly; the annoyed expression on her face; the fact that I was in the picture, floating on an inner tube; the space between my two front teeth; the fact that this picture had been framed at one time and hung in my parents' bedroom. After I made my list, I mulled things over for a few days, occasionally adding to the list. I let things simmer.

When I finally sat down at the computer the story just flowed out of me, because I had already watched and listened to the characters engage in dialogue on the screen inside my head. I wrote the memoir in one day and then revised it for days on end. The final paragraph of this story came to me after I thought I had the ending right. As I studied the photograph, I suddenly realized it was prophetic — the concerned look on my mother's face, her large pregnant belly, the fact that I was floating on an inner tube on the dark side of the picture, the fact that my father was not in the picture at all — clearly foreshadowed the events that unfolded.

The Dark Side
of the Picture

My father's funeral program listed Susan Lea as his third child.
The only other document proving her existence is a black-and-white
photograph taken in 1947.

The matted picture is an enlarged copy of the original. I
remember it in a brown frame hanging on yellow-and-white daisy
wallpaper in my parents' bedroom. I'm sure my father loved this
photograph because my mother is the focal point. She's sitting on the
edge of the dock at our cottage on L Lakes, squinting upward at the
camera. I remember the green-and-blue plaid bathing suit she's
wearing - the low v-neck revealing cleavage between her large breasts,
the flared skirted bottom circling her movie-star legs, which in this
picture dangle an inch above the water. She is beautiful and obviously
pregnant.

I'm in the picture, too, just beneath her feet, floating on my
stomach in my one-piece bathing suit on a black inner tube. My smile
toward the camera reveals a space between my two front teeth, my
mother's and brother's space, an inherited distance among us. I have
pigtails in the picture, actually French braids, my lifetime favorite hair
style, something that connected me to my mother, who braided my
hair every other day until I was thirteen years old.

As I examine the picture more closely, I realize it is an important
document, not just because it shows my mother's belly large with life,
but because it captures my mother as she was when I was a child:
complicated, a study in contrasts. Her light brown hair and white skin
highlighted in warm sunshine, her body relaxed and calm,
contradicted by her face, which conveys concern with the situation,
and maybe a slight annoyance with the photographer. Did she want to
have her picture taken? Did she want to be pregnant? How would a
seven-year-old know that for certain? I was close to my mother, but she
wasn't easy to read, especially regarding her relationship with my
father. My parents argued a lot, but there was an equal amount of
affection between them. I never questioned my father's love for my
mother, but her devotion was more complicated, seemed more
conditional. I heard mixed messages, saw ambivalent facial

expressions, and a vacillating passion for him and what they did on Sundays – what they did after they attended the First Baptist Church with its red neon "Jesus Saves" sign; what they did after we ate roast chicken, homemade noodles, mashed potatoes and gravy; what they did after my brother and I went outside or over to a friend's house to play and the front and back doors were locked. Sometimes when it rained, we were allowed to stay on the glassed-in front porch if we had nowhere else to go, but unless we were sick, we had to wait until after 4:00 p.m. before we could come back inside the house. They always said they were napping, but by the time my brother was ten and I was seven, we knew the Baptist Church wasn't the only place where my parents sought redemption.

Shortly before the baby was born, my parents had an argument over whether or not my father should go on his annual week-long deer hunting excursion. My mother thought it was too close to the expected delivery date – what if the baby came early, what if the weather was bad and he couldn't get home in time? – but my optimistic father argued that my brother and I had not been premature, that he would be home with his twelve-point buck at least two weeks before this baby was born, and that his mother had agreed to come and stay with Mama just in case she needed extra help while he was away.

Finally my mother relented. "You do what you have to do; I don't want to deprive you of something you look forward to all year." But there was an edge in her voice. I'm sure my father heard it. My brother and I learned at an early age that her tone, not her words, was what mattered. My father knew it too, but chose that day to focus on the words because the words said what he wanted to hear. I think he regretted this momentary deafness for the rest of his life.

On the day he left for deer hunting, an air of tension competed with aromas of Mama's famous baked chicken, homemade chili, Dutch apple pie, and chocolate walnut brownies. She had gotten up at four in the morning to make some of his favorite foods, but by noon, when my father and grandfather pulled out of the gravel driveway, only my grandmother, my brother, and I waved goodbye. Mama remained inside the house, stretched out on the living room couch.

I remember watching as my father leaned over to kiss her just before he left. She was lying on her back, the only comfortable position, and as he bent closer she turned her head toward the back of the flowered couch. He kissed her cheek and, with his hand, gently turned her face toward him so he could kiss her on the lips. She sighed loudly and obliged, but with her mouth rigid and closed.

"Are you going to be okay?" he asked, hoping the answer would be yes.

"Of course I am," she responded in a chilly monotone. "Don't give it a second thought."

"Honey, everything will be fine. I'll be home in a week," he tried to reassure her. "Remember, Dr. Fochman said he was pretty sure you'll have another month before delivery." She didn't respond, but he couldn't stop searching for the magic words. "Are you as excited as I am?" he asked.

This got a response. "Excited about what, your deer hunting trip up north or the prospect of me being without you for a week?"

Ignoring the icy sarcasm, he gently patted her huge belly, "You know I was referring to our baby."

"You better get on the road," she said, shifting her face again toward the back of the couch. "You're way behind schedule."

But the baby came ahead of schedule, came three days after my father drove away. I hardly remember the specific details about what happened to my mother and the baby. It's like I was wearing a blindfold and earmuffs. I can only bring back emotions, moments, and snapshots like the one of my mother on the dock with me in the water on my black inner tube.

What I remember instead was a sense of helplessness, of everything going wrong, "going from bad to worse," as Grandma put it.

It took almost eight hours for them to find my mother's doctor and even longer for the State Police to locate my father. There was no phone at the hunting lodge.

By the time he got home, the baby had been born, and my mother wasn't expected to live. My brother and I were not allowed to see our mother or the baby. Only our father could go, and we could tell by his red swollen eyes each time he returned that things were not going well.

"We need to say a prayer for Mama and the baby," he told us at the kitchen table before we ate tomato soup and grilled cheese sandwiches.

One day he came home and spoke privately with my grandparents in the kitchen. Their voices were hushed, but I could hear that he was crying. When he called my brother and me to join him in the living room, I burst out sobbing before he had a chance to talk to us. After he told us the baby died, I felt hugely relieved that it wasn't my mother.

"Does Mama know? Is she okay?" I asked him. "No, she doesn't know, and no, Judy, she is not okay."

I'd never been to a funeral home before, but my father insisted that my brother and I see our sister before she was buried. She didn't look real to me. She was more like a china doll laid out in a little white casket. She was wearing a pink dress with white satin trim and had a little gold ring on one of her fingers. What upset me most was the size of her head. It seemed too big for her body. My dad said a prayer and kissed her mouth. I wanted to touch her but was afraid. My brother turned away. I think he was crying. There wasn't a funeral service, just our private viewing.

As scary as it was to see our baby sister in a casket, it was even more frightening to see and hear the changes in Mama after she got home from the Sparta Clinic.

"Oh my God, they're up there on the ceiling! Get them down. They're going to kill me. Oh God, I'm going to bleed to death!"

"No, no, Grayce, nothing is on the ceiling. It's the medication." Grandma was in the bedroom trying to calm Mama. "You're back home and perfectly safe."

"Where is my baby? Those monkeys took my baby!" Mama was crying inconsolably.

"I'm going to make you some tea." Grandma opened the bedroom door before I had a chance to dash out of sight. "What are you doing, little Missy?" she asked in a hushed voice, pushing me into the kitchen. "You know that you and your brother are supposed to stay away from her bedroom." She looked at me sympathetically while she filled the tea kettle. "After I take your mother some tea, why don't you and I sit here at the table, have some hot chocolate, and read one of your Sugar Creek Gang books?"

Grandma could shield us somewhat in the daytime, but at night, my brother and I could hear Mama screaming from our upstairs bedrooms. She was usually yelling at my dad, "Where is my baby? You killed my baby. Get out of here. I don't know who you are."

The doctor came every day, but Mama didn't get better. "As soon as a bed opens up in Blodgett Hospital, she'll have to go in for a complete hysterectomy," he told my father. "She's still bleeding and the infection just won't go away."

It would require two major surgeries to remove her female organs and repair the internal damage. Some of the damage was beyond repair, like her relentless grief over losing the baby and her bitter resentment toward my father for not being there when she needed him most. For months she refused to attend the First Baptist Church, dropped out of the church choir, which my father directed, and kept her head up and her eyes open during his mealtime prayers at the kitchen table. Sundays would not be about forgiveness or redemption for a long time.

Re-examining the old photograph, I realize there are two distinct sides to the picture: a bright side and a dark side. My pregnant mother sits on the dock with her toes dangling just above the water on the bright side of the picture, whereas I am on the dark side, floating in the lake on a black inner tube. It may be prophetic that while my mother's beautiful face is bathed in sunshine, she is not smiling. It may be equally prophetic that while my father is the one who planted the seed in my mother's belly, he is not in the picture. Instead, he played the photographer, the one who captured and preserved this moment in time.

The Wrong Prescription

"You're a bitch," Agnes shouted at Millie as I entered the gold dining room, a small eating area for residents who required mealtime assistance.

"Stop using that language, Agnes," a nursing assistant named Rhonda interceded from another table where she was hand-feeding a resident.

"She's eating her dessert first," Agnes complained, grabbing Millie's hand and forkful of apple pie before it reached her mouth. "Drop the fork, you bitch," she snapped through gritted yellow teeth. Millie looked bewildered but refused to surrender her forkful of pie.

Rhonda got up and stood between the two elderly women. "Let go of her right now, Agnes. Millie can eat her dessert first if she wants to." She stared at Agnes until she let go of Millie's fork. "If you touch or threaten anyone again," Rhonda warned Agnes, "you're going to eat in your room by yourself."

"You're a bitch, too," Agnes muttered under her breath.

Ignoring the remark, Rhonda turned in my direction. "Hi, Judy," she said, rolling her eyes as she walked to another table to open a milk carton for a woman whose arm was in a cast.

"Hi, Rhonda. I won't ask how your day is going," I joked, looking down at my mother who was swirling her fingers in mashed potatoes and gravy. Two other residents at her table were eating with forks. I bent down to kiss my mother's cheek, "Hi, Sweetheart, how are you?"

"Fine," she grinned, sucking gravy and mashed potatoes from her fingers.

"Do you know who I am?" I asked, wiping her hand with a napkin. I often asked this question to gauge the progression of her Alzheimer's disease. Half the time she answered with, "My beautiful daughter" - the answer I obviously wanted - and other times she identified me as someone else from her past.

On this day she took a long time before answering. I think she was studying my face. I was studying her face, too, because she was wearing a hairnet and someone else's glasses. "You're Fanchion," she said finally.

This response hit a nerve. Aunt Fanchion, my father's sister, was twenty-seven years older than I am and had been dead for eight years. Unfortunately, there were certain things about my face as I grew older - jowls, deep wrinkles, lizard-eyelids - that I feared were somewhat similar to Aunt Fanchion's face. "Mom, it's Judy, your daughter. Do I really look like Aunt Fanchion?"

"You resemble her," she said, plunging her fingers into a pile of sauerkraut.

"Here, let me help you." I filled her fork and lifted it to her mouth. "You know how to eat with a fork, Mom; you really shouldn't use your fingers." The nursing assistants were more lenient because in their words, "she was a good eater," but it bothered me to see my mother, who had always been fastidious and proper, eating like a two-year-old. "Whose glasses are you wearing?"

"Mine." She reached into the mashed potatoes before I could stop her.

"Those aren't your glasses, Mother; they don't look anything like your glasses." The glasses she was wearing had elaborate frames, black and gold bows flared out to diamond studded cat-eye corners and ¼-inch thick lenses. Some resident who was extremely nearsighted was feeling her way around the facility in my mother's farsighted prescription. "I don't know how you can see anything through those Coke bottle lenses. Isn't everything blurry?" I was trying to rationalize why she confused me with Aunt Fanchion.

"I see just fine," she said through a mouthful of mashed potatoes.

"Those are the ones she had on all day," Rhonda, the nursing assistant, chimed in from the other table. "I put them on her after her morning nap." She walked over to my mom's table to get a better look at the glasses. "Are you sure these aren't hers?"

"My mother's glasses aren't as elaborate and the lens is thinner," I told her, reaching to lift the frames off my mother's face.

"Don't take them off." My mother was annoyed.

"We're just going to look at them for a minute," Rhonda assured her, gently lifting the frames from my mother's frowning face. "I don't see any name in these." She carefully examined both bows. Everything was supposed to be labeled at the nursing home, every personal belonging, every item of clothing, including shoes. "Were your mother's glasses labeled?"

"Yes, I watched them do it." The facility had an electric tool for engraving names. I remembered watching the unit secretary engrave my mother's glasses the first day she entered. "Why is she wearing that hairnet, Rhonda?" I asked, knowing my mother wouldn't remember why.

Rhonda laughed. "They put it on her in the beauty shop the other day. Wilma buys them for some of the residents to wear when they're in bed, but Grayce likes wearing hers all the time. I tried bribing her with a lemon drop this morning, but she wouldn't let me remove it."

"I want my glasses back." My mother was reaching for the Hollywood frames with sauerkraut and gravy dripping off her fingers.

"We're going to borrow them for a little while, Grayce," Rhonda explained. "You'll get your glasses back later."

"Hey, hey you, hey —" It was Agnes again, looking at Rhonda while pointing a bony finger at Millie's glass of juice.

Rhonda turned around, "What, Agnes? Now what's wrong?"

"What's she got in that glass, what's that red stuff, is it wine? Where is mine?"

"No, it's not wine, Agnes. It's cranberry juice. I gave you apple juice because a month ago you said you hated cranberry juice. Have you changed your mind?'

"No, I thought it was wine," she muttered.

"Don't we wish," Rhonda said, turning back to my mother and me.

I laughed. "Do you think they put the wrong ones on her in the beauty shop?"

"Happens all the time." Rhonda shook her head. "We'll check all the residents who got their hair done on Wednesday."

"Wouldn't someone have complained by now? That was two days ago."

"Sad thing is most of them don't know the difference," she said. "We could give them frames with window glass and they wouldn't complain."

I thought about how I washed my mother's glasses each time I visited. It was something the nursing assistants obviously didn't have time to do. With 200 elderly residents to dress, feed and take to the bathroom several times a day, lens cleaning had to be one of the lowest priorities.

I never complained because overall my mother received excellent care and the facility was immaculate. Still it bothered me to see her lenses speckled with little particles of food, and I couldn't imagine how she could see anything. I guess it's hard for me to realize that the condition and prescription of the lenses aren't the only factors involved in vision.

"Judy, if you're going to be walking your mom around in the wheelchair for awhile, would you please check with Wilma in the beauty shop to see if her glasses might be down there?" Rhonda asked. "Let us know if you find them."

On the way to the beauty salon, my mother flinched when I kissed the top of her head. "What's wrong, Mother? Are you upset with me?"

"Why do you always think you know everything?" she asked with a frustrated tone in her voice.

"Mother, I know what your glasses look like."

"Don't you think I know what my glasses look like?"

Before we got to the beauty salon, we stopped in the atrium where I directed her attention to some of the pretty little birds in the aviary and pacified her with a strawberry Creme Saver. My pockets were always full of candy when I came to visit her. The aides often called my mother "Sugar" or "Sweetie," not only because she usually fit that description, but because she was addicted to Jelly Bellies, chocolate and ice cream.

"My mom's hair looks great," I told Wilma before asking about her glasses. "And thanks for giving her the hairnet. She likes it so much she won't let anyone take if off."

Wilma looked up from the salon sink where she was scrubbing someone's thick silver hair. "That's not all bad," she chuckled. "That shitty fine hair of hers won't hold a set for anything."

Laughing, I nodded my own head covered with that same shitty fine hair. "Wilma, did my mother by any chance leave her glasses down here when she got her hair done this week?" I asked, as diplomatically as I could.

"I don't think your mother was even wearing glasses when she came down here," Wilma said defensively. "Anyway we're pretty careful not to get them mixed up."

"Well, she ended up with someone else's glasses, and they aren't close to her prescription," I tried to explain.

"You think you've got problems; look at Helen over there." Wilma hollered over the roar of the dryers, "Show them what you lost, Helen."

Helen, a heavy-set woman in a pretty paisley dress, smiled from under a hair dryer as she pointed to her bottom missing dentures.

"Oh, my God, you mean she lost her teeth," I gasped.

"She didn't lose them; some other resident must have taken them out of her room or an aide misplaced them after cleaning them." Wilma shook her head. "That kind of thing happens all the time around here."

When my mother and I got back to the south unit, the aides greeted us with big smiles. "We're over halfway through Wednesday's beauty shop list. We didn't find Grayce's glasses yet, but we did find four other residents who were wearing someone else's glasses." They burst out laughing and I laughed, too. "One woman who doesn't even own a pair of glasses had on Alma Hodges' glasses which have been lost for over a month." Tammy smiled, pleased with her detective work

"I want them back." My mother was eyeing the cat-eye frames in Tammy's hand.

"How come these glasses weren't engraved like all the others?" I asked.

"Just slipped through the crack. Probably belong to a new resident and things got busy when she entered the facility," Rhonda explained.

A nurse sitting behind the circular desk looked up from her work. "Did Francis Zimmerman get her hair done on Wednesday? She's only been here a couple of weeks."

Rhonda looked at the list. "Yeah, great idea, Barb. We'll check her out," she called over her shoulder, already moving toward the green hall, and gesturing for Tammy, my mother and me to follow.

Francis Zimmerman was in room 227 sitting by the window with a magazine on her lap. I could see from the doorway that she was an attractive, sophisticated woman with beautiful silver hair. I could also see that she was wearing my mother's glasses.

"Hello, Francis," Rhonda greeted her loudly, bending close to Francis's ear. She had a hearing aid in her ear, but evidently it didn't work well. "We wondered if you'd let us look at the glasses you're wearing; we think they might be Grayce's," she said, pointing at my mother in the wheelchair. "And that these," - she pointed at the ones Tammy was holding - "might be yours."

"Oh, I don't want a different pair of glasses," she said in a refined voice.

Rhonda smiled and tried again, this time louder. "But these might not be yours," she shouted, touching the bow on Francis's glasses. "We need to check them to make sure."

Francis looked bewildered but she slowly removed the glasses and handed them over. Rhonda held them up toward the window to check for a name. "Bingo. It says Grayce Rohm," she said with a proud smile. "Here, Grayce, these are yours." My mother looked at her glasses as if she'd never seen them before.

Tammy moved close to Francis. "Here, Francis, we think these are yours," she shouted, placing the cat-eye frames on Francis's face.

Francis looked out the window and then down at the magazine in her lap. "Oh, I do see a lot better in these," she exclaimed with a smile. "She can have the other ones," she added.

After I thanked the assistants for all their help, I pushed the wheelchair down the long red hall. "Well, we finally got that solved," I said as we entered my mother's room. "Aren't you glad to have your glasses back?"

"No, but I know you are." She was reaching for the jar of Jelly Bellies on her night stand.

"But, Mom, don't you see better now?"

"I saw just fine with the other glasses."

"No, you didn't; you thought I was Aunt Fanchion."

"Well," she said, looking up at me, "you still look like Aunt Fanchion through these glasses."

Was she serious or was it the dementia? Was she getting back at me for making a big deal about the glasses or did I really look that much like my deceased aunt? The ambivalent expression on her face as she munched on the Jelly Bellies was impossible to read. Handicapped with Parkinson's and Alzheimer's diseases, my mother didn't know how to get to the dining room, the beauty salon or even her own room, but she could still get to me.

TESS WIELAND

As a teacher in elementary school, first in Germany and then in the United States, I was upset when my students always groaned about another social studies class. How could they find the study of history boring when I was intrigued by the impact of time and place on peoples' lives?

I was born in Bremen, Germany, in 1938, a year before Hitler invaded Poland. As a child, I huddled with my parents in bunkers during the nightly allied air raids on Berlin. We were in Berlin when the city fell to the fury of the Red Army. We greeted the American occupation forces in our part of the city and shivered hungrily through the Russian blockade. Little did I know then that one day I would marry an American, come to this country, and share my stories with my new friends.

The year 1999 brought more changes in my life. After thirty-nine years of teaching, I retired. Finally, I would have time to do whatever I wanted.

Think about How the Larger Forces of History Have Affected You

My daughter often asked me for stories about my childhood experiences which were so different from hers. Here was my chance to share my thoughts about the intertwined connections between people and history. I never regretted my decision to relive the good and bad times in my writing. Many of the twists and knots in my relationship with my parents became untangled while reflecting on my life. I realized that beyond horror and fear I experienced the joys of a protected childhood and the excitements of growing up in a big city.

When my husband and I moved to Georgia, I joined a local writers' group. The support of my fellow writers and the interest my husband, Art, shows in my stories encouraged me to continue with my memoirs.

I enjoy working in my garden, listening to the birds and realize that it is little things in life that bring meaning to a world full of turmoil. I hope I will complete my life stories one day and dream about a grandchild who might some day read them and like social studies.

The Blockade

Berlin, Germany, November 1948

My shoulder is cold from sticking out of the comforter. I pull a corner up so that it covers me and try to hold on to my Dr. Doolittle book. "Waltraud, make sure you get your homework done. Put your book aside," my mother calls. I hear her moving around in the kitchen where she is busy preparing dinner. It is snowy and windy outside. Big ice crystals form inside our bedroom window, but it is comfortable in my featherbed. Oh ya, my homework. Reluctantly, I put my book aside and turn my attention to math. It is too nasty to go outside so I will have plenty of time to get my work done. My mother, who is wearing her heavy winter coat, comes into the room. "I have everything ready to go as soon as the power comes on," she says. In answer, my stomach rumbles.

"How come we have to wait until four o'clock before you can cook? I am hungry now," I say.

"I told you before, it's because of the blockade," my mother answers. "You know that the Russians have closed all the roads into Berlin. Trucks and trains cannot get here. There is no food and coal arriving in Berlin."

I nod my head. I have heard this story before. I know. Everything is rationed and I am always hungry. My stomach continues to growl as I wish for a tasty stew with real carrots and potatoes, not the dried ones we eat now.

Our daily lives are strange. Each section of the city has electricity for two hours a day on a rotating basis. When we have power from 2:00-4:00 a.m., we get up in the middle of the night. Mutti cooks and irons while I play a game at the kitchen table.

It is one of the coldest winters ever. Coal for the *Kachel-Ofen* that heats the apartment is very limited and there is no wood. All the trees in Berlin have been cut down for firewood. We spend a lot of time in bed to keep warm. When the sun is out, I spend many hours with my mother all over Berlin hunting for stores that might carry margarine or bread.

I hear the constant drone of the airlift planes. Tempelhof Airport is nearby. Every three minutes a plane takes off or lands, day and night. I have become used to their constant roar and sleep right through it. My friend Ruth told me that she finally caught one of the little candy parachutes that some pilots drop over Berlin. How lucky! The parachutes have Hershey bars and gum attached and are eagerly hunted for by the kids of Berlin. We call the pilots who release them "candy-bombers." Usually there are so many kids pushing and shoving to get one of them that I have given up. Anyhow, my dad does not want me to "beg," as he calls it. Easy for him to say: he works for the Americans at the airport and he can eat whatever he wants.

When I beg him to bring some food home, he shakes his head sadly. "You remember what happened to Herr Mueller?" he asks. One day as I picked my dad up from work, I saw American MPs beating Herr Mueller across the legs with nightsticks. Then they yanked him into the guard building and he lost his job. "That's what happens if you get caught taking food through the gate. I can't risk that, Waltraud," Dad says.

I think the behavior of the Americans is weird. They are usually so generous, passing out candy to kids and feeding us at school. Why are they so mean to Herr Mueller, who only took some of the donuts? They have so much food, enough for all of us. My dad eats at the airport so that Mom and I can use his rations. Yet, how I would love to gorge on his donuts instead of getting an extra portion of powdered soup.

One day while I am playing at home, Dad arrives looking mysterious. "What is the matter with you, Willi?" Mom sounds concerned.

"I don't know," says Dad, "I think I caught some lice at work. I have such an itching on my head. Waltraud, will you take my hat off and check?" he asks.

"Yuck, lice," I yell. Many kids in my class have had them and I know well what he is talking about. I am not too pleased with his request to check his head. But he insists so I take his hat off using only the tips of my thumb and index finger. There, on top of his head is a Hershey bar!

"Now don't expect that every night," Dad says while I rip off the wrapper.

School is also strange this winter. Most of the buildings are closed, and our unheated school operates on a short schedule. Each morning we line up in the schoolyard. In our satchels we carry only notebooks and empty containers for the powdered food that is distributed at school. First, we line up for breakfast. In the American sector, all students get a hot breakfast, *Gries mit Rosinen*, oatmeal with raisins. Each morning I hope for something different, but the sweet smell of oatmeal always greets me in the cafeteria. I hate the raisins: too long in the oatmeal, they make a slimy squish when I bite them. I try to swallow them quickly without chewing.

In the next line, we receive portions of milk powder or scoops of powdered mashed potatoes to take home. Everything we eat is a powder. Just add water and, presto, you have milk, scrambled eggs, or vegetable soup. I get warm in the steamy cafeteria and open my coat just a bit. I know it will be cold in the classroom.

Our teacher, who is waiting at her desk, is wearing an old coat, scarf, and boots. She has to take her gloves off to handle our notebooks. Once in a while she blows into her hands to warm them. I see her breath steaming over her cupped hands. I line up at her desk and take my notebook with my completed homework out of my satchel. "You did a good job yesterday," she says. "Make sure you check your division answers before you turn them in. You remember how to do it?" she asks. I nod my head and we exchange notebooks.

Even through layers of my winter clothes, my chair is so cold I only kneel on it. At first, I try to copy my assignments from the board with mittens on. But it is difficult to hold the pencil, so I remove one mitten and hurry through copying. As soon as all the students are done, we will be dismissed and school is finished. We all go home with a load of practice exercises to be completed for the next day. There are several math problems, a reading assignment, plus some writing. Mrs. Becker will collect everything the next day. I enjoy imagining her in her in her featherbed with piles of our notebooks all around her.

After eleven months, our strange way of life ends. The Russians, worried about U.S. atomic weapons being moved to Europe, open the roads to the city in May 1949. Stores open and three million scrawny Berliners rush to devour the fresh produce.

I still have my love for food and my fast eating habits. My family often kids me at the dinner table. "Slow down, Tess, the blockade is over."

The Russians Arrive

I knew my world was coming to an end in April 1945. Nightly bombings and the dash to the bunker had stopped. Dad told me the war was over in Aachen, where my grandparents lived near the Dutch border, but fighting continued around Berlin. "The Russians are near, but because our soldiers hold the *Stadtmitte*, they will keep shooting at us until the last German gives up," he said.

With grim faces, we moved my bed into the basement storage area along with suitcases full of clothes and pillows and blankets for makeshift beds for us. Our storage area was a compartment at the end of a long hall of similar cubicles with wooden slats separating each renter's unit.

I was puzzled when Dad told me we would all live there the next few days. How would we undress and go to bed in sight of the Werners next to us? And, if there were no air raids, why didn't we just stay upstairs in our apartment? Neither of my parents answered these questions. All grown-ups were preoccupied. Even my dad, who usually smiled and talked a lot, was worried and quiet.

Later that day, Dad and other men in the apartment building dug a deep hole in the courtyard. They tossed home-guard guns into it along with the red and black swastika flag that had flown over the entrance to our building. Some neighbors threw books and even pictures of Hitler into the hole. Then the men covered it all with dirt and trampled the mound flat. In the afternoon I heard a new noise, a screaming whistle followed by an explosion. "Stalin Organ," my father said. "We better go into the basement."

People from our building were down there. There were also about a dozen women, workers from Tempelhof Airport who could no longer reach their homes and sought shelter in our building. Nobody slept.

Shortly after midnight, soldiers with odd uniforms and strange helmets appeared in our basement. Their leader spoke German. He ordered us into a big room and explained that the "Glorious Red Army" had delivered the city of Berlin. He urged us to be quiet and cooperative and to stay in the basement until all fighting stopped.

Then the German people would be liberated from Nazi oppression. A young soldier behind him shouted with a broad grin, "Hitler *kaputt*," drawing his finger across his throat.

I was relieved. The war was over, and the Russians seemed much nicer than people had feared. Strangely, none of the adults around me showed any relief. "Don't believe a word they are saying," said Herr Kupke. His daughter, Marlies, had told me that the Kupkes had fled from the Russians in Silesia. She did not like talking about that and was often upset and cried a lot. "These are their elite troops trying to make us feel safe," continued Herr Kupke. "When the Cossacks come, the raping and killing will begin."

We trudged back to our cubicles. Now the power was out and the basement was dark, with only candles lighting up small areas. We sat waiting, for what, no one seemed to know. I heard screeching shells and staccato tat-tat of machine guns above. After a long time, I heard the heavy clunking of boots at the entrance to the basement. Russian voices yelled "*Stoi!*" and "*Frau komm!*" Women screamed and men cried out. Footsteps came closer to our end of the basement hall. My father told my mother to hide under my bed and put me into my bed telling me to "pretend sleep" and not to let anyone know where my mother was.

Obediently, with my heart pounding, I squeezed my eyes shut. What was going on? Several soldiers entered the cubicles of our neighbors. "*Frau komm!*" a voice yelled. I heard Frau Werner plead, "Go with them, Otto, don't make a fuss." Soon, I heard Frau Werner whimper and the Cossack groaning. I did not dare open my eyes or move. The door to our area flew open and a voice demanded, "*Frau komm!*"

"*Nix Frau,*" my father said. A soldier bent over my bed and lifted me up. He said strange words to me and rubbed my head. I laughed, trying hard to keep his attention focused on me, away from my mother hidden under the bed. I sensed something dreadful would happen if he discovered her. He fumbled through his pockets in search of something he could give me. When he could not find anything, he put me back into my bed, rubbing my cheek. His breath stunk of alcohol.

Turning to my father, the soldier demanded, "*Uri, Uri!*" He pointed at his forearm that sported several wristwatches. My father understood, removed his watch, and gave it to him. Another Russian appeared at the door, but the first one talked to him rapidly and they both left. It was quiet after this. I could hear the Werners whispering to each other. The sound of boots and yelling ceased in other parts of the basement, too.

"We cannot stay here," my father told my mother. They discussed what to do. "We have to leave Berlin. We will go to Aachen and stay there," my father said. When my mother objected that no trains were running, he replied, "Then we walk."

Walk? I had visited Oma and Opa in Aachen by train. It took a full day to get there. How on earth could we walk there? We would never make it. Surely, Dad had a better plan that he did not want to explain right now.

Mom got me out of bed and dressed me in several layers of clothes. She ignored my protests that I was too hot. She also put on several layers of clothes and stuffed a backpack with more clothing items. My father picked up one of the suitcases; I headed for my doll and teddy bear. "Leave them here, Waltraud." My father's voice sounded so stern that I dared not protest.

The early daylight was just barely visible on the horizon. As we left in the false dawn, I saw our street for the first time in several days. Bombs and rockets had hit many houses, and walls and roofs were blown away. A toilet dangled at an odd angle from a building missing its side and part of the floor. Abandoned vehicles cluttered the street – jeeps, cars, and even a tank. Toward the center of the city, the sky was bright from fires. The sound of gunfire also came from that direction.

We walked down streets, staying close to the sides of buildings. The *Stalin-Orgels* began their song of destruction. Dad pushed us into the nearest building, where we waited for the sound of the detonation. The rockets were aimed at the center of the city and exploded in the distance. But my father did not want to chance an errant rocket exploding nearby, so we continued our dash into buildings.

Away from our part of the city the scene changed. Dead soldiers lay on the streets, looking as if they had fallen asleep in strange positions, with their arms and legs spread away from their bodies, their eyes wide open. They seemed almost peaceful. My father tried to shield me from the sights by pulling me close to his body. But I could not stop looking. I was not scared. I was only upset when I saw the carcass of a dead horse in the street. It looked huge, its belly ripped open, the insides spilling out.

By midday we came to the outskirts of Berlin and saw many more

Russian soldiers. One group was laughing and singing in front of a store. One soldier was sitting on a toy horse, hollering and grinning. Many of them were loaded with things they had taken from stores and buildings. My father realized that it was too dangerous to continue now. We would have to find a safe place and go on later. We turned into an apartment building and found our way into the basement. Many people were crowded into a tight space. I had the dreadful feeling of being back at the scene of last night's events. I did not want to stay here, but as soon as I stretched out on a blanket, I fell asleep, holding my father's hand.

We stayed there overnight. I woke up the next morning hearing my father discuss with other men the possibilities of getting to the West. Some of the other children were at the basement door. No adult was paying attention. They motioned to me to come along. Together we snuck out of the basement, leaving the arguing adults behind.

It was a wonderful spring day. The sun was shining, the air felt warm, and it was very quiet, an ideal day for a game of tag or hide-and-seek. We had a great time running around in the backyard and even ventured into the street. Our fun stopped abruptly when we saw a Russian soldier. He smiled and came toward us, jabbering something we could not understand. We froze, unsure of what would happen next. He took the hand of one of the boys, laughed and motioned him to walk with him. The boy looked desperate, not knowing what to do. I longed to be back in the crowded basement with our parents. The boy probably did, too, as he took steps into the building. We fell in line behind them.

When we appeared inside the basement, all talk between the adults stopped. The women grabbed scarves and pulled them over their faces. The boy yanked his hand free and ran to his mother. The rest of us kids stood by the door. I felt awful and guilty. What had we done? The soldier stared at the group of adults, then turned around and left without speaking a word.

As soon as he was gone, everyone began yelling at us. We had given away our hiding place, the Russian would surely return with more soldiers, and it was our fault. A flurry of packing began. My father took our suitcase. Wordlessly he took my hand, and we left. He did not scold me; he did not say anything. That made me feel even worse. I wished I had never joined the group of kids. After a long time, I finally dared to ask whether we were still going to Aachen. I was relieved to find out that we were now headed for Neu-Koelln, a

Berlin borough not far from Tempelhof. We would stay there with Aunt Martha until it was safe to return to our apartment.

Years later, I found out why Neu-Koelln was a safer place, why the Russians did not rape and plunder there. This section had been the center of German Communists and the resistance movement to Hitler. Because many workers were members of the underground Communist Party, there were orders to abstain from crime and pillage in this part of town. Here the Red Army was to be a comrade in the struggle against Nazi oppression. We stayed there several days, until the end of the war in May 1945.

My feelings for my parents changed during this time. I sensed that my parents could not do everything. They were sometimes as helpless and frightened as I was. All their love could not always protect me. I loved my dad even more, understanding that he would try to do the impossible to protect me. But I never again believed "Father knows best." That led to many conflicts later, when he tried to assume his old role again.

The Glass

A strange man stands at our kitchen sink. I watch him from the door as he carefully washes and rinses a glass. Then he does it again. What is he doing? It seems he must rub out a stain that only he can see. Finally satisfied, he turns to my mother. "Thank you, Madam, thank you so much for the drink of water. I truly thank you."

He bows and hands the glass to my mother, who takes it wordlessly. The man shuffles to the door where I stand. He looks thin, stooped, and gray. His eyes, cast down to the floor, avoid looking at me. His head is shaved. When he passes me, he pushes himself into the wall, giving me as much space as he can. He tries to make himself invisible.

Only now do I notice the yellow star on the sleeve of his jacket. I have seen people with the yellow star before. "Jews," my mother explains when I ask about the stars on their clothes.

Later, I want to find out what a Jew is and why we do not have yellow stars. My mother and I are in the dairy store getting our ration of milk and margarine. The store is full of people standing in a long line before the counter. In front of the counter, but to the side, stands a woman with a star on her coat. Nobody looks at her; the clerk does not offer to help her. One after another, all customers are served. We receive our portions of dairy products, yet the woman stands alone there, her ration cards in her hand.

On the way out, I ask my mother why nobody has served the woman. "She was there before us. How come we got our stuff and she did not?" I want to know.

"She is Jewish," my mother replies. When I start to ask more, my mother interrupts me. "You ask too many questions."

That is it. We never talk about the Jews during the war. I see less and less of the people with the yellow star as I grow older, until finally I completely forget about them.

In the 1950s, as a high school student, I remember these childhood events. We were studying German history. After reading about knights, kings, wars, and conquests, we reached the 20th century. My classmates and I were confronted with images of concentration camps. Humans as thin as skeletons walked around in striped suits. From the pages, their hollow eyes stared at us. In films, trainloads of Jews were being transported to camps, like cattle to the slaughter. Auschwitz, Dachau, Treblinka, and Mauthausen were names that started to haunt me.

Amidst all the sorrow and horror I felt, was the lingering doubt that said, "Your people did this. They let it happen." I tried to fight it. Could my parents have done this? Or was it just a lot of anti-German propaganda?

Next time I did not give up when my father tried to avoid the topic. "Is it true what I read about the crimes against the Jews? How could it have happened, Dad?"

My father looked uneasy. After a long pause he said, "Yes, some of this happened. Don't believe everything you read though," he added quickly.

The Holocaust became my obsession. It was hard to find a lot of information about Nazi atrocities in 1953. The German people preferred to ignore the topic. "This is long over. One should forget about it. I don't want to talk about it." These were answers I often heard. But the subject would not go away. The publication of *The Diary of Anne Frank* and broadcasts on the new German TV system added the word "Holocaust" to the German language. Yet few would come to grips with the facts.

Many nights I cried myself to sleep after reading about Hitler's final solution to the Jewish question. I was horrified and deeply ashamed to be a German. My parents, my family, my teachers – had all remained silent as these crimes were committed? If so, where was their humanity?

As a teenager, I struggled with the usual feelings of inadequacy as well as conflicts with my parents. But worst of all was the sense that I faced a generation of grown-ups who had all become guilty: guilty of helping in these acts or guilty of allowing them to happen.

"Nonsense!" roared my father. "We did not know what was going on. How can you hold me responsible for these mass murders?"

He was as angry at my accusations as he was deeply puzzled. He obviously did not feel any guilt. He himself had never done anything to harm another person. I knew that. I knew that my father disliked memberships in any organized group. He had never been a member of the Nazi party. He much preferred evenings on the couch to party meetings.

That left the question of whether or not he could have known what was going on around him. My father was not alone in this amnesia. The entire population of Germany claimed innocence by ignorance.

"How could you not have known, when things happened right under your nose?" I persisted. "The *Kristall Nacht* did not happen secretly. You saw the Jews wearing the Star of David. Did you not wonder why all the Jews disappeared?"

My father looked sad and tried to take my hand, but I pulled away. "I could not have done anything about it, Waltraud. If I had dared to speak out against it, they would have arrested me. And who would have taken care of you then?" he asked quietly.

I was torn between accepting my father's love for me, and the guilty feeling that my own safety had been bought with the death of Jewish children whose parents could not protect them. I pulled farther and farther away from him. I was sure that I hated him and all that he stood for.

My father was hurt by my behavior. He would never accept responsibility for what had happened and scoffed at the notion of collective guilt. Finally he reverted to his role of authority, telling me I was his child and had no right to question his actions. Neither one of us was able to overcome what stood between us.

My mother did not participate in these arguments. She did not try to defend herself. In her mind she could not be responsible because she did not know what had happened. She also thought that the whole notion of collective guilt was nonsense. "Hitler was not even a German. He was Austrian," she huffed. "Your dad did not even join the party. I often thought it could have helped his career. But on the other hand," she continued, "after the war, we were glad he did not need de-Nazification papers."

But even my practical mother must have thought more about the Jewish question. She recalled, "I once gave a Jewish man a glass of water after he cleaned the apartment building. I have nothing to be ashamed of. I was as kind to them as I could be."

There he was again, that man who so urgently tried to wipe off the stain that his Jewish lips might have left on a glass. His spirit had been broken so that even he believed that he was less than a human being.

To this day I feel guilt and shame for the acts committed in my name. I am German and I cannot untangle myself from my country's name. I no longer hate my father. I do understand what he tried to tell me so long ago. Who can say how one would act when doing the right thing could have meant jeopardizing the safety of one's child? What would I have done?

SHIRLEY BREHM

I grew up on a small farm in northern Michigan, graduated from high school at sixteen, taught thirty-six children in a one-room school when I was eighteen, graduated from college to teach elementary children, and eventually completed a PhD. in curriculum and instruction. I retired from a career as a college professor with thirty-two years teaching undergraduates and graduate students the methods of teaching science, mathematics, and environmental education. My teaching overseas included the British Isles, Japan, Okinawa, Taiwan, and Nicarauga.

Music is a central interest in my life. I have played the trombone since I was twelve years old, most recently in local community bands. I began to write after I retired from university teaching. I owe my love of language first to my mother, who insisted that we speak correctly, and second to my junior class English teacher, Elizabeth Hartergrink, for her encouragement.

Relive the Experience

All my writing now is done at the computer. When I wrote in

longhand, I had a series of procrastinating activities I usually engaged in before the words arranged themselves for the opening sentence. I sharpened all the pencils I could find and laid out ruled yellow legal pads. Only then could I begin. Oddly enough, the transition to computer was relatively easy, since the typed draft is more readily edited and produces better copy.

Topics I have selected for stories may have sentimental meaning or they might be amusing incidents from childhood, or travel episodes as an adult. As I begin to recall an experience, I think it through for several hours or several days, actually reliving the experience in my mind. The story seems to write itself in a relatively short period of time. At that point I transcribe it to computer or to paper. I rarely outline the story or make notes prior to writing. I often edit what I write. Working on one story might trigger memories that produce another story. Often as I write a story, some nugget of philosophy might develop. I feel these are bonuses.

When writing a story, I imagine I am writing to a particular person or a group of people. It helps to have someone in mind when writing the story.

I have become more aware of my own writing tendencies in the use and expression of language. Sentence length can be a problem, as well as tending to write with a spoken idiom style. I also have attempted to focus on developing a sense of presence in the description. I find it is a challenge to create the small details that depict the scene or event without using too much description or too much narrative. I try to make my writing more precise.

I am convinced anyone can write his or her memoirs. Think about to whom you want to tell the story. Find a good opening sentence, write the sequence of events, and then find an ending. There!

Buddy

Buddy and I were standing in the door of the horse barn, watching the threshers. I was holding his hand, keeping him by my side. We were both barefoot and dressed alike, wearing denim bib overalls and cotton blouses. The threshing machine was making a fearful racket and producing clouds of dust. Men carrying grain sacks filled with oats scrambled up the steps to the second-floor granary to deposit their loads and return to take yet another. A wagon loaded with oat sheaves pulled up. Dad called "whoa!" to the team, hopped down, and waved at us. Buddy tried to pull away and run to Dad, but I held on tight, for Mom had told me to look after him and to stay out of the way of the men working.

"I want to see Daddy. My throat hurts bad," Buddy cried.

Dad came over and gave Buddy a hug and told us to go into the house. He'd be along in awhile.

We went in to dinner to the place Grandma had set for us. Buddy said he couldn't eat. His throat was hurting. Mom looked and was startled to see the inflammation and swelling. "We have to get him to a doctor," she said. "Shirley, go and tell Dad to come in. Buddy is sick!"

Dad ran into the house and quickly changed from his threshing clothes into a clean shirt and pants, and drove off to the doctor's office with Buddy beside him. Mom was very worried but she had to stay home with Durwood and me. Durwood was only three months old. I had just turned seven. Mom cradled the baby on her shoulder as she paced about the dining room. "We have to be brave," she told me. I felt uneasy and didn't know what to do to help.

A couple of hours had passed when Mrs. Whaley came across the road with a telephone message from Dad. He had to take Buddy to the hospital. The doctor thought it was diphtheria. "Oh, no," exclaimed Mom. "It can't be! He was immunized this spring along with all of the other children at school! It can't be. It can't be!"

Now the worry began in earnest. Mom was silent as she cuddled the baby close to her and kept telling me to be brave. I didn't feel brave. I wanted to cry but I didn't because I didn't want her to think I wasn't brave.

As evening approached we remembered the cows needed to be milked. It was getting so late we worried that Dad wouldn't get back in time. I could help, but I couldn't do the job by myself. Mom had to stay in the house to take care of the baby.

"Shirley, go ask Mr. Whaley if he could come over and help this once. Our five cows probably won't take too long."

When the milking was done and the milk run through the separator, we tried to eat supper. Mom looked so tired and white I was worried about her. I tried to hold the baby to give her a rest but he wanted only her. When he fell asleep, Mom sent me to bed and she stayed up walking around the dining room, too restless to sit still.

The next morning we still had not heard from Dad. Mr. Whaley came back to do the morning milking. Mom gathered up Buddy's sheets and washed them. We hung them on the line, for it was a sunny day and they would dry fast. "We'll make up Buddy's bed nice and fresh for him when he comes home from the hospital," she said, as much to herself as to me. "You can go out and pick some flowers to put in a vase. That will make a welcome for him."

We were trying to keep busy and not show how worried we were. It was late in the morning when Dad drove into the yard. He parked the car beside the woodshed, as he usually did. I ran out to welcome him and Buddy home. But he was alone in the car. He stumbled out of the car and came toward Mom, who had joined me at the back stoop. He had a terrible, twisted look on his face. Mom looked at him and screamed, "Oh, no, Frank, oh no!" and she sank to her knees on the ground.

I didn't know what was going on. I kept trying to ask, "Where is Buddy? When can he come home?" But neither one answered me. I was confused and terrified. Dad was on his knees hugging my mother, and both of them had their arms around me, squeezing me so hard I could hardly breathe. Dad was sobbing. I had never before seen him cry.

"There wasn't anything they could do," he gasped between sobs. "They even cut a slit in his throat and put in a tube so he could breathe better. But it was too late. The poison had gone too far. Just before they put the tube in, he said to me, 'Daddy, when can you take me home?'"

Dad nearly collapsed with the sobs that wracked his body. I didn't know what to do. Mom had told me to be brave. I squirmed away from their hugs and ran toward the barn. I climbed into my secret hidey hole and wondered why my teeth were chattering. No one had said Buddy was dead but it was dawning on me that he was. I wondered what it was like to be dead. It was hard to think that only a couple days ago we had sat washing our feet in the tub on the same stoop where my parents still knelt. I had splashed Buddy with water, making him cry. Mom had come out and scolded me. "Shirley, why must you always pick on your little brother? You are the oldest and you know better."

I had been just a little angry at her for taking his part. He didn't pick on me but he did whine a lot, which seemed to get me into trouble. But now the worst possible thing had happened and he was dead. Was it my fault? The more I worried about it, the more I became convinced that in some way I was to blame for his getting sick and dying.

I wanted to cry but I couldn't. My throat constricted until I could hardly swallow. It hurt awful. Buddy's throat had hurt him. Maybe I was getting diphtheria, too, and maybe I was going to die.

The suddenness of Buddy's illness and the danger of infection meant that Buddy's funeral was hurried. His casket was placed in front of the living room window of my grandparents' house so mourners could view his body from the porch. Afterwards, Mom and I spent a long month isolated in quarantine.

All three of us grieved Buddy privately, the farmer, the young mother, and the seven-year-old sister. And I think each of us felt responsible for his death.

My parents never spoke of Buddy again. I didn't, either, until well into adulthood.

The Ten-Year-Old Cowherd

Cadillac, Michigan, is tucked in the southeast corner of Wexford County. Clam Lake Township is the very corner township abutting Missaukee County to the east and Osceola County to the south. We lived a mile from each county line on what was then known as the McBain Road. It was a quiet gravel road that saw little traffic. A Model A puttering along at twenty-five miles per hour or an old Buick or Dodge raised but little dust. A half-dozen cars per hour would have been considered a real parade.

The year 1936 was a dust bowl year. Michigan was not hit as hard as were the plains states, but we went for weeks with no rain. The few acres of pasture for our seven or eight cows had rapidly dried up. As a result, Dad decided that we had to pasture the cows along the road. I would be the cowherd.

My day began as soon as the cows had been milked. We opened the barnyard gate and drove them out onto the road. At first they grazed just outside the barnyard, but as days passed, we had to move further down the road to the west. We preferred this as there were more neighbors to the east, and they did not appreciate the Brehm cows coming into their yards.

I amused myself with all sorts of imaginative play as the hours dragged on, while keeping an eye out to drive the strays back to the herd or to shoo one out of the road at the approach of a car. Cars poked along at a sedate speed so I could hear them in time to act.

The culvert at the foot of the hill was a favorite place to wait out the morning. It drained the runoff into a swamp and most of the time it was bone dry, especially this summer. It was a big culvert, three feet in diameter with plenty of room for a ten-year-old to crawl through. An occasional frog or toad inhabited the cool space and, as the summer progressed, crickets and grasshoppers occupied the area outside. It was a great place to lie on my stomach and look out, daydreaming about being Heidi up at her grandfather's hut.

The morning crept along at a slow pace. I had no watch to gauge the time, which was just as well, as time did drag its snail trail across the sky. The best estimate of the hour was to watch the cattle. As they overcame their hunger, they became more restless and more curious about what was on the other side of the road. That was the signal to round them up and herd them back to the barnyard. If they had had sufficient grazing they would go readily homeward and to the water trough to quench their thirst.

I can still feel the tiredness as we came back up the hill, passing the grove on the south side of the road and relishing the momentary shade it offered from the hot sun overhead. The cows smelled the water and crowded through the gate, shouldering and butting one another to get to the water tank. I struggled to close the heavy wood-slatted gate and headed for the house and my noon dinner. The cows, full and refreshed, found a shady spot and lay down to chew their cuds.

Suffering Threshing Time: A Woman's Perspective

August was a special time of year. It seemed that things were gradually slowing down. The garden was producing fresh vegetables, the crickets were beginning to chirp their late summer song, the sweet corn was ready, and the early watermelons were beginning to tempt you into thinking they were ripe. It was also the month when we prepared for the threshers. Wheat was cut in July, but oats ripened in August. I recall the threshing bees of the 1930s and 1940s, before the advent of the self-powered combines. This was the time of threshing.

During June and July, the oat crop pretty much took care of itself. The hay seeded with the grain was for next year's hay and would only get started during the current season. By the next year, the oats would have been harvested, leaving clear sailing for the hay crop.

In mid-August, which was usually when the oats had turned yellow, we hitched up the team to the grain binder and proceeded to cut the grain in preparation for threshing. One of the great inventions of the nineteenth century was the McCormick reaper. It changed the harvesting from centuries-old hand harvesting to first, a hand-held scythe, then later, a grain cradle. The binder tied the grain into bundles that were ten to twelve inches in diameter, thus cutting out another centuries-old practice – hand-tying grain. As the binder moved around the field cutting six-foot swaths, the bundles were dumped out on the ground. The farmhands grabbed a bundle of oats in either hand, putting the butts firmly on the ground about thirty inches apart and tilting the heads together so the bundles leaned into each other and stayed upright. This was repeated with another pair of bundles set tightly against the first pair, and so on, until you had eight or ten bundles lined up. Then you placed a bundle at either end so the shock was closed off, and then laid enough bundles along the heads to make a roof of sorts. That comprised a grain shock, and you proceeded around the field gathering and shocking the oats. It was an itchy job, for the oat heads had fine hairs coming out of the grain seed, and the weather was apt to be good and hot.

The operation usually required more hands than any one farmer had available, so the farm community banded together, making it a bee. Usually a half-dozen or so farmers traded with each other to form the threshing crew. The first threshing might be done for the farmer who owned the threshing machine, and then it was a simple advance from farm to farm in sequence.

At home, it was the Petersons who owned the threshing machine. This was a great long device that looked as big as a railroad car, and into it the bundles of grain were fed. Flails beat the grain out, spouting it into sacks to be carried into the granary for storage. From another vent came the straw, which was blown through pipes into the straw mow to be used for animal bedding during the winter.

The star attraction was not the threshing machine but the steam-powered traction machine that provided the power for the thresher. These wonders have made a nostalgic comeback as oddities shown at steam shows around the country. I vividly recall running out to the road to watch the threshing rig slowly making its way from the farm next to ours. The top speed was perhaps three miles per hour as it huffed quietly along, pulling the thresher as well as a trailer, and carrying wood and barrels of water.

The rig would be positioned so that the thresher was closest to the barn, and the tractor was twenty-five feet away, connected to the thresher by a long, webbed belt. Setting the rig up always seemed to take a long time, even as efficient as the crew was. By now all the other farmers would have arrived with their teams and wagons with hay racks. They decided who would collect the grain from the fields, who would handle the sacks of oats, and who would work in the mow – one of the worst jobs, as it was hot and dusty.

In the house the preparations for feeding the threshing crew had been proceeding at a frantic pace. At one time, the women used to help each other with the meals, but not during my time. Mom and I were the main cooks, bottle washers, potato peelers, pie bakers, and dish washers. I don't think I ever worked harder in my life than while cooking for the threshers. There might be ten or twelve very hungry men to feed, and this would include all the meals except breakfast during the time that the crew was at our place. We provided breakfast for the rig crew, who, while they lived only a mile away, slept over in the barn to keep an eye on the steam tractor, possibly so the fire under the boiler didn't go out.

Meal preparations would begin a few days prior to the arrival of the threshing crew.

"When do you think we will have the threshers?" Mom would ask

Dad.

"Well, they are at So and So's, and they have only five acres, and then W's are next and they have eight acres, and if it doesn't rain, well, maybe we'll have them next Tuesday or Wednesday."

The next question was how many meals we would have to plan for. If we were lucky and something didn't go wrong, we may have to cook two noon dinners and two suppers. It wasn't hard to plan menus; we just cooked the same things four different times and in succession. Quantity was the most important ingredient. We peeled and boiled a peck of potatoes for a meal, then made two or three macaroni and cheese casseroles and maybe a tuna and noodle casserole, cooked a ham and a beef roast, and roasted a chicken. We put a fresh loaf of bread out along with peanut butter and jam, and jello with fruit and real whipped cream, glorified rice, baked beans, and if we had it at the time, fresh sweet corn, gallons of coffee with real cream and sugar, two or three kinds of pie, and a big chocolate cake for dessert.

To serve this mob, we'd have to take most of the furniture out of the dining room and extend the table to the longest dimension. Usually we'd have to bring in nail kegs to serve as additional chairs and use the straight-backed chairs from all over the house. We'd set the wash-up area outside by the back door, using the washtubs on their stands for basins. It was important to have plenty of soap and farm towels made from unbleached linen, the kind that were scratchy when new and softened with many washings.

The men would come in to eat, scrubbing themselves as best they could, with the exception of the rig crew who were covered in dust and didn't wash during the week. It was too hard on the skin to get all that dirt out only to get dirty all over again, they said. Then, in almost complete silence except for "pass the . . . ," the meal would be devoured. It was the custom that the women, who were nearly exhausted from the preparation, didn't eat with the men. We had to wait table and, when the men were finished, could at last pull up a chair and hope there was enough left for us. But the chore wasn't over yet. The mountain of dishes awaited. After the dinner dishes were done, it was time to start all over again and begin cooking for supper – the same menu, for the most part, all from scratch, and the same dishes to wash. By 8:00 p.m. we could call it a day. If we were lucky, we'd only have to go through this one more day, and then threshing time at our place would be over for another year.

Farm women hailed the invention of the combine, which put an end to all this agony. Dad got one in the early 1950s and all the threshing processes were scrunched into one. No more cooking for threshers. What liberation!

The Mended Heart

The surgeon gave me the red pillow after open-heart surgery. It was shaped like a valentine and inscribed with the evidence of the operation: the neatly drawn lines showing arteries, the three by-passes, and the location of the aortic valve now fitted with one taken from a pig heart. I could recite the names of the parts and show the locations. It was like a lesson in biology. It belonged to a book. But I was having trouble placing all that inside my own chest, for it seemed so remote, as if it were happening to someone else.

"Squeeze the pillow when you cough!" admonished the nurse. "You don't want to tear the incision in your chest." The eight-inch chest wound splitting my sternum felt fragile and insecure. Coughing and any other movement pulled at the staples holding the two halves together, making the bones grate. The thigh and ankle incisions stapled with metal felt numb and scratchy against the other leg. I hugged the pillow, trying to find a comfortable position, and prayed for strength and patience. It was a prayer I would repeat many times during the following weeks as the doctors struggled to overcome a dangerous staph infection resulting from the surgery.

As time went on, other complications developed: one antibiotic after another failed to stop the infection, then the kidneys began to fail from so many medications and kidney dialysis was required. Lying in bed with all the various tubes and monitors gave me time to think about my heart. So much was a mystery. Not the science part. That was relatively easy to understand. The mystery was having the pig valve sustaining my every pulse, every beat. I could feel my heart thudding, hear it in my head, and feel it vibrating in my chest. Yet I could not imagine that it was mine, that it was real. I began to listen for my heart beating, and gradually was lulled to accept that it was. I would drift off to sleep only to be startled awake to listen for my heart again. It became a mantra. "My heart is beating, beating . . . "

In the middle of the night, when the hospital was without visitors and less noisy, I thought about how my heart had been stopped for the surgery. I marveled that the doctor had held my heart in his hand, feeling its smoothness. I wondered if it had felt cold to touch. I wondered, "Do you die when your heart stops beating?" It was a strange experience to be so abstract about my body, to have this displaced sensation that had no connection to what had happened during those hours, when my heart had been stilled and I hung suspended between life and death. There was no conscious memory, no sensation of movement or pain.

Day after day my condition did not improve and I was placed back in the intensive cardiac unit under constant supervision. The medical staff was vigilant. I was miserable, for nothing was going well. My mind seemed to float freely away, living in other times and places, an observer present but uninvolved with any willful action. Memories scrolled as if on a screen. Each was as crisp and fresh as if it were yesterday's event. One led to another, and I spent the long night hours reviewing incidents of my life. The future was only the next second, the next minute. Tomorrow did not exist. The tug toward the past seemed irresistible and compelling, safe because I knew how things had come out. I was exhausted. It seemed so hard to take the next breath. There was no awareness of the room or the bed, only memories floating somewhere in space and time. Impressions slipped in and out of the shadows, like a night animal not quite glimpsed, skittering away and fading into darkness. Suddenly a thought emerged. "This must be what dying is like."

The possibility, even the probability, of imminent death came into clear focus. I felt a desperate need to make important arrangements that had been left undone, to say goodbye to dear friends. Mundane things needled, taking valuable time. It was so hard to think clearly.

I clutched the red pillow - the touchstone - bringing back the memory of that night, linking me to those moments when my life hung in the balance. There were still serious questions that had not been answered. What does it mean to be alive? If I'm given a second chance, what will be the debt incurred? What does God have in mind for me? Or is it absurd to think that God really cares? Where does the soul exist? What is the life force and what is memory?

That long episode ended when I was at last discharged from the hospital. Weeks of living in the hospital room with windows shaded from the outdoors had displaced me in both time and space. I had entered the hospital in August and it was now October. I was both anxious and hopeful as the wheelchair rolled me along the corridor. I realized it was a great responsibility to go forward and to trust my heart, to trust that it would continue beating, and to be able to feel joy and rejoice with love.

Outside, the brilliant blue sunlit October sky was the backdrop for shocking yellow, red, and orange autumn leaves. This sudden shift from isolation and shadow to the living world was too much. I burst into tears with the incredible joy of being alive, of seeing and feeling the world.

JEANIE AMBOY

I grew up hearing my mother's history as my brothers and sisters and I sat around the potbelly stove on cold winter nights. My father's best stories were told after dessert at the end of Sunday dinner.

Both of my parents were raised in the South, and moved to farmland in the greater Detroit area. Our little farm with cows and chickens looked more out of place each year as people flocked out of the big city and bought up the land around us. Oblivious to the ever-encroaching suburban life, my parents retained their life style and values. I knew I was different when I started school with my plaited hair, biscuits in my lunch pail, and hand-worked buttonholes in my jumper.

I now live in Okemos, Michigan with my husband Chuck. With appreciation for my rich Appalachian heritage, I wrote several songs, including: *Love's Legacy, Cumberland, Song of the Northern Winds, The Hill Spring, and Living Water.* I play the mountain dulcimer and sing for school assemblies, historic villages, festivals, libraries, and retirement centers.

Imagine Each Event as if It Was a Movie

My mother told me this story about fifteen years ago. She told it to me but, of course, not to my dad. It happened so long ago I had forgotten about it. Thankfully, my sister Alice knew the story, too, and retold it to me on the phone.

The notes I took from her phone call formed the basic outline for my story. I closed my eyes and imagined each event as if I was directing a movie, with characters, sights, smells, setting, and dialogue, as I remembered it.

After writing the rough draft, I sent it to Jan, one of my brothers. He helped me fill in specifics about the work Mom was doing that day. I also asked Roger, another brother, for his ideas.

Pop's mother, Grammaw Warren, always said that if a person's story is always told the same way, without significant changes, it's probably true. She maintained that a liar usually gets his story mixed up the more he tells it. Mom's story met this test of truthfulness, as she told this story in the same way to all of us. She told the truth – sort of – to Pop that day too.

An easy way to begin writing memoirs is to start with old family stories. Just put them down on paper the way you would tell them if you were sitting in your living room with your brothers and sisters. These story sessions usually begin with, "Remember when . . . ?"

Since we don't know how long we will have one another, life being uncertain, there is no time like right now to share the stories of our lives. Getting some of them on paper will be a gift to succeeding generations.

Extra Crispy

As Pop grew older, Mom began fixing him special meals. Nothing was too much trouble. Did he want chicken with German-style dumplings? No problem. How about cherry pie? No sooner said than done. She delighted in seeing her husband enjoy his food, the sense of taste being one of the simple enjoyments left in his old age. But some days, even the best of intentions met up with limitations.

One day after she finished cleaning the kitchen, making the beds, and cooking breakfast and the noon meal, she began the arduous task of laying tile flooring on the enclosed front porch. The room hadn't been used for anything but a collection place for homeless things. She lugged out box after box of books, grown children's high school memorabilia, car parts, and broken furniture. Next she prepared the exposed floor for spreading the mastic. None of the walls were straight in the century-old farmhouse. It took creative cutting to make the squares come out right. All this time Pop was working outside in the garden and garage, but Mom didn't mind. She said she could think better on her own. After the floor was finished, she stood admiring its slick new surface. It was when she was scraping her cutting knife clean that her thoughts turned to supper. "What am I goin' to fix? I'm so tired right now I could sleep till Sunday. I know," she brightened. "I'll whip up somethin' really fast. Then I'm goin' straight to bed."

Just then Pop trudged through the kitchen door, looking worn out from working since sunup in the outdoor air. With a hint of a smile, he proudly held up a fat old black hen by her feet.

"Edith, look what I brought you. I killed the one that's been getting out all the time. Could you fry her up for dinner?" With that he let go of her clawed toes and dropped the headless old truant right there on the kitchen floor. "There is nothing quite like the taste of a freshly killed chicken fried up country style."

She looked down at the lifeless heap of iridescent black feathers next to the door. As a farm wife, she was used to making quick work of dressing poultry. However, most of the work preparing this bird was better done outside, and it was dark now. To heat up a tub of water to scald this hen would take some time. Then there was the smell of hot, wet feathers that would stink up the whole house. It would take some energy to pluck out all those feathers. The entrails needed to be removed and the meat butchered into parts. All at once, she felt overwhelmed with fatigue.

"No problem," was all she had the strength to reply.

"Good. Honey, I'm bushed. While you're cooking supper, I think I'll just lie down on the bed for awhile."

At that, Mom sprang into action with an energy-saving plan of her own. There were two stoves in the kitchen: an antique wood-burning heating stove and an electric cooking range. She stoked up the fire in the heating stove. "The hotter I get this thing a'blazin' the better," she said under her breath. From the chest freezer on the back porch, she fished out a package of frozen chicken parts from the IGA and set them on "thaw" in the microwave oven. "I'm glad I bought a package of these last week when they were on sale," she thought. Next, she preheated the electric oven to 400 degrees and began patting out biscuits in her bread bowl.

She grew up in the Great Depression believing waste was a mortal sin. But now, without blush or shame, when the sides of the potbelly stove glowed red hot, she tossed in the dead chicken and slammed the door shut. "What will Pop say if he catches me destroyin' a perfectly good chicken?" she wondered. "He'll not be happy. I have to get this job over with before he wakes up." With her back to the wood stove, she busied herself rolling the commercial chicken in seasoned flour. When the parts were fried golden brown, she removed them onto a thick earthenware platter. With her big metal spoon, she scraped up the browned bits in the bottom of the big black skillet to make gravy.

There was no time to feel content. A new worry surfaced with the acrid odor of burning feathers assaulting her nostrils. She panicked. "Oh my goodness," she thought, "I'd better open both kitchen doors and air this out before the smell wakes him up." With both stoves cranked up full blast, the kitchen itself had become an oven. For a moment she paused in the breezy space between the doors and relished the coolness of the night air. Then, with no time to spare, she got back to work and dumped a quart jar of green beans into a pan along with a dab of bacon grease for flavor. "These will hit the spot," she said softly to herself.

Since she had never cremated a chicken before, she was surprised at loud hissing and popping noises that began sputtering from the stove. "Oh, no," she worried. "It's like the Fourth of July in here. Has

Pop stopped snoring? Did he hear all this strange noise and wake up?" She added more wood to the fire and hoped.

In twenty more minutes the old black hen was merely ashes and Mom laid the table with fried chicken, gravy, re-heated leftover mashed potatoes, green beans, hot biscuits, butter and jam. She was too exhausted and too full of kitchen smells to even think of eating, but she sat down at the table. After all this effort, she wanted to be nearby just to see his reaction. He cleaned his plate by sopping up every last drop of gravy with a broken piece of biscuit, and he pushed his chair back from the table.

"Edith, this was the best meal I think I've ever had," he declared. "City folks just don't know what they're missing. There is absolutely nothing in the world like a freshly killed fried chicken."

"No problem," she said.

Inside Story

"If goats are so smart, why do they eat tin cans?" I heard this question often from my city-raised friends. "They don't really eat cans," I explained. "Actually, they are very fussy eaters. They won't even eat the grass in your lawn, just the broad-leaf plants."

I called my father to ask him how he would reply to this question.

As I expected, he didn't give me a short answer. He answered with a story about the morning that he bought eight cows.

There's something you need to know about Pop. He loved talking with people everywhere he went and he was a real "wheeler dealer." He would trade, buy, and sell on the spur of the moment if the deal was right. Our family never knew what he might bring home on any given day.

That's why we weren't surprised when he brought home a modular office on wheels from the U.S. Army surplus, a truckload of reclaimed bricks, an upright piano, six used clawfoot bathtubs, and two hundred fifty padded and button-tufted bi-fold closet doors.

On the way home, this time with his trailer-load of cows, he heard the weather report on his truck radio. Unseasonable freezing weather was on its way. The barn with gaps between the boards was a drafty place. Before he left for work that afternoon, he had to figure how to insulate it.

As an emergency fix, he decided to flatten out old cardboard boxes he'd been saving and nail them to the walls.

With his nail pouch tied around his waist and not much time to spare, he grabbed his hammer and went to work. Each one-and-one-half inch roofing nail received only two strikes of his hammer, one to tap it in place and the other to drive it clean into the oak boards.

He filled the mangers with hay and the elegant old bathtubs that served as watering troughs with water. Each day he pulled the plugs and replaced them with fresh water. Confident that his new cattle would be warm, snug, and well-fed, he drove off to work.

Next morning, wearing his warm fleece jacket and flap-eared Yukon Charlie hat, he walked through the snow-covered path to check on his cows. He stopped in his tracks and stared in disbelief at the glints of sunlight shining through cracks in the barn walls. Bracing himself for the worst, he stepped in to assess the damage. The cardboard was missing. Only jagged shreds remained clinging around the nails.

"Dr. Turner," he asked his vet on the phone, "are my cows going to die? They've eaten about a hundred square yards of corrugated cardboard."

The doctor's tone seemed reassuring. "They will probably be all right. But let me ask you a couple of questions."

"Sure, go ahead," Pop said.

"Did you give them plenty of hay?"

"Yes."

"Did you give them water?"

"Yes."

"Did you leave them a salt and mineral block?"

"No. I thought they could get by without it for a day or so till I bought one for them at Wixom Co-op."

"Well, that's what they were after. The cardboard contains trace minerals which cattle need. Just be sure to get that salt block right away. And call me if your cows show signs of distress."

Pop paused for a moment here at the end of his story. Then he added, "So you see, Jeanie, that's why goats appear to be eating tin cans. A goat will move a tin can around in its mouth to loosen the glued-on label because it's craving the trace minerals it contains."

I learned two things that day: why goats "eat" tin cans and how to keep insulation where it belongs — on the outside of the cow.

The
Rock

Pop had hitched Molly, our workhorse, to the plow. He was getting the yard ready to replant grass. I found a fossil sticking up in the freshly turned earth when I walked outside to get the mail. The rock was light for its size and stamped with exquisite markings, like the underside of a mushroom. Returning from the mailbox, I dropped my rock so I could open a letter from my grandmother.

"I can always pick it up later," I thought. For the next two days, I walked up and down the furrows in the front yard searching for that rock. "From now on, I will never let go of a good rock," I promised myself. It was the perfect thing to take for show-and-tell.

My little brothers and I liked to play on our property in a big place we called "the hole." It was dug by previous landowners to be the basement of a house that never got built. Its steeply sloping insides exposed parfait-like layers of distinctively colored soils. Starting at the top were browns, moving into shades of red in the middle, and at the very bottom, crystal white sand.

Pop didn't believe in giving children many toys. "Give them a pile of dirt and some blocks of wood and they'll create some fun," he would say. We used to sit on the inner slopes of the hole and engineer mountain roads with switchbacks and build houses out of scrap blocks of wood. We broke off the tips of weeds and twigs to create bushes and trees and laid down moss for sod. When my brother's precious toy truck careened off our "mountain road" and tumbled down to the crater's center, I went down and raked the leaves away to find it. That's when I found the large black rock.

It was dense for its size, with red and turquoise-green marbling throughout. I carried it in both hands up the side of the hill and washed it off with the garden hose. Dark and shiny, its edges were rounded like molten metal. "It might be a meteor or something! I'm going to take it to school tomorrow!" I said.

Marsha went before me at show-and-tell. She brought her pretty Barbie dolls with shiny plastic hair and sparkly ball gowns. The girls in class ooh-ed and aah-ed. "Why did I think my old rock would be interesting to anyone?" I thought. "Suppose someone asks me where I found it?" I would have to explain that I played, not with glamorous dolls, but in the dirt with my brothers. When Mrs. Koenig called on me to come up for my turn, my face glowed as red-hot as the potbelly stove in our living room. "I didn't bring anything today." I answered. Before recess, I shoved the rock a little further forward under the lid of my desk, just for insurance.

Throughout the school year, I managed to keep it hidden there. I was too afraid to take it home for fear my classmates might tease me for carrying it. It's not that I thought about the rock all the time; I only remembered it was there when I needed to put something in or take something out of my desk. The rock took up a lot of room, so this got harder to do as the year went by and we got more and more workbooks and papers. I lifted up the lid of the desk only an inch or two and tried to locate items strictly by feel. This worked okay for pencils and erasers but not for books.

On the last day of school, we were told to clean out our desks. "Oh, no," I thought. "Someone is bound to see me with this dark homely thing."

There was nothing to be done about it. I filled my paper grocery sack with notebooks, papers, stubby pencils, and broken crayons. Last of all, I brought out the rock. I spread my fingers to cover it over in my hands and pressed it against my stomach as I headed for the wastebasket.

Suddenly, pointing at me, Margie Aitken yelled loud enough for everyone to hear. "Hey! What's that you're throwing away?"

I froze where I stood. "You mean this?" I asked meekly.

"Yes. That's the coolest thing I've ever seen!" Her delight heartened me to hold it up in the full light of our classroom windows. I wondered again at the mystery of its brightly colored streaks, squinted into the mellow gleam of its rich blackness, felt the coolness of its weight in my warm hands.

"Can I have it?" she asked. I paused a moment to consider her request before placing it into her hands. She was my best friend, after all. A kindred spirit, she saw the beauty of it as I first had.

School was out. All that summer I dug around in the hole, searching for another one.

Into the Bluest Sky

The morning sky shone such a brilliant blue that it hurt my swollen eyes. Small brownish-gray birds darted around the arbor, now overgrown with pink morning glories. Mom always said she loved anything with feathers. The birds were chirping simultaneously, like a dozen neighbors all talking at once on a party line. Such a beautiful world, but today this world seemed unfamiliar – a world without my mother in it.

I picked up the cheery yellow bottle of dish soap and read its label as if for the first time. "Joy," it read. "Just what I am going to need lots of," I thought. Its lemony fragrance tingled in my nose as I squeezed a stream of detergent under the running faucet. "It's going to be another hot one today here in southern Illinois," the newscaster on the radio warned. "Today's expected high of 102 will be another record-breaker for the second day in a row. Portions of Highway 51 between Ullin and Villa Ridge buckled in yesterday's heat wave and are closed for repairs. Be prepared for detours and delays." I clicked off the radio.

The day after Mom's funeral, everyone went home. Aunts and uncles, brothers and sisters returned to Michigan, Kentucky, and California. Mom was almost twenty years younger than Pop. Now that she was gone, we didn't want our eighty-nine-year-old father to stay alone in the farmhouse. My sister and I planned to alternate staying two weeks at a time. By the end of the summer, we hoped we could talk Pop into living with one of us.

Even though I thought this was a great idea, as the last car drove off, a sense of panic crept over me. It was not the red-hot fear that came one time when a motorist unexpectedly turned left in front of my car and I had to slam on the brakes. That I knew something about. This was a dark and cold fear that I was somehow being sucked into the gaping mouth of an unexplored, underground passage – a dismal tunnel of grief that I would be passing through for the next two weeks.

If given the option right then, I would have gone back to Michigan, to my familiar surroundings and network of friends. Instead, I would be alone with my grieving father, sleeping in Mom's bed in the room next to Pop's, cooking from her pantry and washing dishes in her kitchen sink.

"Why does Pop insist on working out there in this heat?" I wondered. "The morning's just begun and it's already a steam bath outside." Gardening was his passion, but I felt that this time he was working for a different reason. He needed an excuse to chop, till, and sweat out his grief. He, too, hadn't planned on living in a world without Edith. I thought of the white plastic porch chair he kept in the garden. When he got too tired to stand, he would sit on it and hoe everything within reach. When that area was cleared, he would move the chair down the row and continue.

My own tears came to mind as I wrung out the dishrag. Uncle George and Aunt Julie told me not to be afraid of crying. They said that, believe it or not, the tears would help me heal. To my relief, it seemed that when waves of grief washed over me, my tears only lasted a few minutes until, like a fully squeezed-out dishrag, my eyes could give up no more water. This gave me a sense of normalcy until, like the cloth dipped back into the sink, my eyes filled up again.

I desperately wanted to feel normal again. I plunged an egg-stained plate into the sudsy water, scrubbed it, and gave it a rinse. I held it up for inspection. The thick china sparkled as the clean water sheeted off. Like Pop in his garden, I was hoping this task would help me work out my grief, each job providing tangible proof that I could survive and function in this newly defined world.

"There," I stated out loud, as if to convince myself. "One dish washed, and I'm still here." I brushed my fingers across my apron to dry them. I needed to wipe my eyes. I couldn't hold back the flood, though. Salty tears carelessly flowed down and mingled with the dishwater. Through blurred vision, I picked out another dirty dish, weakly scoured it, and rinsed it under the faucet. "There!" I said, my voice shaking a little. "Two dishes washed, and I'm still here."

As I slid it onto the rack, I thought I heard a rustling sound behind me. Not trusting my senses, I paid no attention until I heard it again. Chill bumps raced up my spine. My scalp tingled. I knew then that I was not alone in the room.

It was not the too-familiar sound of mice scurrying through the walls. Since Mom became sick a couple of months back, she stopped setting out traps and they had gotten out of control. Pop was so hard of hearing that their scratching and running at night didn't faze him.

I checked around the kitchen to see if one of Pop's pet bulldogs had sneaked through the kitchen door for a scrap or two. When I heard the sound again, it led me straight to the potbelly stove near the middle of the kitchen.

The cast iron door complained with a screech as I yanked it open. That's when the dark thing flew out at my face. I instinctively threw up my hands. I dodged and whirled around to see what it was, but it was flying so erratically, I couldn't keep it in my line of sight.

It hit the kitchen window and plopped down into the dishwater below. Streams of sooty water flung off its wings as it flopped and floundered on the surface. It was a little bird with a stubby brownish-gray body and long narrow curved wings.

It must have been a chimney swift. Their nests are made of twigs and saliva then fastened to the inner walls of chimneys. When the babies are ready, they are supposed to fly up the chimney. This one went the wrong direction.

"How long had it been in that dark, lonely place?" I wondered. He had been desperate to get out into the light. Now he was desperate to stay afloat.

"Don't die on me, please," I pleaded softly. His wings thrashed against me as I scooped him from the water with both hands. Rivulets of dirty water ran down between my fingers and dripped from my elbows as I cupped his struggling body in my hands and walked to the back door. My next thought forced me to smile a little: "There, that's one bird washed, and I'm still here."

I shifted him to my left hand so I could grasp the doorknob with my right. I could feel his wings vainly flailing against my fingers. He was trying to get away. "Not yet, little bird," I said in my gentlest voice. "I'm taking you out where there's room to fly."

The sky I released him to was so sunny and blue it hurt my eyes. He flew straight to the morning glory arbor where the other little swifts were singing for joy. "Fly, little bird," I urged him. "It really is a beautiful world."

J. CHARLENE GENTHER

When I was five, I watched a T.V. show about women in prison. At the end of the show one of the women prisoners turned out to be a cop. I was sitting next to my dad and quickly turned and asked him, "If she is a police officer, what is she doing in jail?" He explained that some police officers wear a uniform and get the bad guys that way and that some officers wear regular clothes, called "plainclothes" and get the bad guy that way. Before he even finished his sentence I knew that when I grew up I was going to be one of the police officers wearing plain clothes and getting the bad guys that way. Sixteen years later, I was doing exactly that.

My manuscript, *Badge 3483: A True Story*, is based on the five years before I was a police officer when I volunteered to work undercover for the Roseville Police Department; the fourteen years I was on the Detroit Police Department, and five years after I retired from the force as I adjusted to being a suburban civilian again.

I currently reside in Royal Oak, Michigan with my beloved husband of twenty-seven years. We take care of our college daughter's three dogs, three cockatiels and cat.

Since 2001, I have been employed in the private security sector, in plainclothes, of course.

"Nightmares of an Undercover Volunteer" is an excerpt from my memoir, *Badge 3483: A True Story.*

Remember that It Is Your Story

I developed my story by sitting down at the computer and writing just what I remembered off the top of my head. After reading it, I went back and added more detail. Then I had several people read it to tell me if it made sense to them – for instance, if I used "cop speak." Other police officers would understand what I was talking about but the average civilian might not. That was important with every aspect of my stories, not just with the police language. Having other people read the stories and ask me questions gave me the insight to put in more detail. My writing certainly has improved. Paying attention to my friends' and families' suggestions about punctuation, spelling, and detail has made a difference.

When I wrote about being unexpectedly let into Tony's house, the time his daughter found my transmitter, and when I was caught in the alley with five guys coming after me, it caused my heart to race and my blood pressure to go up. I certainly relived the experience and was nervous even typing it.

Once you have written your story, have many readers read it for corrections and other information you might need to put in to make the story clearer to the reader. I had twenty-seven people read my manuscript. Remember that it is your story. Stick to what you want in your story but use others' comments to make your story better. It is a fine line but you will know it when someone wants you to cross it and make it their story and not yours.

I had many other stories I could have included. Even now I'll be driving down the highway and I'll remember another story I could have put in this book or in the manuscript I am writing. But this story is the start of my dream come true and I thought the beginning is always a good place to start.

Nightmares of an Undercover Volunteer

Marijuana on the Shelf

In 1971, when I was twenty, I got a ticket for not stopping at a stop sign. There was a lot of construction at the end of our street so I made a habit of stopping a few feet before the stop sign to make sure no one was coming my way. The officer just saw me take off, not stop. I explained what I had done, but he would not budge. I went to court, the judge believed that I had indeed stopped, and the ticket was thrown out.

The day in court was nothing special, except that while waiting for my case to come before the judge, another man had his case brought up. This thin, dark-haired, good-looking man had been stopped by an officer on a traffic violation. As he pulled his license out of his wallet, a packet of heroin fell out with it. Do not collect $200, go directly to jail. Even that would not have stuck out in my mind if it were not for what the judge said to him. He admonished him for being involved with this drug, telling him that he probably had the highest IQ in the courtroom, that he knew he had been a science teacher, and that he was now wasting his life. A high school teacher turned druggie? I had just been out of high school four years and could not picture any of my science teachers selling or using drugs. This man would come into my life again, but the next time I would be buying the heroin out of his wallet.

In May 1973, I went into a local hippie shop to buy some clothes. I struck up a conversation with the clerk, who was about my age and into selling weed along with bell bottoms and wide belts. After a long conversation, he asked if I wanted to try a sample that just came in. I just about jumped out of my skin. I stayed real cool on the outside and calmly said, "Sure." He went in the back and came out with one joint, which was free. He told me if I liked it to come back for more. I took it home.

Whenever anyone offered me drugs, I always used the excuse that I wanted to be a cop and couldn't do drugs. Really, I just wasn't interested. I was always shocked by how easily the druggies said OK, and that they never hassled me about it. Therefore, other than alcohol, I had never used any drug. I didn't tell the clerk that. I put the joint on a special shelf in my bedroom that my dad had handcrafted and installed for me a few years earlier.

This was the early seventies. I was twenty-two. I stared at this joint on the shelf and had a discussion with myself. I was curious about how it would feel to smoke it, so I debated smoking it or turning it in to the police. Maybe if I was lucky, they'd ask me to work for them. For God's sake, I'd be walking into a police station with a marijuana cigarette. They could arrest me!

I looked at that joint on the shelf on and off for about two weeks before I finally removed it and walked right into the local police station. I told the officers that I wanted to be a cop and explained how I got the joint, leaving out the part about debating whether to smoke it or not. Lo and behold, they asked me if I would volunteer to take an undercover officer into the store to further the deal. This was my dream came true. I took the cop in and he took over the rest of the buys. On Thanksgiving Day the same year, the local suburban police department made its biggest marijuana bust to date – twenty-seven huge green garbage bags full of prime reefer. To protect my identity, I was not at the bust. Even so, the officer I was working with gave me the credit.

I had also put in an application with the City of Detroit to work as a police officer and while I waited to hear from them I continued working undercover as a volunteer for the local police department and part-time at a doctor's office. The access to medical supplies came in handy because back then they didn't have the kind of bandaging tape they have now. Every time I wired up I had to put several pieces of that old white sticky tape on my chest to hold the wire in place. When I took the wire off, white sticky residue was left on my chest. Luckily, the doctor's office had a bottle of ether that smelled very bad but took the stickiness off with a little rubbing.

Wrong Way Down a One-Way Alley

After so many months of buying dope on the street, the kids get to know you, at the least by your reputation. One day an officer and I went to a little restaurant that had many complaints of kids selling dope. It was on Gratiot in a city now called East Pointe. We went in separately and sat at different tables. Sure enough, in a short while our targets came in. After a few minutes, before one of us could approach them, they started talking about me, saying that I was the one who bought dope from their friend at the Trading Post, another large local hangout that sold clothes, candles, incense, and dope. Their friend eventually got busted and they figured out I was the one who started the ball rolling. That was enough talk for me. I got up and exited the back door of the restaurant instead of the front door. As I entered the alley I knew instantly I was in big trouble. The alley was completely sealed off from any quick escape. On one side of me were the backs of the businesses; on the other side was a six-foot brick wall. The one way out was to walk down the alley to the south and hope for a space between the buildings.

I was about thirty feet out of the restaurant when the boys came after me. There were five of them. Two were taller than I was, and beefy. The other three weren't as big as the first two but they were just as determined to get their hands on me. I instinctively knew not to run because it would trigger a pack response from them, but I was walking as fast as I could, with no relief in sight. It was the longest alley I had ever been in. I could hear their feet hitting the pavement. They were gaining on me. Their voices grew louder and I was almost in a full panic when the heavens opened up.

I had finally come to the end of the alley and was walking as fast as I could right in the middle of a parking lot. A car squealed into the parking lot doing a 360 degree turn almost on two wheels and screeched to a halt. The driver threw open the passenger door and ordered, "Get in."

At that exact moment, the boys turned into the parking lot and started running toward me. I looked into the car and saw what appeared to be a police radio microphone lying on the front seat. The car pulling up in the parking lot and the boys turning the corner, and running toward me all happened in three seconds. I figured my chances were better with the guy in the car, so I got in. My door wasn't even shut when the driver pulled away, burning rubber. He then immediately told me he was a police officer and that my partner had called "officer in trouble" as soon as the boys left the restaurant. By this time I was in tears and shaking in my boots. We met my partner at the local police station.

The cop who had come to my rescue was at home, off-duty, listening to his police radio when my partner called in my predicament. I don't remember his name. It is well known among police officers that the most beautiful sound that officers can hear is the sound of a siren responding to their call for help. Squealing tires have the same effect.

My street buying days ended in that parking lot. From then on, I bought dope from just one person.

My Last Volunteer Assignment

My next and last volunteer assignment for Roseville P.D. was a man who was once a big-time dealer, a genius so slippery that no police department could grab him and keep him. I'll call him Tony. Tony and his wife lived with their child in a brick home in the suburbs. He had dealt drugs mostly in Detroit, and no matter what Detroit law enforcement did, they couldn't arrest him. The officers knew Tony was breaking the law. They just couldn't catch him. One time Detroit narcotic officers had just made a raid at a Detroit location when Tony drove by. They knew Tony was dirty (had drugs on him), but since the officers did not have a legal reason to stop the vehicle, he drove away. Tony was slick and trusted no one. It was rumored that he had killed a man. One other thing they told me: he used to be a high school science teacher.

That's right, Tony was the man I had seen in court a few years earlier. Tony had fallen from his glory years. His wife was now a customer and using up the profits. He was dealing out of his house and was no longer considered a main player. Since he was living in and operating his drug business out of our town, our department still wanted him. I was the girl they would use to try to get him.

A young woman who had been arrested on drug charges was going to take me into Tony's house. She was nervous because she didn't trust this man. The narcotics officers said Tony was so paranoid he would never let me in even though he knew her. He never let anyone in on the first try.

When I went out buying dope, I would start mentally preparing a few hours before the buy, but since I was convinced he wouldn't let me in, I didn't bother to prepare. I wasn't even nervous as I "wired up." I thought I wouldn't need it. The young woman and I left the station.

I parked in front of Tony's house and we both walked up onto the front porch. Tony opened the door and talked to the young woman as he sized me up. I was nonchalant about the situation because I knew it wasn't going anywhere that night. That's when I heard the tall, lanky, good-looking man with dark brown eyes say low and softly, "Come on in." I don't remember my exact thoughts. I'm sure they had something to do with manure.

She walked in first and I followed. Across from the front door was a closet. After she had walked past it, Tony opened the door, pulled out a shotgun, held it vertically in front of us and said, "If you're the police, you're gonna get this."

"I ain't no police," I mumbled. Underneath I was beginning to panic. He pointed out all the strategically placed mirrors in the home. He could see both doors of the house from the front room or kitchen. He said he wanted to see the cops before they saw him.

The first thing I always did when I entered a dope house was to look for all possible exits. I noticed that both the front and back doors were secured with double deadbolt locks. Once we were in the house he locked the door and put the key in his pocket. The officer I worked with told me this was his set-up.

He said, "As soon as you get into the room, look for something very heavy to throw through the front room picture window before you jump through it to make your exit easier."

He told me to jump out on the right side of the window because he and the rest of the guys would be coming in on the left. Since they didn't have a battering ram in their immediate possession for the doors, the window was going to be our exit of choice, if needed. This was not something I would go home and tell my mother when she asked me how my day went.

We all sat down in the front room and were talking a bit when out of the hallway staggered Tony's wife. Her right arm was bent up at the elbow and her head was wobbling. She slurred her words as she talked. My attention switched from trying to understand what she was saying to noticing a path of blood flowing from the crook in her elbow. She had just shot up. Within ten minutes of entering this house, I had been threatened with a shotgun and seen my first heroin addict fresh from shooting up. For a twenty-two year old white female suburbanite who had wanted to work undercover since she was five, it didn't get much better than this. Not being mentally prepared kept me on my toes. I didn't dare make a mistake by saying or doing anything wrong.

In the early seventies, if you wanted drugs you had to go into the room and sit with the dealer so he could check you out, make sure you were OK. You really had to be cool to pass the dealer's test.

We sat down and talked about cops. Tony actually named an officer who was within one block of the house listening to everything that was being said over my hidden mike. When Tony said the cop's last name, King (not his real name), I joked and said that his name sounded like something somebody would call a dog. I knew the officer was hearing all of this and I got a charge out of it, even though I knew he would rib me about it later. I also listened as they talked about a drug bust.

A few years earlier the cops had a tag on Tony's mail. They knew that a drug shipment had come into his house so they got a warrant and raided it that night. The house had been under surveillance. No one had come in or gone out of the house all day so they knew the dope was still inside.

But during the search they couldn't find the dope. They looked and looked and looked, to no avail. They finally left, completely perplexed. Where was the dope?

There I was, sitting with that dope dealer, and he divulged it all. He and his wife had had a baby just before the search, so they took the cardboard bottom out of the diaper bag and laid the dope flat in there. Mystery solved! The cops were hearing it firsthand from the dealer himself. I loved it. This was really cool.

The conversation turned serious after a while as Tony talked about how he had killed a guy. I don't remember if the guy was going to squeal or if he just didn't pay his dope bill. I remember Tony saying he killed him and I remember the way the room went deadly silent. The thought crossed my mind, "He might kill me if he finds out." I can't remember if we bought dope that night. After an hour or so we walked out the door.

We weren't ten feet from his front door when the girl I had accompanied started freaking. She was actually bent at the knees as she walked, unable to stand up straight because she was shaking so badly. She was freaking because Tony had admitted he had killed the other man. Her voice was shaking with the rest of her body as she said, "I heard the rumor that he'd killed a friend of ours but I really didn't believe it." She said she didn't care what sentence the judge gave her, she wasn't ever going back into that house with Tony. She kept repeating it over and over. When we got back to the station, we gave our reports and I never saw her again.

The next time, I went back alone. For some reason Tony and his wife liked me. Over the next six months I visited their home often, mostly to buy heroin, but sometimes just to visit. I was always wired and had a heavy band of enforcements just down the block. In any other world, the dealer, his wife, and I would have been friends.

To fit in, I started donating blood whenever I was able. I wanted to have "track" marks on my arm, in case there was ever any question. You can still see the faint scars on my left arm from all the times I visited the Red Cross. Every time you enter a dope den to deal with these people, it is risky and dangerous. You wonder, "Did they hear something or find something out since I was here last time?" I only had one close call and that was with Tony's eighteen-month-old daughter. My heart still jumps when I think of it.

I'd become like a member of the family. Even their cute little girl felt comfortable with me. She would stroll over to me and sit on my lap. I always wore a microphone when I bought drugs from them. The transmitter was about the size of a cigarette pack and made of metal. This was in the days when almost everyone wore bell-bottom pants with large belts and even larger belt buckles. The large belt buckles hid a transmitter perfectly. It couldn't be seen, but if someone thoroughly frisked you, you would be found out, especially if the person was looking for it. The guys told me to always wire the mike to the right side of my chest. In a panic situation, they didn't want to sit there and just listen to my heart pounding. Very funny.

One of the hardest parts about dealing with that family for so long was that I was getting comfortable with them while I was also going through all the steps to become a Detroit police officer. I would pass one hurdle and be so excited I would tell every one of my friends. I had to tell myself before every deal with this man to keep my mouth shut. I took time before each visit to prepare things we could talk about. Tony came to like me so much he even gave me a bottle of red wine he had made. I never could bring myself to drink it. It's not that I thought there was anything wrong with it; I just knew where he was going to wind up. I also knew I would be the one to put him there. I felt it would be wrong to celebrate by drinking wine that he himself had made.

On one visit, I was sitting on the front room floor with my back against the couch. The little girl waddled over to me to climb on my lap. As she climbed over me, she put her hand on the top of my transmitter, which was protruding just about a half an inch above my belt buckle underneath my shirt. She immediately became fascinated with it. Her mother had just walked out of the room and by the sound of her footsteps was about to return. I took the little girl's hand and started playing patty-cake. I kept my voice light and friendly while praying she would forget about the hard rectangular object she had just come across. Her further investigation could cost me my life. Thank God for the short attention span of an eighteen-month-old child. Patty-cake made her forget about the potential package of dynamite I had strapped behind my belt buckle. Thank God, also, that this kid's verbal skills were nil. Never again did I hold her. I wouldn't have gotten the chance anyway.

One dose of heroin I purchased from Tony was very pure. He told me to make sure I stepped on it (cut it, or mixed it with other ingredients) because it was so pure. It had come from the Philippines. When the report came back from the police lab, it stated that the heroin was so pure that if it was not cut, that anyone shooting it up would be killed. That's exactly what happened. All over the area heroin addicts were dying from this shipment. One casualty was Tony's wife's brother. Just released from prison, he used this pure dope and died. When they found him, he was lying on his back, sprawled out on a bed with his right leg on the floor. His right arm, which was dangling off the bed, still had the tourniquet around it and the needle was in his vein. He died almost instantly, never even getting a chance to take the needle out of his arm. The most ironic thing about the scene was that above his bed hung a huge poster, the kind you see in police stations, that show pills with medical identification written underneath the pill. At the top of the poster, written in huge letters, were the words "NO HOPE WITH DOPE." The cops took pictures of this scene and showed it to me later. It was time for my dope man to come down.

Based on my information, the police department I was working with got a search warrant and raided the house. The first words Tony said were, "Did you get Charlene, too?"

The officer I worked with told him, "No, she works for us." I'd spent about six months with this man and he'd never guessed, but somehow I wasn't jumping for joy. What dealers do is wrong, illegal, and evil, but they are people, too. Tony wanted the same thing for his child that other people want for their children. He just went about it in a different way.

For many years I never told anyone how guilty I felt about my spending six months first befriending him and then busting him. I never told anyone that I felt guilty about feeling guilty. This was December 1974, and I felt that way until February 1987, when I talked to the number one ranked female narcotics officer in the nation, who worked for the Detroit Police Department. She told me that what I was feeling was normal but that I was still legally responsible to get him put in jail because what he was doing was wrong and I should keep that foremost in my thoughts. I no longer felt guilty. But this would not be the last time I would see Tony or his wife.

In mid-March I had to go to court to testify against Tony about the last heroin buy I had done for the suburban department. I was now employed as a City of Detroit police officer. I had been instructed by the officers about how to effectively testify so that the truth would be heard. It sounded simple enough: look at the defendant's attorney when he asks you a question but look at the judge when you answer. If the defendant's attorney asks too many questions trying to confuse you, ask him to repeat himself. The officers warned me that I could be up on the witness stand for hours because Tony had an excellent attorney.

"After about two hours you'll feel sweat run down your back and into the crack of your butt," the officers said.

"No way," I said. "This is March."

I was on the stand a total of five hours the first day and, sure enough, after about two hours of testifying, the trickles began sliding down my back. I was sweating in March.

Tony was convicted on my testimony and sentenced to Jackson State Prison.

Two Coincidences that Eased My Nightmares

In the summer of 1975, I started having violent nightmares about the man I put in Jackson Prison coming back and hurting my family. One night I dreamt that there were huge square roasting pans on a table, the kind a restaurant might use. I walked over to the pans and looked in. Floating in blood were my mother's and father's severed arms, legs, and heads. I woke up sitting straight up and screaming at the top of my lungs. My mother, whose room was at the other end of the house, came running in to see what was wrong. She told me later that my screams were so violent she thought someone was in the room stabbing me. After she came in the room, I realized my pajamas and sheets were cold and wet. "So that's what they mean by cold sweats," I thought. It took my mom over a half an hour to calm me down.

The nightmares continued. Once I woke up with my whole body shaking. I tried to convince my mother that someone outside was going to come in to kill us. She tried repeatedly to convince me that I was having a nightmare. I even demanded that she call the local · police to have them walk around the house because I knew someone was there. Of course, no one was. It took me a while to come to the realization that it was a dream. I didn't know it then, but it was the price I was paying for having put the heroin seller and murderer in jail.

One day in June I had been assigned inside to take reports and answer the phone. I was standing behind the front desk when I observed a woman giving an officer information about a vehicle accident. She resembled Tony's wife, except that she was quite a bit heavier. I asked another officer to go over and look at the report to check her last name. I said if it was Tony's wife, I wanted to go into the back room until she left because she might be very upset with me since my testimony put her husband in "Jack Town," law enforcement's slang for Jackson Prison. The other officer walked over, looked at the report, looked up at me, and nodded his head yes. It was Tony's wife.

I slowly made my way from behind the front desk, but I must have caught her eye because she called out, "Charlene!" I stopped and turned toward her. I told myself she couldn't kill me there with all the other cops present. I called her by name and said hi. At that she ran over and threw her arms around my neck, hugging me.

The cop who had verified her name for me mouthed, "I thought you put her husband in prison."

"I did," I mouthed back, with Tony's wife still hugging me.

"We don't hate you," she said. "You were just doing your job. You believed in what you were doing and we respect you."

I told her I was glad she didn't hate me, but I would understand it if she did. She said her husband would be getting out of prison in September and that when he went to prison her supply of heroin ended. She went through cold turkey and was clean, except that she had become a wino and had gained thirty pounds because she drank so much. She lived with her mother ever since Tony's attorney had gotten their house as payment for his defense. She was upbeat and genuinely surprised to see me.

Out of all the precincts in Detroit and out of all the cops who are in the precincts at different times of the day, it was an incredible coincidence that I was there when Tony's wife walked in. Her words helped me make peace with myself about befriending them and then busting them. The nightmares weren't as bad after that.

A few years later, I ran into Tony's attorney on the ornate wooden staircase in Detroit's beautiful old court house. He recognized me and called out to me as I passed him. Unlike his pushy, belligerent attitude toward me in the courtroom, he was relaxed. We talked for five or ten minutes about being a Detroit cop and then he said, "I couldn't believe that was the first time you had ever testified in a case because you were textbook in your responses. I hope I'll never have to meet you in court again."

YOUNG SUK PARK KIM

I was born and raised in a small town called Young-Joo, Korea in a noble family.

In Korea, I was a chemist, forensic science instructor at a college of pharmacy, and a pharmacist with Bachelors of Pharmacy and Masters of Science degrees.

Coming to the United States as a student, I pursued advanced degrees and worked for the state of Michigan for twenty-seven years, until retirement.

Jobs I have really enjoyed were being a teacher, chemist, biochemist and senior scientist.

Prepare Mentally

My mother was the greatest educator. She strongly influenced me and I was able to achieve a college diploma and study further in the U.S.A. with many unbearable hardships to conquer. If my great mother had not planted the seed in me so strongly to "study and learn," it would have been impossible for me to even come to the United States.

I wrote my own life story as my duty to complete a chapter of my life, which God has given me. I feel a need to leave these stories to children and the next generations to read and learn. These living moments of my past and extended periods in my life define who and what I am. I am constantly being defined, refound, reborn, rediscovered, reaffirmed and challenged. Writing helps me realize, discover, and reflect many aspects of myself. This helps me to respect my life and love myself, and that is the purest way to pass on lessons from my experiences to anyone else.

In order to write my memoirs, I had to recollect details from past memories. There were so many emotions involved even in tiny events. Happiness, sorrow, love, and hate filled the long, rocky, lucky road. I thought my seventy-eight years passed like a wind or fog in a valley, but it wasn't so. It has been a very serious, long period lived with full emotions. I am very thankful.

"Joyful Outing" is my happiest and most peaceful and innocent memory of passing through mountains on visits to my grandmother's house, accompanying my mother. When my mother was about my age, she said to me with tears in her eyes, "I miss my mother." I did not understand then what she meant, but twenty years later I am mature enough to understand. Now my mother has passed away. With tears in my eyes, I say, "I miss my mother."

When I write a particular story, I think it over for some time, taking notes on a pad of paper. If I am prepared enough mentally, I am able to write the story without any problems. Since English is my second language, I consult the English dictionary often.

I encourage new writers to journal – to write down notes of what happened on the same day. Some memories will always be vividly remembered in detail but it is still a good idea to write a description for that special event when things are still fresh in the mind and soul.

Joyful Outing

When I was a little girl, my mother and I often went to my grandmother's house. Usually, it was for an overnight stay or a one-day visit. It was a one-hour walking distance, four kilometers, from our house. We walked about fifteen minutes and then came to a bridge. After crossing the bridge, we walked another fifteen minutes and met a narrow mountain path on the right-hand side. Turning to the right, we walked another thirty minutes to a place where we could see grandmother's house far, far away in the distance.

We had to pass through many big and small mountains on the narrow path to finally get there. I loved to go to my grandmother's house but I was so afraid when passing through those beautiful layers of mountains because I had heard that leprous patients who hid in the mountains kidnapped children, killed them, and ate their livers to cure their illness. When I passed between the two biggest mountains, I held my mother's hand tightly and sometimes I felt my knees shake with fear. The leprous story maybe wasn't true, but it stuck in my childhood brain as a very scary thing.

After passing the mountains, there was a huge rock by a stream. The rock was taller than people's height, and it was covered with thick, bluish green moss. We walked for about five minutes by the rock, and then Grandmother's house loomed just beyond the rice fields.

The mountains and the fields were beautiful. I can still hear, see, and taste the flowing clean rivers and murmuring mountain streams that washed away our thirst. I can smell the sweet pretty flowers. In the spring, the mountains were decorated with deep pink azaleas. Dark reddish white Pursatillia Korea bowed their heads shyly, and varieties of wild flowers colorfully came to full bloom. Birds were singing merrily. Farmers, working under the warm sunlight and sweet spring breeze near the mountain path, smiled and waved at us. All of nature welcomed us as we passed through their mountains and fields.

We quickened our step on the ridge between the rice fields as we got closer to Grandmother's house, sometimes even running to get there faster. Grandmother's family was as excited as we were. They ran toward us and we ran toward them. We were so happy to greet each other.

Grandmother's house – which was my mother's childhood house – was located in a small village of many layers of the big mountains. There were only about ten farming families and fifty to sixty people living there. My grandmother's family – twelve people, three generations – were living under one roof in peace and harmony. They were a very polite, scholastic family who always had smiles on their faces. Whenever we visited, there was a big feast of freshly picked vegetables and fruits, and meat from their own farm.

At my grandmother's house, one thing I was afraid of was going to the restroom. Located outside the main gate, the restroom door faced the huge mountain. Some people said that there were tigers in the mountains that ate little children, especially at night, and that a tiger actually took and ate a baby. When I had to go to the restroom at night, three adult uncles accompanied and guarded me outside the restroom until I was ready to come back to the house. It sounds like a "once upon a time" ancient story, but it is what I experienced about seventy years ago whenever I visited there. I know for a fact that tigers actually lived in those big mountains and were a constant threat to those villagers.

When I look back at those days after many years have passed, it seems like a wonderful dream I had a long time ago. My mother, in her mid-twenties, was happy not knowing yet about unjust wars and the cruel world. I sometimes wonder whether my mother thought back on her younger happy days before she passed away in her lonely apartment.

I had a chance to visit Korea some fifty years later. I was told that the village had been developed into a modern city with high rise buildings and there was none of the old days' appearance at all. The beautiful mountains we had passed through had become level lands. As I heard the news, I lamented for the destruction of the natural beauty I once admired. Still, it is a thankful thing to have sweet memories of those joyful outings to my grandmother's house.

College
Diploma

I graduated from a four-year high school under the Japanese government. It was six years for elementary school, four years for high school, and four years for college. After Korea became independent from Japan, the Korean government changed the high school educational requirements from four years to five years, then one year later to six years. When I wanted to study in college after World War II, I was not eligible for the college entrance examination because I had graduated from a four-year high school. The Department of Education, Republic of Korea, established the qualifying college entrance examination system for four- and five-year high school graduates.

I took the lunchbox my mother prepared for me early in the morning and left for the library around 7:30 a.m. and studied all day long until 5:00 p.m. It was bearable in the summer with warm weather but it was unbearable in the winter with only cold rice for lunch and no heating system in the room where I studied. My hands, toes, and feet got very cold. Winter in Seoul is always very cold. I checked out thick books from the library and I memorized most of their contents from cover to cover. For nine months, I devoted myself to preparing for the test.

On the examination day, I went to the examination place with about 1,000 four- and five- year high school graduates under the Japanese government. On the announcement day, I saw my name on the successful candidate list. Only twenty-two out of about 1,000 were successful candidates; only two females were included, and I was one of them. It was almost a miracle to me and I was very happy. It felt like I was dreaming.

I applied for and passed the entrance examination for the College of Pharmacy, Ewha Women's University. The university was, is, and always will be the best traditional women's university in Korea, and the College of Pharmacy was the most popular college, especially among women in those days. In Korea, drugstores only dealt with medicines, not as it is in an American drug store. Female pharmacists could have a business and, with some hired help, be a housewife at the same time because the drugstore and living quarters were usually under one roof. Therefore, the competition rate for the entrance examination was stronger for pharmacy than for any other field. In addition, only high school honor students were allowed to apply.

Seventeen days after my college life started, the Korean War broke out and the university's doors were closed. About one year later, the university built a temporary school in Poo-San. After recovering from wounds received in an air raid on the way to take refugees from the war zone, I went to Poo-San to study.

In the university, the curricula were very hard for me. At that time, the school system changed from four to six years of high school. To make things worse, in my high school days we learned less than one-tenth of the regular school load because of World War II. By the time I entered college, high school graduates were very capable in all subjects because high schools faithfully gave regular education to students even when the country was unstable politically.

When I compared what I learned in my high school days with what they learned in their high school days, there were great differences in quality and quantity. Consequently, it was difficult to understand and follow the lectures. Every curriculum was difficult for me. Civic science was a little easier to follow than some other subjects, such as foreign language (especially German), calculus, physics, chemistry, and others. I had never before heard of nearly all of these lectures, while other students looked like they understood everything and just seemed to be reviewing what they learned in high school.

In addition to the difficult school subjects, I suffered from a poor financial situation. Constantly, I worried about tuition and living and school expenses. Two roommates and I lived in the entrance hall of the house of one of my high school friends. The entrance hall was made of wooden floors. The cold came through the gaps between the boards and penetrated my thin quilt. My body was freezing throughout the night. I was cold and hungry. Though my life was getting harder and harder, I assured myself that I had to succeed in the study that I started, no matter what.

I graduated from the university after studying at the original campus in Seoul for one and a half years. The difficult subjects gradually got easier and I graduated number one in my class due to studying hard all the time. At graduation, I also received a pharmacist license. It was the most memorable, meaningful, and valuable period of my life.

Unforgettable
Little Figure

The Korean War broke out on June 25, 1950. Seoul turned into a scene of bloodshed. Fighters flew over the city and rained bombs everywhere, day and night. Everything was destroyed. Tall buildings crumbled and residences fell to pieces. There was no means of transportation whatsoever in the city. Dead or wounded people sprawled all over the streets. The city smelled bad from dead bodies, their flesh decaying under the hot sun. Everything was closed – the government, schools, businesses, and all stores. No food was available for purchase, not even with diamonds. People streamed out of Seoul to southern parts of Korea, where it was thought to be safe, where the communists had not yet reached.

In the midst of those days, I went out to the Southgate area, usually the busiest and noisiest center of the business section in Seoul. There was no trace of the hustle and bustle that I expected. Whichever way I turned, there were the dead or bleeding, moaning people. Then I heard a child's cry and I turned to where the crying came from. There I saw a little girl, maybe two or three years old, standing with blood flowing down her face, spreading all over her body. She was terribly wounded. The left side of her face was hit, maybe by fragments from the air raid bombing, and they disfigured the little girl. Her left eyeball was gone from its socket and her left cheekbone was crushed and bleeding heavily. She stood there, stretching out her arms trying to touch somebody for help. Maybe she was crying for her mother or father. She was surrounded by many dead and deeply wounded people. One of those people could have been her mother or father.

That was not the time to be able to help anyone because fighters could return at any minute. There was a deeply wounded little girl, who maybe just became an orphan, crying for help. I could not do anything for her. With heavy heart I just left her there. That was fifty-five years ago and I have not been able to erase her memory. That day is engraved in my heart and brain. In those circumstances, nobody was able to help her except maybe United Nations soldiers, but they were soldiers, not civilians. The civilians had not arrived from the U.N. yet.

I've always wondered what happened to that little girl. She most likely died from her wounds or from starvation. So many people became needless victims of the war. She was one of them. The pure little soul, God's creation, suffered so much.

War is one of the worst things to face and live through. It kills and tortures people by ripping off their bodies, piece by piece. War kills people by torturing mercilessly, tearing off body parts and making people suffer for a long time.

I wonder what happened to that little girl. I hope God worked a miracle on her. I hope the eyeball she lost has been restored with an artificial eyeball, and that the disfigured half of her face has been repaired by a skillful plastic surgeon. I hope she had a happy adolescence with a handsome young man and they built a happy family with healthy children. But I doubt it. My feeling tells me that did not happen.

They said that there is no test from God that we cannot conquer, and also anything that happens in this world is God's plan. I had many hardships in my life, but God always gave me enough time to appreciate his test on me and I am eternally thankful for that to God. I do not have any rebellious spirit toward God. I love him and he knows that. However, I felt it was just not fair, and not right, to simply think that it was one unlucky fate she had. I just have to ask God with sad feeling what was his purpose for this little girl to suffer as she did at two or three years old. What was my purpose to experience her pain and hold tragedy in my mind? Even at my age, I still have no answer to this experience in life.

Sacrifice
for Freedom

On June 25, 1950, seventeen days after my college life started, the Korean War broke out. I was living with my little sister, who was an elementary school student. Fighters flew over and rained bombs all over Seoul, day and night. Communist leftists were everywhere and nobody knew exactly who was on the left side or who was on the right side. People did not want anybody to know that they were not on the communist side so they mostly kept their mouths shut. Close neighbors suddenly became suspicious, untrustable strangers because nobody knew what they would do to you simply for their own survival in that turbulent, unstable political situation.

One of my aunts, with her three children and my grandmother, decided to take refuge to prepare for the nearing, severe, cold winter in Seoul. I was ambivalent about living in a war zone and decided to join them. In early August 1950, we were on our way to take refuge after loading our luggage on a small cart that we pushed and pulled by hand. The aerial bombardment was very severe and fighters flew over us on the road where we walked. They rained bombs on the road unconditionally. The fighters could not differentiate the people on the right side from those on the communist left side. Wherever the road was crowded with people, the fighters dropped bombs on them. Consequently, many people who were ahead or behind us fell dead or were lying on the ground, bleeding. Roads near Seoul just turned into a scene of bloodshed.

We faced dangerous situations countless times. Fighters flew over our heads and we hid in ditches by the road and waited for them to fly away after finishing their aerial bombardment. Three days after we left Seoul, the most dangerous situation occurred as we were passing through a small farm village. It was surrounded by especially high mountains on two sides facing each other. We were passing on the path between the two high mountains. I pulled the loaded cart in the front and my aunt pushed the cart from behind.

Suddenly a fighter appeared from one side of the big mountain and flew over our heads and disappeared to the other big mountain side. Then the fighter reappeared, flying very low over our heads and showering bombs on us. At that time, my sister was one hundred meters behind the cart. The bombed area was between my sister and the cart. My sister and I were not bombed directly, but were wounded by fragments of bombs which hit the ground and blew out. My aunt, who was pushing the cart, was hit by fragments on the back of her head and died shortly after, without speaking even one word, leaving her three little children behind. The youngest one was only one year old.

My sister and I were hit in many areas of our bodies. It was sometime between 2:00 and 3:00 p.m. when we were bombed. There were no clouds in the sky, and summer day was blazingly hot. My sister was behind the cart and I was in front of the cart, and we were both down on the ground, bleeding from every hole where the fragments hit. Many fragments penetrated my body, and blood gushed out. The blazing summer sun made us fatigued, and the pain of the wounds was unbearable. I felt the warmth of my body gradually going out.

As I lay there bleeding, many thoughts went through my mind like a kaleidoscope of a dying person. I prayed to God to keep me alive even for a short while longer. I felt that I had to take care of many things before I died. It was an urgent time. I was not ready to die. Then I asked God to forgive all my sins and accept me in his warm arms, if this was the time of my death.

We lay on the road for a long time. It felt it was for eternity. The bleeding decreased some and I crawled into the shadow under a tree on the hill near the road and told to my sister to do the same. My aunt just lay there saying nothing. Of course, I did not know that she was already dead. I said to my little sister, "Goodbye, have a safe journey to heaven. I will meet you there." I felt so sorry for her and so very sad because I sure thought that we would die there.

Because we were wounded in too many places and had bled too much already, no one even came to check on us. My grandmother had gone to the village and begged for help several times but there was no guarantee that anybody would come to help us. I tore off the blouse I was wearing with my right hand and teeth, since my left hand was injured. I tied the upper part of my wounded legs and raised both legs and my left arm high to stop the bleeding. I could not tie my left arm so I just raised it high. I told my sister, who was lying under a tree about one hundred meters away, to raise her wounded leg high.

Six or seven hours after the bombing, the evening glow started to show and it started to get dark. Then village people came to check on how many people were dead or alive. They told us that they were afraid the fighter might come right back and bomb again and that they were sorry they could not come to help us sooner. They also told us that the fighter may have misunderstood us as supplying goods to the communists.

They put my sister and me on a carrier cart and took us to the empty house whose owner had taken refuge. Finally we were in the house and the villagers started to take care of us.

Grandmother sent a messenger to her home in Seoul to tell of the accidents, and another aunt came to take Grandmother and my deceased aunt's three children back to Seoul. Grandmother and the three children left after the kind villagers buried my aunt. I'll never forget and will always feel deeply indebted to the villagers for my life and especially to a few people who were unconditionally kind to us from the beginning until we left there. God bless them forever.

We did not have any medicine on hand so there was no way to treat our wounds. There were no doctors and no pharmacy in the village, and most of the villagers had left to take refuge. Even if somebody had some medicines, who would want to share them with strangers? They had to keep them for their own use in case they might need them.

We tore up sheets and bound our wounds with them. It was the middle of the summer and flies were all over. Filthy, bad smells from our wounds filled our room. When I saw shining, fat, wriggling white maggots crowded in the pus of my wounds, I realized that we would never be able to get out of this village alive, and I felt goose bumps all over my body.

First, we were severely wounded. Second, in those days, the North Korean army and the communists were all over. If the right wing thought we were communists, we would be killed by the right wing without an explanation, or if the communists did not like us, we would just disappear without a trace. So we would be dead either way, by the left or the right wing, if somebody wanted to harm us. It was a very unsafe and dangerous time.

One day, a villager brought some green leaves called plantain and told us the leaves were good for sucking pus away from wounds. We covered our wounds with clean plantain leaves. The leaves surprisingly sucked out all the pus, completely cleaning the wounds. Miraculously, healthy new red tissue started to grow there. However, new skin should have covered the newly growing tissue and healed the wounds, but the plantain did not make new skin grow, so the new red tissue kept growing and growing without new skin to cover it.

On one of those bedridden days, a communist executive dropped in to inquire about our health. He asked me whether I could raise my legs and said that he would drop in that night. After he left, I thought about his awkward questions, and my sixth sense warned me that there would be some danger that night if he returned. So we went to the old couple who lived across the path. Using arms to push against the ground, I moved my wounded legs slowly forward. I told the couple what had happened. The old gentleman gladly welcomed us to stay at their house. As we suspected, about midnight there were loud voices, gun shots, and noisy sounds from the house we escaped from. We spent the night safely with the old couple and they continued to let us stay there.

Two days after the incident, I thought I heard my mother's voice from the house where we used to stay. I heard my mother's hurry-scurry. It was my mother and little brother. After she heard our news, they came from Seoul to look for us. They traveled almost eighty kilometers through mountains, over the stream, and on the dangerous roads. How happy and thankful we were to see them. It was truly beyond description. Then I really knew I did not have to worry about anything. She would take us back to Seoul, somehow, some way. Our mother's love was able to handle all these adversities and even more.

KATHLEEN NORTHEY GIDDINGS

I am a retired social worker, having worked in the child welfare field for thirty-five years. My specialty was adoptions. I was raised in Michigan's upper peninsula.

My family moved to Lansing when I was a high school junior, but in my heart I am still a "Yooper." I earned BA and MSW degrees from Michigan State University. My husband and I have traveled throughout all the United States, Europe, Asia, Africa, and Scandinavia, often accompanied by children and grandchildren.

My parents always encouraged me to write and I have enjoyed renewing this interest in my retirement. Getting stories to family members in the form of "books" has been my goal.

Keep It Simple, Keep It Fun

I knew the facts of my mother's emigration from Finland at the age of one and my paternal grandfather's arrival from Cornwall, England, at the age of twelve. These facts were developed into stories, which begin my "books."

My books close with stories of my grandchildren, family songs, and even old memorable radio jingles from the U. P. I never lack for a topic: a niece's wedding, an aunt's eightieth birthday, a dinner conversation, a picture, and incidents from everyday living are certain to fill my mind with ideas. I have also written some fiction. And it is fun!

After three years I have written many stories and given books of them to family members. Each Christmas I give them new, recent stories for insertion. I scan pictures pertinent to the stories onto them.

My first story in this book, "It Isn't Any Trouble," is an example of my writing. As much as I have tried to deny and ignore my rheumatoid arthritis during my lifetime, it has stuck to me like Velcro. So I told the story of its beginning, as I remember it as a child: my feelings, my thoughts, the influence of my father's positive attitude on me.

I have written other stories of events from my perspective at those particular times. I find it easy to write in this manner.

I decide what to write about, think it through in an attempt to gauge the length, and then "go to it." I do final corrections to my stories before giving them to family members. I read them through before class to eliminate confusing sentences and shorten the stories, if necessary.

I like dialogue and feel a little dialogue can often take the place of a whole paragraph of words in a more interesting manner. I am thankful to my friend, Tom Ruhala, now deceased, who introduced me to this writing endeavor. My main motto in writing is, "Tell your story, keep it simple, and keep it fun!"

It Isn't
Any Trouble

"It isn't any trouble just to S-M-I-L-E,
It isn't any trouble just to S-M-I-L-E,
If ever you're in trouble, it will vanish like a bubble
If you only take the trouble just to S-M-I-L-E."

Daddy and I sang happily as he drove from Negaunee to
Marquette. Every Thursday he left the school in charge of somebody
else while we made this trip. I was seven and in second grade, but not
really in second grade. I wasn't going to school at all that year. I was at
home. I had read all the Bobbsey Twins books, *Five Little Peppers*, and
now I was reading *Little Women*.

I remember when it all began. I sat down on my way upstairs and
cried because my knees hurt, so Daddy carried me. He said I was three
the first time that happened. Dr. James said I had "growing pains."
Then I had the measles. Dr. James said my knees still hurt because it
was a "bad case" of measles. They kept hurting, so he said I needed a
tonsillectomy and adenoidectomy. I had to go to the hospital for that.
Then I had an ear infection and my cheek was a round hard ball. I
had to go to the hospital again for a mastoidectomy and couldn't hear
out of that ear ever again. I was getting very good at saying all the
"ectomy" words. But my knees still hurt and sometimes swelled.
Sometimes my fingers swelled, too, and Mama and Daddy were really
worried. Dr. James had run out of reasons for this.

The previous summer, when I was six, Daddy went to classes at
the University of Michigan and worked at its Fresh Air Camp. Karen,
Mama, and I stayed in an apartment in Pinckney, near the camp.
Mama and Daddy took me to the big hospital at the university. I had
to get in a hospital gown and go under big X-ray machines. They took
blood out of my arm.

One doctor said, "Mr. and Mrs. Northey, your daughter has
juvenile rheumatoid arthritis. She will be in a wheelchair."

He didn't even talk to me. I didn't say a word, but thought sassy
thoughts. "No, I won't, I'll show you! Grandpa Northey said I can be
a stubborn Cousin Jack and Aunt Aino said I have Finnish Sisu, so I'll

show that doctor he's wrong."

So that's why I had to stay home from school that year. I had to rest. Every Thursday, Daddy and I went to to see Dr. Roberts and I got a gold shot. I didn't have to hold Daddy's hand anymore when we got to the Clinic. I knew the way to the elevator and could push the button for the second floor. I was always happy when I got there because Daddy and I had sung and talked all the way. Irene Numinen, the nurse, always came to the waiting room to get us and take us back to a patient's room. Nurse Irene would say I was getting richer and richer with all the gold I was getting. We'd all laugh, even though we heard the same joke every week. Dr. Roberts would come in and sometimes I'd have a blood test. Then I'd bare my bum for my gold shot.

One day, Nurse Irene took my hand and said, "You know a war started, don't you?" I nodded my head. "This is my last day here. I'm going to be an Army nurse."

My throat hurt. I wanted Nurse Irene to stay with Dr. Roberts. I couldn't talk for a long time on the way home. Daddy seemed to understand. But I wanted to keep to our weekly routine. "Daddy, look out the window, there's that dog we always wave to, that collie!" Daddy looked and we both waved. Then we began to sing,

> *"It isn't any trouble just to L-A-U-G-H,*
> *It isn't any trouble just to L-A-U-G-H,*
> *If ever you're in trouble, it will vanish like a bubble*
> If you only take the trouble just to L-A-U-G-H."

You Have to Be Carefully Taught

Two men with black skin came walking down our street while I was outside playing with Roger. Martha, Roger's mother, raised her kitchen window. "Roger, come in right now!" Roger did not usually obey right away, but this time he did. Martha raised the window again and hissed, "Kathleen, you should go in, too. Those are niggers out there."

I had seen black-skinned people before, when we were in Lansing and Ann Arbor. I didn't have the feeling it was bad to see them, so I stayed outside and sat on the step. I knew it wasn't polite to stare, so I just watched as they walked by. It was the first time I had seen people with black skin in the Upper Peninsula. Roger didn't come out again, so I went in.

I told Mama what happened and she said, "Oh, they must be working at the carnival in town." When we were eating, I told Daddy, and he scowled one of his worst scowls.

"'Nigger' is a bad word," he said. "People with dark skin are called Negroes. They are people just like us, only their skin is darker." We went to the carnival, but I never saw anyone with dark skin. Maybe they were inside the tents.

The next summer we lived in Ann Arbor again while Daddy went to the University of Michigan and worked at its Fresh Air Camp. One day we went to visit Daddy's Uncle Bart and Aunt Mabel in Detroit. We arrived in the late morning and they had to unlock their front door to let us in. In Negaunee we didn't even lock our doors at night.

"We keep the doors locked all the time," Aunt Mabel said. "You never know when Negroes might come by."

I looked at Daddy's face and knew he didn't like what she said. After lunch, Daddy asked Uncle Bart, "Is it OK if Aune and Karen stay here with you while I take Kathleen downtown on the bus?"

I prayed that Uncle Bart would say yes, and he did. What an adventure! The bus took us right down to all the big buildings in Detroit. There were a lot of dark-skinned people. Daddy said, "All these people are riding on the bus and walking around, just like us." He didn't say so, but I knew then that Daddy took me on this adventure so that I could see people with black skin doing the same things we were.

A couple weeks later, Dr. Martin, a professor at the U of M, was going to Fresh Air Camp. He picked up Mama, Karen, and me so that we could spend the afternoon with Daddy. He told Mama, in an apologetic manner, that he also had to take the new cook. She had black skin. Dr. Martin spread a white towel on half the back seat for her to sit on. I sat on the other half. Mama sat in the front seat with Karen on her lap. I thought it was mean that the cook couldn't sit on his seat. Nobody talked to her. Whenever I glanced at her, she was looking straight ahead, so I didn't talk to her, either. I didn't know what to say anyway. When we got to camp I told Daddy about it and his face scrunched up again. The next week we had company for dinner. His skin was very black. He was from Africa and was in one of Daddy's classes at the U of M. Mama made one of her best dinners and we used napkins. He told us some things about Africa. I had to listen very carefully because he didn't speak English well.

When we moved to Lansing in the early 1950s and I entered Eastern High School, I realized what a gift I had been given. I was not uncomfortable with dark-skinned teens as fellow students. The efforts to expose me to other than the Caucasians of the U.P. had paid off.

My husband, Tom, and I were both raised in Caucasian, Methodist homes. Through marriages, our extended family now includes Catholic, Muslim, and Jewish faiths and people who are black, Middle Eastern, and Hispanic. It is the proverbial "melting pot." Yet sometimes I wonder if the world has really changed in the years since Martha hissed at me to go in because there was somebody different on our street.

The Pest

"Do you want to go to camp (Yooper-term for cottage) with us this weekend?" I waited for the inevitable question.

"Is Karen going?" my best friend, Phyllis, asked. She always asked about Karen, even though she knew what the answer would be. I didn't blame her. When she and I took Karen to the movies, she burst into tears every time people kissed. It was pretty embarrassing for us, a couple of young teenagers. No matter how much we warned Karen about it beforehand, each screen kiss brought forth heart-rending sobs. Loud heart-rending sobs.

But Phyllis had other reasons for asking about Karen going to camp. "We can't go without her, you know." It was a real pain having Karen for a younger sister. Lynn was a baby and was cute, but Karen! After the preliminaries, Phyllis always answered in the same resigned manner, "OK, I'll go."

We started out, Mama and Daddy in the front seat with Lynn on Mama's lap. Phyllis, Karen, and I were in the back. It always started as soon as we got through Palmer. The first sharp curve and the litany began.

"I'm sick," Karen moaned, clutching her coffee can. Phyllis and I scowled at her. "I'm really sick!" Fifteen tortuous miles to go! "Have we come to the waterfalls yet?" The two-lane road seemed endless with its many curves and hills. "Are we almost at Uso Suomi?" whined Karen, as she dramatically made gagging noises. Phyllis pulled as far from Karen as she could, hanging her red hair over her face in an attempt to further shut her out. "Are we almost at the green bridge?"

Each landmark was counted off in like manner as Karen hugged her coffee can. "I'm sick!" she kept wailing.

When we reached Horseshoe Lake, we all breathed a sigh of relief. One more big curve and we were home free. Karen sat up in anticipation. We turned off on a gravel road, right on the next gravel road, and went another mile to a rut road. From this point on each blackberry bush, blueberry bush, raspberry bush, and chokecherry tree was a personal friend. Another hundred yards and we were at our own lane through the woods, just wide enough for our car. The lane was surrounded by poplar, birch, aspen, and evergreen trees. The forest floor was covered with ferns, wild strawberry plants, violets, and mosses. There were our swings, part of and encircled by protective trees. We pulled up into a clearing between the cottage and the outhouse, a two-holer. I was so happy. We were at Shag Lake, Karen was quiet, and my best friend was with us.

A marble sidewalk led up to the back door. This slab was formerly the counter in a cigar and candy store that Grandpa and his brother owned when Daddy was a child. The cottage was wood frame, painted a rusty red, and supported by large wooden blocks. We entered into the "shed," a room holding a cast iron sink with hand pump and icebox. We used the icebox as a cupboard and carried perishables outside to a buried stone crock. There they would stay cool. The kitchen held a big table and wood-burning iron range. The guest bedroom was off the kitchen and the other two bedrooms were off the living room. The middle bedroom was for Karen and me, the front one for Mama and Daddy and Lynn. Kerosene lamps and flashlights were our lights at night. There was no ceiling, but open rafters, so that dividing walls were open on top. Because Phyllis was a guest, she got the bedroom off the kitchen. I was going to sleep in there with her. Karen climbed on the headboard in the middle bedroom and peeked over the top of the wall as we unpacked.

"Mama," I yelled, "Tell Karen to leave us alone."

Karen ran to the screened front porch, grabbed the paddles off the ping pong table, and begged, "Let's play."

But Phyllis and I walked haughtily past her and down the front steps toward the lake. The path was covered with pine needles and crisscrossed with tree roots. Karen came running after us, "I want to go in the boat, too, pleeeease." We relented and let her climb in. Phyllis grabbed one oar, I the other, then we steered around the dock and along the shore. Our oars gently dipped up and down, up and down, among the lily pads.

The future was not then ours to see. We sold this property when we moved to Lansing. Several years ago I searched and found this old favorite spot. The woods had been cleared and other cottages built. Phyllis died of cancer before the deaths of my parents. My sister and I are grandmothers. Karen is no longer a nuisance to me. Buds need sunshine to blossom and our relationship needed time. I wouldn't have believed then that she could become a best friend. But she did.

Good Things Can Come from a Bad Date

In May of my junior year in high school, the first year I lived in Lansing. a student could be inducted into the National Honor Society as a second semester junior, and I was a new member. Maxine, Tom, Bud, and I were in the Methodist Youth Fellowship at our church and knew each other. Maxine, who lived across the street from me, was a senior. Tom was a senior, also. Bud was in college.

"Are you going to the Honor Society picnic?" Maxine asked on the way to school.

"No," I answered, "I don't think any juniors are going."

"I'm going to ask Bud," she said, "Why don't you ask his brother, Tom, and we'll go together?"

I thought for a minute. The picnic was going to be at Lake Lansing Amusement Park and I had never been there. In fact, I had never been to any amusement park. I had heard they had a nice merry-go-round. "OK," I said, "I'll ask him Sunday night at MYF."

So it was arranged. Bud would drive. He and Tom would pick us up.

The day before the picnic Maxine sheepishly told me that she and Bud couldn't go. "But don't worry," she said. "Bud arranged for Tom to get their dad's car that night and he'll pick you up at the same time we agreed on before."

So go we did. My mother packed us lunches of pasties, fruit, and cookies. And sure enough, I was the only junior there. I couldn't eat my entire pasty, so Tom ate the rest of it. I ate one piece of fruit, Tom ate the rest. I ate one cookie – well, you get the idea. He ate everything I didn't. After eating, we were handed complimentary tickets for the rides and let loose for the evening.

"The Dodgems first," Tom yelled. I saw cars going around in a circle and thought I could handle that. Wrong! Shortly after we got started, I was facing the wrong way. I didn't know beforehand that everyone was going to try to run into me. The operator stopped the ride and straightened me out. We started again and soon I was perpendicular to the flow of traffic. The ride stopped. Again I was straightened out. If only people would stop bumping me! The third time I went astray, the ride stopped and everyone had to get out. How embarrassing! Did everyone get short rides because of me?

Undaunted, Tom's voice rang out. "Now the roller coaster!"

There were no seatbelts on rides then, and I bounced around like a ping-pong ball. "Hang on to me!" I yelled, terrified and clutching Tom's arm. "Hang on to me!" So he did.

As soon as we alighted he led the way to the Tilt-a-Whirl. That seemed to have a shell to sit in. Maybe that wouldn't be so bad. But my seventy-six pounds ricocheted in the shell-like compartment and again I screamed, "Hang on to me," and he did. I staggered off that ride, saying, "Don't they have a merry-go-round?" and thinking, "Doesn't this guy ever slow down?"

"The airplanes are right there," he answered, pointing, "Let's do that first."

The airplanes went up, down, around, down, up, down, around, down. My pasty and cookie started a gymnastics competition, then a fight, in my stomach. Then churning and soaring, they spurted right out of my mouth. Up, down, around. This time I leaned over the side and my vomit hit some people below. Up, down, around, over the side again! The ride stopped. The operator very briefly handed me some rags to clean myself off, then grabbed them back and started cleaning the plane compartment. I didn't dare look at the people who had received some of my spray. Good thing it was getting dark.

As I stood there stinking, Tom said, "Let's go on the lake in a motor boat." I couldn't believe it. He still wasn't ready to quit. But maybe the breeze would blow off some of the smell. Out on the dark lake I shivered and Tom put his arm around me. I thought, "I didn't tell him to," and concentrated on breathing through my mouth so I wouldn't smell myself. I still smelled awful, even with the cool breeze. Then, oh no, he kissed me, my sour mouth still open.

We were both quiet going home. I really reeked in the confinement of the car. When we reached my house, I said "bye," and sped inside, grateful to be home, and thinking, "I'll never see that guy again."

Tom and I were married four years later. He just wanted to see what I'd do for an encore.

The Cat Who Had to Go on Steroids

Tom and I had been married nearly a year and I was pregnant. Mom must have thought we were responsible enough to leave us in charge of my sisters, Karen and Lynn. For the first time, she accompanied Dad to an out-of-state conference.

On July fourth, Karen suggested, "Let's go to see Wanda's kittens. They were born Memorial Day weekend."

We were all agreeable, so we enthusiastically set out for the home of Karen's friend. The kittens were, of course, darling. As we held and snuggled with them, Karen and Lynn bemoaned the fact that our mother would not allow any pets. I said, "We could get one. OK with you, Tom?"

He was more than happy about the idea. The problem was, which kitten? After much deliberation, the four of us decided on a cuddly little tabby. She couldn't quite get out a big "meow" yet, just a little bleating "maaa." We all fell in love with her. We named her Yankee Doodle because she came to us on the Fourth of July. It was too big a moniker for a tiny kitten and was soon shortened to Doodle.

I didn't return to graduate school in the fall because I was awaiting Melanie's birth. Doodle was, in all respects, my pet. I taught her to fetch her catnip mouse, just like a dog. She slept with us. She was our baby — until Melanie was born. Then we had a problem. Doodle wanted to sleep with the newborn infant and we could not allow that. We were then in a one-bedroom apartment, so the crib was in our bedroom. If we closed the bedroom door, the cat would yowl and scratch at it all night, giving us no sleep. One night, in desperation, I laid the crib mattress in the bathtub, tucked our baby on top of it, closed the bathroom door, and opened the bedroom door. Doodle was quickly in our bed and we all slept. The next morning I called my mother.

"Will you take the cat awhile?" I asked, explaining our dilemma. What first-time grandmother could say no? Karen and Lynn were ecstatic: at last they had a pet. And they weren't the only ones pampering Doodle. Our mother fed her tuna fish, cream, codfish, and liver. It was a cat's utopia!

Although we had moved into a two-bedroom apartment, we didn't take Doodle back until Melanie's second birthday, when we moved into our first house. We weaned her back to cat food, but every time my parents came, Doodle would meet them at the door, knowing my mother would bring "leftovers" for the cat, real or made-to-order. Sometimes I ate them! When we left town, my parents would cat-sit. When we took Doodle to their place, she would jump out of the car and joyfully run into their home. However, the cat seemed reasonably content with us, until we got our son, Mark.

Mark was six and a half months old and had his own bedroom with a door. We didn't have the problem this time; the cat did. She was very obvious about it. She retreated upstairs and hid under Melanie's bed for two weeks. Occasionally, we would see a ball of fur streak down the stairs to the litter box, with a quick stop for food and water. When she finally joined us again, her hair started falling out in clumps. The vet said she was having an allergic reaction caused by stress. We had to push cortisone pills down her throat to keep her from going bald. We got a dog a few years later, but Doodle handled that with finesse. She slashed his nose a couple times and retained her place on top of the pecking order.

Doodle lived twenty-one and a half years. Then her kidneys failed and we had to have her euthanized. In her last days, Tom was carrying her up and down the basement stairs to the litter box. She was still dragging herself to meet my parents when they came, even though she could not eat their tempting offerings. When Tom brought her body home from the vet's, Melanie came home from college to say goodbye. Mark went through the linen closet and chose the prettiest pillowcase for her shroud. A large rock marks her burial place in our backyard. She truly was our Yankee Doodle Dandy.

Rest Room Blues

"Grandma, you're back!" Four-year-old Justine jumped up and down as I parked my car at the campsite. "Grandpa and I already had breakfast and went swimming. He said you'd read *The Boxcar Children*. Will you, pleeease? Are you going home again tonight? I met the people camping around us. I made some new friends at the beach, too. Can we play cards tonight? Grandpa said we can have a campfire tonight and make s'mores. Do you like s'mores?"

Tom picked up his book. I got the message: it was my turn to handle the flood of words and questions. Not quite in order, I answered. "I brought some blankets for the back of the station wagon. I'll put my sleeping bag on top of them and sleep there tonight. Yes, I like s'mores and you will, too. A fire tonight would be great. Sure, I'll read a Boxcar Children book. Pick out the one you want."

Thus did our second day of camping begin. It was warm enough to say it was a beautiful day and cool enough not to sweat. Leaves rustled in the soft breeze. I spent a lot of time in the public rest room. Justine saw it as a social center and had to go to the bathroom every hour.

"Are you sure?" I'd ask, searching her cloudless blue eyes for any hint of hesitation or guilt.

She steadily met my gaze, nodded her head solemnly, and said "Yes." Once inside, she started conversations with our fellow tenants. "I'm camping in site forty-three, where are you? We're having hot dogs for supper." Et cetera, et cetera. If I used a stall, I told her to stand right outside the door so I could see her legs, then I'd hear her add to her verbal repertoire the fact that her grandma was in there.

When people asked, "Where did you get that beautiful white hair?" she'd answer, "Must be from my dad, because he's losing his hair." She stamped her sandaled foot in a puddle on the floor. I tried not to think what the puddle might be.

Melanie, Steve, and eleven-month-old Anna came out to visit. Anna's eyes stared up as they stepped out of the car. She would not look at us, even when prompted, "Look, Anna, here are Justine, Grandma, and Grandpa." We called her name, but got no response.

"Tree," she said.

"Tree," we echoed.

Then she looked at us and smiled. The fluttering leaves had had her attention. As soon as her family left, Justine had to go to the bathroom again. Of course, she didn't even think of it when her mother was there to take her. Now when we went in, someone was sure to say, "Hi, Justine, how are you doing?" After her many trips to the rest room, trips to the beach, and walks with Tom, she had many "best friends."

My night in the station wagon went well. It was cool enough that I could leave the windows up and avoid mosquitoes. Tom, on the other hand, said the tent did not close up well. A steady stream of mosquitoes sneaked in and attacked him. We dropped a happy Justine off at her home on Sunday.

Tom and I agreed that it was a good weekend.

"But," I said, "I'm too old for board beds and rest rooms with puddles of unknown origin."

"And the mosquitoes got to me at night," added Tom. "If we're going to continue taking grandchildren camping, we need to consider getting a motor home."

"Amen to that," I answered, and so we did.

BETTY DROBAC

I am an easterner, born in New York City, with many beloved relatives spread all the way up and down the east coast. My first job was teaching physical education majors at Cortland State Teachers College, some of whom were older than I was at the time. After three years, realizing that I needed advanced degrees to continue this wonderful work, I went back to New York University for a Masters Degree.

That accomplished, a restless friend and I decided to take a vacation trip to the midwest where my sister then lived. At her suggestion, we stopped at the Chicago Teacher's Agency to investigate the possibilities in the area. My friend was a secretary and could fit in anywhere. Michigan State had an opening. Where was that? We turned my plucky 1937 Ford coupe north and I took what I intended to be a short stop teaching in East Lansing, Michigan before going back to the east coast.

So what happened? A tall handsome tennis player arrived at MSU that year from Milwaukee, a veteran, and we got married. After five years I retired to be a homemaker and he coached and taught at MSU for thirty-two years.

To our dismay, not one of our three children decided to stay in East Lansing. All are happily dispersed across the country. One lives in Colorado, one in California, and one in South Carolina. Nice visiting, yes, but I have decided this country is toooo big.

Write about What You Know

The episode described in my story, "A Walk on the Beach" is, as much as I can remember, a completely true story, but written years after it happened. The details of the place are very clear in my memory from many visits to that beach, both before and since my writing of the story. The description of my father and his actions and the earlier memories of our days at the farm, the horse, chestnut tree, the wasps, and the puppies flowed easily, as though they happened in a fresh dream. This is pretty typical when I am writing a memoir.

When I am writing a story other than an actual memoir, I find that my settings are often partly memoir. In other words I'll write a fiction story but the setting will be a place or places that are familiar to me, so that I find describing them quite fulfilling.

I always write my stories in longhand as I am not familiar enough with a computer, or even my typewriter, to interrupt my thought processes when I am composing. My subjects come from anywhere. Often while I am driving alone in my car, I see or think of a subject and will jot down notes on an ever-present pad of paper to remind me of it later. Sometimes these notes stay around for years and come in handy when I need them. In fact, now that I think about it, almost all my writing, prose or poetry, is memoir of a sort. Someone once taught me: write about what you know. I took that lesson to heart.

A Walk on the Beach

That June day, soon after I was seven, my aunt and I went down to the shore of the Sound.

"I love the sea," she said. "I come to the beach whenever I have something on my mind. The Sound is so strong and quiet that I can feel strong and peaceful here."

I slowed my skip to a walk, still holding her hand. My bare feet sank in the soft sand which separated us from the low tide rocks at the water's edge. The early spring breeze blew through my hair and I smelled the seaweed, the fishy, salty smell that I love because I love the things I do here. I have come often with my cousins when it's warm enough to swim.

My aunt gazed out at the water, which was the same blue color as her eyes.

"Betty, do you know why you are living with me and Uncle John instead of with your mother and father?"

"Yes," I said.

"Tell me," she asked. "What do you think is the reason?" I wondered at the question but knew the answer. "Because Daddy is sick in the hospital, and Mother has to work very hard all day."

She nodded. "That's right. He's been sick for a long time and your mother thought you'd be happier here with us while he was away."

"I know." I made my face as serious as hers.

"Do you remember him, Betty?"

"Yes," I said. "I remember him a little."

"What do you remember?"

I thought a minute, shuffling the flashcard scenes in my mind. "Mostly I remember the Johnny Bear stories he told me every night."

There had been a room, but the edges were blurry in my memory. And a sofa, dark brown and so soft that the pillows rose up around me as I climbed across them into his lap and we both looked into the fire. There was always a fire.

"Whose story tonight?" he would ask, and the sound of his teeth on his pipe, as he shifted it in his mouth, was the signal for me to settle into the comfortable place against his chest. It was hard to decide, for there was not only Johnny Bear and Black Miji of the sudden meow, but the ten little puppies. Little Three Dog was one of my favorites.

"Did you know Little Three Dog?" I asked my aunt.

"I knew them all," she said. "I used to hear him tell you the stories."

"I didn't know you were there."

"Sometimes," she said. "Not always. Your father and I have been very close all our lives."

I tried to fit her into the memory but I couldn't extend the picture of the room, only the sofa, the fire and now . . .

"There was a bear rug," I said, in some surprise.

"Yes, Johnny Bear."

"Of course." And it seemed as if I knew it before she spoke.

"It's funny," I said. "I don't remember any of the stories, only the animals who were in them." I felt a sudden excitement. "Do you?"

She shook her head sadly. "I'm afraid not."

"Maybe when he gets well," I said. "Or do you think I'm too old for them now?"

She turned away from me toward the pile of rocks that marked the end of the beach. Thick brown cattails grew between them and grass with flat sharp blades that could scratch your legs if you brushed against them.

"Let's sit here for awhile," she said. She brushed the sand from a big, smooth rock which tilted only slightly forward. We settled ourselves against it.

"Well, anyway, I know I'm too old for the 'animal' game." I laughed as I thought of it.

"The 'animal' game?"

"Yes, the one on the stairs. Where I fed him through the bars."

The stairs turned their carpeted way upward from a middle landing to parallel the upstairs hall. When he stood on the landing, his head was even with the hall floor where I knelt, reaching through the bannister bars to feed, first, the raging lion, then, the friendly Billy Goat, sometimes even a sniffing bunny. "I always knew what animal he was by the sound he made."

"I guess he didn't really eat the papers," I said to my aunt. "I thought that he did."

"There wasn't anything he wouldn't do to make you laugh."

"I don't know where the stairs went," I said. "I can only picture a door in the hall at the bottom."

"That was the farm."

"The farm," I said. "That's right. We lived there, too."

"Only in the summer," she said. "But you were very little then. You haven't been to the farm since you were four."

I struggled with the memory. "There was a huge tree. A horse chestnut tree in the middle of the driveway."

The tree was so big that I couldn't see around it. I knew it was a horse chestnut tree because horse chestnuts grew on it and I knew what they were. When they fell, it was like rain falling one drop at a time. Some of them were so big that I could pick up only one alone in my hand. Lots of them fell into the sandbox that my father built for me, and we made roads with them, smooth brown roads, like paths of cobblestones, which wound around the sandy hills. We made sidewalks with the little ones.

"There's nothing as smooth as a horse chestnut," I said to my aunt. "I haven't held one for a long time."

The cars came up the driveway and went around the tree before they went out again. Usually they stopped on the way. Everyone told me over and over never to get out of my sandbox when a car was in the driveway. Everyone. I never did and I wished they'd stop telling me.

"Your father loved that tree," said my aunt. "It shaded the whole front yard."

Between the kitchen steps and the garage, the ground was all paved. I rode my three-wheeler there, round and round. When the garage doors were open and the cars gone, I could make bigger circles and go faster, into the shade, out in the sun. But one day a wasp bit me. He flew down my back inside my shirt and bit me – three times, I think. I screamed and screamed until my father came running from the kitchen door. I didn't ride there much after that.

"Did you know about the wasps?" I asked my aunt.

"No."

"I got one down my back once," I said. "It was awful."

After that my father decided to kill the wasps. He was dressed in heavy clothes with long white gloves and a hat with nets hanging over his face. I wanted to watch but he sent me into the house before he went up the path toward the puppy shed. There were no puppies then but there used to be.

"I remember the puppies," I said to my aunt. "Lots of puppies."

It was a long walk from the kitchen to the puppy shed, halfway up a steep hill. He held my hand and we stepped over the rocks, half buried in the dirt path. Then we walked in the door and all those baby puppies ran in the straw to meet us. The whole shed smelled like sweet puppy breath and that was the first time I ever smelled it.

"Whenever I cuddle a baby puppy and he licks my face, I think of the smell of the puppy shed."

"Nine of them," said my aunt. "Nine baby Airedales."

"Whatever happened to them?" I asked. "Later I only remember Laddie."

"He was the gentlest," she said. "The others were sold before they grew up."

Laddie was as tall as I was and I had to reach up to put the soap on his neck and ears. He didn't want to hold still, so I tied him to the door at the bottom of the stairs. My mother called from the top. "What are you doing to Laddie?" I told her I was only washing his face, but she ran down, wiped off the soap, and wouldn't let me finish.

"Mother gave Laddie away," I said, and there was a sudden lump in my throat.

"Only after your father got sick," my aunt said. "She couldn't take care of a big dog in the city after she went to work. She kept him as long as she could."

"She should have left him on the farm until we could go back."

"Betty, I think your mother knew, when your father was so sick, that you were never going back to the farm."

"You mean he isn't getting better?"

"No, I'm afraid he isn't. As a matter of fact . . ." she hesitated and then went on. "The farm is sold, you know."

"And Laddie died," I said. "The people let him chase a car and it hit him. Mother told me." I felt myself starting to cry and blinked hard. "He didn't mind living in the city. The doorman took him for walks in the park. Sometimes I went, too." The pavement was marked in even squares and every third step brought me to a line which I stepped over carefully, like the stones in the path at the farm. My finger made an even thumping sound as I held it against the iron pickets in front of the brownstone houses that we passed. The pointer finger of my glove got all black from the fence but I couldn't miss a post or I'd have to go back to the corner and start over.

"Daddy could stop traffic with his cane," I said. "When we came to a crossing, he just raised his cane and the cars stopped. Why?"

"He used to walk you to kindergarten sometimes," said my aunt. "I don't know why the cars stopped except that he looked so distinguished with his mustache and tall hat."

"Uncle John doesn't have a hat like that, does he?"

"Not many people wear them anymore," said my aunt. "Anyway, not here in the suburbs."

"That's about the last thing I remember about Daddy," I said. "I mean, the oldest I was."

"That's about right," she said. "That was the year he went to the hospital. Later you came to live with us."

"It seems like a dream I had a long time ago. I feel as though I've always lived here, with Mother coming to visit every week."

She put her arm around my shoulders. "I want you to remember those things about your father, Betty. Try always to remember them." Her voice sounded different and I looked up at her face. Her eyes were bright and glistening and she held her top lip between her teeth.

"Your father was a wonderful man," she said. "He loved you more that anything in the world except your mother. Will you remember that?"

I nodded and waited. I could feel her fingers moving on my shoulder as if they were playing the piano. "Your mother is coming tomorrow, Betty. There is something I want to tell you before she gets here. Something that will make it easier for her if you know."

I was surprised. I tried to think if it was the right day for my mother's visit. I didn't think it was.

My aunt went on. "Sometimes when someone has been sick for a long time, like your father, God decides he's been unhappy long enough."

"Can't He make the person well?"

"Not always. And when He can't, there comes a time when . . . " she broke off. "Betty, it's like Laddie. When he got hit by the car and hurt, we wouldn't want him to stay alive and always be hurting. So he died and then the hurt was gone. So it is with your father. God decided it would be better if he weren't sick any longer, and so . . . ,"

I watched her face as a tear escaped from the edge of her eye and started town her cheek. She wiped it away quickly with her finger.

I felt grown up all of a sudden. "Is my daddy dead?" I asked, looking carefully at her to make sure I understood. I saw more tears try to start over her bottom eyelash but she caught them with a wipe of her finger.

"Yes, Darling, that's what I'm trying to tell you."

After a moment I stood up and her arm fell from my shoulder. I walked away from her toward the water, feeling the sand between my bare toes, soft and warm at first, then hard and cool as I came to the damp part. I was careful not to step on any of the little pebbles left in the smooth moist sand, when the tide went out. Then I came to the rocks. They were cold and slippery. Some of them were sharp.

A little crab, no bigger than my toe, scuttled sideways off a stone and slid into a puddle between the rocks. His body, so light that I could almost see through it, floated, rocking gently on top of the water. His eyes, on tiny stilts, looked steadily up at me. I stretched my finger toward him and he scrambled into a pile of seaweed. I could have caught him. Some days my cousins and I caught them by the pailful and raced them.

My father was dead. A numb feeling hung heavy inside me like a stone on a rope. He was dead, the tall man with the pipe and long cane who stopped traffic, who loved the horse chestnut tree and ate paper through stair bannisters. My father was dead, this man my aunt told me I must remember.

I looked back at her. Her head was bowed. I saw the white of her handkerchief crumpled in her hand as it lay across her knee. I had never seen her cry before.

Suddenly I knew that I should be crying, too. The tears wouldn't come. I tried to think myself into the little girl on the brown sofa. She was the one whose father was dead, but I couldn't seem to find her in me.

I knew I couldn't go back across the beach to my aunt until I could cry. Everyone who loses a father cries, and my aunt was crying. There was this stone on a rope, but the tears wouldn't come. I tried to think of a time when I'd been sad enough to cry.

Then I remembered. It was only last summer, when my mother told me about Laddie. She said he ran down the street, racing a car. He slipped, or the car turned. I made myself think how it had been to pet his soft brown ears, to feel his rough red tongue on my cheek.

The lump in my chest moved up to my throat, and at last my eyes were wet. I clung to the vision of Laddie, lying on a strange city street.

Tears ran down my face as I crossed the sand to my aunt. She stood as I reached her and held out her arms. I buried my face against her. Her hand stroked my back. I couldn't stop crying then, because it was so sad that I could cry for my dog but not for my father.

The Year Short Skirts Came In

My mother died the year short skirts came in. I bought one, between visiting hours. I wore it to her room and postured for her, back and forth, around, the way one postures for mothers. She nodded, as if approving the new style, yet only half-concerned, already focused forward. She was not one to look behind, especially at trouble.

"I never cry about spilt milk," she'd say. "The time to worry is before." I never saw her cry.

She was with me, convalescing from her first attack, the day my old dog died. Her eyes were grave and slow.

"Don't cry that way for me," she said.

At her funeral I tried to think of that. I tried not listening to the words, pretending to be someone else. I tried to think of Jackie, Ethel, Coretta, veiled and controlled. I made it only to the anteroom before I broke down.

The year my mother died, short skirts came in and I postured my pleated kilt, pink and yellow, no, coral and gold.

"Do you think it's way too short?" I asked.

"No, it's really quite attractive. You have nice legs."

"It's in my genes," I said.

I sat close by her bed, telling the nurse of when my mother was a girl, of her dazzling beauty and charm, of her many beaus. She listened, as if approving my performance, yet only half-concerned. The nurse was rapt with interest and impressed.

The skirts got even shorter after that, too short for me. But I remember when they first came in. Funny what you remember about your mother.

The Metronome

My child at the piano practices her Bach, patterning staccato keys with careful fingers. I find the well-known notes patterned on my ear as I pursue my daily practice, smooth sheets and polished tables.

Click, click, the sweeping wand clicks out the well-known beat: the daily broom, the constant sink, no tears for improvising melodies, impromptu rhythms, the sweeping wand presses me on to one fresh start after another.

Click, click, relentless beat. I hear her headlong fingers fight the measured rhythm, a waterfall of fingers cascade to discord and despair. The empty beat gathers her on to one fresh start after another. I hear her crying.

Click, click, the sweeping years click out the well-known beat, modulating my impatient fingers, patterning legato days with steady fingers. I hear the faithful beat. My child at the piano practices her Bach.

Visiting My Son at College Gives Me Hope

He arranged our stay in the apartment of absent friends, four levels up on Mass. Ave.

The quiet elevator lifted us to carpeted halls.

Inside, the light switch activated the stereo, crimson fish finned through the lighted aquarium, the floors reflected the leaves of plants.

In the closet, coats hung without touching; utensils in the kitchen drawers lay in geometric patterns.

I thought about my cluttered cupboards, unread books, grease on the floor of my garage, my sickly spider plant.

"I hate to think how much they had to clean," I said to my son.

"It always looks this way," he said.

Visiting my son at college gives me a pain in the neck.

Reunion

By your own assessment, you're not much good at Christmas. It irks me that you won't even try. All through the holidays you have relegated yourself to a place behind the tree lights, to putting your finger on ribbon ties, emptying the dishwasher. You have reached to high shelves, laid fires, cleaned out the car for trips to the airport.

I have lost you in the children's arrival, their wants, my wanting to serve them. You spent the days folding paper napkins, fetching from the basement freezer.

Now they are gone. The last guest has left, waved out of sight beside the open door. The weather is ten degrees but the fire is burning.

I find you where I left you.

I am glad to see you.

Small
Gifts

From the snow-covered kennels, my sunlit dogs, trailing bits of straw from feathered coats, wagging their glad shoulders into the warm kitchen, bring me small gifts: a frozen ball, a half-chewed stick, a rubber shoe, an empty dinner pan, a pencil left on a low table.

Long ago, my father at the station, at sundown, waves the evening news from a slow-moving window. He bends and lifts me, a small gift in his pocket: a piece of sweet, a box of crayons, a garnet birthstone ring.

My child in the afternoon, gone the long morning, flies the driveway with unbuttoned jacket, running to meet me, clutching small gifts: a crayoned paper plate, a Christmas ball of spangled Styrofoam, a soap-carved puppy.

PATRICIA WINTERS

When I was a young child, growing up in Chicago, I lost my
mother. Following that event I had few opportunities to talk of her or
share my memories with others who had known her. Consequently my
memories were few and scattered. I was drawn to writing the stories in
this collection as a way to revive my sense of our relationship.
I am consistently influenced by the stories of other peoples' lives and
to the details of their experiences and emotions, both in fiction and in
biography. These interests have influenced my style of writing. For me,
life is the journey, not the arrival, and writing about this early part of
my journey has made it a richer, clearer and more meaningful
experience.

I moved to Michigan as a young woman, and raised my family
here. I am a practicing psychotherapist.

Choose a Richly-Remembered Event and Allow the Story to Unfold

I wrote "Dancing with Fred Astaire" as a love letter. I have always
warmly remembered playing among my mother's clothes, gazing at her

jewelry, makeup, and trinkets, and listening to her sounds and her music coming from the kitchen. I love my mother and I also love that imaginative, cautious little girl that I was back then. When I approached this story in my mind, I gathered the memories that I loved about us, and out the story came. I wanted to tell my mother about these events for the first time. Perhaps other writers might choose a richly remembered item, event, or place and, by focusing attention on it, allow a story to unfold.

When I begin to create a story in my mind, I try to see it and then to register what I feel about what I see. When the story is first on paper, I ask myself if I can once again step into my own shoes and recognize something of my own landscape. Am I writing the mood, the sights, and sounds in a way that someone else might be able to see a bit of what I am seeing? Have I found a way to draw in words a picture that is true to the event, true to its emotional meaning?

Sometimes I find that I have extended the story too far and that it is beginning to take on additional meanings. When this occurs I cut out the redundancies and write my story ending. I have been willing to take deepening risks in my writing. I remain surprised at how challenging it can be to write about parts of my life. Inside of myself I know where the painful parts are and what they are. These events have been visited many times in my thoughts. But to write about them with a beginning point and an ending point concretizes them and forces me to come to conclusions about my past. In some instances I have come to new conclusions.

They say that reality is in the mind of the beholder. I believe that is true, and that parts of who we really are can be shown to us in a new way as we write our memoirs.

Peony
Memories

As I sat down to begin writing about my childhood and about my mother, I was flooded with unexpected memories. There came memories of games and the faces of little children who had been my friends. And then there came rich feelings, filled with sights and sounds and the geography of my Aunt Erna's home. For three years, off and on, from ages seven to ten, my sister and I lived with my aunt, uncle and cousin in their south Chicago home. My family had been torn apart by tragedy – the loss of my mother – and my aunt had stepped in to help my dad by giving my sister and me a home.

Geraldine Freeman, my best girl friend for a summer, comes first to mind. We became friends in July, with my frequent visits to the peonies in my aunt's backyard. They were my mother's favorite flower, my aunt told me, and that was enough to keep me coming back often. And they were worth the trip. I wondered, Did my mother like their smell and how soft they were? There were two colors of peonies, and both reminded me of her. The deep pink ones reminded me of her lipstick and the bright colors she loved to paint on her nails; but the yellow ones with the tender, pale creamy centers, these felt more like something I had known about our relationship, even though at this moment I cannot capture what I knew then.

Geraldine was as shy as I was, and it took us from November until July to say our first words to each other over the fence that stood behind the peony garden. I had been instructed to be careful of the Freemans. The caution had something to do with Mrs. Freeman being a single woman who was away at work all day, leaving her seven children "uncared for" and free to trouble the neighborhood. Everyone alluded to something bad about the family's situation, which was a warning to me to not bring my "situation" to anyone's attention, fearing they would find out something bad about me. But Geraldine and I had been eyeing each other for months, and one day I told her about how much my mother loved peonies. She must have thought this inviting because she reciprocated by asking me to come and play with her in her backyard where, she said, there were lots of flowers. Being eight years old, caution was easy to toss to the winds in favor of discovering what was to be seen in the world next door.

While the flowers turned out to be largely wild ones – weeds I later learned to call them – I had known these from the backyard at my old house and I was eager to escape back into a bit of the world of play that I once knew. Gerry and I spent days that summer running a restaurant, like her mom did at the hospital where she worked. Gerry had dishes, and pots and pans, and a hand-made wooden stove, and lemonade. We made delicious salads out of plantain and dandelion leaves, tossed with lemonade and tiny white flower dressing, garnished with the small green seeds that we spent considerable time individually plucking from their stems. I didn't know why my Aunt Erna allowed me to play there after her warnings to me. I kept thinking she would stop me, but she said nothing as I went to Gerry's yard almost every morning that summer.

I can still clearly remember the impressions of my first visits into Gerry's house. It smelled of food left a little too long in the sink and garbage can and, by most people's standards, certainly my aunt's and her friends' standards, the house was messy. It wasn't dirty, but messy, mostly because Gerry and her brothers and sisters had tons of toys, clothes, pets, books, photo albums, and more, all kind of falling out of cupboards or left casually on the floor where someone had last played with them. However, these conditions were not disagreeable to me. And the basement, oh, the magic of the basement! It was warm and dry down there, with a dusty smell and a promise of unending discovery. It seems that Gerry's father, who was dead, had loved to make toys for his children as well as buy them many things that their hearts had desired. But then, most of these loving gifts had been gathered and taken to the basement, where they were left in a forgotten mess.

I realize now the profound connection these experiences had with my own dad and with what had happened to us the previous fall. But I did not understand this connection then. Years would pass by before my sister and I would find a short note among my dad's things after he had died. His handwritten note simply said, "$350 dollars for everything. Dear God help me." The note was attached to an invoice from the man to whom my father had sold everything in our home, including all of our toys and everything of my mother's that remained.

And the toys in Geraldine's basement were waiting there, waiting for her to find a friend who had a passion for lost treasure. I was that girl and together we dug in.

Schneider School

George C. Schneider Elementary School and its building that I grew up in remain in my memory. My sister had already been going to Schneider School for two years when it was my turn to go. I neither wanted nor hesitated to go there on that warm September day when I was five. My sister, Dad, and I had walked past the school many times on our way to play at the swings in Hamlin Park, so I had a vision of it in my mind. Like many families of that time, neither of my parents prepared me in any way for what school would be. But, fortunately, I knew from my sister's demeanor and from her willingness to go to school each morning that it was something that big kids liked. That alone gave "school" a mystery I wanted to find out about. Besides, my father had told me that he wanted me to become a teacher, and this was where I had to start.

That morning my mother put me into a pretty dress. Was it pink? I don't remember but it was pretty. And she braided my hair and put a whole banana on my Wheaties. I knew that this day was something important to her. She had sent my sister on ahead, so it was just the two of us walking out the door into my first school day. Down the sidewalk across from our apartment, past the big playground where my grandmother had often taken me to play, under the brick arch and into the far-away apartment courtyard where I was never allowed to go by myself, my mother and I walked. And then there we were, ready to cross Clybourn Avenue, in view of my new school.

Schneider School was a large stately building of dark red brick. I really had not realized how tall it was. And then just a little edge of fear opened up in my chest. The building's corners were made of large white stones, and these same stones decorated the enormous windows that swept across the building's front, from one floor to the next. But I had little time to think about much because my mother walked us steadily towards "going to school." I remember that we passed a small grassy yard. Now here was something familiar. And the friendly sunshine was all around, helping me to recover my bouncy gait and reopen my big brown eyes.

We swept up the sidewalk leading to dark brown, heavy doors that were hard to open and had funny glass that you could almost see through except for the waves in it. Through the doors, it all went so fast. Then there I stood, looking up this great, broad staircase that went on and up and up and on into spaces I could not imagine. Later, after many years of standing like a good soldier on these same stairs, waiting for my class and me to be lined up for our turns outside for recess, or even later, running up and down in happy defiance of the rules, these grand staircases became symbols of open avenues and places to go. But on this day, my knees buckled and I could not follow my mother up the stairs until she looked back at me with those crunched up lines beginning in her forehead and said, "Patsy, catch up." My terror of her anger had always worked, and up I went.

I think that she read a sign that told her my kindergarten class was room 101, just around the corner from the first staircase. I followed her into the room. The tallest ceilings in the world, blackboards, strange kids, a piano in the corner, colored pictures around the room, a clock that I could hear ticking even as I stood at the door – this and more assailed my senses. I remember getting tears in my eyes. Then an old woman in a dark blue dress and black shoes, with a mustache that made her look like Hitler's wife, approached my mother. I was frozen. A rock had fallen on me. I couldn't swallow and I couldn't say hello to Mrs. Hitler, the principal, when instructed to do so. I didn't look at my mother's face. I couldn't remember what I should do, and I knew that I was about to wet my pants. So I closed my eyes and held on, waiting for the next big never-known thing to happen.

"Patsy," a soft voice said. "Hi, Patsy. I am glad you came to see me today." My stricken spirit flew instinctively toward the gentle love in her voice, and tears streamed from my eyes as I opened them to see who the voice was. She told me she was my teacher and asked if I would let her show me some of the nice things in our room. She acted as though my tears and the lead in my legs were not there. I let her take my hand and followed her as she showed me around. She showed me toys. She pointed out David, who lived near where I did. She asked me if I liked to paint and showed me lots of stuff for painting. She showed me some rather large pieces of lumber that children could make houses with, and go inside of and play. She showed me the little coatroom next door to our room where there was a hook for my coat and a shelf for my books and my name, Patsy Winters. But most of all, she held my hand and told me about things that were here in this building that I would come to know and like.

Then we went back into our room and my mother said goodbye to me. With a little wave, I watched her go and thought that she would be proud of me. Then I remember turning back to look at our classroom. I noticed again how very large the windows were from the inside, but the ceiling was not as big as the whole Schneider School, and the yellow shades were pulled down, which somehow made the windows a little pretty and the sky was still blue and sunny.

Dancing with Fred Astaire

Isabel was sitting in her mother's clothes closet. It was after lunch and her sister had gone back to school but, being in morning kindergarten, Isabel stayed at home. These days, sometimes it was good to be home alone with her mother, sometimes pretty bad. She had no judgments about the situation, but saw that her job was to watch for the signals of what kind of day it would be and try to keep her mother happy.

She was sitting in the closet because she wanted to play dress-up and because she wanted to stay out of the way. From the other room, Isabel could hear music playing on the radio and sounds of her mother doing things in the kitchen. Studying the situation, she remembered that there were a number of things that she was never to wear or play with. Among them were a few things that she found almost irresistible. For one, there was her mother's fur coat. It was long and soft, and she would run her fingers through the black-tipped, honey-colored fur. It had a deep collar, embroidered black buttons, and a shiny silk lining that had the fearsome habit of catching on her barrettes when she stood inside of it as it hung on its hanger. Also on the "can't play with" list was the three-foxes collar, where the foxes bit onto each other's tails. Mother would wear these draped prettily around her neck with her black coat. But for now they hung on a hook near the door and were probably watching her with their glass eyes. Isabel felt sure that she needed to be very good today.

So, after some consideration, she pulled out her special box. She was allowed to keep her important dress-up things in her mother's closet. She selected a little yellow sweater with broken buttons that her mother no longer wore, a mirror, a pair of white gloves that her mother said young ladies wore when they dressed up, and a small pair of white lacy socks. From two handfuls of jewelry she selected the colorful necklace that she had made herself from a Christmas bead set. Finally, next to her planned costume, she set down the Mercurochrome bottle that she had taken out of the trash and that now held her pretend perfume. Isabel daydreamed a bit as she put on her costume and stopped for awhile to listen to the words of a familiar song: "Sleepy time gal, you're turning night into day, sleepy time gal you've danced the evening away." She wondered how you could be sleepy and dance too, but grownups did that kind of thing. She went back to dressing. When finished, she looked for the shoes she would wear before making her appearance. Deciding on something new, she chose her mother's black rubber boots, the ones that looked like high-heel dress-up shoes that had fur around the zippers and the tops. She slid her little feet in and, walking up on her toes, she found that she could scooch her feet forward, step by step, so that the empty rubber heels would not collapse in on her.

"Dressed to the nines," as her daddy would say, she glided out of the bedroom, down the hall, and into the kitchen, where her mother was washing something at the sink. At first Ann didn't notice that her daughter had come into the room. But then, hearing the excited scuffles and rustles coming from the doorway, she turned to see the little girl standing there.

"Well, how do you do, young lady?" she heard her mother ask. "Are you going out for the evening? Are you going to a dance?"

This was a wonderful idea, and Isabel said "Yes!" as she began to twirl around and around. But something went wrong, for the empty heels of the boots gave way and she fell backward onto the floor with a big plop!

For a moment the little girl felt something hot creeping up her face and her bottom hurt, but then, there was her mother picking her up from the floor and smiling. She held Isabel in her arms as she danced them around and around. "You must be Ginger Rogers," her mother said as they twirled through the kitchen door and into the hallway. The boots flew from Isabel's swinging feet, and the room was filled with music and happy laughter as she clung tightly to her magical, beautiful Fred Astaire.

Broken

It seems that I am floating slightly above the ground. I am mildly frightened by the sensation. Even so, I can't keep my eyes from the three people standing there, side by side in a line. They are standing in the hallway of our apartment, looking into what once was our living room. But something is terribly wrong. Although all that I can see of them are their backs, I know that they are dumbstruck. Daddy is on the right, his gray shirt hanging large and loose from his bony shoulders. I don't remember him being so skinny. His body is hiding within the folds of his clothes. I fear he is dying.

My sister is standing beside him. Her hair is in braids, and rubber bands hold the ends together, not pretty ribbons like before. Her dress is a checkered green, the back crumpled from sleeping in it. She asks, "But, Daddy, where is everything? Where is the sofa? Where is the radio? Oh, Daddy, where is my desk?"

Hanging there in the air, I float a little farther away, for I know immediately how big this question is and how awful the answer will be. Her little wooden desk – with the three drawers down the side, the magical rolling up top and the four hidden compartments – this desk is her joy. I remember her face and happy tears when she got it last Christmas. I also know from a few pinches and shoves, one that toppled me over, that my sister owns this wonderful thing. "Oh, where is it, Daddy?" Her words are bouncing into my mind, and I can hear whirring in my ears. You see, the living room is completely empty.

I do not have the courage to look down the hall. From where I am floating, I would see my own little bed that I used to sleep in. I would see my blue, soft, bumpy bedspread, with my pillow hiding under a fold at the top. And on the yellow wall over my bed would be my picture of Bambi and Thumper sniffing noses. My bed was there the day my mother took my sister and me to my grandmother's house and left us behind. I don't remember now how long ago that was. My daddy, who had been in the hospital, had gotten out and come to get us. I don't remember how long ago that was.

Now I hear Daddy telling my sister that he had to sell everything because he can't work and we are poor. He is telling her that her desk, our toys, our clothes, and everything of my mother's are gone. He is telling her that my mother ran away. And he is telling her that maybe she and the little girl standing next to her will have to go and live in an orphanage for awhile.

I am floating in the air, just a little above the floor, watching the three people standing together in a line in the hallway of our apartment, looking into our empty living room. There is my daddy, my sister, and a little girl, who stands without moving, broken.

Confessions
of Dick and Jane

Her teacher was speaking at the front of the classroom, but Isabel wasn't paying attention. She kind of knew what was being said. One of the nicest things about school was that it was so predictable and safe because things happened again and again and could be counted on. Not that she did things in a predictable manner, but the safety made it easy to be there and figure out what she wanted to be doing. Right now it was just after lunch, and time when the fourth grade class worked to earn stars on their reading cards.

She had been zooming through the books and her card was filling up fast. As a matter of fact, she had again been given the job of working in the principal's office, collecting the other kids' milk money orders, because she was so far ahead of where the teacher wanted the good readers to be. Her seat was next to the boxes of small storybooks that lined the windowsill, all arranged by how hard they were to read. And there, sitting next to the last box of stories, was her milk money stuff.

Every day Mrs. Wright, the teacher, laid out the milk money stuff for Isabel – and only Isabel – to use. There was a grown-up notebook with lines and columns where she added up the pennies and nickels that she had collected that day. And there was the small sack that she took with her, carefully putting into it all the money and room tickets filled out by the teachers. She almost always felt happy and engaged as she did her job. She brought the money back to the office with a sense of excitement, and would do her figures in the big room next to the place where the principal and her secretary sat.

She loved being in this room with the warmth and smell of its aged wooden walls, whose carved lines carried her eyes up and down. The tall, broad ceiling that added to the room's strength. The enormous windows that were always lidded by drawn shades whose sun-backed khaki color filled the room with a soft amber glow. These filled her with a sense of peace as she did her job. She had earned all of this because she was a smart, good girl.

Except, she had a secret. She wished she could ask her teacher about it but she knew that she couldn't ever. Her secret was that she was not a good girl.

So here it was: free reading time. When the other kids began to stir, Isabel opened her desk and found her reading card. Then she joined the others in selecting her own book. Would she find something she could really read this time? She always had hopes that she would find a way to do it right, and be good. She found seven books that were at her next reading level, and although she would have to read them all, she hoped to find the best one to start with. There was usually something nice about the stories, and many of the books still had pictures and bright colors. Isabel selected one because its binding looked new and not raggedy and returned with it to her seat.

The story was about a family that was going on a trip to California. She plunged in, reading about two girls engaged in happy conversation about where they were going and what they should pack. One of the girls ran to ask her mother, "What would be the best kind of shirts to bring? Would she want her jacket? Which one? Could she bring her toys?" Isabel began to feel sleepy. The girl in the story thought about the choices her mother suggested while she drank a glass of milk and ate some cookies.

Isabel began to think about the Oreo cookies and milk that she had had for lunch. She should have had a bologna sandwich, even some of the cold chicken. But she hadn't wanted them. The strong chocolaty taste of the Oreos washed down with milk was a favorite of hers, and it was easy to make, no time wasted on fixing things or cleaning them up. She turned her attention back to the book, and then, just like so many previous attempts, she stopped struggling to keep reading the story. She didn't even feel particularly evil today. She just gave it up.

The sleepiness was stronger now, and her mind wandered to other things. Outside it was rainy and cold. She had worn her woolen plaid jacket back to school that afternoon, and she wished that she could put it on now to keep herself warm. The gray muted light and the drops on the windowpane brought back thoughts of her mother and of her tears. Rain did that. But it now worried Isabel that she could hardly remember her mother's face. She had seen that woman in the Chinese restaurant who smelled like her. And she had stared at the woman for a long time, trying to remember if that was her mother or not, watching to see if the woman recognized her. But when the woman gave her a bad look, she had felt afraid and turned her gaze away. Then she did not dare to look again. And now it was too late to ever know. She thought perhaps she had missed her last chance.

Some minutes passed before she pulled herself together again. The other kids were still working, and the teacher was at the door talking to someone in the hall. She went over to the book boxes and got out the quiz sheet. Here were the story questions that she had to answer right in order to get her star for this book. Returning to her seat, she read each question slowly once. Next, she went back to the first, read it again, and then thumbed through the book, skimming the words until she found what seemed like the answer to the question. Carefully, with good penmanship, she wrote down her answer: "The family was going to California because the parents wanted their kids to see the world." For some reason she suddenly felt angry and thought that the book was dumb. "Who wants to see the world?" she thought. "Who wants to be a good girl anyway?"

One down, five more questions to go.

MARY ANN EICHMEIER

I was born and grew up in Lansing, Michigan. I am a retired school psychologist. A friend of mine told me about the Life Stories: Writing Your Memoirs class and I decided to try it. I liked the class immediately even though I thought my stories would not be as good as the other writers in the class. My mother wrote in her diary every day until she could not write anymore. Her diary was factual but proved very important when she needed to find specific dates for something in the past. I loved to write papers in school. A friend of mine loaned me his typewriter to use and I helped him organize and write his papers. I learned that when I think about the past for a story, other things come to mind that I hadn't thought about for years.

Set a Deadline and Keep It

When I write a story, I think about it over the weekend several times and tell it to myself. The first of the week, I write it on my computer and print it out. Then I read it and see what it lacks or what sounds wrong or confusing. Then I call it back up on my computer and change the story until it sounds better and all of the mistakes are corrected.

I print it out again and have my husband read it for his comments. There is usually something he sees that I have missed. I make the corrections and print it out for class.

My writing has changed since I have been in the class. My writing flows much better, and as I write one story, I think of other stories to tell the next week. The class gives me discipline. If there was not a deadline, I would never get around to writing, as there would always be something else to do. If you are thinking about writing, a class gives you structure, support, and helpful criticism.

My Last
Blind Date

My cousin Connie called me, which was not unusual. We still call
each other at least once a week, although now it is long-distance. This
time she wanted me to go out with a friend of Connie and her
husband. I had had several blind dates with her husband's old friends
from military school and had not been impressed. This time it was a
Michigan State University student who lived in Okemos. I finally
agreed to go and Connie, her husband, and Jack picked me up on
Saturday night. We went to a movie at the Gladmer and for a drink
afterwards. Jack was a couple of inches taller than I was, had short
dark hair, beautiful brown eyes, and a dazzling smile. He was polite
and a good conversationalist. We were both seniors at MSU. He was
working part time as a conservation aide at Rose Lake. I had a stipend
for the summer and was working on a research project for a
psychology professor in one of the Quonset huts. I was much more
impressed with Jack than with Dave's other friends. When Jack called
for another date the next Saturday, I agreed right away. When I told
Connie that we had another date, she said, "Jack always did like
scrawny girls."

We double-dated with another one of Jack's friends. He and Jack
had built a boat together. On Sunday we all went out in the boat on
the Grand River. Jack's eleven-year-old brother Jim went with us. I
don't remember much about the boat trip other than worrying about
Jim sitting on the bow. After that weekend, Jack and I saw each other
frequently. On one of our early dates, he told my mother and father
that he had something in the trunk of the car to show them. We all
followed him out to the car. He opened the trunk and showed us a
rattlesnake in a cage. My mother was not impressed! He and another
student had caught it at Rose Lake that day and, after scaring the
secretary in the office out there with it, Jack brought it home to show
everyone. When I was sure it couldn't get out, I did go with him.

After school started in the fall, we studied together, sometimes at
the library and sometimes at home. We also picnicked a lot. We would
buy some hot dogs and buns, go out to Rose Lake, and wander
around. Jack tried to teach me how to shoot a shotgun and took me

pheasant hunting. I never was able to shoot anything but an occasional clay pigeon.

By Christmas, I was wearing Jack's fraternity pin. In the fall, we both started grad school. The next Christmas, Jack bought me a ring and we were engaged. A year later, three days after Christmas, we were married. We had about ten days for a honeymoon, then I had to go back to school to finish up my course work, and Jack had a job teaching at Saginaw High School. At the end of winter term, we found an apartment and I had an internship at Saginaw Child Guidance Clinic. Jack had to go to Lansing twice a week to get a math minor, as he was teaching math instead of science. I usually went with him and visited my parents while he was in class. We put a lot of miles on Jack's little VW. When I got a job as school psychologist in Saginaw, we had enough money to buy a new Nash Rambler. It was a real luxury, as the heater really worked!

We were in Saginaw a year and a half, and then moved back to the Lansing area. We bought a trailer in a trailer park in Okemos. Jack went back to school and I went to work in Lansing as a school psychologist. Jack went to MSU for a year, but decided he liked teaching better and got a job at Lansing West Junior High School.

The following summer, Jack decided we were going to take a camping trip to Alaska. He built a car-top carrier and we bought a tent and all sorts of equipment. I had never camped and I didn't think we'd make it that far. As it turned out, it was a really great trip. Jack was so capable and made everything easy and comfortable. We made it there and back with no trouble. The next year, we invited another couple to go along to the Seattle World's Fair. Jack had built a small trailer to carry the equipment, and we made the trip in the little Rambler. It was a wonderful trip, and we were still good friends when we got home.

On that trip as throughout our marriage, we had some adjustments to make. My birthday is in November. After Jack bought me a bow and a shotgun, I made it clear that I did not consider them an appropriate present. Jack made it equally clear that he did not consider clothing as a suitable present, so that problem has been solved. I always liked things neat and everything put away. Jack didn't care. After I tripped over Jack's shoes in the living room of our very small apartment, I hid them. Obviously that didn't work. When we moved into our current house, with lots of closets and hooks near the back door, I thought that would help. However I had a desk near the door, as well, and it soon became a repository for tools, hats, and coats. Every time I wanted to write bills, it took more time to clean off the desk than to pay the bills. When we built an addition to our house, we moved the desk to another room, far from the door. There is a coat rack beside the door. There are still coats on the living room chair and on the chairs and couch in our solar room. It almost seems natural, as now my son and daughter do the same. These days I just have them put everything away once a week when they clean the particular room. Jack does put his tools away now, or else he can't find them next time he needs them. I don't nag anymore about the clothing.

We have been married forty-four years. I am happy that I let Connie talk me into one more blind date. Jack has been a wonderful and supportive husband who has encouraged me to experience many things I never dreamed I would.

Raining
Cats and Dogs

When my husband Jack and I moved to our farm, our son Karl was three years old. We bought a black Labrador retriever puppy, which we named Nyx, after the Greek goddess of night. We were given a calico kitten, which we named Tinkerbell. Nyx was a cute little puppy. She soon decided she liked to chew on the kitchen chairs, then the doorjamb. When she started to chew on some of Jack's tools, he decided enough was enough. He built her a large pen in our garage and a large fenced-in area beside it.

Tinkerbell was a cuddly little ball of fur and loved to sit on my lap while I read to Karl. Karl delighted in both of them. Nyx was always gentle, even when she became full grown. When I got pregnant the following year and was home most of the time, Tinkerbell got more attention. Then my daughter Ann came along and I didn't have as much spare time. Tinkerbell was very jealous and angry. One day when I was changing Ann on a table, Tinkerbell bit me on my calf so hard that the teeth marks were there for two weeks. We had to watch her around Ann.

That year Tinkerbell had kittens. We kept one of the kittens and named her Pandora. She loved everybody and most cats she met. Pandora had kittens at least twice a year. One summer, just before we were leaving on vacation, she presented us with seven white kittens. They all had one green eye and one blue. We left them in the basement while we were gone and we arrived back home to a house full of fleas. Pandora disappeared shortly after that.

The next winter Nyx presented us with eleven puppies on New Years Eve. The father wasn't a Lab and they looked odd so we gave away as many as we could and had to take the few remaining to the animal shelter.

One evening Jack came across a thin, bedraggled kitten. He brought him in and now we had two cats again. Curious grew quickly into a large tomcat. On one of his early excursions he came home with one eye hanging out of its socket. The vet removed the eye and sewed the eyelid shut. He also neutered Curious, as his fighting skills were not good enough to keep him from losing the other eye. The closed eye gave Curious a kind of raffish look. One of our problems with Curious had been his habit of marking territory and although that continued it didn't smell so bad. He would stand on the back of the couch and mark the window, or file cabinets and he always marked the Christmas tree skirt and some of the packages. He dragged any piece of loose clothing around, even heavy afghans. He also liked to jump into cars and pick up items. We were always finding under our shrubbery t-shirts that didn't belong to any of us.

He was definitely Jack's cat. He followed Jack all around. One day Curious was on our back porch watching Jack as he clipped wing feathers on one of the geese. The goose suddenly grabbed at Jack's arm and Curious flew down there and leaped onto the goose's back. The goose jumped and Curious fell off, still trying to scratch the goose. He had rescued Jack.

Curious caught lots of mice and always offered them to Jack. Sometimes he brought them inside to play with. One night he ran in with a live bird that got away and frantically flew all over. Curious gave chase and it was utter chaos until Curious was put outside and the bird was caught in a butterfly net.

One Sunday afternoon, we had a birthday reception for my mother. Since we didn't want Curious running in and out or getting into the buffet, we shut him in the barn. His curiosity got the better of him, so he crawled into a groundhog tunnel. He couldn't turn or back up, and when he got to the entrance outside the barn, there was a piece of wire fence that Jack put there to keep the groundhog out. After the party, Jack went to let Curious out and couldn't find him. He and the kids hunted all over the barn. They finally heard a weak "meow" and found him in the tunnel behind the barn. He had scraped his nose trying to get out. He was a very muddy, but happy cat, and he never tried any more tunnels.

Nyx was growing old and didn't hear very well, One morning, Jack's father came into the house, fixed himself some coffee, went into the garage and got in the car, and drove down to the woods. Nyx never stirred and neither did we. A few weeks later, Jack's brother came out, got our house key out of the garage, came in, fixed himself a sandwich, then walked down to our airstrip and took off in the plane he and Jack owned. The dog didn't hear him and neither did we until we heard the plane motor. We finally decided we needed a small noisy dog to wake up the big dog. I found an ad in the shopping guide and we soon had a tiny black toy poodle. Her name was Penny. She looked fragile but could run circles around the big dog and loved to play with Curious. They would chase each other around the house, then collapse in a heap and lick each other. Tinkerbell ignored them both. Whenever someone she didn't know came in the house, Penny would jump on my lap and growl and bark at them. She loved to go to my mother's house. We'd ask her if she wanted to go see Grandma and she would beat us all to the car.

Soon after, my mother's neighbors had to get rid of their Irish setter, Duchess, and asked us to take her. Now we had three dogs. Duchess and Nyx got along well and shared the dog pen.

The next winter Jack found a small kitten in our backyard. She had a steel trap on her front paw. She must have dragged it up from the creek, behind our house, because we have never used those kinds of traps. The vet amputated her leg at the shoulder. Now we had a one-eyed cat, a three-legged cat and a very old bad-tempered cat. We dubbed the new cat Callie, short for Calamity Jane. She got around really well. The only thing she couldn't do was jump high enough to get on tables or counters.

Tinkerbell and Nyx both died soon after we got Callie. We only had Penny for ten years before she died of a heart attack. Dutchess got out on the road and was hit by a car.

While Curious was Jack's cat, Jack was Callie's human. She was very jealous of his attention to any other animal or human. When Curious would get on Jack's lap, Callie would jump on, too, and would end up pushing Curious off. We were out of dogs, so we picked up a mixed Labrador and Great Dane from four girls who lived in an apartment. The dog, Dutchy, had grown too big for the apartment. Jack brought him into the house and Callie went ballistic. She ran upstairs and defecated all over our bed. By bedtime, Dutchy was out in the pen, Jack had washed and changed all the bedding and we were laughing about it when we went up to bed. Just then, Callie streaked past us and did it again. She was put out for the night. Dutchy was with us about six weeks when he got out on the road and got hit by a car.

Callie always slept with Jack on his side of the bed. She would stretch out beside him under the covers. If Jack displeased her in any way, she was quick to let him know. She'd walk away and wouldn't even look at him. She would completely ignore him for a couple of days and then she would graciously forgive him. When we bought a yellow Lab puppy, I carried her into the house and Callie couldn't have cared less. Jack was the only one that couldn't have other pets.

We named the new puppy Sunny. She was a cuddly lovable puppy. However, she had some problems. She would run into things sometimes. We had a low fence around part of the backyard to keep our chickens out. When Sunny would run from across the yard, she would sail right over the fence, but when she was inside the fence, she would try to walk over it. She would get her stomach hung up and she never learned the difference. Jack always tried to train our dogs not to cross the road, but Sunny didn't learn that either and she, too, got hit and killed.

About a year later, we bought another black Lab and again used the name Nyx. She was cuddly and affectionate and never understood that when she was full-grown, she couldn't still sit on our laps. She chewed up all of her water buckets and anything else in sight. She liked to watch Jack work on things but she also liked to pick up parts and carry them away. Nyx liked everybody, even the UPS man, but her favorite was the meter woman, who always brought dog biscuits.

Sadly, shortly after we got Nyx, Curious got cancer, and when he seemed to be in pain, had to be put to sleep. Now we had one dog and one cat. When Callie died of old age a few years later, Jack said "no more cats." About six months later, Jack happened to come across a large, skinny, and very matted cat that meowed at Jack and rolled over to be petted. Guess what happened?

Tommy was going to be a barn cat. He ate like he was never going to get full and would lie there quietly while Jack cut all of the matted fur off of him. Nyx didn't like stray cats so Jack carefully introduced the two. Surprisingly, Tommy ran over to Nyx and rubbed up against her. Nyx wasn't too comfortable about it, but this cat had obviously grown up with a dog. As soon as Tommy got in the house, he made himself at home. He had a bed in the garage attic but being a tomcat, he rarely used it. Tommy would go out every night, then would come dragging in next morning, eat a big breakfast, and then sleep in the house all day. Then one day he disappeared. We figured he might have mistaken a coyote for a dog.

Now we just had Nyx. She died of old age last spring. Jack said, "No more pets." In November, a weak, skinny cat came up our drive and Jack fed her. We call her Callie and she obviously had lived in a house. She had even been spayed. She sleeps in the garage attic at night but is always ready to come inside in the morning. She goes out hunting in the daytime and brings her mice home.

Our cats and dogs have given us many years of companionship, laughter, and tears. It would be a dull world without pets.

A Difficult
Diagnosis

I was about forty-eight when I finally got an answer to a question that I had been asking since I was around thirty. The first time I was really aware of the problem was when Jack and I were moving a table. When we set the table down, I couldn't let go of it for several seconds. I had already noticed that sometimes I had trouble letting go of pens and pencils at work. I would ask my doctor about the problem, but he always told me it was probably just a little arthritis. The problem kept getting worse. The doctor retired.

I went to a new doctor, who also said it was nothing. After several years of my asking questions, he finally ordered tests after we shook hands at one of my visits and I couldn't let go. He ordered the right tests: an Electro Muscle Gram and a muscle biopsy. After the tests were completed, he informed me that it was just something to live with and not worry about. He gave me a prescription that I looked up in our Physicians' Desk Reference when I got home. It was a heart medication and I threw the prescription away.

My hands continued to get worse. Cutting Jack's hair got to be really difficult. When I closed the scissors, I couldn't reopen them, and when they were open, I had trouble closing them. I had to lay the comb down every time so I could use both hands on the scissors. Finally, after a very frustrating haircut, I called an old friend who was a doctor at MSU. I asked him to give me a referral to a neurologist. It didn't take the neurologist ten minutes to diagnose my condition. He told me that I had myotonic dystrophy, and that it was progressive and incurable. He set an appointment for me to come back in a month.

I was devastated. I managed to drive home before I started to cry. I tried not to cry in front of my daughter, Ann, as it would have upset her. Karl, my son, was in North Carolina for three weeks at Outward Bound. I read everything I could find about myotonic dystrophy, which didn't make me feel much better. We had to pick Karl up at the outer banks in North Carolina the weekend after. Ann stayed with her grandmother, so Jack and I had time to talk about the changes in our lives and how it would affect our future.

My feelings about the doctor who ordered the initial tests and then prescribed heart medication were mostly angry. At first I thought he was stupid, and then I figured that he was playing God. He would have denied me the opportunity of setting my own priorities for the future. I went and demanded all my records from him and took them to the neurologist at MSU. I spent most of the month on Valium so I wouldn't cry so much.

When we went back to the neurologist, he said the tranquilizers weren't good because my muscles were too relaxed already. He also told us that both children had a fifty-fifty chance of having the myotonic dystrophy, as it is an autosomal dominant gene. He set up an appointment with the Muscular Dystrophy Association Clinic. Now I had something more to worry about.

We went to the clinic in early November, and Karl, Ann, and I were evaluated. We saw a physical therapist, occupational therapist, social worker, Muscular Dystrophy Association coordinator, and the neurologist. The results were the worst possible. Both kids had myotonic dystrophy. This was more devastating than finding out that I had it. Karl was seventeen and Ann was only twelve. What would the future hold for them?

I retired at age fifty-three on sick leave. With time, a person can get used to a chronic situation. As I learned more and more about the condition, I could make better plans for the future. The Muscular Dystrophy Association website has been a big help with research updates and other information.

Jack and I had been to Kansas City for him to have multiple heart vessel angioplasties. After that, Jack had to go on a strictly nonfat diet and I had to do most of the cooking from scratch. I was able to find tools and gadgets to compensate for my weakening hand muscles.

That same year, I had cataract surgery on both eyes. Cataracts are another side effect of myotonic dystrophy. Another side effect that we later discovered is narcolepsy. We learned that when Karl was sent for a sleep study. I always had trouble getting him up. Ann said he slept all the way to high school on the bus. After he graduated, he totaled two cars because of falling asleep at the wheel. He wasn't injured in either one and was alone in the car both times. This had been a long-standing problem for him. When he was six years old, our neighbors' barn burned down. I tried to wake Karl up twice to get him out of the house and away from the burning barn nearby, but he would not wake up.

I also had narcolepsy. Jack used to get really mad at me for falling asleep in the car. I couldn't stay awake unless I was sewing or playing a game with the kids. Just sitting still in meetings would send me off. I used to fall asleep reading to the kids. When I was near retirement, I would drive home and then wonder if I had stopped for the red blinker at Holt Road. Karl and I both have sleep apnea as well. We take Ritalin to keep us awake and oxygen to keep us breathing at night. Ann doesn't seem to have these problems. The symptoms or side effects vary from case to case. Ann has no hand cramping but is not really strong. Her main problem, so far, was a learning disability in school.

We are fortunate that Jack is so handy. He has figured out many ways to compensate for our problems. When I was still able to drive, he made a tool for me to open car doors and turn the ignition. He modifies equipment and thinks of ways to make things easier for us. I have a golf cart to get around on outside. Last summer, I was able to be in our woods for the first time in many years.

The first year after the diagnosis, Jack and I went on a guided tour of England, Ireland, and Scotland. We went back the following year for another tour, partly in England and partly in Scotland. Our hotel was within walking distance of the British Museum and we spent time there. We also took the tube out to a World War II airfield and museum. The walking was very tiring, and I was glad that they had benches all over. We still do a lot of traveling, all of it in this country. We did go to Cancun every winter, but accessibility is not great and it would be a real problem if either of us got sick. Flying is not that easy, either, with the equipment we need to take. We visit a lot of Civil War battlefields. At most of them, walkways are paved and the entire visitor center is accessible.

It is possible to have a full life even with a chronic condition – with some adjustments, the right attitude, and the right equipment. You also need a supportive, loving family and I've been fortunate in that regard.

VIRGINIA WOOD

I enjoyed almost everything from as far back as I can remember. I loved school. Music filled every extra moment. I practiced the piano until asked politely to stop. I learned the cello, the big bass fiddle and even played the bass drum in a parade. Life was fun! I went from soda jerk to advertising manager of a large department store.

I chased boys until I found the right one to spend my life with. Suddenly it was time to decide if selling tractors and decorating store windows was what life was all about. We decided to leave it all behind and go to Africa as missionaries. After four years of theological training we left family and homeland. Now fifty years later I can write about those wonderful years woven with joy, fear and heartache, but for me it is what life is all about.

Write about the Sad Times to Heal a Broken Heart

More than thirty years ago our daughter told us about something that happened while she studied nursing in a local hospital. It remained stored away in a far corner of my memory for many years. I began to think about it a glimpse at a time, then more and more, and eventually it became an almost constant companion. Details developed in my mind both night and day. When I did sit down at my computer to write, it came pouring out almost faster than I could type. I could see the whole story clearly in my mind and found it easy to describe every detail. I added some details where the memories had faded away.

After I finished, I carefully read my story to remove any passive verbs, replacing them with more descriptive, active verbs, sometimes rearranging sentences in order to achieve this. I also eliminated any words or phrases that did not contribute to the plot.

This pretty much describes how I write all my stories. I write in order to record my memories in the hope that others will find them and enjoy them. I also have a desire for others to understand what my life has been like. Hopefully they will be a little surprised. Sometimes in writing about the sad times, I write for my own benefit. This provides healing for my broken heart. As I continue to write I find that I improve in my ability to express my feelings rather than hide them among the words.

To me the most important thing is to share with others. Read aloud to someone. Find a writing partner or join a writing class. You must agree to keep personal stories safe in the confines of the group or with your writing partner. The joy and satisfaction in a finished story will be treasured by you, the writer, and by others that you may possibly never dream of.

The Empty Room

On a bone-chilling evening in July 1992, the hospital in Johannesburg, South Africa, struggled in turmoil. A few women employees fought to get to work, torn by the need for a job and a desire to help those in the overcrowded wards. They feared persecution or even death.

Outside, on the hospital grounds, racial demonstrations escalated to violence. Militant blacks roughly refused entry to frightened black nurses. Frustrated patients and their relatives desperately sought medical help.

On the third floor, our son Doug fought a different life-and-death battle. Two years before, Doug called from South Africa to Michigan, where we then lived, after twenty-five years as missionaries in southern Africa.

He said those dreaded words, "Now I don't want you to worry," and explained from 10,000 miles away that he was scheduled for surgery. He glossed over the words cancer, swallowing, and stomach, and skillfully eased our worry. He would let us know how things came out. He had good friends who would look after him.

Several months later, after many phone calls, much prayer, and a knot of fear growing in my stomach, we made the long journey back to our adopted homeland.

Doug met us at the airport. Although he was gaunt and pale, he was determined to show us a wonderful time and to make it like old times.

He took us to restaurants, where he pretended to eat and have a good time. He installed us in a racially integrated hotel on the beautiful Indian Ocean beach-front city of Durban.

This provided an exciting new experience for us, since we had lived through the intense racial strife of the apartheid era. The law had just made everyone equal, but an uneasy feeling of suspicion, hatred, and fear still prevailed. Crime was rampant. We spent many hours looking down from our high-up hotel window into the crowded streets below.

We went with Doug to his doctor, who put things into perspective for us. He called Doug's cancer a "lifestyle disease." We heard a diagnosis of incurable stomach and esophagus cancer, caused by smoking, drinking, poor health habits, drugs, and on and on.

Respected for his brilliant mathematical mind and natural leadership of the black South African workers, Doug had managed to keep an excellent job. He fluently spoke the corrupted dialect which combined many local tribal languages, popularly called kitchen *kaffir*.

Twenty years earlier, as a teenager, he charmed us all. We were so naive!

We couldn't see the signs: the lying, the cheating, the school skipping, the wrong friends.

A brave missionary friend told us about our son's drug problems. I was angry!

At that time we lived in a huge rambling house in the beautiful city of Pietermaritzburg, called the Garden City of South Africa. Flowering bougainvillea vines reached for the sky, climbing the trees and the tiled roofs of houses. Flame trees blazed their beauty. Jacaranda trees carpeted the streets with their sweet-smelling lavender blossoms. Two huge clumps of stralytzia or bird of paradise plants, dominated the front yard.

Our home, partly converted into office space, guest rooms, and family living quarters, hummed with continual activity. We always had a cluster of lonely teens looking for and needing attention. Our guest rooms welcomed missionaries visiting the city for supplies or for a brief rest from isolation, or parents visiting their schoolchildren. We rarely ate a meal without extra people at the table. Louie's position as field director, caring for more than one hundred missionary families throughout South Africa, kept him constantly sorting out some kind of problem somewhere.

We lived in a totally white world. Blacks lived in a corrugated iron and cardboard shantytown a few miles from us.

Fifteen-year-old Doug attended an all-boys school, reluctantly wore the required uniform, and conformed to the strict rules. He was small, quick, handsome, and very smart, and was probably bullied by the boys at school. He didn't like being half-American, a missionary kid with parents who never understood what was going on. I still regret buying the wrong socks for his first rugby game. His excitement turned to shame when the team laughed him off the field for wearing first-team socks in a beginners' game.

The night when I told Louie what I had learned about Doug's

drug problems, he exploded. "How could he do this to us? Don't we mean anything to him? What did we do wrong? How can I continue to do my job if I can't even raise my own son? What will people think? What will people say?"

We had known for some time that Doug played at witchcraft, the current teenage fad among the upper-class kids. They met at the home of a prominent magistrate, thus we didn't take it seriously. They apparently organized seances and attempted levitation and other strange behavior.

Tired and angry, I focused on what to do. Louie seethed. Doug kept a low profile.

I quit all my very important Christian activities and began to focus on my son and his needs. He always showed complete respect for us, his parents. His life outside our home was appalling. I finally realized how deeply imbedded he was in the drug culture. We wracked our brains for solutions but found none.

I involved myself in every part of his life. It turned into a game for him. He even took me to drug dens, introduced me to his far-out friends, and tolerated my constant presence.

Back home in the States, my elderly parents desperately needed care. Several people wrote to us saying we should come home. We stored everything we owned in an empty garage, tried to untangle our responsibilities, and prepared to return home.

My mother suffered from a brain tumor. The resulting operation failed, leaving her severely mentally disturbed. My innovative dad tried everything he could think of to care for her but it was a losing battle. When we arrived home, we found furniture nailed to the floor, lamps wired to tables, and, among other things, a metal contraption over the stove to prevent her from turning on the gas. My dad took his wedding vows very seriously. With tears in his eyes, he begged us not to put her in a home. He had promised to take care of her until death and he couldn't go back on that promise, still tenderly reminding her of his love. Her strength made it hard to control her during violent rampages. She almost never slept. She could not talk or, as far as we knew, understand anything we said. At night she would become agitated, walking quickly around the house.

I constantly looked for ways to help Doug. I decided to go to a local community college to take all their courses in drug rehabilitation. Every time I learned something new, I wrote to Doug, explaining it all to him. I wanted him to know that he could not fool me anymore and that I probably knew more than he did on the subject. I think in some weird way we had genuine respect for each other.

Occasionally we asked some of our friends to check on him. They didn't say much in reply. Bev, his sister, saw him a few times. She said he looked and smelled terrible.

Doug finally did come home. I remember him sitting one day on the bottom step of the stairs to the basement, where we were sleeping at the time. He just sobbed, saying over and over, "Dad, I just can't do it. I tried. I just can't do it. I'm sorry."

He stayed with us for a short time while looking for a job. He showed kindness and patience during that time, helping us with my mother as much as possible. One night as I took my turn staying up, Doug decided to stay up with me. My mother, in extreme agitation, walked quickly around the house. This was strange because during the day she could hardly function at all. Finally she sat in her favorite chair, a brown wicker rocker with a bright chintz cushion. She sat up straight, looking furtively around the room. She pointed toward the far corner and whispered directly to me, "There he is, over there. It's the king. Do you see him? He wants you to see him. Do you see the little ones? They want you to see them, too."

Her eyes were shiny with excitement. I shivered from goose bumps and prickles of fear on my head. Doug woke my father. We all managed to get her into bed. Neither Doug nor I ever spoke of this to anyone.

Eventually, Doug's girlfriend came to live with us. They arranged a wedding before a judge in Lansing and tried to get their lives in order. Doug continued to go from job to job. His employment was usually provided by friends of ours, and usually of short duration.

They found a small apartment which had recently fallen into disrepair but still showed traces of the elegant building it had once been. Doug wanted nothing to do with us by now. Our anger and hurt had subsided and we decided together to reject the tough love theory, choosing rather to show him the gentle constant love that was in our hearts. This was not easy. Every Sunday after church we went to the apartment lobby. Louie pressed the buzzer, then waited for the familiar voice.

"Who's there?"

"Doug, this is your dad. We wondered if you would like to go out to lunch with us."

"Dad, we can't go now, thanks. How about next week?"

The slurred voice spoke volumes. In the background we heard vulgar laughing and crude remarks and people milling about.

"We love you!"

The intercom clicked off. This went on week after week. Finally we heard, "OK, I'll come down. It'll just be me."

We waited an eternity, anticipating and dreading what was to come. He chose a local steakhouse. We wondered if they would let him in. He looked and acted terrible. We struggled to subdue our revulsion. Here we were in our prim-and-proper Sunday best. Doug was in his unkempt worst. We remembered that he had called us hypocrites many times. Now we had a chance to prove otherwise. When our friends came by, we introduced them to Doug with pride and love. This is our son. Things improved a little after that.

Doug and his girlfriend finally returned to South Africa, restless and homesick, wherever they were. By this time Doug was too ill to care much about anything. He abandoned the marriage. He did not want anyone watching him die.

Doug did come back home again. I think he came with hope of a cure, but he had no insurance and the experimental programs all refused him. He faced the reality of the situation and decided to go back to Africa for a final good-bye to his friends.

For the short time he stayed with us, his emotions rose to great heights and plummeted to despair. He said hurtful things, interspersed with loving thanks. He was literally starving to death.

He made that long trip again, hardly able to carry his luggage. He moved in with good friends. Doug was now too weak to make the journey back to us again, so we went to him.

We were finally able to understand this son of ours. His friends, employers, and caregivers clearly expressed his talent. He was embarrassed when so many praised him to us. We had not truly known this great young man. Pride mingled with heartbreak.

One night we received a call to come quickly to the hospital. His friends brought him in because he was barely able to breathe. He was diagnosed with pneumonia. The hospital now became his home.

The hospital staff, including his doctors, had an unusual affection for him. A famous cancer specialist spent many hours sitting with Doug on the edge of his bed, and discussing everything from politics to racial problems to death and heaven. A young Zulu girl who came up from the basement laundry every day stood at the foot of Doug's bed to pray aloud in Zulu, tears streaming down her face.

We had wonderful talks with Doug and he eagerly expressed his desire to return to the faith of his childhood.

Doug continually encouraged the many mourning visitors. Old acquaintances came and looked, not knowing what to say. Doug always put them at ease.

We had gone there with the hope of bringing Doug back home and had described the newly painted, bright, cheerful room we had prepared for him. All this time he refused the generous offer of morphine because he wanted to savor each moment of life.

He finally said he wanted to go home to die. We scurried around organizing the complicated trip. All his worldly possessions, brought in by his friends, added to the chaos. Doug sat up, giving directions of what to take, what to leave behind, and what to give to all his friends and admirers. No one was left out. Happiness dominated, with the relief of a decision made. Word filtered throughout the hospital, and many came by to say good-bye. Tears flowed freely. Hugs and advice concealed emotion.

We paraded through those familiar halls, past soldiers carrying machine guns. We all went by ambulance through the busy metropolis to the South African Airways jumbo jet. We entered the jet through an emergency door and went to an area where they had a special place for us to sit. We had arranged for oxygen, but someone had slipped up. After a flurry of activity the oxygen arrived and was hooked up. Doug was happy. The half-hour drive through the wild traffic thrilled him. It was dark enough that he could see familiar sights, brightly lit.

He sat between us in the plane, comfortable and happy. He ate some dinner and soon fell asleep. The plane stopped at Cape Verde Islands for refueling and a change of crew. We tried to rouse him for a sip of juice but he didn't want to wake up.

A few minutes later he slipped away to heaven. From then on everything became a blur – the numerous offers of tea, the call for a doctor among the passengers, the very young stewardess sitting a few rows back in a state of shock, the patient passengers waiting for the end of international red tape, the removal of the body to the hold, and the deep kindness of everyone involved.

In New York we arranged for Doug's body to be given to medical science, as he had wished.

It was not the end, because the love and memories never go away.

The Day Buddy Went to Heaven

In the late 1960s, on a lazy hot afternoon in a small South African town, old Buddy sprawled on a concrete step, soaking up the sun like a cat. He almost purred. Probably someday he would die right there. There was, however, the disconcerting thought about where he would go then.

He must be getting old. Someone just the other day asked him if he was retired. "Retired from what?" he mumbled, leaving a trail of rancid breath as he shuffled off to the mission.

Periodically he suffered through three miserable days of no drinks and no smokes, just wholesome food and praising the Lord. This was necessary payment for an occasional much-needed change of clothes.

Buddy settled into his favorite afternoon resting place on the wide steps of the hospital teaching unit. No one disturbed him there. He liked the sedate atmosphere, and the company was good. He especially enjoyed the occasional fellowship of the young nurses and their guardian angel ogress.

Soon the people passing by blurred and the huge marble pillars towering above his head swayed pleasantly. Buddy smiled a toothless smile, hiccupped, waved to everyone, and passed out.

One day, the nursing instructor was outside for a breath of fresh air when Buddy erupted in a particularly loud drunken snore.

"Oh, no! Not that dirty old man again," she thought. "Someone should really do something about him. He is disgusting."

Suddenly, overwhelmed with inspiration, she looked at her watch and quickly disappeared through the huge oak doors.

A few minutes later she returned with four young girls carrying a canvas stretcher which they placed on the step below Buddy's limp body. He rolled easily onto it with a little help from the girls. A few curious eyes watched as Buddy was carried into the hospital classroom.

They gingerly removed the ragged coat, pants, and shoes. Buddy wore no socks or shirt. His once-white underwear matched the same dirty brown color of his coat and pants. Buddy had a badly worn billfold with a few discolored pictures of a boy and two girls, with an address scrawled on the back of them.

They placed Buddy – still snoring peacefully – on the examination table and covered him with a clean white sheet. Next they shampooed, cut, and combed Buddy's long, matted, lice-infested hair. They learned how to disinfect his scalp. They learned to give a patient a sponge bath and to treat open sores and blistered feet. They cut and cleaned his nails. They found clothes that had belonged to a patient who had died and put them on his immaculate body.

Buddy looked almost handsome in the dark navy suit and white shirt. The girls put some money in the billfold with the snapshots and returned it to Buddy's pants pocket. One of the nurses brought a food tray which held a complete chicken dinner, apple tart and all.

Finally Buddy began to stir. He opened his eyes a little, then quickly closed them again. He cautiously opened one eye. The girls, one on either side, took an arm and propped him up against some soft white pillows and placed the dinner tray in front of him.

Buddy looked at his navy blue sleeve with the pure white shirt cuff framing a clean manicured hand. He looked at the tray with its array of gleaming silver. He felt for his missing hair and looked at the beautiful girls all dressed in white surrounding him.

"It happened," he whispered. "I'm in heaven. It's even better than I thought. Angels everywhere."

In awesome silence Buddy ate his dinner while the angels watched. He sighed with satisfaction as the angels gently helped him up and guided him to the door. They each kissed him good-bye and old Buddy went out into the late afternoon sun.

Buddy was different after that. He had a peaceful, knowing look on his face and often talked about spending some time in heaven and being fed by angels.

People laughed about the old drunken fool.

The
Snake

In the foothills of the rugged Drakensburg mountains of South Africa, at a little village called Sweetwaters, clouds hang heavy on the hills most of the year, filling the valleys with thick wet silence. Each house stands isolated from the others by the mist that dims visibility to a few feet.

Some days the mist stays all day. Other days, the tall eucalyptus trees emerge like ghosts at about 10 a.m., and by noon the hills turn from gray to green and the sun is king.

It was on one of those days that I met the deadly green mamba and came face to face with my greatest fear.

As the mist lifted, I stood at the sink finishing the breakfast dishes. I had already made the beds. I hated the clammy feel of the sheets and blankets. The washing, ready to hang as soon as the sun came out, would hopefully dry before the four o'clock clouds rolled in.

I felt a surge of loneliness. The hundred or so college students were home for a long break, to care for their crops. The other faculty members were away for one reason or another. My husband left early on a trip to one of the remote areas of Zululand. My children had felt their way through the thick fog as they walked down the long winding drive to catch their ride to school.

The school bordered a black residential area. The house backed up against a fence separating our home from 50,000 Africans. The farther side of the eight-acre campus formed the border of an elite residential area for white people.

We lived in the buffer zone between the two. South African law required at that time that people live in separate racial areas. Six miles and three thousand feet down the hill nestled the beautiful town of Pietermaritzburg, often called the garden city.

Many nights I would lie awake all night unable to shut out the ominous beating of drums just over the fence behind our house. My husband never seemed to hear them.

Sometimes in the night, Zulu men would come carrying their spears and cowhide shields. They danced all around the house, calling and knocking on the windows to wake us. Usually someone had been stabbed in a drunken brawl and they would ask us to call the ambulance. We always did.

One night a man came walking, asking for help, with a spear right through his body. Later I heard that he had walked from the ambulance into the hospital, had the spear removed, and walked out again.

When I stayed home alone, the nights stretched out long and frightening. The fear started when I opened a dresser drawer to put some clothes away. I reached in and something brown moved right by my hand. I jumped and at the same time slammed the drawer shut, just catching the fingers of the other hand. I am terribly afraid of spiders, even the little ones back home in Michigan.

My South African neighbors told me that big furry tarantulas (wolf spiders) like this one don't really poison people. They carried the spiders around to prove it.

I looked at the blue marks across my hand. My swollen fingers throbbed with pain.

The sun shone brightly now, turning the dampness into a steamy heat. I decided to make some lemonade and take some fruit and a good book out under the trees just to relax. All I had to do yet was to empty the garbage and hang up the washing.

The last time I hung out the wash, there had been an ugly chameleon sitting on the clothesline, following my every move.

African chameleons do not resemble the small smooth lizards called by the same name in the States. Rather, they are like miniature dinosaurs with rough scales and large hissing mouths. Their eyes bulge out, always watching.

I had the courage to use only two of the five lines so the clothes didn't really get dry. They already smelled of mildew, and I dreaded hanging them out again today.

As I looked out the window I relented a little and enjoyed the beauty. The silver pampas grass must be twelve feet tall, I thought, and the brilliant red bougainvillea has completely covered that huge old pine tree. It made me think of a giant Christmas tree covered with bright red lights.

"Well," I sighed to myself, "I had better take out the garbage." I hated this job most of all. Little flies always flew into my face when I lifted the lid of the big can, and it smelled so horrible in the tropical climate.

I picked up the garbage dish, opened the screen door, and walked into the carport. The garbage can stood in the back outside corner of the open garage, which had two-foot-high brick walls around the back and side. I hurt my already sore fingers trying to get the lid off. I put the lid on the wall, and just as I was going to bang the garbage pan against the inside edge of the big tin can to clean it out, I felt something on my foot.

Goose bumps crept over my body. After what seemed a very long time, I managed to look down at my feet. Two jewel eyes blazing with fiery hatred looked straight at my face.

My thoughts were very clear and calm.

"This is a green mamba, the deadliest snake in the world. Everyone is gone. No one will hear me if I scream. He is the most beautiful creature I have ever seen. If he bites me, I may live for three minutes."

The snake, at least six feet long, had wound himself completely around my ankle. His skin was an arrangement of iridescent bright greens. He held in his mouth a limp chameleon, which had already received the deadly poison.

He can't bite me, I thought, because his jaws are locked on the lizard.

I slowly moved my rigid muscles, bent down, took hold of the shimmering green body, and unwound it from my ankle. I left the lid off the garbage can and walked back into the house and sat in the living room for a long time.

Later, I told the old Zulu caretaker about the snake, but he refused to kill it because of the chameleon in its mouth.

Zulu folklore says that long ago God sent the chameleon to tell the Zulu people that they could have eternal life. The chameleon, seeing himself reflected in a pond, admired his beautiful color changes for so long that he never delivered the message, thus preventing the Zulu people from entering heaven. The harmless dead chameleon terrified the old man.

Huddled on the shabby couch, still shaking, a dark cloud of doubt crept over me, reminding me of the loneliness, the constant danger, the never-ending fear, and the struggle to provide adequately for our family. I dared to wonder why. Gradually my brooding turned to prayer. I thanked God for my children and my husband, and for bringing me to this amazing place. With a sigh I got up and started preparing our evening meal. I set the table, anticipating the return of my family.

RALPH KRON

A natural-born U.S. citizen, my parents brought me to America from my Romanian birthplace as an infant. I grew up mostly in Kansas City, Mo., a place I thoroughly enjoyed. The public schools fostered a love of learning, which my parents encouraged.

I earned several degrees at the University of Kansas, culminating in a counseling psychology doctorate. It was a privilege to join the nationally recognized staff of the Michigan State University Counseling Center in 1959. My psychotherapy skills were further honed there, and over the years I taught psychology and education courses, too. Most rewarding were the opportunities to provide clinical supervision for advanced graduate students and interns.

After becoming a Professor Emeritus in 1982 I had a private psychotherapy practice in East Lansing. My final two years of professional work were as the clinical director of a private faith-based counseling clinic.

Now I have more time for extended travel with my wife, Linda. Considering blended families, we have five adult children, eleven grandchildren, and one great-grandchild.

Make a Mental List of What to Include

At the outset it was easy to choose topics to write about. My approach to a memoir was to be chronological, starting with earliest memories and continuing on a linear timeline. When I had written my way to age eight, it was suggested that it might actually be possible to skip around. So began an adventure with time warps. I thought of some more recent significant events and even wrote of current happenings, a broken foot bone or treatment for prostate cancer. What other class members wrote about might trigger a memory about a similar event to explore.

Jumping back and forth in time means I don't yet have a seamless narrative of my life. Maybe I never will, and maybe that's all right.

One discovery I made after writing a lot of prose was that I could express some experiences only through poetry.

I also wondered what would happen if I tried some fiction, perhaps a short story. The introduction to "The Very Special Watering Can" relates an actual event. Anna really did ask me to make up a story, and I did. My task was to write something that would fit with where a seven-year-old's imagination might be while also reflecting some of her actual experience with grandparents.

Once I have a topic in mind, I think it through, making a kind of mental list of what to include. Then I sit down, pen in hand, and write it out in longhand. For good or ill, that means there is usually little revising during the process.

The piece about boys and fireworks on the Fourth of July was done in this way. While it is a generalized description of a number of celebrations, it moves from preparation to execution to conclusion. Each item was thought about ahead of time in hopes that the writing would flow and incorporate the fun and excitement of those days.

Peace
Bird

Highwire mourning dove
White feathers flash floating down
Softly settling.

First Communion Gift

By the time I slid into Calvinism,
I had long since abandoned my rosary,
And Mother had claimed my plaster Jesus,
Her souvenir of my days as a Catholic.

She always kept him on her dresser,
Standing tall amid the bobbypins, combs and colognes,
Where she might see him close at hand
Though I never heard her pray.

I could never believe in him,
So straight and rigid in his yellowed robe
With face painted to look benign
Through all eternity.

He was no Sugarloaf Jesus
With arms outstretched to all the world.
Yet looking back I can see his hands
Parting the garment of his being
To reveal a flaming heart
Pulsating with the energy of creation.

In my here and now
I raise my hands to my breast
To feel my oneness
With that Sacred Heart of the Self.
Now that's something I can believe in, by Jesus.

A Boyhood Independence Day

Summers in Kansas City were as hot as the blast of a firecracker. My brother, Carl, and I could try to stay cool drinking homemade root beer in the basement. The back porch might be all right for playing Monopoly if there was a breeze. At night there was the sleeping porch or cots on the front porch for us. Even then the heat and humidity would feel unbearable if the air wasn't moving.

But there was something to look forward to as soon as school was out in mid-June. That was when we could begin to anticipate the Fourth of July. The comic books had ads for various collections of fireworks. But it was much more fun to go down to the corner where the Crown Drug had a big supply you could see and touch. We dreamt about getting a huge quantity of firecrackers. The Black Cat packages were best. It would be great to also get ladyfingers and cherry bombs and rockets and Roman candles, and everything. But then we had to check our saved-up allowance money to see how much we could afford. And maybe Dad would be willing to add to what we had.

Once we knew what we could spend, we had the job of deciding exactly what to buy. Of course we had to have firecrackers and ladyfingers. We decided "no," on the cherry bombs. We needed some things for after dark – maybe some fountains and Roman candles. We also needed a punk so the fireworks could be lit.

Once our supply was home, we had to count and sort in order to plan how to make it last all day. And maybe we could save some firecrackers to shoot off at midnight next New Year's Eve.

Finally the Fourth arrived. We woke up early and the day was already hot. Already there were the sounds of firecrackers all through the neighborhood. Our dog, Daisy, spent the whole day in the crawl space that extended under the back porch. She was a small Collie mix, white and orange. We loved playing with her but on the Fourth she never came out.

Carl and I each lit a punk and started shooting off firecrackers, one at a time. At first, we held one in our hand and, as soon as the fuse started to burn, tossed it across the backyard. Then we found ways to get creative by placing a firecracker in a piece of log or in the dirt to see how much got blown up.

We found empty tin cans and lit firecrackers under them. It was a challenge to see how high the cans would go. Sometimes a whole package of crackers would be lit at once. Of course there was always the chance that some would not go off. It was a game of chicken to see if either of us would be willing to approach the errant explosive. Was the fuse still burning? Could the punk re-ignite it if not? Might it go off in our faces?

When shooting off regular firecrackers got boring, there were always the ladyfingers. They just made a small pop. But one game was to see how quickly they could be lit and thrown in a series of pops. One flaw was that the fuses frequently came out of them. When we tired of all these games we told ourselves we needed to save some for later. By now the air was filled with the smell of burned powder.

As dusk arrived the cicadas would start their raucous, scraping songs. Much earlier we had investigated how destructive a little ladyfinger was to their discarded old shells and had blown all of them up. But evening meant trying to decide if it was dark enough to get out the rest of the collection. Sometime during the day "snakes" had been placed on a rock and lit to watch the body of the snake emerge. Then we tried it in the dark. We thought we were too old for sparklers but each year we lit "just a few" and twirled them. There were Mt. Lassen cones or fountains. They were pretty but often they fizzled out too quickly for our taste. The Roman candles were exciting though we usually thought there weren't enough fireballs coming out. Across the city we could see rockets soaring into the night sky. When these fireworks were over, it was time for just a few more firecrackers before going off to bed on the sleeping porch. With all the windows open we could hear distant explosions far into the night.

A Stranger in the Land of Enchantment

I drove through the Old Town of Las Vegas. On each side of the wide street were buildings and storefronts that could pass for a Hollywood set. No gunslingers, though, that I could see.

Beyond the Old Town I found a little store that passed for a supermarket. I picked up some beer, cold cuts, and bread. Some friendly "howdys" and a little small talk were exchanged with the checkout clerk. Back in the van I headed north on the state highway for the nearest state park.

A couple of weeks before, I had driven out of East Lansing with my youngest daughter, Lori, on our way to Houston. The van was new, bought two months before, and I had the month of August off. Lori and I spent a week with her sister, Carol. Then I was off across West Texas on my own. Lori would stay another week with Carol before flying back to Michigan. I would be camping in New Mexico.

It was early afternoon when the van turned in at the park campground. No one else was there, so I had my pick of spots and pulled alongside one of the shelters. I popped up the top of the camper van, zipped open the canvas window, and opened the back end to capture any breeze that might saunter by. To the west was the mountain range called Sangre de Cristo, the Blood of Christ. Beyond it was Santa Fe, Holy Faith.

I had a little lunch, and with the afternoon ahead of me, I decided to explore. The sun was hot in a cloudless sky. I hiked down the roadway that was supposed to lead me to a lake. Most of the view was of grassland. But the road passed a wooded area where what seemed like a group of high-schoolers was having a party. They were whooping it up. "Probably drinking beer," I thought. The lake was a huge disappointment because it had dried up. On the way back, the party in the woods was still evident. As I approached my campsite, I saw that a dusty old pickup with a cap on the bed had pulled up behind my van. With a whole campground to choose from, this guy was at the same shelter where I parked. But he was nowhere to be seen.

Now I was dusty and sweaty, so I cleaned up a little in the van.

When I came out again, the pickup driver was seated at the picnic table under the shelter. A short stocky guy, quite a bit older than I, he was wearing tattered jeans, an old shirt, and beat-up work boots. He had gnarled hands and a face to match. What hair he had was graying. We said "hi" to each other and exchanged first names. Joe said he wasn't camping but just liked to come into the park sometimes.

It was hard to have much of a conversation with Joe. He spoke in partial sentences and so quietly it was difficult to hear him at times. We were glad to be under the shelter, but it was still hot.

"I'm going to get a beer. You want one?"

"Yeah."

I came out of the van with a couple of cans, and Joe took one. The table had been bare before. My eyes must have opened really wide when I noticed a huge revolver. Joe assured me it wasn't loaded and added that it was a pretty rare piece.

"Not a six-shooter. This one took nine cartridges. But it's all froze up now."

I admired it and allowed that I'd never heard of a nine-shooter. He seemed proud of his gun but sad that it wasn't working anymore.

"It's a lot different than the weapons we had in the war."

"World War II?"

"Yeah. I saw a lot of action in the Pacific. Did a lot of island-hopping." He was quiet for a moment before continuing. "I used a flame-thrower. Jap soldiers would be firing out of a cave. I'd fire the flame-thrower into the cave. If they came out, they'd be burning up."

"It all sounds really terrible."

"Yeah. A lot of guys were getting killed. I've seen a lot of dying."

We were both quiet for a while. Joe didn't seem to want to talk anymore right then. I went back into the van, opened a can of Dinty Moore Stew, heated it up for supper, and took it to the picnic table. The revolver was gone. In its place were several large onions with garden soil still on them. Joe wanted me to have them, saying something about how he had more than he could use now. I thanked him.

Joe murmured that he'd been married ever since he'd come home from the war. "My wife has cancer all through her female organs. She's at home dying."

My first impulse was to think, "What's he doing here if his wife's at home dying?" Then I remembered what he'd said about the war. Yes, he'd seen a lot of dying. I searched fruitlessly for words of comfort and reassurance. Joe said he had to go and climbed into his pickup. I thanked him again for his gift of onions.

The Art
Of Dying

"*Dying*
Is an art, like everything else
I do it exceptionally well."

From "Lady Lazarus" in *Ariel*, by Sylvia Plath

The Hours have ticked away
and left us reeling.
Virginia has pocketed the stones
of her misery
and waded into the stream of our consciousness
only to slip beneath the surface of understanding.

Now comes Sylvia
wearing her bell jar
and singing the post-partum blues.
Perfect mother
thoughtfully leaves mugs of milk
with bread and butter for the children.
Perfect housewife
descends to her kitchen of despair
to stuff with towels the leaking seams of her life.
Gently she pillows her head on the oven door,
jetting away to oblivion.

How sad to have practiced the art of dying
so exceptionally well.

The Very Special Watering Can

The beat of the wiper blades was hypnotic as we drove home in a steady rain. The whole family had been with Anna's great-grandmother for Mother's Day. At her request, Grampa told Anna some stories about when he was a boy of seven. Then Anna asked him to make up a story for her. "All right," he said, "but I'll have to think about it for awhile."

Anna loved to visit her Grandma and Grampa. One sunny day that was warm, but not too warm, she rode her bike the few streets over to their house. She could do that now that she had finished second grade.

After taking off her helmet Anna put on her baseball cap. Her Grandma was working in her garden in the front of the house. She gave Anna a big hug and kiss as always. For awhile Anna helped with some of the weeding but then she sat down on the front steps.

Grandma said, "Oh, Honey, why don't you go around back and see what your Grampa is doing?"

"OK," Anna said, skipping her way to the backyard. Grampa was watering flowers off the deck. "Hi, Sweetheart, I'm glad to see you."

Anna was surprised because Grampa was using the watering can with the pretty flowers painted on the sides. It had been given to Grandma by Aunt Kate and Uncle Pablo. She never used it but kept it in the house for a decoration.

Grampa handed Anna the can. "I was getting tired of doing this. Why don't you finish watering around the garden while I sit on the bench under the crabapple tree?"

"OK, Grampa." Anna started going around the garden along the edges of the backyard, watering all the flowers as she went. It seemed magical to her to use this special watering can. And no matter how many flowers she sprinkled, it never ran out of water. Even so, it was never too heavy to carry, either.

Finally she arrived in the back corner of the yard where the big bushes were. Some birds were chirping above her head. A couple of bees sleepily buzzed by her into the bushes. Then she thought she heard the tinkling of tiny bells. The sound of the bells turned into happy laughter. Peeking out from behind branches and blades of grass were seven tiny fairies. Anna's eyes opened as wide as her mouth. The fairies called for her to join them. Something brushed Anna's hair. One fairy had touched her with a wand. Slowly Anna got smaller until she was just their size. They joined hands in a circle playing ring-around-the-rosie until they all fell down laughing.

Queen Bonita jumped up, grabbed a fluffy white dandelion, and flew up into a branch. "Come on," she called, and they all joined her high in the bush. Two of them had taken Anna's hands and flew her up with them. Each then took a dandelion seed parachute and floated down to the ground. Their happy squeals sounded like bells again.

"Now," Bonita said, "it's time for tea."

Anna and the fairies sat in a circle, drinking their tea from tiny cups and saucers. "The tea is delicious and so sweet," Anna said.

"Yes, the bees have brought their honey for our tea," they told her.

The fairies began to yawn and stretch their arms. "It's nap time," one of them said. "Come again soon."

Slowly they fluttered their wings and slipped away through the grass. Anna was sorry to see them go but realized she was starting to get bigger again. As she crawled out from under the bush on her hands and knees, she looked down on the ground. There beside the watering can was a very shiny penny. She slipped it into the pocket of her overalls as she stood up.

Grampa was resting on the bench. His straw hat with the bright cloth headband and red feather was covering his face. Anna put down the watering can and pulled a blade of grass. She tickled her Grampa's right ear. He lifted his hat and smiled at her.

Grampa said, "I had the strangest dream just now. I dreamt that some fairies had left a magic penny for you under a bush."

Anna reached in her pocket and found the penny there. She was going to tell him of her adventure when Grandma appeared.

"How are you two?" Grandma asked. Then she spied the watering can. "Grampa, please don't bring that outside. I certainly don't want water in it," she fussed, placing the back of her hands on her hips.

Anna and Grampa looked at each other with crooked little smiles. Grampa winked at Anna and said, "Would you take the watering can in the house, please?"

She picked it up. As she carried it into the house she looked in the can. It was perfectly dry.

Jean Powers Gaa

I grew up in the town of Dumaguete, Negros Oriental, in the Philippine Islands. I was an accounting major at the University of Illinois and worked as a bookkeeper during World War II at a war plant that made batteries for tanks and planes. From 1970-1982, I worked as a librarian at Hope Borbas Library in Okemos.

Family has always been important to me and I want to pass on my memories to my children and their families. I have also shared my memories with my sisters. Memories are only important if they are shared – preferably in the written form so they can be passed on to another generation.

Family Documents Can Tell a Story

One summer afternoon in 1988 our doorbell rang. My sister Ann and her husband were standing on our doorstep with a very large "coat-sized" box from Marshall Fields. "What in the world is that?" I asked.

"We are moving to Colorado soon, as you know. I thought you should be the caretaker of this box now. We found it under Mom's bed when she died. Dad kept it under his bed until he moved into the retirement home. I have had it under my bed ever since. It is your turn now."

Mom died in 1955. Dad moved to the retirement home in 1964.

"What is in it?" I asked.

"None of us have any idea. Neither Dad nor I looked. Just put it under your bed. Do what you want to do; you always do."

I could not stand not knowing, so I opened the box. I found hundreds of pictures, letters, and newpaper clippings. A few of them were very early relatives, born in the 1700s; the pictures were taken in the 1800s. There were several Civil War letters and pictures! It was an inheritance beyond belief.

I wrote to the members of my extended family, asking questions and sharing information. I was astonished to remember so much. I assembled the documents and stories into sagas.

Finally, I wrote to and visited my sisters to get help and more ideas to write about. I also contacted my four children and their cousins, asking them to write a few paragraphs telling me about their memories of their Powers grandparents. These are all included.

I discovered the encouragement of other writers for years in a writing class.

Born with a Handicap

I was born in Manila, Philippine Islands, on July 13, 1919, the third daughter of Clyde V. Powers and Willabelle Wilson Powers. The first child, June Powers, born in 1913, lived only ten months. Ann Powers was born in 1915, and my younger sister, Marian, was born in 1924.

I was born "damaged" with a large red birthmark on my left leg, toes to waist. This kind of birthmark is called "cavernous hemanogioma." It is not inherited but was probably caused by a pre-birth accident – I have been told my mother had fallen.

I wonder now how much this bothered and upset my parents, although they never even mentioned to me that I have a "mark." The left side of my body is much larger and longer; even the bones are larger, as shown by X-rays. My parents must have been really worried, for before I was a year old, at a doctor's urging, they agreed to let the doctor rub dry ice on a spot to see if it could obliterate the redness from my toes to my knees, so that I could wear dresses without it showing. I have been told that when my dad heard me scream, he ordered the doctor to stop. All my baby pictures until I was nearly two years old show a bandage on my left ankle. I still have the scar and it is still the same shade of red as the rest of my leg.

During all my growing-up years in the Philippine Islands, no one ever mentioned my leg within my hearing. I am sure, however, much was said. Everyone, I assume, agreed to treat me as normal. I know I was not ever given any extra attention, nor was I even restricted in what I wanted to do. I could and did climb the highest trees; I could and did walk the rafters in the structures Dad was building. I climbed and walked on very strange places, like the third-floor roof on the College Science building. It was my favorite place to eat lunch. My parents were strict with all of us in many ways. I was no exception. Nor did I get more love and attention than my sisters got. I was as special as I was – no more, no less.

I was never aware I should hide my mark. I do not think I was really aware of how prominent it was. As a child, I swam every day of my life in as skimpy a bathing suit as was allowable. I wore skirts (no shorts in those days, of course) and I went barefoot whenever I could get away with it.

When I was thirteen, Ann was ready for college, and Mom brought her three girls to the U.S. Even during that year, my leg problem was never discussed in my presence. I was never aware it could become a major problem in my feeling of self worth.

I came to the U.S. again in 1937 to enter Rockford College. No one seemed to notice my leg. If they did, I certainly did not realize it. I never thought I was different in any way, except I was classed as a "foreign student" and, as such, was in a different category. There were five of us foreigners: one from China, one from France, two from South America, and me. I was different all right, but so were the four other freshmen.

As I had been very active all my life and was in good condition, I joined in all the sports, including the Rockford College Varsity Crew. I was made the coxswain in a four-man shell. I was in charge of our shell when we won first place in a tournament with Beloit College men's crew. I was tossed into the river. I was so thrilled! I never once thought my body was different.

Between my freshman and sophomore years, I worked as a counselor and the only life guard at a camp for children who lived with a family member who had active tuberculosis. I had no worry about catching it. I had to wear a bathing suit almost all day long. I had no problems; the smaller children always asked me how I hurt my leg. I grinned and told them it was a secret. They were all giggles.

In the fall of 1939, Mom, Marian, and I moved to Urbana, Illinois. I enrolled in accounting at the University of Illinois. There, I was just a body. There were thousands of us in all sizes and colors and with a lot of lumps and bumps here and there. No one noticed me except when I was in an accounting class, because I was invariably the only girl.

In 1940, I got engaged to a young assistant professor of accounting. My mom did ask me once if I had talked to him about my leg. I remember stretching my left leg out and saying, "Yes, but why do you ask? He isn't marrying my legs; he wants to marry me for who I am, and not how I am made."

I was so right. He seemed never to notice it. I explained to my kids that it was sort of a burn scar I had when I was tiny and didn't remember. Later, when they were mature enough to understand, I told them all I knew, which was almost nothing. I did say it wasn't anything to be embarrassed or alarmed about.

So I lived ignoring the whole issue until one spring day in 1977. I was wearing shorts while weeding in the front yard on a hot day. My new neighbor, who was from India, came over to introduce her mother, who was visiting her. As we chatted, Mama's eyes suddenly widened and she became agitated. She spoke wildly to her daughter in Hindu. They had a long discussion that was loud and almost angry. "What in the heck is going on?" I wondered.

Finally my neighbor said, "I must apologize. I am very ashamed to ask you this, but my mother insists I must. She says she has to know if the red mark on your leg is from an accident or were you born with it. I am embarrassed to ask you."

"Well, the answer is I was born with it. Why does she want to know?" After more discussion my neighbor said, "She says a person who is born with a mark is lucky, very happy. If she rubs it with her eyes closed, she can share some of your happiness and luck for herself."

What would you do? I stuck out my leg so she could rub it! She did, then held her hands in a peak in front of her face and bowed to me several times, all the while murmuring to herself, maybe in prayer. She walked backward, still nodding and holding her hands up in a point, with tears running down her cheeks. She mumbled what sounded like, "Thank you, bless you." The daughter tried to explain it to me but really couldn't. Finally she nodded to her mother, touched my leg, and ran back to the house. I didn't know why, but I did not mention the strange encounter to my family at dinner.

In June of that same year, my sister Ann and I embarked on a trip through the Orient to visit our old home in Dumeguete, Philippines. When we were in Thailand (old Siam) we visited with a dear friend of mine, Ad, from the Foreign Student Organization at Michigan State University. Ad spent a couple of days with us, visiting temple after temple, and shop after shop.

The afternoon of the second day, Ad told us her mother had invited us to high tea at her home. Ad's father was a general in the Thai Army and a confidant of the king and had a very nice home on the military compound. We enjoyed tea, and she showed us the whole house, including her private shrine room full of lighted candles and polished Buddhas. Ad explained that Buddhists do not attend a church as such, but pray in their own shrine room.

While we were there, Mama started talking firmly to Ad. Ad

answered, "No!" Mama went on and on, waving her hands and pointing at me. What was going on? Finally Ad turned to me and said, "I am so embarrassed. I really don't know how to say this, how to ask you if the red mark on your leg is a scar or if you were born with it."

I answered, "I was born with it." Mama's conversation became louder this time, even angry. Finally Ad said, "She says she must touch it. In our culture, a marked person is marked for a very special reason. The mark will bring much happiness into other lives. I am even more embarrassed to tell you she insists on touching it." Ad was very light-skinned and she blushed a bright red. I moved toward Ad and her mother and held out my leg. Mama gave it a slight rubbing touch and then folded her hands in prayer!

Ad made a motion toward me. I laughed and said, "Go on. Are you scared? You must do it to make your mother happy."

With tears and a big grin, she did and said, "Thank you for understanding so well and for being so kind."

On the way back to the hotel she asked, "Did you see my two little girls run to their brother and rub one of his arms while we were at a Temple?" I had seen it and wondered about it. Ad explained, "He has a small dark spot on one arm. The girls became frightened by a loud noise we heard and ran to him to rub his arm so they would be safe. When they felt they were safe, they rubbed it again so they would be happy. My mother taught them this; they didn't learn it in Lansing, Michigan, you may be sure." When we got back to the hotel, I told Ann what the Indian lady had said and done in Okemos.

In a week or so we landed in Manila, left our tour group, and flew to Dumaguete to see our home and our friends we had left so long ago – forty-five years for Ann and forty years for me. About thirty or forty people were waiting for us at the airport, which was really an old beat-up cornfield on the edge of town. We had to zoom over the field to chase the caribou and several dogs off the field before we could land.

One of the men waiting was a doctor at the mission hospital. I had known Dr. Garcia rather well before I left in 1937. He was educated and trained in St. Louis at the Barnes Hospital and at Washington University. His wife was a nurse and midwife. She also trained at Barnes and Washington University. As we walked along, he carried his black bag in one hand and clutched my hand in the other. He looked quite intently at me, maybe to see how I had changed. Finally he said, "Are you the daughter that has a birthmark?"

"Yes."

"I knew when I looked in your eyes just now, they were happy eyes. You have led a good life and brought happiness to others." He went on, "During World War II, my wife and I went up to the mountains to be with and work for the guerrillas against the Japanese. While there we learned that the mountain folk all but worship a marked child. Such a child will always be happy and bring happiness to others. We always wondered about this belief. I think perhaps you have proven that to be true. I can hardly wait to tell my wife; you must allow us to entertain you." I did have tea with them, and she told me she was now convinced that the mountain folk were right.

How should I handle all this? I did not know then, nor do I know now. I don't talk about it much; I am not sure there is any truth in the whole superstition. Or is there? I am living as I have always lived.

I do know I have lived a good and happy life, for whatever reason it has been.

My Tablecloth

When I was nine or ten, my dad said, "Jean, you are already collecting, saving, even hoarding seashells, coral, stones, butterflies. I can't count them all. Someday you will have more collections than your mom and I have." He must have had a vision. I am sure I now have more collections than they did. I really didn't realize what a collector I had been until I was sorting, giving away, and actually throwing away "things" when preparing to move to Texas in 2003.

In our retirement community, we talk a lot about the things we got rid of and the things we kept. Before packing, I had already decided that only memorable things should be kept, and maybe not all of those. What would I pick as my most valuable thing if I had to downsize even more? My tablecloth.

Charlie and I left Army life in 1947 and moved back to Champaign-Urbana, Illinois, where we lived before we were married in 1941. Early in 1948 we bought our first house, and had room to entertain friends who had entertained us before we left Illinois and after we got back. A dinner party for our four best friends was the first project. I got busy. First came the list making and menu planning. I practiced making the main course so I would not fail as I had when we entertained this same group after we were first married in 1941. I polished the little silver we had and washed the few pieces of good china. I cleaned the whole house, had a few long talks with John, age five, and Chuck, age three, about how important it was when we had guests for dinner to stay quietly in their room in bed. We moved the table next to the twelve-foot-long, knee-high radiator because some of the guests would have to sit on the radiator, as we had only two stools and four chairs. We had put all the table leaves in the table and everything was going well. But disaster hit when we realized the tablecloth was about two feet too short. What to do now?

I finally went to the dry goods store, where they had bolts of bleached muslin in wide widths which were sold to make sheets or draperies in those days. I bought four yards. I did not have time to hem it, of course, but it looked like a real tablecloth. Miracles never cease, do they?

The guests arrived and the food was good. We all laughed hilariously about the Melmac we used to supplement the china, the jelly jars for glasses, and the old, well-used spoons and forks. The dessert was just right, as were the coffee and wine. We made toasts to the food, to the set-up for ten people, and to the kids, who had behaved the whole evening.

We were sitting around the table with our last cups of coffee when Jim, Charlie's oldest and best friend, announced, "Jean, we all just love your real Irish linen tablecloth. I understand it is new, so now we will christen it by writing our names on it." He pulled out a pencil and wrote big and bold, "James Malcome Carritheres." Then he turned and gave the pencil to Bob Mautz, who did the same. He passed the pencil around to the others, and the signatures seemed to get bigger. By now everyone was laughing. They could see, of course, that the tablecloth was not really Irish linen.

The evening ended well. I was left with all that marked-up white yardage. I did not complain because it topped off a good, fun-filled evening. The party was such a success we decided to have more parties.

But we could not have a Christmas party in 1948 as Jim was born in late November. In the spring of 1949, I decided to have our first annual "Christmas in July" party. I still did not have a tablecloth, so I fished out the length of bleached muslin. Now, what to do about getting the signatures off? I decided I probably couldn't, so since it was a Christmas celebration, I embroidered all the names in bright red, hemmed the tablecloth, and even added a fringe. Voila! I had a Christmas tablecloth. Our original guests laughed and found their names. I brought out a pencil and many more guests signed their names. They actually stood in line to sign. This was a 1940s cocktail party with Christmas decorations. We even served eggnog to anyone foolish enough to drink it. Our first Christmas in July party was a roaring success, as was the tablecloth.

Christmas in July and the tablecloth became a tradition. I embroidered all the names and became a better stitcher in the process. We had even had names written in Greek and Chinese.

We moved to Ann Arbor in 1954, held more parties, signed more names. Our four boys were now big enough to help, thank goodness, and to sign their names, all except Tom, who was only four. He has signed it four more times as his penmanship changed.

Tom started wearing his Santa suit at that time. The first time he wore it, we were surprised. Chuck had decided that Tom, the door opener and greeter, was to be Santa. Tom was dressed in Chuck's red pajamas with a pillow insert. His Santa hat and red socks were on, but his beard wouldn't stay on. In desperation, Chuck glued cotton balls on Tom's face with Elmer's Glue. The greeter was a great success, and a happy success, but disaster struck when Chuck removed those cotton balls. Santa let out a scream. Elmer's glue is not soluble in water.

We moved to Okemos in 1958 and held more Christmas parties every year, both in July and in December. Perhaps our best parties were the ones in Okemos, as in the 1960s we expanded them to include our children's friends. Each boy could invite his school friends and their families to our Christmas parties. We also invited neighbors and friends to bring their families. We always had crowds, and lots more names to embroider.

Early on we made a rule: you can't sign until after you have eaten. Sometimes, even if I did not use The Tablecloth, they signed it anyway.

The tablecloth was part of our celebrations during the nearly ten years that Charlie was on the American Accounting Association board. We almost have a history of the officers and members on our tablecloth from the annual meetings of the association that we hosted at the University of Illinois in 1954 and in 1972 at Michigan State University. At MSU we also entertained Charlie's graduate students each year and collected many more signatures.

In Okemos, the tablecloth was also signed by PTA friends, church friends, library parents, knitting friends, stitchery friends, and investment group friends. There were also pioneer ladies and, most importantly, my writing class friends.

Our families visited us in both Illinois and Michigan. My mom and dad are on the tablecloth as well as my sisters, their husbands, and most of their children. Charlie's parents, his sisters, and their three children have also signed it. Our four sons married and the cousins married, and some of them had children. This last year at a Thanksgiving reunion we wrote in the names of three great-grandchildren.

Now I have moved to Texas. What shall I do with my tablecloth? Should I add more names? There is really not much room. Should I retire it too? Should I start a new one? I think I just have to wait until it seems time to make the decision.

We all had pets whose paw prints have been lovingly embroidered too. This past Thanksgiving, Reid, our thirteen-year-old grandson, looked at the tablecloth and saw the corner with all the pets' names and then whispered in my ear, "Could we put our cat Quickby's name on it?" Together we drew a paw and Reid signed the name. We then added John and Cindy's cats' names (Thai and Thud) and paw prints to the tablecloth.

Some months after Charlie's death in 1991, I saw the old tablecloth in a drawer. In a burst of loneliness and mellowness, I spread it out to look at all the names of our friends, all of our dear, good friends with whom we had shared good times and good memories. It opened the doors of memories.

I decided to count the names and I measured and divided the tablecloth into eight squares and listed all the names in each square. Then I categorized and alphabetized them. In 1991 there were:

26 from the American Accounting Association – all accountants plus their wives

22 from the University of Illinois – accountants plus their wives

8 from the University of Michigan – accountants plus their wives

28 from Michigan State University – accountants plus their wives

198 friends

53 family members

10 extended family members

12 paw prints

A total of 421 humans signed the tablecloth from 1948-91. This exercise was good therapy. I had many laughs and a few tears, as many of the signers have passed on. I felt good about my life.

I wonder how many have signed from 1991-2005. I don't think I will count and list them, although I really want to.

We joke and laugh about the tablecloth. My kids all have many warm memories of this tablecloth. "Don't mess with Mom. If she gets really mad at you, she will rip your name off the tablecloth." I hate to confess, but I did once. And with great ceremony. A neighbor made me so angry that I didn't know how to handle her, so I came home and ripped her out.

Another joke is who will inherit it.

John says, "I am the oldest. I know most of the people on it. I get it."

Chuck says, "I get to have it. I have the most girlfriends on it and two ex-wives."

Jim says, "I am an accountant. I go to all the American Accounting Association meetings. I know all the old and young accountants."

Tom says, "I am the youngest. I was around the longest. I helped to set up, to serve, and do the dishes many more times than you guys. All my life, I also watched her embroider it."

So, what will happen to it? Who will inherit it? Really it is the history of my adult life. "You make the choice, Mom."

After a lot of thought, I feel that I have only three choices:
1. I could cut it into four pieces.
2. I could have them draw straws.
3. Each could have it for one year and then pass it on.

I won't tell them what I have decided. Can you guess? The family will have to look in my safety deposit box someday. It will contain a note for them.

NANCY SEUBERT

Although I spent two years in Seoul, Korea during grammar school, I grew up in Eugene, Oregon at the southern end of the Willamette Valley. I moved to the Great Lakes bioregion in 1979 where I earned a Bachelors Degree in criminal justice and a Master of Divinity degree. I coordinate the social justice, peace and ecological sustainability work of the IHM Sisters in Monroe, Michigan. I've taught the "Life Stories: Writing Your Memoirs" class through community education for ten years.

Stories have been the most effective way for me to understand people whose experiences are different from mine. I've written my memoirs to share my life, help people I know to understand my perspective, get a new view of my experiences through the process of writing, and situate myself in the human story and within the larger cosmic story.

The strongest influence on my writing has been my mother, who instilled in me a love for language that she retains herself even now as she copes with memory loss at age eighty-six. I have long-admired the work of Joan Didion, who wrote, "We forget all too soon the things we thought we could never forget . . . forget what we whispered and what we screamed, forget who we were."

Through Talk Pretty Press, I published "Something that Happened at Night: Writing Exercises to Begin Your Memoirs or End Writer's Block," based on the writing exercises I developed for the Life Stories class.

Let Your Story Guide You through a Change of Perspective

The story I call "Visitation" recounts an experience I had twenty-six years ago when I was twenty-eight. I wrote about the events as they unfolded in a journal I kept. The journal became the raw data, colored by my personal bias.

The following year I wrote up my experience as a story in which I, the heroic and dedicated teacher, overcame the obstacle of an unyielding principal to rescue a child snagged by the juvenile justice system. Although I rarely spoke about my time at Visitation, I remembered and understood it in a general way that was consistent with the story I wrote that first year after it happened.

About five years ago, twenty years after the fact, without referring to my journal or the original story, I wrote up my experience again. I was surprised to discover a new character – the child's grandmother – and a new plot – the wise elder who saves the naïve teacher from her well-intentioned illusions. This version of the story continued to reserve the strict principal as an antagonist, but planted within it were the seeds of a changing perspective.

Last year I returned to my story and began to see it less in terms of heroes against villains and more as part of the greater human story of flawed heroes limping toward salvation, getting distracted along the way.

That memoirs change depending on when and from where you approach them, does not mean they are not true; it merely underscores the power of story to shape the way we think about ourselves and the world around us. Another five years from now I may rewrite "Visitation" again. I won't be surprised if I discover in the process that my take on the year I was twenty-eight has been altered once again. But you have caught me in 2005 and this is the story I can offer you today.

Visitation

While I was in the process of entering a religious community, a friend invited me to spend a weekend in a large convent on the south side of Chicago. The shabby linoleum in the kitchen and the smell of old grease that clung to the lace curtains repulsed me instantly. Over the weekend I met several of the families from the neighborhood and glimpsed their experience of community, something I was longing for myself. That hint of vital community boosted me past the drawbacks of living in poverty.

I met with the sisters in charge, told them I wanted to work with the poor, and requested that my first placement be at Visitation. Three buildings – the convent, the elementary school, and the church – would make up my world. I soon joined eleven nuns in a steamy, five-story building that became my new home. In letters to my family, I wrote with excitement about my new calling to work with the poor. It felt right just to say it: to work with the poor.

Just about everything in my life changed that year. I had lived alone for five years in a cabin in the foothills of the Oregon Cascades. The home of my childhood was within an hour's drive. My community was secure and my world as familiar as an old lover. Now, instead of the lapping of flames from my evening campfire, the howl of coyotes in the distance, or the rumble of a train across the lake, I fell asleep with the waves of traffic as the signals changed on the street below my L-shaped bedroom on the second floor.

For a couple of weeks after I arrived in Chicago, I had time to become acquainted with my new housemates and the two priests who staffed the church. Almost as quickly as I learned the daily routine at Visitation, I was thrust into the hubbub of the new school year: the smell of floor cleaner in the mornings, the floods of children in the hallway when the bell rang, the contained excitement in the basement lunchroom, the new personalities that became defined as my co-workers and students.

The principal, Sister Bridget, kept order in the school with strict discipline. Lines for the bathroom were straight and silent. Any child caught with a weapon was immediately expelled. The benefit to the children was obvious: school was safe – perhaps the only safe place in their lives.

Coming from my wilderness cabin, the disciplined environment that Sister Bridget created was completely foreign to me. Again and again I met with her disapproval over this or that unwritten infraction. I began to avoid her in the convent and at school.

A troubled fourteen-year-old transferred into the eighth grade at the same time I was to begin teaching in the school across the boulevard. Angela observed the world through distrustful almond eyes. She wore white high-top sneakers with her plaid school uniform and did creative things with her hair.

All of the children to whom I taught science and religion tested me, but none more severely than sullen Angela. She wouldn't answer when I asked her a question. She refused to join in when we broke into small groups for discussion. Her homework was mediocre. She stared.

As the weeks went by I noticed she was kept after school almost every night by one teacher or another. I suppose I saw mirrored in Angela's resistance my own frustration with Sister Bridget and the living situation in the convent. She wore sadness like a habit.

Sometime in November, Angela was absent for two days. One afternoon while I was instructing, Sister Bridget entered my classroom and handed me a note. I read the neat script: "Angela Johnson will not be returning to school." Alarmed, I turned to Sister Bridget. She stopped my question with a firm look and abruptly left the room.

After class I sought out Sister Bridget in the principal's office. "What's happened to Angela?" I asked.

Sister Bridget protected the information that weighed on her. "Angela won't be coming back. That's all I can tell you," she answered, concluding the conversation before it began.

I had never deliberately disobeyed Sister Bridget, but I knew something was terribly wrong. I copied Angela's address from the school directory and, after school, for the first time since arriving in Chicago, I checked out one of the community cars and drove to Angela's home. A stout woman in her fifties answered the door. I introduced myself and said I was concerned about Angela. In a Haitian accent the woman said she was Angela's grandmother and invited me in. She began sobbing in great gulps. When we sat down, the story poured from her.

At home a few days earlier, Angela had again acted out. Whatever she had done was typical of her misbehavior, but this time her grandmother had had enough. She locked Angela in the basement and left the house. When she returned a couple of hours later and opened the basement door, Angela flew out in a rage and began smashing things in the living room. Terrified, her grandmother called the police, who carted Angela away. She had been in Cook County Juvenile Detention since then.

My heart went out to Angela's grandmother, who was clearly beside herself with anguish. I told her I'd contact the authorities and see if I could meet with Angela. She thanked me profusely and pleaded with me to keep in touch.

The next day I took the car out again, this time to the downtown detention center. Visitation was strictly regulated, I learned, and the next scheduled visiting time was in the evening two days later. I met with Angela's teacher at the center, who told me that Angela was not doing well. He used the word "defiant." I pressed him to tell her that I had come to see her and would be back during visiting hours on Thursday.

On Thursday, Angela was called to the visiting lounge. As I walked over to meet her, she turned on her heel and began to hurry away. I called her name and she turned back again. I pointed to a table and sat down. Angela followed. I hardly recognized the girl in the detention uniform with the hard look sitting across the table from me.

"Angela, what happened?" I asked.

It was evident that Angela did not know what had caused her incarceration. She had crossed a line somewhere without realizing it. She responded to questions about her week in detention in shrugs and monosyllables, and she seemed baffled and betrayed. As we talked, I willed her away from a kind of psychic cliff. Eventually the schoolgirl returned. At the close of the visiting time, I asked her if it would be all right if I came again. She nodded yes.

I met again with Angela's grandmother. She agreed to see Angela, and I continued to go to the detention center during visiting hours. Angela said she wanted to go back home, and this was eventually arranged.

As I was leaving the lounge on my last evening visit before Angela's release, I passed Sister Bridget on her way in. Neither of us acknowledged the other.

About an hour after I returned to the convent that night, I heard Sister Bridget pull in. It was time to face her. In the downstairs parlor,

Sister Bridget didn't wait for me to begin.

"I don't have any control over you, Nancy," she said. "You just do whatever you want. You always have." Her voice was tight. I wished in that moment that I had been more compliant, that I had won her trust, not her suspicion, in the months I had been at Visitation. I wished that we – the principal and the teacher – could have worked together to assist this family. I felt the terrible weight of my shortcomings and hers and Angela's grandmother's. It seemed that we were all working against each other.

Sister Bridget surprised me then. Without going into any detail, she said quietly, "Maybe I was wrong."

Some time later I stopped by Angela's grandmother's house. She was looking forward, with some apprehension, to Angela's return home. We talked for awhile and, at one point in our conversation, as any new friend might wonder about another, Angela's grandmother asked me why I was there, meaning in Chicago, meaning inner-city Chicago, meaning in her kitchen at that moment. Without thinking, I gave the canned answer that seemed so right when I had written to my family five months earlier. "I want to work with the poor."

Angela's grandmother pulled her eyebrows together slightly. "I'm poor," she said.

It's hard to explain what those two words did to me. In a flash I realized that working with the poor was not what I had imagined when I first took up the phrase. It was not calculated self-sacrifice for people who were wanting. It was not a soul struggle the way living in a religious community had been for me. If working with the poor meant anything, it was the friendship this middle-aged Haitian offered me and the love that propelled me beyond my principal's authority to help a child out of the abyss. Angela's grandmother had no pretensions about her life and no expectations of me. Her honesty cracked open the prison that my fantasies had constructed and that religious life had become for me.

Angela was released and returned to Visitation following Christmas break. After a week of difficult discernment, I decided to leave the order.

On visits to Chicago, I sometimes drive by the old Visitation buildings at Garfield and Halstead. The school was still open the last time I was there but the convent had fallen into disrepair and was unoccupied.

Today I am about the age that Angela's grandmother was in the few months that I knew her. Angela would be forty. I wonder whatever happened to her, how she makes her living, what her family is like. I doubt that Angela's grandmother has any idea about the effect she had on me, lingering all these years. Does Sister Bridget realize that her lifetime gift to me was not her discipline, but her doubt?

Do any of us really know what we are doing? We wake up to the click of a door locking behind us and wonder how we got there. When a chasm separates us from the thing we want most, we discover an even more compelling choice that our original quest would have prevented.

I hope Angela's grandmother and Sister Bridget are enjoying good health and a comfortable retirement, and that somewhere along the way, Angela found a place that suits her. I am grateful to all three of them for their gift to me twenty-five years ago.

Mythic Encounter

I sat at my desk one morning, enjoying a cup of coffee. It was a brilliant August day. I opened the door to my cabin to let in some fresh air. The vivid green of the fir trees and the sapphire Oregon summer sky captivated me. I was lost in a kind of meditation, a lazy lingering that is easy to slip into when no one has a particular claim on your time.

Four years earlier, I had dropped out of college. Now, along with the poignant beauty of the Oregon wilderness, the late summer worked on a preconscious, ingrained schedule in my memory: *I'm not ready to begin the school year. It will be exciting to see everyone and get back into learning again. I don't want my freedom to end. Where did the summer go?*

But I wouldn't be returning to school that year. In fact, I didn't have any plans at all. At the same time that I felt I was losing my freedom, I was lonely knowing I was going to be in that cabin for another long, wet winter, even with its illusion of freedom.

If I had known I would be leaving my cabin – leaving Oregon completely – the following year, the visceral conflict that lay just beneath the surface wouldn't have interrupted my coffee meditation, transforming a moment of pleasure into an edgy sense that something was not right.

Suddenly, I heard a whirring behind me: the sound of a cat with an amplified and accelerated purr, but moving swiftly, flying. I turned to my left and saw a blur of wings against the window opposite the entrance to my cabin. A hummingbird had flown through the open door and was now trapped by the large window over the kitchen sink. I froze momentarily. I knew what the hummingbird did not: there was no way to pass through the glass to the tall trees visible beyond, and I could not open the window, which was firmly nailed in place.

The tiny bird frantically flew back and forth, jabbing and bending its delicate beak against the unyielding glass. I was afraid the hummingbird would seriously hurt itself before it thought to turn around and fly back through the doorway. "Hummingbird," I said, approaching slowly, "you can't get out that window. It doesn't open.

You are so beautiful and I don't want you to hurt yourself. Let me take you outside."

I lifted my arm, cupping my hand as if I were about to carefully turn a doorknob. I placed my hand over the iridescent blur and closed my fingers. I didn't really expect to catch the hummingbird. I didn't feel anything in my hand, and there wasn't a lot of room in the space between my fingers and my palm. But the blur was gone, and I thought I must be holding the hummingbird.

"I'm going to take you outside now," I explained as I took the ten steps to the door.

When I reached the front porch, I carefully opened my fingers. The hummingbird lay motionless in my hand. I was afraid it had died of fright. It was no bigger than a cottonball.

Then, with a whirr, it flew away.

The Monkey
Who Loved Amy

My sister was going to be back in the States for six months.

Phyllis is a year younger than I am. We were great pals through high school and had kept in touch through letters over the years. Because she had settled in Australia, we rarely got together in person. I hadn't seen her in the four years since her visit home after her daughter Amy was born. She had just given birth to Zoe and had arranged to spend several months in Oregon.

I loved having Phyllis back with such an extravagant opportunity to get together. Zoe was a cuddly baby who slept well and smiled a lot. The most delightful surprise, however, was Amy, now four and a half. "Foah ond a hoff," she would say in her perfect Australian accent. Like many four-year-olds, she struggled with the letter "r," replacing it with a "w."

"Let's go pick some black bewwies," she would suggest.

Besides her Australian accent and her charming speech alteration, Amy was impressively self-possessed. She loved to play Concentration, the card game in which players alternate turning over two cards to get a pair. If you make a pair, you get another turn. The more accurately you remember previously overturned cards, now turned under again, the more cards you collect. Amy won this card game against everyone she played, and nobody threw her the game. She had a quick mind and was great fun to be with.

I had recently been given a monkey puppet. This toy was so realistic that when I was practicing handling it on a ferry from Seattle to Port Angeles, a uniformed orderly told me I'd have to put the monkey back in my car. I called the monkey Chiquita. The monkey had a wrinkled face with plastic ears and eyes, and a plastic nose that had nostrils I could move as if she were sniffing. I could open her mouth with my fingers and thumb. No teeth. She had a squeaker that I could activate if I wanted to convey her excitement. Velcro snaps attached her long furry arms to my neck and her matching legs around my waist. Chiquita couldn't talk, of course, but she could nod yes or no and she could tuck her head under my free arm if she was scared.

The morning I took Chiquita over to my folks' house, Amy fell madly in love with her. Her clear brown eyes widened and her little girl energy froze as if she were momentarily paralyzed. Then, walking deliberately closer, she asked if she could pet her.

"Mm hmm," I answered, "but be very gentle because she's shy."

Amy reached up and began to pet Chiquita's head carefully, without bending her wrist.

"Chiquita," I said to the puppet, "this is Amy. Do you like her?"

Chiquita turned her head slowly to Amy, paused, and then nodded her head soberly.

Amy couldn't contain herself. She put two little fists up against Chiquita's face, squeezing her with joy, and kissed her on the nose.

"I like you, too, Chata," she said, and kissed her again.

"Chi-qui-ta," I said.

"Chi-qui-ta," repeated Amy.

Amy wormed her body closer to mine and wound her arm around Chiquita. She released her grip, looked up at me, and asked, "Can he talk?"

"She's a girl," I said. "She's a monkey so she can't say words, but she can understand what you say. Can't you, Chiquita?"

Chiquita stared at Amy a moment, then looked up at me and nodded her head up and down.

"Are you hungwy?" asked Amy. "What do you like to eat? Do you like bananas?"

My eyes flicked over to my parents' counter, decked with half a crate of bananas. "The perfect food," my mother always says. I had visions of Amy trying to feed one of the overripe bananas into Chiquita's plastic mouth.

"Chata, do you like bananas?" Amy asked insistently.

Chiquita wagged her head a couple of times.

"But you're a *monkey*," said Amy. "Monkeys – like – bananas." She puzzled, wrinkling her eyebrows as she considered this breach of logic. A new thought registered in her eyes and she asked slyly, "Are you joking?"

Chiquita nodded her head vigorously up and down and made a high-pitched sound with her hidden squeaker.

I could see Phyllis out of the corner of my eye, as transfixed with Amy as Amy was with Chiquita.

"Ask Chiquita if she likes biscuits, Amy," said Phyllis, bouncing Zoe in her arms. Biscuits are the Australian term for cookies.

"Do you like biscuits, Chata?" asked Amy.

"Chi-qui-ta," I corrected again.

"Chi-qui-ta, do you like biscuits?" asked Amy, impatiently.

Chiquita nodded her head, yes, she liked biscuits.

"Are you hungwy? Do you want a biscuit?"

Chiquita shook her head. Her plastic mouth wouldn't take a cookie any more easily than a banana.

"Ooooooh, are you joking?" asked Amy.

Chiquita shook her head. No, she wasn't joking this time.

"Come on, Chiquita, don't you want a biscuit?" Amy persisted.

Chiquita tucked her head into my free elbow. I scratched the back of her neck with my hand. "You don't have to eat a biscuit if you don't want to, Chiquita," I said.

Amy melted immediately. She bent over to reassure Chiquita. "You don't have to eat a biscuit," she repeated. "Come on, Chiquita, don't be shy."

Chiquita slowly lifted her head and looked at Amy. Amy wrapped her arm around Chiquita and kissed her twice. She looked up at me and asked reverently, "Can I hold her?"

"Better not, Amy," I said. "Chiquita gets really shy around other people."

Amy was satisfied with this. She kept her arm around Chiquita and began a monkey interrogation of likes and dislikes, often challenging Chiquita's response with, "Are you joking?"

Over the six months that Phyllis was in Oregon, Chiquita was with me whenever I went out to visit, and Amy welcomed her without fail. One time, I didn't bring the puppet in with me but left her balanced on the back of the passenger seat in the car, with her legs and body dangling behind the seat and her arms hanging down in front. I think I was trying to teach Amy delayed gratification, or maybe I wanted to temper her powerful will.

Amy instantly asked where Chiquita was. I told her the monkey was sleeping in the car, and I'd get her later. Amy objected immediately, but I was firm about letting Chiquita sleep. Amy insisted on seeing the monkey NOW. Phyllis snapped, "Amy! Chiquita needs to sleep! Nancy told you she'd get Chiquita later! You're just going to have to wait!"

Amy puffed out her lower lip and left the room.

Phyllis had talked with her husband, David, the night before, and she began filling me in on his activities back in Australia. Phyllis played patty cake with Zoe while she talked.

All of a sudden, Amy was at my elbow, pecking insistently on my sleeve. She looked at me intently, her eyes deadly serious. "Nancy, you have to come quick. Chiquita isn't moving. She's in the caw and she's just sta-wing. She's not moving. She's just sta-wing."

I swooped Amy up in my arms. "Oh, that's how Chiquita always sleeps, Amy," I reassured her. "She's fine. She's just sleeping. I'll go and wake her up in a little bit."

Because I don't have children of my own, it was the children of my siblings who gave me the incredible gift that children often bequeath their parents: an invitation to view the world again with innocent eyes.

I had an unexpected cross-over later in the summer when I took Amy to the zoo. I wondered how Amy would respond to the real monkeys in cages after she had developed such a strong emotional bond with the monkey puppet. I brought Chiquita with us to the zoo. As we followed the signs to the primates' section, I wondered if the caged monkeys would have any reaction to the lifelike Chiquita. I completed the cross-over with my next thought. "I wonder if Chiquita will be afraid of the real monkeys?"

The six months passed too quickly. It is always hard when Phyllis leaves Oregon. The distance nags at her even though she has adapted to her second homeland. My folks wonder when they'll see her again. I knew the next time I saw Amy she wouldn't be four and a half anymore, and I regretted not living closer so I could be part of her life while she was growing up. One car wasn't enough for all of the luggage and all of us, and we were clinging to every moment that remained, so we drove two cars to the airport.

At the gate, Amy saw the monkey hanging onto my neck. "Chiquita!" she exclaimed, greeting her summer friend. Turning to Phyllis, she asked, "Mum, can Chiquita come home with us?"

Phyllis seemed relieved to have the momentary diversion from her sad good-bye. "No, Amy. She has to stay here with Nancy."

Amy knew this was so. She embraced the monkey fiercely and said, "I love you, Chiquita."

I so desperately wanted Chiquita to tell Amy she loved her, too, but Chiquita couldn't talk. She nodded her head and squeaked, but it was not the same.

After a moment, Amy seemed to remember Chiquita's language limitations. "Chiquita," she asked tentatively, "do you like me?"

Chiquita nodded vigorously but she was powerless to convey her love. Amy would have to solicit that from her.

Amy put her face right by the monkey's ear and, in a voice almost too quiet to hear, asked, "Chiquita, do you love me?"

Chiquita was ecstatic. Squeaking loudly, she nodded her head vigorously again and again. Then she ruffled Amy's hair with her mouth. Amy wrapped her arms around Chiquita and kissed her many times.

Then Phyllis was handing the flight attendant her tickets. She looked at me over her shoulder before she rounded the corner of the boarding tube. "Bye," she said, with wet eyes.

CHARLES FOSTER

I grew up in Cadillac, Grand Rapids and Muskegon, Michigan. I attended seven different schools. Strong friendships came easily in each situation, and some of them remain to this day.

I knew early in life that I wanted to be a high school math teacher when I grew up. Two of my math teachers also coached the football team, and that inspired me even more.

One day, the results of a career preference test that I did with a high school guidance counselor showed that I had greater aptitude for a career in social work. I laughed off that idea, and continued to pursue a teaching career. I took all the math courses that I could find.

I recently retired after a nearly forty year career in social work.

Use Images and Engage the Senses

One day, the mail included an invitation to the fortieth reunion of the first football team at the high school where I graduated. That brought instant memories of my high school days, and I decided to write them down. Later, full of stories from the reunion, I decided to write a story about my experiences at this new high school.

About that time, my wife and I both enrolled in a writing class. I started writing about my life from the beginning. As I came to the time in my life when polio struck my four-year-old sister, my story changed from focusing just on me. I began telling my sister's story through my eyes. The class' reactions to my writings helped me broaden my focus as to how I saw this illness affecting the entire family.

I developed the story chronologically to match the way that I wrote my other life stories. I replaced "to be" verbs with stronger ones. I also tried to write my stories using "show, don't tell" techniques.

This story, like all the other ones, flowed easily as I wrote it on the computer. I started by doing a rapid recall of the major events as fast as I could remember them happening. I went back and revised the story. I struggled with this part of writing, especially when it led to restructuring sentences. I felt victorious when I found the right words, frustrated when I did not. The class' reaction to my reading told me whether or not the changes worked. Sometimes, the class helped me find the words that I could not find on my own.

I saw my writing change as I moved from mere recitation of facts and taking more space to set the scene for my story, to using more images and engaging more senses. I find that my enjoyment with my writing is reading it to someone else and hearing how he or she hears it.

When Polio Struck Our Family

Gloom hung over my grandparents' home. One sultry summer day in 1952, my grandmother seemed very sad, too sad for a ten-year-old boy to ask her why. She stared at the phone as it hung in its cradle after she finished a conversation with my father. My parents had never before called from summer camp. My four-year-old sister, Nancy, had gone with them that year, leaving my twelve-year-old sister, Pat, and me at my grandparents' home.

I just waited for my grandmother to say something. Finally, she said that my parents and Nancy were coming home early. She told me that Nancy was very sick and might have polio. I did not know what that meant. I did not ask. She did not tell me. She later told me that Nancy could not reach out with her right hand to touch my father's hand when he held it out to her. It all scared me so much that I hid in my grandparents' dark basement when my parents arrived with my sister. I did not want to see her or touch her.

The doctor confirmed that Nancy had polio with paralysis in her right arm and hand. My parents followed the doctor's orders and put Nancy in Cadillac's Mercy Hospital right away for treatment. She joined several other children who also had polio in various parts of their bodies. Pat and I could not visit with her, except through pictures that my parents took of her and the other children. She stayed in the hospital for many weeks, but made no improvement.

My parents prayed and prayed and prayed for her recovery. People in the church and others who knew our family also prayed. But the paralysis did not leave her. I just hoped that she would be able to come home.

Sometime later, my aunt convinced my parents to move Nancy to Munson Hospital in Traverse City. They knew a specialist there who had helped other children with polio get better. My parents agreed to make this move, hoping that the possibility of healing for Nancy would overcome the pain of a fifty-mile separation from her. They also knew that my aunt and uncle would be close and watch over her. Our family made frequent visits to Traverse City to visit Nancy, and she could come outside so Pat and I could see her and talk to her.

The doctor fitted Nancy with a steel frame that strapped around her entire upper body. It held her arm in a rigid splint at shoulder level like an airplane wing. There was another brace that fastened to the frame over her wrist and held little metal bands that fit like rings over each finger and her thumb. These braces never did fit her quite right, and the need for repair increased as she grew.

After all this, still no noticeable improvement. My parents and lots of other people kept praying for her recovery.

Our hope changed as the doctor decided that Nancy needed the special treatment at Mary Free Bed Hospital in Grand Rapids. My parents agreed to the move. The doctors there were doing special treatments for children with polio. This encouraged my parents as we made the hundred-mile trek to my sister's new home. My aunts and uncles living in Grand Rapids visited my sister regularly, and they could take her to their homes for day-long visits. All this helped my parents as they struggled with making this long trip more than once a month.

About a year later, my father gave up full-time employment for a career change that resulted in our family moving to Grand Rapids. Nancy, now a six-year-old, could live at home. A taxicab transported her to a school that included an orthopedic clinic connected to Mary Free Bed Hospital. Part of her day included physical therapy and occupational therapy. At home, she still had to wear the big brace and have lots of help with her daily living. Much of this help had to come from my sister and me. My father attended school part-time and worked part-time. My mother worked at a downtown store on a full-time basis. Pat had to leave school early every day, and give up other high school activities to provide child care for Nancy. Being a natural left-hander, I had to show Nancy how to do things with her left hand. I found it hard to be helpful. I would not give her any special treatment. I considered her as my bratty little sister who seemed to delight in tormenting me. I did not want her to have privileges any more special than being the baby in the family. One time in desperation over having to tie her shoes over and over again, I devised a way that she could tie her own shoes with one hand. It worked, and she seemed to enjoy doing it for herself. No more having to get down on my knees and tie her shoes.

Later on, our family moved to Muskegon. My parents had to find a school where she could continue with the daily therapy that she needed. They found one quite near our home; however, it meant that she had to ride the same school bus that Pat and I rode. I handled this news with howls of protest. Our bus was for high school kids, not for somebody's little sister.

"Why does it have to be me who has to be different," I objected to my parents. I didn't care that they had no alternative. However, not much later, I found myself defending Nancy in a shouting match with another freshman, who complained about her being on our bus. From then on, I even made certain that she had a seat near the front of the bus, although I made sure she didn't know this.

I later graduated from high school and went off to college. Nancy started attending regular school, as she no longer needed the therapy that we all thought would help her. She did have corrective surgery so that she could have some use of her arm and hand. She could tie her shoes easier, too. She learned how to twirl a baton, play the French horn in the high school band, drive a car – and she could bowl quite well.

Today, Nancy is a woman married over thirty years, the mother of three, the grandmother of three, an avid football fan, an active and fiercely competitive soccer mom, and a highly respected home day-care provider for several years. Now she manages the scheduling office at a major hospital in the state. She organizes family reunions that usually result in everyone making the effort to get there, even from hundreds of miles away. She wraps packages, she cooks and bakes, and she ties the tightest knots of anyone that I know.

My Baseball Card Collection

I started collecting baseball cards in 1951. My father gave me a pack of five cards as a gift for my ninth birthday. I looked through the pack for New York Yankee players, and I found one for a player named Mickey Mantle. I liked his name. He instantly became my baseball hero.

The neighborhood where we lived in Cadillac, Michigan, included several boys about my age. Most of us collected baseball cards. Whenever I could come up with a nickel, I bought another pack. Each pack came wrapped in shiny paper with five cards. We eagerly opened each pack with a high hope that it included cards that we did not have already.

We each kept our cards banded together with a rubber band. Sometimes a new purchase included cards for players that we already had. Those we kept in a separate stack for trading with the other guys. At least once a day all summer long, we would go through each other's cards, looking for ones that we might want. Then we entered negotiations for the cards that we wanted, offering the ones that we would give up. Any of us could get the card that we wanted if we made the right offer of cards that we had. Sometimes it took a combination of cards to get that desired card. Or we might have to wait until we found someone else who also had the desired card and wanted one that we would give up.

We all wanted to have as many different players as possible. No one kept track of who had the most. Each guy only paid attention to what he had and what he wanted. We avoided cards for rookies because they were first-year players and did not have major league data on the back of their card. The more data on the back of the player's card, the more we wanted that card. Rookie cards had only minor league data, and we feared that rookie players might not stay in the major leagues. Nobody wanted their card if they did not. Sometimes we threw their card in as part of a trade for the card that we really wanted.

We had favorite teams that we especially wanted to collect. I traded for any Yankee player that I could get, including those, like

Charlie Silvera, who seldom played but continually had major league data on the back of their card. I quickly offered Detroit Tigers for them, and this usually worked. The good Tiger players, like Al Kaline and Harvey Kuenn, I could trade away for good Yankee players, like Yogi Berra, Mickey Mantle, Allie Reynolds, or Ewell "The Whip" Blackwell.

Not having Kaline or Kuenn meant that I might have to give up two or three other Tiger players and sometimes a few from other teams to get a Yankee card. I tried to keep from appearing too eager for the Yankee cards as we bargained. I did not want to give up, at least not too quickly, any card that I wanted to keep. Nobody offered any money in the trades. We dealt strictly cards for cards. When I lost one of my special cards, I could only hope that another one showed up in a new purchase or in someone else's cards.

Duplicate cards that we could not trade away stayed with us. Nobody threw them away. Some of us fastened them to our bicycle spokes so that we could make a motor-like sound as we rode.

Each summer we started the ritual all over again for the new cards coming out that year. They still cost a nickel a pack. This continued year after year for as long as I collected cards. As each baseball season ended, I banded together that year's cards and put them with the banded cards from earlier years in a shoebox in the bottom drawer of my dresser.

In September 1954, just after my twelfth birthday, my family moved to Grand Rapids. Baseball card collecting changed for me. We lived in a city neighborhood where I knew only one other boy my age. He and I traded some cards, but his interest did not match mine. It seemed that I had to talk him into buying the cards, which he did only a few times. This forced me to make-do with the cards that I could buy, still a nickel per pack.

My baseball cards became a new fantasy for me as I spent more time alone at home than I did when we lived in Cadillac. I organized my cards into my own league of teams, playing the teams against each other on a mechanical baseball game. I put my Yankee players on all the teams in my league. I even kept a scorecard for these games, and I set up a World Series at the end of the summer for the two teams with the best records.

Two years later, my family moved to Muskegon. I continued to collect baseball cards, and I had more friends to trade with. One friend especially had many more cards than I did. As a self-described

"Yankee-hater," he easily gave up Yankee cards for just about any other player one-for-one. I found that I could convince him to give up two or three Yankees for one Chicago White Sox player. I made certain that I had my White Sox players cards with me whenever we got together.

The next year, my interest went away. My friends lost interest, too. We found other things that we wanted to do with our money, like meeting girls at the new hamburger stand in town named McDonald's.

I eventually lost track of my baseball cards. I did not even look for them. A few years later, my mother called me at college to ask what she should do with "all these baseball cards." I didn't need them anymore. I told her to toss them out. She did.

Taking the Early Out

Retirement came too early for me. I started my working career in 1965, thinking that retirement would come after my sixty-fifth birthday. I signed the mandatory retirement beneficiary form designating Halen, my wife of one month, as my sole beneficiary. I gave no more thought to retirement over the next several years. I even considered Social Security as an income shift from the employed junior citizens to the unemployed senior citizens.

I began reaching the point in life where I qualified for letters offering an incentive for early retirement. These letters came about every four years. I did not keep them long enough to read them a second time. I stayed the course toward my original retirement plans. Nothing could change my mind.

Early in 2002, the agency where I worked exploded with a frenzy of excitement about a new early-out incentive that topped all the previous ones. I assumed my customary position of "not interested, period." But I could not escape all the chatter, including one colleague who talked with a financial planner who specialized in the State of Michigan Retirement System. I decided to check this planner out, and I came away with a clear picture of why I could take this incentive and retire earlier than I planned. After talking with Halen, I drove to the retirement office and signed the retirement papers. I would retire at sixty years of age.

I picked the latest possible date to leave work. This gave me the time that I needed to prepare for the day when I would wake up without a job. My last day of employment started just like the previous ones – with my usual early morning routine. I felt more and more detached from the agency as the day progressed. As I moved my personal effects out, a colleague began moving into my highly coveted work station near a window. I had seen enough. I put my office keys and my security badge on my desk and walked out the door.

The next day started with my decision to treat myself to an extra half-hour of sleep, waiting for Halen's alarm to go off. When it did, she seemed surprised to see me still there. I told her I wanted to determine if I could do this retirement thing. She suggested that I was a bit late to wonder about that. She commenced with her usual morning routine. I, however, did not get out of bed until she left the bedroom, just before 7:00 a.m.

I headed straight for the breakfast table, not reading the morning newspaper, not listening to the 6:00 a.m. news on a local radio station, not meditating for a few quiet moments, and not getting dressed – all things that I had done routinely before breakfast for many years. After breakfast, I stared out the window, looking into the backyard as Halen closed the garage door and left for work around 7:30 a.m.

I filled my four-cup coffeepot and drank coffee listening to National Public Radio until the news ended. I do not like NPR, thinking of it as "Not-very Public Radio" for many years. It seemed just like all the rest of the national media shows. Their report about Minnesota politics following the tragic death of Paul Wellstone grabbed my attention. I met Senator Wellstone a few years earlier at a child abuse prevention conference in Minnesota. I previously thought of him as "a controversial senator from Minnesota," just as the national media usually described him. Since meeting him and hearing him speak, I came to appreciate him as a passionate spokesman for those who have no voice, such as children who are abused or neglected. My daughter, who lives in Minnesota, talked with me often about his work. Now she fears the local talk about his likely replacement.

It was 8:00 a.m. Now what would I do? I couldn't sit around and watch television or listen to sports-talk radio all day. So I got dressed and saw that I still needed to shave. This took all of ten minutes. I saw that Halen's absentee ballot was ready, and I decided to hand-deliver it to the township clerk's office. The people there had no interest in chatting. I decided to walk in the mall. On my way there, I decided to go farther west on Saginaw Highway and I ended up at Menard's. I walked through the entire store, bought nothing, and headed for Wal-mart. I saw nothing in the entire store to buy, and I went over to Lowe's. I liked this store, but I wandered aimlessly with an empty cart for a while, then put it back and left. Next I stopped at Horrock's. I could not think of anything that we needed from there, and I left. I arrived at the mall and started walking in silence while staying out of the way of the serious walkers. I stopped in Barnes and Noble bookstore, where I could easily spend hours. I saw a friend who works there and said hello to her, noting that customers kept asking for her help. I went home and waited for noon so that I could have lunch. I watched an old television show all the way through. I remembered seeing this particular story before.

I actually tried to check my e-mail at work, and I learned quickly that I was already off the system. Just as well. What would I do about anything that I saw if I did get in? Shortly after 1:00 p.m. the telephone rang loudly. One of my former colleagues, and still a friend from work, wanted to consult on some case situations she was handling. That conversation went on for about an hour, and she seemed satisfied. I suggested that my fee would be a cup of coffee someday.

Another phone call. My sister wanted to wish me a happy retirement. She retired from a nursing career a couple of years ago and wanted to know how I was handling my first day. I described my day and asked her what she does with her days. I know that she enjoys retirement very much. We talked about the two of us taking a couple of days to visit our ninety-year-old aunt who lives up north. She is about the only remaining source of information about family history, and perhaps she can put some names with the faces in the countless pictures we have in family albums. My sisters "adopted" all our aunts and have worked at keeping in contact with them since the death of our mother in 1980.

I decided to work in the yard for a while. I saw that the newspaper was still on the porch, and I threw it inside the house for reading later. I mowed the lawn two times: once to mulch up the leaves, and then to tidy up the yard. I swept up the middle of the garage, noting that soon I would have to get rid of the junk that had accumulated in the corners. That would wait for another day. At the moment, I felt weary. I went inside and took a nap, an afternoon nap. Then I read the newspaper and waited for Halen to come home from work. I wondered what I would say if she asked me what I did all day.

The Day My Daughter Was Born

Our air-conditioned home made for a good night of sleeping. The warm, humid July 1973 weather hung around right into August. Not in our home, however, as we enjoyed the great indoors night after night. This night was no exception. As usual, the quiet drone of the air-conditioning unit eventually lulled us to sleep.

Suddenly, I hear, "Charles, I think that my water broke."

Did I dream that? I never heard words like that before. I open my eyes carefully to see Halen standing by the side of the bed, waiting for me to say something helpful. I can sense her concern. However, I can also see that it is 5:00 a.m. I could only think to ask, "Do you want to go to the hospital, now?"

We needed more time for this baby's arrival. All of Halen's prenatal visits pointed to the birth coming later in the month. Our doctor arranged a short family vacation out of town with plans to return well in advance of the due date. We thought that we did not need a backup plan. Plus, the family who planned to provide child care for three-year-old Bruce also left town on vacation. We had responsibility for their goldfish during their absence. My work calendar included meetings every day for the next several days.

Halen dialed the number for the doctor's answering service and left a message along with our phone number. We got dressed and sat in the living room while we waited for the call back. At 7:30 a.m. the phone ringing finally wakened us. Our doctor's partner sent a message for Halen to go to the office when it opened at 9:00 a.m. That gave us time to make a new child care plan for Bruce. We called friends with children about the same age as Bruce, and they could take him for a couple days before they left on vacation. That helped.

We took Bruce with us, as we arrived early at the doctor's office. The partner's son, a new doctor, saw Halen. She returned to the waiting room quickly, saying that the doctor wanted her to go directly to the hospital. Her face magnified her concern about this guy's lack of experience with obstetric patients. I made no attempt at humoring her. She voiced hope that her doctor's partner would do the delivery, even though she had never seen him and knew very little about him.

Before going to the hospital, we stopped back home and called our friends, who assured us that they and their kids had already made plans for Bruce's stay.

After we got Bruce settled and headed for the hospital, Halen announced that she wanted a Whopper from Burger King. I found this stunning, as she did not like Whoppers. We stopped at Burger King, which just started its lunch menu. She ate the Whopper and fries and a medium Diet Coke. Wise purchase, I thought.

Back on the road, we talked about where to park the car and decided to leave the car in a church parking lot about a block from the hospital. We did not know how long we would need to leave it and we wanted to avoid paying for parking. We walked to the hospital and crossed a busy Michigan Avenue. Halen was obviously pregnant; I was obviously carrying her overnight bag. I felt the burning stares of all the people in cars passing by and seeing us walk up to Sparrow Hospital.

Upon arrival, Halen decided that she wanted to visit her friends working in the medical records office. They visited while I read a newspaper and drank coffee. Finally, we walked into the admitting department at 1:30 p.m.

Even though we had attended expectant parents' classes for several weeks in anticipation of this birth, I intended all along to not be in the delivery room. The hospital offered the choice, and the decision came easily for me. The memory of seeing films about childbirth showing the actually delivery and having to put my head down every time told me that I could not really be there. I could see myself doing something stupid. I further rationalized that I wanted the doctor's complete attention on Halen and delivering the baby. Halen seemed to agree. After all, I could handle being in the Fathers waiting room.

The labor and delivery area had lots of noise and busy activity with other expectant parents calling for attention. That left us alone for longer periods of time than we'd had with Bruce's birth. Not much happened as we waited, and waited. We talked intermittently about the breathing exercises that we learned in the expectant parents' classes. We waited some more, and then frustration set in. We talked about going home and had started to do so when the first real labor pain hit. Then everything sped up as the baby kept coming. At about 6:00 p.m., the nurse said that the time for delivery had arrived. She told me to go to the adjacent room, where I found a staff person in scrub clothes washing his hands. This did not look like the Fathers waiting room. Without looking at me, he described the activities I needed to do before I entered the delivery room. "The delivery room?" Before I could tell him that I wanted the Fathers waiting room, I put on the hospital gown and started washing my hands.

Soon, I walked into the delivery room and an attendant directed me to a chair placed next to where Halen was lying. She did not see me as she talked nonstop with all the hospital staff attending to her. I preferred watching them and the other activity and keeping my mouth shut. I heard it all, but understood none of it. I forgot to worry about fainting. I could see clearly how much these people all focused only on our baby arriving safely. That helped. Our doctor's partner entered the room and introduced himself, and Halen seemed real pleased to see him. He engaged Halen in a conversation that seemed like they had planned this all along. I stayed out of it.

One of the attendants offered to move large mirrors around so that we could watch. That did not help. Before I could ask her to move them back, the doctor asked if we wanted a boy or a girl. We said that we hoped for a girl, but a boy would be OK. He introduced us to our new baby daughter, and handed her to an attendant, who quickly prepared her for Halen to hold and feed. I missed the delivery. But I did not care as I silently watched Halen enjoy holding our daughter. While everyone talked about the baby and checked her over, I said a quiet prayer of thanks for Meredith Karen's safe arrival on August 6, 1973, and for Halen's safety during the delivery – and, oh yes, for my surviving it, too.

Over the next several days in the hospital, Meredith spent quite a bit of time under the bilirubin light, for treatment of jaundice. We found the length of her treatment hard to accept, remembering that Bruce seemed more jaundiced than Meredith, but had a shorter treatment. During my visits, we watched in silence as she lay under that light. We hoped and prayed that this amount of exposure would not negatively affect her. Still we did not know how long it would take.

On Halen's discharge day, we learned that Meredith had to stay for a while longer. She needed more bilirubin light treatments. We offered to bring her in as often as needed. They preferred to keep her there. We went home and made plans to return to the hospital early the next day. Later that next day, we rejoiced at the good news that we could take our daughter home to join our family.

We decided that having one boy and one girl now makes us a million-dollar family.

HALEN FOSTER

I grew up in St. Paul, Minnesota, in a working class neighborhood with two older brother who ignored me. My grandparents lived upstairs and I loved to be with them. My grandfather used to scold me when I swung on the drapes that separated the living room from their bedroom. When Grandfather had a stroke, I would stand by his bed silently. Once when making a housecall, the doctor asked me to leave. I replied, "Oh, it's OK, because I'm going to be a nurse when I grow up"

Now I live in Michigan. I recently retired from my nursing career. I want to spend more time with my family and friends, do some traveling and enjoy my little Maltese, Comet!

Think of Ordinary Life Events as Story Material

My father's autobiography, whose yellowed pages are brittle with age, inspired me to write my stories. He typed his autobiography on his portable Underwood typewriter as a graduation requirement for every student at St. Olaf College. My father was an ordinary man writing about everyday life events. I treasure this autobiography because I got to know him as he grew up on a western Minnesota farm in the early 1900s.

I try to think of everyday ordinary life events as story material. What could be more ordinary than losing a fork? The fork I wrote about had no monetary value. It was a gift from a supermarket back in 1965. From years of use and misuse, part of it was even broken. The children are grown and gone, the mortgage is paid, we've owned many cars, bought new furniture – but this fork has remained a constant and valued part of our lives throughout our marriage. I was beside myself when it turned up missing, like the woman in the Bible who lost some coins, and searched until she found them.

I started writing life stories as part of an adult evening class. Our teacher gave us some broad categories for ideas of where and how to start. I needed the discipline of being in a class to write in a timely manner. It forced me to write. The more I wrote, the easier it became. Because my handwriting is illegible and physically painful, I use a computer to compose and revise. I might jot down ideas on paper as a rough guide. I keep my class materials, completed stories, and works in progress in a zippered three-hole notebook. I used sheet protectors for the finished works. The stories I wrote are not in chronological order. I like to write about funny things that happen to me and think would make a great story.

Beijing

Choosing one of the doors, I entered to find a "squat" toilet, which was level with the white tiled floor and had a plastic wastebasket nearby. I hung my jacket, hat, scarf, and travel bag on the door hook. I positioned my feet on either side of the white hole, pulled down my slacks, pantyhose, and underpants, and assumed the position of squatting over the toilet, unsure of which direction to face – the wall or the door, which did not lock. The thickness of the slacks, pantyhose, and underpants hit just behind my knees and it hurt to do a very deep knee bend. My aim improved nanoseconds after the first stream splashed outside the rim.

The wad of toilet paper in my hand was not adequate. I remembered I had taken the partial roll of toilet paper from the hotel as well as baby wipes and antiseptic hand wash, but they were hanging out of reach on the door hook. My arms could not reach the travel bag, let alone lift it off the hook. Shuffling forward, I grabbed the bag. While squatting, I rummaged through the bag, which contained not only the extra toilet paper, baby wipes, and antiseptic hand wash, but also my camera bag, extra film, a can of pop, a container of yogurt, and brochures. The items I needed had settled to the bottom of the bag. Not wanting to set the bag on the dirty floor, I held the bag with one hand and rummaged with the other, still attempting to hold my position over the squat toilet, balancing on the balls of my feet and trying not to think about the pain at the back of my knees. The plastic wastebasket next to the toilet was already primed with discarded toilet paper and I added mine. The pipe for the water supply had no flushing apparatus, so that part remains a mystery. Outside the stalls, I saw a bucket with a long-handled scoop-shaped strainer. I didn't even want to think how that would be used.

Throughout our time in Beijing, China, I attempted to find places that had western-style toilets. Even with this information, it turned out that in each row of stalls, perhaps one was the western style. It was like playing roulette. My shoes stepped on many unknown substances in the bathroom floors during our journey. When packing to return home, I left the shoes behind in China.

Lost Diamond

The sharp points poking my finger alerted me to look down to see what they were. I was horrified to discover that the solitaire diamond was missing from my ring. At first, I stared in disbelief before uttering, "Oh no, oh no, oh no!"

"What's wrong?" Charles asked.

"The diamond is missing from my ring!" We looked on the floor next to the computer where I was sitting. It was not there. I shined a flashlight on the floor, looked under the furniture, and tried to remember the last time I knew I had it. I remembered having difficulty putting on vinyl gloves in the morning at work. Even small gloves are too big for my hands. The diamond could be anywhere – at work, in the car, in the parking lot, at home, in the garage. The next morning, Charles called the insurance agent. We had no coverage, as we did not take out a separate policy and the loss was not due to fire or theft.

Eight years ago, Charles and I purchased the diamond ring. This was not an engagement ring, since we were married twenty-eight years at that time. I tried on a full-carat diamond and it looked disproportionate on my size four finger. We settled on just over a half-carat. My mother was thrilled that I finally had a diamond. I wore this ring nearly every day, leaving it at home only when on vacations. But now I had a ring that was soldered to the wedding band and no diamond solitaire, just empty prickly prongs. "Don't buy me another diamond, Charles. I don't want to risk losing another one. Now I know what to do with my parents' rings that have been sitting in the medicine cabinet for the last four-and-a-half years. I will have them repaired and soldered to my wedding band."

I put the ring in a small plastic Ziploc bag. The following Saturday, I went to a family-owned jeweler.

"I can't tell you how many other nurses and doctors have had this same thing happen to them," the jeweler said. "The prongs that hold up the diamond catch on gloves. We recommend only baguette settings for nurses or doctors."

I didn't want to ask what a baguette setting was.

"It's too bad the jeweler didn't educate you to have the setting checked," she continued.

"They did, but I never had it done. I was always too busy, or the jeweler was closed, so I put off doing it for these past eight years. Here is what I have in mind. I would like to make this a combination of my wedding band and my parents' rings. Is this possible?" I pulled the rings out of the plastic Ziploc bag and poured them into her hand.

"I can see that two prongs are damaged. No wonder it fell out. We also recommend six prongs."

"If you look inside my mother's diamond ring, you see the inscription: EJ to BG 10-24-36."

"Oh, I see it is hand engraved, something that isn't done anymore. It's very special and has a lot of sentimental value."

"When her wedding ring got too thin, she wore my father's wedding band, sizing it to her finger. Her fingers got gnarled from arthritis and they cut the rings off so crudely at the nursing home."

"Yes, I can see that the engraving is still there, and I think we can save that. They just barely missed the year thirty-six."

"My father's ring also has a bit of design around the band. Can that be saved?"

"I'll write up the description and give it to the jeweler to estimate the cost and let you know on Monday. He is not here today."

Back home, my hand felt naked with no rings. The base of my finger looked thin. The pasty white skin started to peel. I waited impatiently for the jeweler to call and tell me the rings were ready for pick-up.

The day finally arrived. Out came the rings, sparkling in the bright overhead lights. The diamond dazzled my eyes.

"Do you think my mother's diamond has much value? They were so poor when they got married, and I'm sure it didn't cost a lot."

"Your mother's engagement ring has an illusion setting with filigree around the diamond that enhances the size of the diamond by reflection. This alone makes it valuable as an antique setting." Looking at it with an eyepiece, she continued, "The diamond is nearly colorless and flawless." She made a mark on the scale indicating the value. It's definitely worth an appraisal."

"Well, after the holidays. I want to wear it for a while and enjoy it."

"Yes, I definitely need the appraisal!" I said, glancing down to admire the sparkling diamond. I felt incredibly happy that my parents' rings have a permanent home on my left hand.

Nature's Miracle

While finishing my bath, my eyes are drawn to the all-too-familiar site of our Maltese dog's poop. Again it was almost completely on the pad next to the toilet where he does his business, at least some of the time.

Comet's eliminating in the wrong place started when I became a full-time employee and was unable to come home at lunch to let him outside. The experts call this separation anxiety. I have complied with all their suggestions: no long good-byes, give him chew toys, play music especially for pets, and give him small food in a ball that he has to roll to make the food spill out. I keep him on washable surfaces, praise him when he does eliminate in the right places, and never scold when he misses the disposable pad.

Stepping out of the tub, I wrap in a towel and grab some toilet paper to pick up the poop and what looks like a piece of glass. I almost throw it in the toilet along with the dog poop, when something prompts me to examine it more carefully. I put on my glasses, for it is just too blurry without them. It looks like glass, smooth and perfectly round. Could this be my diamond solitaire that was lost seventeen days ago? Could this be possible, since we had the cleaning ladies out twice, fourteen people here for Thanksgiving, and countless changes of Comet's wee pads?

I stare in disbelief and call Charles to come up from the basement. "I think I found my diamond!"

I am not sure it is a diamond, for I've never seen a loose diamond except on TV or in movies. We agree it must be the diamond; no one has broken glass in the bathroom.

"We can take it to the jeweler's on Saturday after volunteering at the museum. The store is open until 4:00 p.m., as it is Christmas hours," says Charles.

I call the housekeeper to let her know I found the diamond, and leave a message on her answering machine. On Friday, there is a message from LuAnne. She and her team have cleaned our home for nearly ten years. She says the cleaning ladies always wipe up the bathroom floor, even behind the toilet, but she offers this theory.

When they are finished, she sends the girls out to smoke, and then does a tour of the house. I have left messages to remind them to close the bedroom doors and to be sure a pad is placed on the floor for Comet. This time the bedroom doors were closed, but no pad for Comet. She pulled one out of the package and placed it on the floor next to the toilet, in its usual place. The diamond probably fell out of the setting and settled to the bottom of the bag when I pulled the pad out seventeen days ago. It was protected there while the cleaning ladies came twice and we had our Thanksgiving company. Then when LuAnne pulled the pad out, the diamond must have fallen on the floor near the pad.

I don't know what to do with the diamond, so I place it in a tiny Ziploc bag and put it in a dresser drawer. I don't even have a jewelry box. Saturday comes, and we got to the jewelers, who are surprised and happy for me. I have mixed feelings. In my mind, I am resolved with the lost diamond and happy to have my parents' wedding set repaired as a replacement and no longer sitting unprotected in the medicine cabinet.

"Now what do I do with this?" I ask the jeweler.

"The prongs need repair, the band is worn and too thin, and the setting certainly needs six prongs instead of the original four. You can look in this book of 4,000 settings or look at the displays to see what you like."

"I am overwhelmed! I have no idea what I like at this point. I think I just want it to look like it did."

"Yes, I thought you would like the traditional solitaire setting. The cost of a new, stronger setting is the same as the cost of repairing your old setting."

"OK. Then I will have it set in the stronger setting." So many decisions. I just want to go home.

"We can have that ready for you in two weeks," the jeweler assures me.

Now I wear my wedding set on my left hand and my parents' set on my right hand. Many people have told me their stories of lost and found diamonds, but I never thought I would have one. For once I'm glad Comet missed his mark.

The Fork

"Honey, I can't find the fork." That's all the description it needed, for it is understood which one I am looking for. This ordinary fork, a freebie from a grocery store in Amarillo, Texas, has been in our lives for the more than thirty-eight years of our marriage,. The fork survived countless moves across the country.

It's a sturdy fork. The tines are unbent, although some of the black handle portion is missing and the metal part no longer shines. On the back it is stamped "stainless" and "Japan." Five stars are engraved on the handle. It doesn't match our other flatware, so it is reserved for specialized tasks, such as turning bacon, poking holes in potatoes for baking, and crimping the edge of pie crusts. It is even kept separate from the matching flatware, in another compartment in one of the many miscellaneous kitchen drawers.

When it turned up missing, I wasn't too worried, knowing I would find it sooner or later. But months and months passed and still no fork. Intermittently, I went through the drawers, looking for the fork. This resulted in neater drawers, but no fork.

I eventually settled on the fact that the fork had just been thrown away along with table scraps. I went for weeks without thinking of the fork. Then last week, while eating lunch with people from work, I saw the fork!

"Let me see your fork! Ah ha! That's MY fork, the fork I've been looking for! Where did you find it?" I said to my co-worker.

"In the drawer with a bunch of other odds and ends," she said while eating her tuna fish hot dish. I had to control myself from grabbing it out of her hand and wait patiently for her to finish. "I'll wash it up when I'm done and you can have it back."

I must have brought it to work for one of our many potluck lunches and then forgot to get it when cleaning up.

I carefully placed it in my purse so I wouldn't forget to take it home that night. I washed it by hand and placed it in one of the miscellaneous drawers. I check on it occasionally to make sure it is still there.

Summit to the Sea

Biking down the inactive volcano, Haleakala, on the Hawaiian island of Maui was the highlight of our October 1999 trip. My husband Charles and I had read about it in the travel books and were intrigued.

Pick-up for the adventure was at 3:15 a.m. We set our alarm for 2:45 a.m. and were awake before it went off. We dressed in layers, which we would remove as we descended into warmer air. Over my underclothes I wore a short-sleeved t-shirt, a lightweight jacket, a hooded sweatshirt, walking shorts, long johns, and the pants of a jogging suit. This was strange-looking apparel for Hawaii, but no one saw us waiting in front of the hotel except the family we invited to join us. Our ride came a few moments early and we drove to the staging place.

"This company must be on a low budget," I thought as I looked around the not-so-glamorous building. I couldn't believe there were so many people getting up this early to ride a bike downhill for thirty-eight miles! There were cups of hot coffee and donuts and Danish served in their white bakery boxes. Juice was available for the non-coffee drinkers.

Then we had to pick up our gear: one very tight-fitting bike helmet, one yellow rain suit in size medium for me, and one very thick pair of gloves. The bikes were already loaded on a trailer. Our van had twelve people plus the two guides, Gregg and Big K. Then off to the top of the crater we went. I never looked at my watch to see how long it took to get up there. I was amazed at the traffic all going to the same place at the same time.

All along the way, the guides were instructing about the safety rules and what to expect. When we got to the top at 10,000 feet above sea level, it was raining and very cold! We donned our outfits, and everyone looked alike in the yellow rain suits, red bike helmets, and black gloves. It was hard to distinguish which group was ours! There were hundreds of people all crowded at the rail, waiting for the sun to come up around 6:15 a.m. and it was now 5:45 a.m. The vans then got in line to begin. We found out that the first two groups of riders had to leave ten minutes apart, and the rest, five minutes apart. We were number twenty-two. It didn't take long to figure out that we would be there a long time on that cold rainy day. Big K called to one of the park rangers. We were allowed to move to a lower starting point if the group agreed. We all agreed. Big K told us we would bypass two hairpin turns. We decided we could do without them. We drove to the new spot. We had cups of hot chocolate and coffee. I worried whether I would manage all the fluids without stopping. We were able to watch the sunrise in a private sheltered area. We took pictures of each other, dark figures against the rainy sky. Then the sun came up and we could see in color. The clouds hung like necklaces around the volcano's cinder cones.

Our guides took the bikes off the trailer and gave us a chance to practice. I hadn't ridden a bike for years. The bikes were all one size and I barely made the height limit. My bike had to have the seat put all the way down so I could reach the pedals. It was a boy's bike and it was hard for me to swing my leg over the bar, with all the layers of clothes and a rubber rain suit that stuck on the metal. I found I could not straddle the bike like the other riders did. I had to swing my leg over and stand next to the bike. Perhaps if I hadn't had so many layers and the sticky rain suit, it would have been better.

"Get on it like you're riding a horse," Gregg said to me. "The right brake is the rear brake, the left one is the eject brake. Be sure to squeeze with both hands in a steady movement. Go ahead and ride around the parking lot." I squeezed the right brake to test the eject theory and found it to be true.

Big K was the forward guide and I was next. My husband Chas was much farther back so I wouldn't embarrass him. The chase van was behind us. Big K gave us hand signals, which all seemed the same to me. I decided to follow him and do whatever he did.

"Be sure to ride in the middle of the road," Big K told us. "Look at the scenery now, then keep your eyes on the road. You tend to ride in the direction you look and that can be disaster. No camera. There will be stops and photo opportunities. Keep twenty to thirty feet apart and brake slowly but steady. There are two rangers out here: Rocky and Cliff."

With so many instructions, I hoped I could remember them all. Off we went. What a rush of adrenalin. The black gloves were bulky, making it hard to squeeze the heavy-duty brakes on the heavy mountain bike. I felt uneasy. The road was steep, with hairpin turns that I couldn't see around. "Stay in the middle and squeeze with both hands," kept going though my mind.

Radio contact was constant between Big K, the chase van, and the home office. From time to time we did stop, and Big K and Gregg did a check to see how we were doing and complimented us on remembering the rules. We could retrieve our cameras from the van or deposit unwanted clothing. Big K rode most of the way with only a shirt and shorts. He also turned around while biking to see how the group was doing. He had been a guide for the bike trips for seven years, so he knew every turn. The scenery changes were dramatic. At the top was a huge crater with cinder cones. The National Park was at the uppermost part of Haleakala, then open-range cattle, then residences, then the town of Piaia, and lastly the sea. We passed through a eucalyptus forest with its wonderful fragrance. We saw the blooms of the silver sword, a plant that only grows there and blooms every thirty years. I took a picture of the scraggly looking plant with the strange, tall, green projection of spines. At one point, we were able to see the ocean on both sides of Maui.

At one stopping point, Big K assisted the bikers in poses on the bikes that were far from the strict safety rules. These turned out to be my favorite pictures. Our breakfast orders were taken at this stop and phoned in to the restaurant below.

We knew it was raining on those still waiting at the top as we ate our hot breakfast and visited with the other bikers in our group. We received more instructions, as we were now going to go through residential areas and would have to ride closer together and closer to the edge of the road or even stop so cars could pass. Occasionally we had to pedal the heavy mountain bikes, and it was hard for me. I had to stand to pedal to keep going. My heart pounded, and I worried about Charles, knowing the cardiologist told him not to overdo it. The entire group made the journey from the summit to the sea, ending up in a park next to the beach where bathing suits were optional. No one was curious enough to see who might be there. Greg and Big K loaded all the bikes on the trailer for the short ride back to the staging area. All too soon the adventure was over. We were back at our hotel by 10:00 a.m. with wonderful memories and many photos.

Illegal Operation

The message reads: "This program has performed an illegal operation and will be shut down. If the problem persists, contact the program vendor."

I decided to contact the program vendor to see just what could be done about this persistent problem. It was one of those 800 numbers. I had nothing to lose, or so I thought.

"Hello, my name is Halen Foster and I am responding to the Windows message that I have performed an illegal operation more than once. I feel so ashamed. Usually I am a law-abiding citizen, although I have had a few traffic tickets in my life. I want to turn myself in and wonder if you have an amnesty period for first-time offenders. You don't have that program? I am very sorry about performing an illegal operation, but quite honestly, I'm not sure what I am doing to get in this trouble. I feel I should get some consideration for being a 'newbie' with this computer stuff. Maybe you can help me to understand some of the common mistakes so I can correct them in the future.

"What? You won't report me? How will I know you won't report me? I think I should get something in writing, after all! It won't be necessary? Is this one of the phone calls that will be monitored for quality assurance purposes? I don't recall hearing that message. I want your name so I have it for my records. No, I am not paranoid and I resent that remark."

At that point, I hung up. I could no longer keep from laughing. I still get these messages and have been ignoring them ever since.

Weight Watcher

I found my weight creeping up and up. I decided to take action. Health Promotion through work would offset some of the cost for joining Weight Watchers. My weight was too much for my height. The survey said I needed more exercise, less weight, and lower cholesterol and blood pressure. Weight Watchers met on Mondays over the lunch hour, making it very convenient. The cute young leader wore a size six. Proclaiming her successful forty-pound weight loss, she assured us all that we could do it. She described the program, which sounded easy enough: just count points, add exercise, and weight loss will happen.

As a new member, I received the Weight Watcher member organizer that looked like a black planner. It contained program materials, membership book with supermarket and dining-out companion, POINTS calculator, and a place for your pen or pencil.

"Get organized today and keep all your program material in one place," she told us.

The 10 percent weight loss goal seemed reasonable.

We were told to journal everything we ate and did. I could eat eighteen to twenty-five points per day. Well, I starved the first week, having a house full of high-fat food. No wonder I weighed so much! I had to go out and buy prepackaged frozen dinners with the points posted on the front of the box, lots of carrots and fresh fruits, and fat-free bread, to name a few. Part of the program was drinking at least six to eight glasses of plain water every day. Diet pop, juices, milk, and tea did not count as part of the water. I ran to the bathroom every twenty minutes. I guess that is part of the weight loss program. At the first-week weigh-in, I had lost two pounds.

Each week, the cute instructor handed out recipes. I decided to make the one-point bran muffins. I was warned to eat only one a day for starters, as there was a lot of fiber in them. It took a couple of weeks before I had all the ingredients for the muffins. The recipe makes fifty. I picked a cool day to make the muffins. Remembering that some of the members said they forgot to put essential ingredients in, like baking soda and sugar, I double- and tripled-checked my assembled ingredients, but I forgot to see if I had muffin liners. I counted fifty-three. Just enough.

"Be sure to mix in a large bowl."

I used the biggest bowl I had. The recipe called for one box of 100 percent bran cereal, two generous cups of boiling water, twelve egg whites (I hated throwing away those egg yolks), five cups of whole wheat flour (the one with the highest fiber content), one and a half cups of sugar, a cup of applesauce, five teaspoons of baking soda, and one quart of 1 percent buttermilk. Mix well.

"Be sure to mix in a large bowl."

Well, I couldn't even budge that big bowl of ingredients. There was just too much to mix well. I tried moving the bowl into the sink so the bowl would be lower. I stood on a stool for more leverage. Nope, still couldn't budge that sludge. My husband helped with mixing the initial first few turns.

Even though it was a cool day, the 400-degree oven made the kitchen hot. I baked and baked and baked, and it seemed never-ending. Where do you cool all the muffins? I ran out of muffin liners. Oh well, too bad. I sprayed the muffin tin with non-stick spray and continued baking. I had sixty-four muffins cooling on every flat surface in the kitchen. When they cooled, I packed one dozen per freezer bag. But the freezer was full. I ate the butter pecan ice cream to make room for the one-point muffins. There will never be a shortage of natural gas as long as there are bran muffins.

I was on week six of a ten-week program and dreading the weigh-in. Too many eating occasions – a high school reunion, potluck at work, Labor Day weekend and birthday occasions, and then the cruise to Alaska – all to sabotage The Program. By the end of the program, I lost six pounds. We still have one-point muffins in the freezer.

Paula Zang

I grew up in Sturgis, Michigan, which is located about fifty miles south of Kalamazoo. I received my public school education there beginning with kindergarten in 1956 until I graduated from Sturgis High School in 1969.

My best friend, Linda, and I visited her sister, Sandy, for a week during the summer before we began eighth grade. Sandy was attending Michigan State University. I decided within a day that I wanted to become a Spartan and green and white would be my primary colors.

I began my college career at MSU on September 22, 1969. My academic endeavors yielded a Bachelor's degree in Education and a Master's degree in English. Only one other student, a guy, shared two classes with me. I never could have imagined on my second day of school that my classmate, Paul Zang, would become my best friend, the love of my life, my husband, and the father of our two children, Eric David (03/19/79) and Anna Christine (06/14/85).

I had a rewarding career as a high school English, speech, and drama instructor for twenty-seven years. Even though I am unable to walk due to Multiple Sclerosis, my life has been a fascinating journey.

Write for Enjoyment

After developing secondary progressive multiple sclerosis and desiring to keep my mind and body as active as possible, I investigated intellectually challenging opportunities through Okemos Community Education. I joined a writing class in 2001 and have continued ever since.

All of the stories I have written actually occurred in my life or to someone in my immediate family. In every case, each story made a major impact on my life, either in a positive or negative way. Before I begin writing, I usually spend an hour just thinking about the experience. In my story "Mugged," I learned of the violence perpetrated against my son on a Tuesday night in New York City. The next day, I sat down and wrote the entire story while the details were still fresh in my mind. My journaling is in longhand because I lack the trunk strength to sit at a computer keyboard.

My ideas flow spontaneously and I do not revise my stories much at all. I taught various forms of writing to high school students for twenty-seven years. I don't make formal outlines because my ideas are usually well-formulated in my mind before I begin writing. Besides, drafting an outline would make it seem like I was writing a required school assignment. I write for enjoyment.

I am writing my memoirs so they may be passed down to my children and grandchildren. I believe it is important for family members to understand their origins. In my children's case, they may want to know what life was like growing up in the 1950s. They may ask, "How did Mom and Dad meet?" There are so many fascinating stories to tell. I hope I will be able to continue writing them until the day I die.

Mugged

Tuesday, January 18, 2005. I am sitting in front of the fireplace, warming my hands and feet. I love the gas logs that Paul bought me for Christmas three years ago. We used to burn real wood in the fireplace, but that was cumbersome and transient. Now we can have an enduring fire at the flip of a switch. I am so relaxed watching the flames flicker in different formations. I am mesmerized. I am in my own private world. It's twenty minutes before *Judging Amy*, one of my favorite television shows, and I have no cares, no worries. My most relaxing alone time is in this setting. Even though I spend a lot of time by myself, I am usually paying bills, making business calls, or attending to other necessary duties which are not typically relaxing. I cherish my alone-time in front of the fire.

I am startled by the ring of the telephone. Paul has already gone to bed, since he gets up at 5:30 a.m. on weekdays. The digital clock on the VCR reads 9:46 p.m. It's too late for my friends or solicitors to call. It must be my brother, Philip, or one of my children, Eric or Anna. I'll keep the call short so I can watch my show.

"Hello?"

"Mommy, I just got mugged!" Eric is clearly holding back tears, and the sound of his voice takes me back to when he was thirteen, not almost twenty-six.

"Eric, I'm so sorry. Tell me what happened. Do you need medical treatment?" I'm trying to sound strong for him, but I am unable to keep my voice from quavering.

"It's so cold here, it's insane. I dressed in layers so I wouldn't freeze my ass off. Thank God I put my cell phone in the inside pocket of my fleece jacket or I wouldn't have a thing. I wore my really warm jacket with the hood, which I had covering my head. I was looking down to protect my face when all of a sudden, with no warning whatsoever, I was jumped from behind and punched hard on my cheek. I don't know if it was a bat or a fist, but I fell flat on my face on the sidewalk. Before I could get up, four legs started kicking me in the lower and upper back and on my sides. Then I felt my wallet being pulled out of my pants pocket. They ran with their backs to me. I made $140 in tips tonight, and I had my credit card, and my bank card. They got everything."

"Honey, where are you now?"

"I'm in my apartment. I called you first 'cause I need to talk to you. I don't know what to do. Mommy, what do I do? I'm looking at my face in the mirror. It's super swollen and I'm getting a black eye already. I don't think I need to go to Emergency. Besides, I don't have insurance."

"Eric, put an ice pack on your face to help with the swelling. Look for unequal pupils because that could indicate a concussion. You need to call the police and have an officer come to your apartment so you can file a police report. Then call your credit card company and bank and report that your cards have been stolen. Also, see if one of your friends can come over and spend the night. I think you will feel better if you're not home alone tonight."

"I'm not alone. Trinity came running to the door as soon as I walked in and began purring. Also, what good would a police report do? I have no description of the suspects."

"It's important for you to explain exactly what happened and where it occurred. Maybe there's a pattern and other people have been victimized, too."

"This is MY neighborhood. I've lived in New York for two-and-a-half years. I've always felt safe. I feel violated."

"You have been violated, Honey. I'm thankful that you are alive! I'll call you around midnight to find out how things transpired with the police. Love you forever."

"Love you, too, Mom. I think this was a sign. I don't have to work until Friday. I'm going to take time to reassess my situation these next two days and decide exactly what I want to do with my life."

"You are still in a state of shock, Honey. This has been a frightening experience and it may change your life's direction or it may just change your route home. Give it some time, but I want you to know that you are welcome to live with us while you figure things out if that's what you need."

"Thanks for the offer. I may take you up on it."

"Call you at midnight."

"Thanks. I have a lot to do by then. Love you, Mom."

"Love you, too, Honey. Bye."

As I hang up the telephone, my anxious eyes return to the serenity of the dancing flames in the fireplace. I think about the fragility and uncertainty of life. The fire warms me and its perpetual flames remind me that a mother's love is the umbilical cord that eternally binds our hearts and is the wellspring of healing when her child is wounded.

The Magic Pumpkin

My first day of classes at Michigan State University arrives on September 22, 1969. A cool breeze caresses my body as I make the trek to Bessey Hall. I enter the building and find my room number. I anticipate that the room will be a large, impersonal lecture hall. Much to my surprise, it looks like a regular high school classroom. There are about thirty desks.

I arrive twenty minutes early. Two guys are sitting next to each other in the last desk in their row. I say, "Hi," as I walk in. They answer, "Hi," and that is the extent of the conversation. I am deciding where to sit. Not the very front desk in a row, but definitely not the back. There are five rows of desks going across. I sit in the second desk from the front, in the second row from the door.

People start to filter in, most moving toward the back. By 9:00 a.m., many of the seats are occupied. Only one person sits in a front desk, and it is the desk in the center row directly in front of the podium. I can't help noticing this guy – staring at him is more like it. I have never seen anyone like him, at least not in person, only on the news. He has straight blond hair that reaches all the way down to his shoulders. He turns around and notices me because I am occupying a desk in closest proximity to the desk he chose. He says, "Hi," so I say, "Hi" back. He wears gold wire-rimmed glasses. He faces front again, in silence. In fact, the classroom sounds like the waiting room in a doctor's office. Only a few people are speaking in whispers. We're a bunch of nervous freshmen.

All of a sudden, an elderly gentleman shuffles in with a briefcase in hand. I hope this isn't our professor.

"Good morning, I'm Dr. Squint (not his real name) and I'm your instructor for American Thought and Language, commonly referred to as ATL. I'll begin by telling you a little something about myself. I have been teaching here at MSU for thirty years. I have been the chairman of this department for the past ten years. My primary responsibility is to establish the curriculum for all three terms of this class and to supervise the other ATL instructors, particularly the graduate assistants. In order to manage these duties effectively, I teach one class per term. I'm sure you will be gratified with the realization that you have the most knowledgeable ATL instructor at MSU."

I look around the room. Maybe it's me, but I don't see any grateful facial expressions. The instructor is wearing an outdated sports coat with a shirt and tie. He wears glasses and he squints and blinks a lot. His face looks pinched together, as if a doctor used forceps when he was born and his features never righted themselves. His nasal voice has an irritating sound. He begins to pass around a syllabus and starts to go over the class requirements.

We will be studying early American Literature from the Puritans until just after the Revolutionary War. I love American Lit, but I'm thinking more John Steinbeck and Ernest Hemingway. I'm confident that Dr. Squint will facilitate captivating discussions on this time period. Yeah, right. As he goes over the syllabus, he directs a few questions to the class, though I'm not sure he necessarily expects a response. However, one individual eagerly raises his hand. As you may guess, it is the hippie in the front seat. I figure he is a brown-noser. Who else would sit in the center front desk?

When Dr. Squint dismisses the class – of course there aren't any bells – I notice the hippie leave the room. He is on the tall side and extremely thin, almost emaciated. I collect my belongings and go to my next class.

On Tuesdays and Thursdays, I have another required class, Natural Science, Nat Sci for short, which meets in the Natural Science building. The class runs from 1:50-2:40 p.m.. There are twenty minutes between class periods, probably because it takes that long to walk across such a large campus. The building is one of the older ones, brick with ivy growing on it, like Campbell dorm. The classroom appears antiquated. There are two rows of heavy wooden tables nailed to the floor. The table where I'm sitting has graffiti gouged into it everywhere. "Class of '39'." You've got to be kidding me. There are three chairs per table with an aisle between the rows. There are eight tables on each side, with a gas outlet on each table. Yippie! We'll be able to do science experiments without leaving our seats. Students are talking as the instructor walks in.

He bellows, "I expect absolute silence from all of you the moment I arrive. The fact that three of you sit at the same table is not a license for chatter or tomfoolery. My name is Dr. Nerd (not his real name). I want to begin by taking roll, and please raise your hand as I call your name." Blah, blah, blah, blah, blah. Does he think we're in grade school or what?

"In an effort to learn your names, I am instituting a seating chart. Everyone please stand." My seat is next to the aisle, the second table from the front, in the row closest to the door. All students obediently follow the nerd's instructions. After everyone has been assigned a seat, Dr. Nerd believes he has a cool idea.

"I am going to allow you to converse with your tablemates. Shake hands with your tablemates. Shake hands and introduce yourselves. Then do the same with the table in front and behind yours." Two other girls are seated at my table. Three guys are behind us.

"Far out. You're the girl who was sitting kitty-corner behind me in ATL yesterday. Hi, I'm Paul Zang," the hippie says as he extends his hand.

"This is really weird, not just because we have two classes together. My name is Paula, Paula King."

"That is serendipitous,"

"You mean, 'coincidental'."

"Attention please, your five minutes are up."

Dr. Nerd is younger than Dr. Squint, but not any more interesting. We spend the rest of the class period going over the syllabus.

After we are dismissed, Paul says, "I guess we'll be seeing each other every day from now on. Where do you live?"

"I live in Campbell. It's an all-girl dorm on north campus. It's known as the nunnery. Our head advisor is a nun, literally. Where do you live?"

"I live in Wonders Hall. It's a co-ed dorm on south campus. It's a jock dorm. My roommate is at MSU on a baseball scholarship. It's such a nice day. Would you like to sit on the hill behind the ad building?"

"Sure. It's really nice there. I enjoy being near water."

"Me, too. I like to look at water, but I don't like to be in it. I never learned to swim." As soon as we get outside, Paul lights up a cigarette. "Do you smoke?"

"Not really, I've tried it. I have a lot of allergies."

"Unfortunately, I'm hooked. My older brother got me started when I was sixteen."

We have a nice time sharing stories. He walks me to Campbell. Nat Sci is the last class of the day for both of us.

Of course, Paul and I see each other daily from now on, so it only makes sense that we hang out each day. We are not dating; we are just friends. It is so refreshing to have such a close friend of the opposite sex and have the relationship be completely platonic. I like him so much. The weather is getting chillier, so we need to wear jackets outside. The leaves are currently at their peak of perfect splendor.

"You know, Paul, it's Halloween this Saturday and it just doesn't seem like it without a pumpkin."

"What do you mean?"

"Every year we go as a family to a local pumpkin patch. We all pick out our favorite pumpkin. Then we go home and carve our pumpkins into jack-o-lanterns. It's really fun. We put candles in them and display them on the front porch. Mom and Dad dress up in costumes to hand out candy to trick or treaters. The kids love it."

"We have never had a trick or treater because we live out in the boonies. Sounds fun though."

The next day is windy with thick, dark clouds and a cold drizzle. After classes and dinner, I hole up in a study carrel. I'm not going anywhere tonight in this weather. The nun finds me and says that I have a guest waiting in the front lobby. I run down the stairs and as I reach the lobby my eyes fill with tears. Paul is standing there holding a perfect pumpkin in his outstretched arms. Overcome with emotion, I can't speak for a second, so I run up and put my arms around his neck and hug him tightly. He doesn't hug me back; of course he can't since it takes both hands to hang on to the pumpkin. I've never hugged him before but it feels right.

"Thank you, thank you, thank you! This is the sweetest thing anyone has ever done for me. Where did you get it? How did you get there?"

"I made a few inquiries and found out that they are selling them at the Frandor Shopping Center, so I got it there."

"Who drove you?"

"No one. I walked."

"Do you mean to tell me that you walked all the way from Wonders to Frandor and then back here to Campbell?"

"It was no big deal."

"What do you mean 'no big deal'? That would be at least five miles in this yucky weather. That's a huge sacrifice. I'm overwhelmed. This is incredible. I can't believe it. Set the pumpkin down. Sit down. You must be exhausted. Come into the lounge with me and rest your weary legs."

"Thanks for the offer but I haven't eaten yet and the cafeteria only serves food for another half hour."

"Go nourish your body. I can't tell you how much this means to me. Thanks again."

"Oh, one more thing. As you know, it's Halloween on Saturday. Wonders is hosting a Halloween-themed mixer. There are going to be all sorts of Halloween decorations and a D.J. to provide the music. There are signs all over the dorm advertising it and I think it's going to be cool. I know how much you like Halloween, so would you like to go with me?"

"Are you kidding? Of course I want to come."

"Gotta go. See you tomorrow in Nat Sci."

"See ya. And thanks again from the bottom of my heart."

Maybe those words sounded a little strong, but so what if they did? I need to properly acknowledge the incredible gesture that Paul made for me. I don't feel like studying anymore. I need to show Linda, my roommate, what Paul brought for me.

"Hey, Linda, you won't believe what Paul just came and brought me."

"Paula, that is so cool. He is so nice to you. I wish Bill would do special things like that for me."

"You have been together so long that he takes you for granted."

"I guess you're right. Why don't we carve this pumpkin right now?"

"I would love to but we need a sharp knife."

"No problem. The day my brother drove me here he gave me a going-away present that he told me I would find indispensable. It's a Swiss Army knife. I'll get it now so we can get started."

Linda is a really good artist, so I tell her what I want the jack-o-lantern to look like, and she does the carving. I have a candle and when she is done carving, I put the candle inside and set it on the window ledge.

"Linda, you have done a great job. Now people will notice it when they walk by."

"You're right. It does look pretty cool."

The next day after Nat Sci, I ask Paul for some details regarding the Halloween mixer.

"So, Paul, is the mixer a costume party or what?"

"The flyers say nothing about costumes. I'm not wearing one."

"The party starts at 8:00, right? Do you want me to walk over at about 7:30?"

"No, you know that I like Campbell's food better than Wonders'. I thought I would pick up a cafeteria pass so we can eat together at Campbell, and after we eat we'll walk over to Wonders together. Besides, I don't feel comfortable having you walk by yourself all that way, particularly in the evening and especially since you're so pretty."

Paul has never mentioned anything about my appearance before. Hippies aren't supposed to care about a person's looks. It is inner beauty that counts.

"Sounds like a good plan. I have a big paper to write. It's due Monday and, you know me, I hate to wait until the last minute. I'm starting it tonight and I hope to finish it tomorrow night. I want to have fun on Halloween, and I don't want to have the paper hanging over my head."

"It sounds like you don't want to see me until Saturday evening."

"It's not that I don't want to see you. Of course, it's not that. I will have a better time if the paper is finished. You understand, don't you?"

"I'll let you off the hook on one condition. Promise to give me your undivided attention Saturday night."

"I promise."

"See ya."

"Bye."

Paul and I have hung out together on a daily basis for the past six weeks. We are getting to know each other really well. My intuition tells me that the mixer is going to be different, sort of like a formal date. I finish my paper late Friday night. My roommate, Linda, went to Royal Oak for the weekend. I intend to sleep in so I have plenty of energy for tomorrow. I don't know what is the matter with me. I say my prayers and relax into bed but I can't fall asleep. My heart is pounding too fast. I didn't have any caffeine tonight, no chocolate. My paper is done. Actually, I think it's quite good. So, what is my problem?

I fall into a restless sleep. I try to sleep past eight in the morning. Not once have I made it to breakfast on a weekend morning all term, but since I'm not sleeping anyway I might as well eat. I throw on some sweats and have a hearty breakfast by myself. While I'm eating, I get a great idea. It is Halloween after all, so I will wear a costume to the mixer. It won't be a traditional costume, but something different nonetheless. Paul has never seen me in anything but the most casual clothes, jeans and sweatshirts mostly. I always wear my long blond hair down and perfectly straight, except if I wear two long braids. He has never seen me wear makeup. For tonight, I will curl my hair, apply makeup, and wear a skirt and blouse. I run down to my room and look through my closet. I decide to wear my long-sleeved purple blouse and my purple pleated miniskirt with a really cool psychedelic sash that I bought in San Francisco this summer. I find my hot rollers and makeup bag on the top shelf of my closet. I haven't taken these out at all since I got here. I spend the whole day getting ready. By the time Paul is expected to arrive, I check out the finished product in the full-length mirror on our door. "Damn, I look good!" I'm getting really excited now. In a few minutes the phone rings.

"Hi, Paula, it's Paul. I'm waiting in the lounge."

"I'll be up in a minute."

I make a mad dash to the bathroom. I always have to pee when I'm nervous. I run back to the room and grab a jacket, but decide to leave it in the room for now. I don't want anything to interfere with making a good first impression. I peek into the lounge.

"Hi, Paul."

"Oh, my God, you're absolutely gorgeous."

I curtsy. "Thank you, kind sir."

Paul is wearing an outfit that I have never seen before. He is wearing brown bell-bottom slacks with almost imperceptible vertical rust-colored stripes and a long-sleeved rust dress shirt that really highlights his blond hair. "Paul, I guess this is going to be a costume party after all."

"You're right. We'd better go to dinner so we can make it to the mixer on time."

Paul usually fills up his food tray until it overflows. Tonight, he takes small portions and fewer items. After we finish eating, I run to my room to grab my jacket, and we make the trek to Wonders Hall.

We go to the room where the mixer is taking place. The only lighting comes from a series of black lights, so it is difficult to see anything. Paul takes my hand and leads me into the room. Once inside, I notice some ghosts and a witch on a broomstick. Next to the D.J. are some jack-o-lanterns on the floor with candles in them. It is so dark that it is difficult to see.

Once my eyes adjust, I see other couples; I don't see anyone who isn't paired off. The song "Nights in White Satin" begins to play. "Let's dance." For the first song, we dance in the traditional position. Later, Paul puts his hands on my waist, so I put my hands on his shoulders. He pulls me even closer with his arms around my waist. I put my arms around his neck and rest my cheek on his chest. My heart is pounding fast. As the music fades away, Paul puts his hands on my cheeks and raises my face to his and kisses me. At that moment, I know our relationship will follow a different path, quite possibly a long term path.

Indeed it has. On September 18, 2005, we celebrated our thirty-fourth wedding anniversary. We have two children. Eric David Zang was born on March 19, 1979. Anna Christine Zang made her debut on June 14, 1985. As soon as Eric and Anna learned to walk, we started our family tradition of taking the trek to the local pumpkin patch so all of us could pick out our own "magic pumpkin."

KATHLEEN F. WEBSTER

For eighty-one years I've lived in the Webberville-Williamston, MI area. With the exception of living in Webberville from the seventh grade until I graduated from high school, I've always lived on a farm. At the present time my home is located on the same property where I began my married life in 1941, between those of my two daughters, five grandchildren and nine great-grandchildren.

When my girls were in high school, I began working at jobs off the farm. I worked for the Agriculture Economics Department at Michigan State University, the Agricultural Stabilization Office in Mason, and I was the Wheatfield Township Clerk for six years.

I was a 4-H leader for cooking, sewing and knitting for fifteen years. My daughters were active in 4-H with me.

Find a Comfortable Place and Time

I think a lot before writing anything down. After I decide what I'm going to write about, I put other topics out of my mind and just think about the story I want to tell. I think all week about what I am going to write, and then when I get under the hair dryer at the beauty salon on Friday mornings, I write it down.

I might think about Mrs. Hunt, my ninth grade English teacher. I moved between two counties and had missed a lot of school. She made me stay after school every day for a month and worked with me. She was meticulous in her approach. She would assign me a topic and I had to write about it. She gave very clear directions on how I should organize my writing. Then she checked to make sure I had good sentence structure and that my spelling was perfect. Everything had to be just exactly like she said. I still find the things she taught me are the best approach to writing.

First I think about a topic, then I write it down, and it becomes my story. Just write down what you are thinking about, and you will tell your story. Writing a story really isn't any different from thinking it or telling it.

In my writing class I listen to everyone else. I have learned that I lived out in the boonies. I never went to shows and did things like other people. Cows take a lot of time. Writing what I did is my story. You can do the same thing. Just write down what you are thinking about and you have your story.

Try it and you'll see that it will work for you, too. When you are ready to write, find a comfortable place and time. Mine is always under the hair dryer on Friday mornings. It is a good thing to stick with the same approach after you find what works best for you.

I started out writing in the order that things happened. That is a good way to get started. Now I write about what is on my mind at the time.

When the House Burned Down

The year was 1933. My father died on January 3. As we were farmers, my mother had an auction sale and got rid of all the cows and machinery. She put the money from the sale in the local bank. On February 16, the banks all closed and you could not get any money from your accounts. The very next day our house burned to the ground. When my mother discovered the fire, she was washing dishes and just automatically picked up the dishpan and carried it out to the backyard. I still have five of her good teaspoons that were in that pan.

Since my mother was not well, my three older sisters had been taking turns staying out of school to help her. My oldest sister, Lucy (whom we always called Peggy), was home with her that day. After Mother found the fire, Lucy kicked off her shoes and put on boots to walk to the nearest phone, which was a mile away. Later, Mother tried to get some money from the bank to buy Lucy shoes, but she couldn't withdraw any. She had to take her to the Red Cross for shoes.

Mother always said I was a very independent child. While the three older girls ran around in the morning yelling, "I can't find my books," or "Where are my shoes?" she would look for me and I would be standing by the door ready to go. The day of the fire, we were having a birthday party at school so I decided to dress up for it. I had put on my best dress, coat, and shoes. Mom didn't even notice that I was the only one in good clothes after the fire. We stayed the first night with some good friends. Then my oldest sister went to another friend's, and my brother and I were sent into the village of Webberville to live with another couple. They had no children so every night they would rock us to sleep. It was great for us. We still went to our rural school. The teacher lived just one block from where we were staying, so every morning she picked us up on the way to school. Later, Mom had a cement floor put in the garage and we lived there until the house was replaced.

When my husband died several years ago, I was asked how I coped so well and I said I learned early in life that you get up in the morning and put your shoes on and do the best you can do. It does no good to worry about things.

KATHLEEN F. WEBSTER ■ 233

Tough Times after My Father's Death

After my father died, my mother had to depend on welfare to keep the family together. She was not well either. The county nurse picked her up once a month to take her to Ann Arbor Hospital for treatments. She did take in washing and ironing, because it was something she could do at home. We all had to help around the house, but Mom could iron so fast that I just never learned to do a good job at that until after I was married.

We all had our assigned tasks. Mine was to do the grocery shopping. I walked to the store, which was only four blocks away. Mother said I was the best shopper. I learned early to make substitutions if something else was cheaper. My sisters didn't do this. They got exactly what was on the list. I sure preferred to do the shopping over dishes and cleaning.

When the house burned down – six weeks after our father died – the older girls took turns staying out of school to take care of Mom. One day they all had final exams, so they let me stay home with her. I felt I was really someone to be trusted to look after Mom. Later, I realized she was really worried, because I had to keep the wood stoves going and fix dinner on the kitchen stove. She worried, but I was sure of myself. I had no problems that day.

Peggy, my oldest sister had to walk three and a half miles to school, all alone. She finally quit school to stay home with Mom for awhile. The rest of us were going to the country school a mile from home. Dr. Mercer finally persuaded Mom to stay at their home and help his wife with the house and their two little boys. She went to his house, and then the next year we moved into the village.

Many people in those days resented people on welfare. Times were hard for everyone, and they really watched you to be sure the welfare money wasn't wasted. The summer before Peggy was a senior, she did housework all summer for a doctor at the Howell Sanatorium. She and her husband had a daughter just one year older than I was, so they gave me all the clothes she had outgrown. Another neighbor who gave me clothes, Mr. Lalocano, was a buyer for Hudson's in Detroit, so I really had beautiful clothes.

Also that year, Peggy was to graduate, and Dotty and Ginny were in high school. When they all showed up at the high school prom with new formal dresses, several people called and reported it to the welfare department. When the caseworker came to the house to check it out, my mother explained that Peggy had bought her formal with money she earned, and Dotty's and Ginny's dresses were made with material someone had given her.

Mom worked really hard to keep us all together and happy. After we moved into town, Mom's father stayed with us for a year. Grandpa Rose was almost eighty years old. He spent a lot of time just talking with us and rocking us. One thing he taught us was to play cribbage. This was an excellent game to improve our math skills. I'm not sure what his nationality was. When we asked, he would say, "English, Irish, Dutch, Scottish, Welsh, and Yankee." I always thought he might have been German, as he arrived on the scene during the early 1900s, when Germans were not accepted by others. He never admitted his heritage. Even my mother never knew. Many of my philosophies in life were formed from all the talks with Grandpa Rose. In his younger years, Grandpa earned his living by trapping in Michigan's Upper Peninsula. My mother grew up near the Pictured Rocks area and she always said she learned to swim when her brothers threw her in at the base of the Pictured Rocks.

We always had a big garden. We learned so much because even though Mom couldn't do much work, she could tell us kids what to do. We all had our jobs around the house, but with three big sisters, I didn't have to do much besides the shopping. Even with her poor health, Mom took in washing and ironing for other families. She was very independent and hated having to accept welfare.

Living with
My Father-in-Law

Coridon and I married on September 28, 1941. I was seventeen and had just graduated in the spring. Coridon was twenty-two. In those times, very few people had large church weddings. We were married at home with all our brothers, sisters, and families present. My favorite uncle was also there.

Our honeymoon was three days spent with Coridon's sister, Gladys, and her husband, Don, in Detroit. Don got tickets, and they took us to a burlesque show. I hadn't been to one, and I don't think Gladys had ever seen one either.

Because Coridon worked on the farm for his father, Sherman, we lived there with him. Coridon's father did not approve of me because I wasn't a big strapping person. He was really hard to live with at first. I soon found out that I had to fix a big breakfast with eggs and potatoes every morning. He wouldn't leave the table until he'd had them. As time went on and he found I could do most things on the farm, he was easier to live with.

The first years were very difficult since I couldn't drive and Coridon was too busy on the farm to take me anywhere. I always said that if I could have driven, I might not have stayed. Sherman's father controlled almost everything. He insisted on doing all the grocery shopping. I would make a list, but if he thought something wasn't needed, he didn't get it.

I remember how upset Coridon's father was when we converted the front parlor into our bedroom. He did not speak to us for two weeks. We didn't have good heating, and the old farmhouse had no insulation. At night, in our upstairs bedroom, a glass of water by the bedside would freeze. It was much more comfortable downstairs.

The second year of our marriage, Sherman planted a whole pound of pea seeds. We were picking peas by the bushels. I would start picking before breakfast, and then he would start podding peas while I finished picking them after breakfast. I canned eighty-eight quarts of peas. This was before the time of pressure cookers, so they had to be cooked three hours in a hot water bath on a wood stove. Before we were done, I said I never wanted to see peas like that again. Needless to say, I never have.

In the fall, they took wheat to the mill and had the year's supply of flour ground. It was put in twenty-five pound bags and we stored them on the stairs. It was a big job to keep the mice out. I baked all of our bread, cakes, pies, and cookies. It was a real treat to have bakery bread. We had only a wood stove and no refrigerator. We had a large water tank in the corner of the kitchen. All water for the livestock was pumped in there first and then pumped out to the barnyard, so the water was always fresh and cold. We put milk in two-quart glass jars, which we sealed and stored in the tank. Since we had fresh milk twice a day, sour milk wasn't a big problem.

My first Christmas gift from Coridon was a refrigerator. As it was wartime, he had to get a priority in order to get one. He bought it from Montgomery Ward. When they brought it, it was larger than what he had ordered. The deliveryman didn't want to take it back, so he said, "Their mistake. Just keep it." We had to keep it on the porch until we had the cupboard cut down to make room for it. That refrigerator lasted until 1965.

We had no car, just an old pickup truck that Coridon had purchased for fifty dollars. Since there were no cars available due to the war, we drove that truck for six years. When new cars became available, we put a down payment on one. We didn't offer an extra payment under the table, so we never got a new car. We were finally able to get a fairly good used car.

Coridon's Uncle George and Aunt Susie lived just down the road. She was so helpful to me. She helped me the first time I had to get dinner for threshers. We had a large oblong dining table with six leaves to extend it. I could easily seat all the men at one time. Feeding fifteen or sixteen men all at once was quite a job, but with Susie's help it all went well. I had homemade bread and pies, lots of mashed potatoes, and corn and green beans from the garden. Sherman insisted we have hot dogs for meat. I was horrified. I just didn't realize what a treat it was for these farmers, who had their own beef and pork, to have store-bought meat. Coridon always laughed about it.

One day the threshers were at the neighbor's and she had chicken that wasn't well-done. One of the men, Ray, didn't want to embarrass the cook but didn't want to eat the undercooked chicken, either, so he hid a drumstick in his pocket. Another thresher caught him. Ray never heard the last of that.

Farm Life

Since we had a dairy farm, it was a seven-day-a-week job. When Coridon and I were first married, we milked the cows by hand, so we only had about fifteen cows milking at a time. We also had sheep, pigs, and chickens. After we purchased our first electric milker, we increased the dairy herd to thirty-five and sold the hogs and sheep. As the diary herd increased, we needed more hay, straw, and silage. We still hired very little help, so there was always too much to do. Coridon and his brother Maynard bought one of the first balers in the neighborhood. It took four people to operate it. Coridon or Maynard drove the tractor while the other stood on a platform and forked the hay or straw into the baler as it came up the chute. When the bale was large enough, he would put a board in to divide the bales. Meanwhile, Maynard's wife Marion and I rode on seats next to the baler. One of us pushed the wire through the groove in the board that separated the bales. The other twisted the wire to fasten the bale. We baled all the hay and straw for our two farms and then did a lot of custom baling for the neighbors, because no one else in the area had a baler.

These bales still had to be picked up on the wagons, taken to the barns, and put in the mows. Later, we purchased a baler that was automatic and required only one person, the tractor driver. This allowed us to pull a wagon behind the baler, which received the bales coming out a chute on the baler. As I drove the tractor, Coridon stacked the bales on the wagon. Then we'd take the load to the barn, and I'd place the bales on the elevator going up into the barn, where he stacked them in the mow. This was a lot of hot, heavy work.

While we were in the field baling, the girls were placed on a blanket under a tree with toys and books. This would probably be considered child abuse nowadays. When the girls were about eight and five, their job was to make Kool-Aid and bring us a drink when we brought each load to the barn.

Since we were farmers, our daughters always had chores to do. When they were small, we still had sheep, hogs, dairy cows, and chickens. At five years old, Ida was in charge of the chickens. She had to be sure they had feed and water each morning before she went to school. In the afternoon, she fed and watered them again, gathered the eggs, and bedded the coop with straw. We sold fresh eggs, and she didn't like cleaning them. There was one old rooster who used to chase her and pecked at her. She sure hated him.

In the early sixties, we built a new milk house adjacent to the dairy barn. We purchased a new milking machine and a bulk milk cooler. Later we added the pipeline so the milk went directly to the cooler. Of course all of this equipment had to be kept spotless, so each morning after breakfast dishes were done, I went to the milk house and washed all the milking equipment.

With so much time needed for the dairy operation, we finally sold all the chickens, sheep, and hogs, and concentrated on dairy cows. The girls were delighted to see the chickens go.

When the girls came home from school, they had to go up in the silo and throw down the silage (usually Corinne's job), and then bed the barns where the heifers and steers were kept. They also fed fresh milk to any small calves.

After my husband was ill in 1958-59, I had to help him more outside, so the girls were responsible for doing the dishes and other inside chores. They also had to do their own laundry and make sure they had what they needed for school the next day. In the morning they fixed their own breakfast and packed their lunches. Many times I didn't even see them before they went to school.

Our daughters both went to the country school that their father and grandfather had attended. When Ida started school at five, she was so tiny she was still wearing size three clothes. She walked a mile and a half from home to the school. We had two elderly neighbor couples who thought she was too small to walk to school, so they would try to time their trips to town so they could give her a ride either to or from school. The following year, there were two more children who started school from the direction she was walking, so she no longer had to walk alone. She was never unhappy at school, as all four girls who occasionally babysat for us went there.

When Corinne started in the country school, there were two more children on our road, and they had even farther to walk than she did. Their parents thought we should carpool and take the children to school. A couple of years later, we purchased bicycles for the girls. Ida didn't really like to ride hers to school and we discovered later that she would ride to the corner where we couldn't see her and then push it the rest of the way. What a determined child.

They were so different. Corinne would make sure her homework was done the night before, while Ida would do hers on the bus on the way to school. Corinne always made sure the night before that her clothes were pressed and ready. Ida would get up in the morning and press hers. If it were winter, she would press the front of the blouse and then wear a sweater so the back and sleeves didn't show. Most times I had no idea what they wore. Later, when they were in high school, their homeroom teachers asked why they were more mature than most kids were. I guess they just had more responsibilities than other kids did. Between my mother's illness and their father's, I just didn't have time to do much waiting on them.

The Hazards of Farming

Farming is one of the most dangerous jobs anywhere. When we were first married, Coridon and I put our hay up loose. One day while bringing in a load of hay, we were coming up the lane and the wagon tipped over. I was riding on the top of the load. I fell off the top and landed on the fence, with my legs on one side and the rest of me hanging on the other side. Coridon had to remove about half the load of hay to release my legs and get me out. After that I always walked to the house behind the load of hay.

One day Coridon was coming up the road with the corn picker. It was a mounted picker, so it was difficult to get off the tractor. He stopped to pick up something in the road and decided it would be easier to jump off the front rather than the back of the tractor. But as he jumped, his coattail caught on the hand clutch and put the tractor in gear. He lost his balance and fell. Realizing he was in trouble, he rolled as he hit the ground and just got clear of the tractor as it went by. It took his hat off his head. Quick thinking saved his life.

The Cyclone

When we had a cyclone on Memorial Day weekend in 1942, I was eighteen. My husband Coridon was milking cows in the barn, and he saw the big black cloud coming across the fields. He ran to the house and hollered at me to go upstairs and shut the windows, as there was a storm coming. I really didn't believe it, so I took my time going up. As I closed the last window, a big livestock truck was going by, and the wind took the rack off the truck, right in front of our house.

I really speeded up as I went down the stairs. As I crossed the kitchen on my way to the basement, something hit my legs. We spent some time in the basement to be sure the storm was gone. When we went back upstairs, we had no electricity and the house was a mess. I found what had hit my legs. It was the curtain rod from the living room window. I later found the curtain hanging on a nail behind the piano. All the lamps were broken, and it looked like the rooms had been stirred with a big spoon.

We were really concerned about my husband's brother and his family, who lived a mile away. We had to walk to their house because there were too many trees in the road to drive. They were OK, but the neighbors had lost their big dairy barn.

When we got back home, we had to check the beds. All but one of the five had glass in them. The big tree in front of the house had taken out the front window, so there was a lot of damage in the house. The wind had also lifted the roof off the big dairy barn and leaned it against the silo. There were lots of repairs to be made, inside and out.

During the Memorial Day weekend, Coridon's sister and her husband were supposed to come to stay overnight. We couldn't let them know about the storm because the phones were out, so they came and were a big help cleaning up around the house.

Harvesting Spy Apples and Black Walnuts

As a child, I remember harvesting apples and walnuts. We had a lot of Spy apple trees, and each year we picked the apples, wrapped them in newspaper, and put them in barrels in the basement. They went well with the popcorn on Saturday or Sunday nights. We also really enjoyed Mom's apple pies. They went well with the school lunches every day. We were always sad when the apples were all gone each year.

We also harvested walnuts. We carried them all into the old log house and then hammered the husks off. We always had stained brown hands all fall. After the nuts dried for a few weeks, we had to use the hammer to smash open the shells so we could dig out the nuts. We always had nuts in cookies and cakes. Mom also put them in jars for gifts for Grandma, Grandpa, aunts, and uncles. I still like black walnuts.

Both Spy apples and black walnuts are not very common any more. The walnuts are too much work, and the Spy apple trees take so many years before they produce fruit that no one wants to grow them. You do see new varieties mixed with Spies to come up with a tree that yields fruit sooner. Michigan State University had some wonderful Spy-Golds, (Spy and Golden Delicious), but I have not yet seen them on the market.

We had such wonderful times just talking and laughing while we shelled those nuts and wrapped apples. With five of us, the jobs really went quickly.

We also had strawberries and raspberries every year. With a big garden and the fruit, we really ate well. Mom was a great cook. My daughters loved to go to Mom's and eat her sugar cookies. I never could get mine to come out like hers. They loved to stay overnight.

Olga J. Santiago

I grew up in Ponce, a city located in the southern part of Puerto Rico, a beautiful island in the Caribbean. The sixth of seven children, raised with Catholic values, I loved nature and have always enjoyed its simple presents.

I earned a Masters degree in health services administration in 1990. In 1992 I married Carlos. I worked as a hospital administrator for fourteen years in Puerto Rico before moving to Michigan in 2004. Now I am a full-time mother enjoying our two most-valuable treasures, Carlitos and Carelis. In the fall of 2005, I began my doctoral degree in kinesiology at Michigan State University.

I fell in love with the beauty of writing and reading when I was a child. The intense experiences of my life have been the motivation for writing my memoirs. Missing Puerto Rico and enjoying the blessings of living in Michigan give me other good reasons to write my memoirs. Writing my memoirs has shown me how I have lived through different experiences in my life, while still being the same human being. Our bodies can change, our minds can mature, but our souls are the same as when we were children.

Just Sit Down and Begin

When I wrote the story "Metamorphosis of a Marriage," I wanted to communicate to my husband my feelings and my point of view regarding his physical changes. I began with the day that I remember as the beginning of all his transformation. When I sat down in front of the computer, it was like watching a movie in my mind. While I was writing the story, my mind rewound the movie for details that I skipped, or fast-forwarded the movie to important parts. When I finished the story, I read it, and more details came to my mind – details related to the body's five senses: colors, shapes, sounds, smells, textures or flavors. When I finished the story I realized that it could help others to start a new body and mind transformation.

Sometimes when I decide on a theme and I begin to write, I change my mind and finish writing a different story. It may be related to something that has happened during the day, something that brings me memories.

I prefer to write on my computer, especially because my first language is Spanish and the computer helps me with the grammar. Since being in a writing class, I write with more details and with more happiness. I want to give a positive message to others by sharing the lessons that my life has given to me.

If you are thinking about writing your memoirs, just begin. Sit down, take your favorite pencil or pen and your favorite piece of paper or just sit in front of the computer and begin to write. Let your feelings flow, whether they make you smile or cry. Share only those stories that you want. Just keep the others for yourself and enjoy the healing power of writing.

Metamorphosis of a Marriage

When I got married, my husband Carlos and I were thin, not too thin but definitely we were not fat. The years passed and we gained weight each year. I was always very concerned about my weight. On my seventh year of marriage I was size twelve, so I decided this had to stop. In one month, I lost twenty-eight pounds and went from size twelve to size six. I kept the same weight for about two years. Then I got pregnant with my second child and gained some weight, but I did not gain as much as before. I changed my eating habits. That means that I lowered the salt, sugar, and fat. While I was worried about my weight, my husband did not care about his weight; at least he did not do anything to lose weight. He did not want to eat my diet's meals because to him, they did not have a good taste.

His snoring was getting worse all the time; as his weight increased, the snores increased, too. He was sleepy all the time. Every time he felt bored, even in a middle of a family reunion, he fell asleep and snored very loudly. Everybody in our family was concerned about his weight and his sleepiness. You could not argue with him because you could be sure that you would lose the argument.

I remember the hospital Christmas party in December 2002. He was at a meeting, so I had to arrive at the party without him. I was very thin for the party; I felt gorgeous in my long, feminine dress. It was getting late and he did not show up, so I decided to wait for him outside. I really felt bad about being alone at the party. Everybody expected the hospital administrator to be with her spouse. Suddenly, from the shadows, I saw him walking in the parking lot.

"Oh my God. He looks so fat!" I thought. His way of walking had changed because of the weight. I honestly felt a little uncomfortable with the situation, but I smiled and I did not tell him anything of my feelings. When it was time for dancing, the situation got worse because he was exhausted very early. I felt very angry but I did not say anything. I just smiled.

One morning he asked me to arrange an appointment with an internal medicine physician. Even with the excess weight, the snoring, and the sleepiness, he was always a healthy person. I was surprised by his request. I chose the best of the best internists. I got an appointment for the next Saturday.

Very early in the morning we were on our way to visit the doctor's office. The office was one hour from our house, and we had to take a winding, rural road to find it. There we were, waiting for the physician. I was very nervous because in the fourteen years of our relationship he had never visited a physician before. He did not even take any medications. "He has to be very bad or feel very sick to decide to visit a physician," I thought.

He was with the physician about thirty minutes, which to me seemed a long lifetime. Finally, he joined me again. I asked him what had happened but he didn't answer. I also asked the doctor what had happened, but he did not tell me.

That same day, we went to the drugstore and bought blood pressure and heart rate monitor equipment. The next morning he took his blood pressure and heart rate before breakfast. That became a routine every morning for about a month. The only thing that he told me was the physician said to him that if he did not decrease his blood pressure level, he would have to begin taking some pills.

Several weeks later a-state-of-the-art and very expensive stair-climbing machine arrived at our home. Soon an exercise routine began. Every day at 5:30 a.m., while I was sleeping on the second floor of our house, I could hear the unpleasant high-pitched sound that came from the first floor: the stepper machine was turning on. At the beginning, he could exercise only three minutes, then worked his way up to ten minutes, then fifteen minutes, then twenty minutes, then thirty minutes, and finally sometimes one hour on the stepper. It bothered me because I felt jealous about the attention he was giving to the exercise routine. It began to be the most important thing in his life.

In our library, books about diets and healthy eating began to increase. He was reading and doing research about diets and nutrition all the time. He began to cook and to buy healthy food, fruits, and vegetables. He changed from one gallon of soft drinks to eight glasses of water a day. He began to lose weight quickly, so he had to buy new clothes – new and very different clothes. Every day he arrived at our home with new outfits in bright colors, clothes that showed his desire to live, his love for his new self. He changed his glasses for contacts lenses, too. In about a year, his clothes size changed from forty-two to forty to thirty-eight to thirty-six to thirty-four to thirty-two. After several months on the stepper, he began to visit a gym. The stepper was not important anymore because he had lost about fifty pounds, and now the priority had changed. The priority was not to lose weight; now the important issue was to build muscle.

He invited me to go with him to the gym every day. I went two or three nights, but I was very tired after a hard day's work and I felt very guilty because while I was doing exercises on the treadmill, my three-year-old daughter was looking at me through a glass window of the child care area. I cannot forget that sad and tired face. So I decided not to go to the gym anymore. Then he changed the routine and began to visit the gym on mornings. While I was at my job, working like a slave, he was at the gym, working out like a king.

One night when he arrived at home, his teeth were different, too. He had gone to a dentist where he got a new bright smile. Everybody was talking about Carlos' transformation.

My feelings were becoming worse about the whole situation. I felt jealous about the flexible time in his work, about the pounds that he was losing, and about the person who was growing inside him. For eleven years I had asked him to lose weight, but nothing had happened.

What was the reason for the metamorphosis? What was happening inside of him? Would it be temporary or would it become an attitude of life? I did not know the answer to those questions. I only knew that I had a new husband, with new eyes, new smile, new size, new clothes, and new attitude – and with so much desire to live, to feel alive.

Now my attitudes have changed, too. I do not try to find the answers to the questions or the motivation for this transformation; I am just enjoying it and living it with passion. We are swimming, working out, practicing yoga, cycling, cooking, and even writing together.

As of today, I do not know what happened in that visit to the physician. Probably I will never know. I just know that it was the beginning of a real physical, mental, and spiritual transformation of my husband and myself, the metamorphosis of my marriage.

A Puerto Rican Picnic

My kids love to hear memories from my childhood when they go to bed. "Please, Mami, tuck me in, tell me stories about your childhood." I love to hear those words.

Once upon a time, in a small and beautiful island of the Caribbean, lived a little girl with her big family. She was the sixth of seven children. In her childhood there were no fast food stores, no Play Stations, Nintendo, or Gameboy. No computers. No toy stores.

To handle seven children, their parents had to take them to the church or to devise adventures for them. Like magicians, parents could turn a day from the usual to the extraordinary and unforgettable.

They lived in Ponce, a city in the south. Living near the sea was great but too hot. A cracker tin was enough for the children to have fun and enjoy a sunny day and the ocean. All seven kids were at the seashore in silence, waiting for the crabs to show up, the warm sea breeze playing with their hair and caressing their faces. As soon as one crab came out from the golden sand or from the velvet-green slippery rocks, the kids ran after it. When a crab crawled in front of the kids, the kids shouted after the crab, "*Corre que te cojo.*" (Run or I will catch you). Finally, one of them caught a crab and put it inside the cracker tin filled with seawater.

All the family traveled the island in a 1965 green Nova. Two adults and seven children could fit inside the car. The kids used to fight for the side windows of the back seat. Olga Josefina was one of the last born, so she never had the side window.

"*A mi me toca la esquina.*" (I will have the side window).

"*No, me toca a mi. Mami!*"(No, it is mine. Mommy!)

"Junior y Doel will have the side window," the mother used to say.

"But Mother, it is not fair. They always sit by the side windows because they are the two first born," some kid would say.

On certain weekends the mother woke up very early and cooked a large pot of the traditional *arroz con gandules* (rice with peas). They placed the *olla* (pot) full of rice in the trunk, got inside the car and a new adventure began.

To travel around the island by *la número 2* (Highway 2) was the entertainment. Moving southwest on the island, from Ponce to Mayaguez to Arecibo, they learned to love the simple big presents from Mother Nature. Sometimes they stopped the car to buy and taste the sweet yellow *piñas* (pineapples), and the sweet green sugarcane, or calm their thirst by drinking the clear cold *agua de coco* (coconut water), the best drink on a hot summer day.

When they were driving by the *llanura* (plain) and the road allowed the father to increase speed, the sugarcane plantations looked like green waves created by the tropical breeze.

When *las tripas sonaban* (someone's stomach growled), the father parked the car on the shoulder of the road, in the shade, a free gift from the mango trees to the Puerto Ricans. It was a perfect spot to savor *el rico* (the delicious), aromatic *arroz con gandules*. The mother smiled, watching the kids enjoy the rice and the peace given by the sound of the leaves dancing with the breeze and the song of the birds.

The grandparents lived in the middle of the island in Aibonito (Oh Beautiful), a little mountain town with cold dawns and hot days. The grandmother from the mother's side was a widow. A strong Christian woman who loved to do things the way they were done in the old, golden days and by herself, she lived alone in the mountains with a collie dog. To watch *Abuela* (Grandmother) Felicita praying the Holy Rosary and working in her backyard garden were some of Olga Josefina's pleasures that later would become priceless treasures. Living in the city of Ponce had not given her those experiences. Olga Josefina enjoyed helping *Abuela* Felicita pick the pungent cilantro, the green peppers, the big pumpkins, and the sour oranges and grapefruit and transform them into delicious meals with *sabor a campo* (country taste).

But the adventure that Olga Josefina enjoyed the most was the process of creating fresh coffee from the coffee beans. At sunrise *Abuela* Felicita used to wake all of them up with the sound of the coffee grinder and the smell of the fresh coffee, aged cheese, and the recently laid eggs, fried in lard. What a banquet!

"I don't want to go! Stay with me," some kids said.

"But I want to go," said another kid.

"But I don't!"

"Don't argue! Everybody has to go!" Father said.

"*Muchachito no seas vago,*" (Boy, don't be lazy) shouted *Abuela* Felicita in a bossy voice.

All the family members participated in the process of making coffee. After a delicious breakfast, the family began to climb the mountains. They carried a homemade rustic basket and some *sacos* (pouches or bags made with a hard cloth), and wore comfortable clothes and tennis shoes. In the tree's leaves, *el rocio* (the dew) was evaporating as the day became warmer. The family passed cows, banana and plantain trees, and more banana and plantain trees, which made it seem like they stayed in the same place. On their way, they stopped at the top of the hills to shout, "Echo, echo, echo," and to wait to hear the answer from the mountains, "Echo, echo, echo." The trees were so tempting, that the family did not resist snacking on some ripe bright yellow bananas, sweet wild berries, and oranges. When they finished the snack, their hands were sticky, but that did not bother them; they licked their fingers and they cleaned their hands on their clothes.

For Olga Josefina, the path seemed to never end. Finally they reached the coffee trees. Green coffee trees, three or four feet tall, blossomed with white flowers and were full of beans. The little beans had different colors, from green to red to brown. The red ones were the right, ripe ones to pick to begin the coffee-making process. The soil was full of leaves, like a brown, green, and beige carpet, which fed the coffee trees. The ground was steep and great skills were needed to maintain balance. Sometimes one of the kids slipped because of the dried old leaves on the ground. They tried to grab the coffee trees looking for support, but the branches were very weak and therefore broken easily. That did not help much, sending the kids rolling down the hill.

"*Ja, Ja, Ja, sobate,*" (Rub yourself where you hit the ground), the other kids laughed.

The parents were watching the kids all the time, so they did not have as much fun as the kids had.

The kids were exhausted after intense exercise in the mountain. It was time to go back to *Abuela* Felicita's house but not without first stopping by *Tio* (Uncle) Sabino's house. He always had some fruits, vegetables, or *viandas* (starchy food) to give us. It was a rustic modest house, where the hen and its chickens and the cat walked around the house as members of the family. Olga Josefina loved that. There were rabbits, dogs, pigeons, ducks, birds, and turkeys. A wild garden full of red, orange, and purple flowers surrounding the house, made the visit even more special. She always felt sad when she had to say good-bye to *Tio* Sabino and his family, because that meant that soon she would have to go back to the city of Ponce.

The beach, the sea, the Puerto Rico roads, the mountains, and the plantations were more than enough for the kids. Adventures full of nature, emotions, and experiences stimulated all their senses and their souls. Pure happiness! They did not need money to have fun. They just needed their parents and their car to begin a new adventure with Mother Nature.

The kids grew up and became adults and had children of their own. The shopping malls, the toy industry, computers, technology, cable television, and the Internet conquered Puerto Rico. Today these grown-up children bring their children to visit their retired grandparents. *Abuela* Olga and *Abuelo* Tatin need more than a car and their imagination to provide fun for their grandchildren.

Second Thoughts about Writing Memoirs

Ever since I was a kid I enjoyed writing. During my elementary and middle school years, the teachers enjoyed my writing and asked me to read in front of the class. Writing in those years was like therapy. The teachers gave me the theme. I became part of the theme, and began to write and live what I was writing.

Most of the time my writing was about my love for God, Mother Nature, romance, or simply about trivial things. For me, all of the themes were good – all of them were an excuse to write. I loved to write poetry. When I read the stories, poems, or an essay, I felt proud. I read as though I was on a cloud or in front of a theater audience. The years passed and I did not write anymore. A daily life with a lot of changes and responsibilities made me forget the beauty of writing.

When I was a young girl, I never asked myself why I loved to write so much. Twenty-five years later, destiny changed my life. I enrolled in a memoir-writing class. I was not working and it was a good opportunity to learn more about writing.

When I arrived in the classroom, I got confused. I was the youngest, but why? Do people of my age not want to write their memoirs? Maybe people of my age are working. They are busy with their jobs and their families, as I was some time ago. Anyway, I was happy in the middle of so much wisdom. While the other writers were reading their papers, I was smiling or crying inside. Listening, I felt the same way as the person who was reading. How could they do that? "Being themselves," I answered to myself.

The teacher asked me to be the second to read in front of the group in the next class meeting. I tried to start writing so many times. I never thought it could be so hard to write something that can grab others' attention, something that they would like. I wrote about three stories. All of them were painful and sad, but real. When I was reading the second story to my husband, I realized that I did not want to take the class anymore. "This class is giving me headaches." I was suffering. That week was a nightmare. I remembered my childhood. Why did my mind insist on remembering only the bad stories? Why do I allow my mind to control my life? I had to do something. I made a big effort to be able to remember good memories but the bad ones won the race all the time. Why did God let me find out about this class?

While I was writing, a lot of feelings surfaced. I cried, I smiled, I felt love. Sometimes my body was shaking and sweating. Sometimes my heart was pounding inside my chest. When I was not writing, all kinds of memories surfaced. When I was sleeping, nightmares haunted me. I thought I did not have good stories to tell and wondered if this was a way to feel sorry about myself. What could I do?

In the second class, I decided to change my mind. "Today is the day," I told myself. "Today is the moment. I will do it as a present to myself and my children." The first semester I thought that I was there by mistake, but I enrolled for the next semester. My memoirs began to show happiness in them and even some humor.

Our teacher asked us to write some articles for our first book. At first I was sure to be part of the book, but then the doubts assailed me. What if the people don't like how I write my memoirs? But what if our memoirs help others in their day-to-day living? What if our memoirs could motivate others to begin to write their own stories?

I was thinking about the book all the time on Christmas vacation in Puerto Rico. On the day before we returned to Michigan, I found the book of my mother's memoirs in my baggage. It was her first book of memoirs. She gave us the book as a Christmas present. It had a treasure painted on the front page that I had not noticed before. I did not have time to read the book; I was very busy packing. I gave it to my mother-in-law, so she could read my mother's stories before we left for Michigan.

I felt so proud of my mother. I asked my mother-in-law to read the stories dedicated to my son and my daughter. She read Carlitos' story first and almost cried. She read it loudly, slowly, with meaning, with toning. She made me cry. Carlitos and Carelis were with us in her bedroom. They were watching television. When they heard their names, they began to listen to the poetry written by Abuela Olga, dedicated to each one of them.

"Mami, it is about me. The story is about me," Carlitos said. He felt proud to hear a story about him, a story in poetry. How did Abuela Olga remember every detail of special moments of his life? How could she give so much attention to her grandchildren's life? The words were used in an amazing way, describing the heart of each one of them. The children's faces showed happiness, pride, even nostalgia. Some minutes later my mother-in-law began to read Carelis' story. She began to cry. "No! I can not read it now. Later. I will read it later."

About one hour later, I was cooking in the kitchen when my mother-in-law came in. She was crying again, but at the same time she was happy and her face looked like a naughty little girl.

"What happened to you? Are you OK?" I asked her.

"Yes, I just finished reading Doña Olga's book and it reminded me of my childhood. Most of all it reminds me of my mother."

"How could a book of Puerto Rico stories make her remember Costa Rica's stories?" I asked myself.

My mother's book is her legacy to her thirteen grandchildren and her seven children. That day I realized that the memoirs she wrote with passion and love could enable the readers to identify themselves, and could awake feelings that have been sleeping for a long time – maybe a lifetime.

My mother's book of real stories is full of love and emotion. Since her first grandson was born, she has written stories about family occasions. The children are proud to be part of the book, and I know that later they will understand that they have an even greater treasure in their hands.

Writing memoirs is good therapy for ourselves but can be a treasure for the people we love.

RAYL CONYERS

I was born in Marion, Ohio in 1915 to John and Aimee Conyers.
I was educated in and graduated from Marion Public Schools.
I got a B.A. degree from Ohio State University and worked in a small
family business until 1942 when I enlisted in the Navy. I was to spend
nearly all my time in VR-1, a naval air transport system and was
variously stationed in Norfolk, Houston, Corpus Christi, and Patwent
River in Maryland. I was married in May 1944 in Washington D.C. to
Mary Gracely, with whom I had attended high school.

When the war ended, I was in Honolulu waiting for a scheduled
invasion of China that was supposed to precede an invasion of Japan.
After the war we returned to Marion. I was disillusioned by my
experience as a salesman and impressed by what I heard from Mary.
After some summer education courses I was hired on a temporary
certificate in Marion City Schools and enjoyed nearly every minute of
my time in the classroom and as an administrator.

We both retired in the year we reached our sixty-ninth birthdays,
but Mary continued to teach on a part-time basis at Ohio State
University-Marion, the local branch of OSU. We traveled quite a bit in

in our retirement years and did not spend another February in Ohio. We had a daughter, who is now a senior faculty member of the Michigan State University College of Nursing. She has two daughters, both now married. I am now a great-grandfather, which shows what happens when you carry longevity too far.

Play with Your Muse

With pad and pen I sit down and wait for the muse, Clio, whose province is history. In my teens I had a flirtation with Erato, but by the time I was mature, incompatibility was evident enough for a conviction, and I turned to Clio.

She is shy, even as muses go, or the laziest slut in history. Sometimes she doesn't show at all, and again she drops just a hint and disappears.

Sometimes she consents to give enough inspiration that I am only a scribe, but that is seldom. I don't think the old girl is as spry as she once was. She seems to enjoy dropping an elusive clue that makes me feel that I almost have it, but noooo. She has flitted back to the Elysian Fields.

Ancestors

Everyone always says, "Start at the beginning." The problem is, the beginning may not be where you think it is but I have some clues as far as the Conyers go.

Conyers, my family name, goes back to the Norman conquest in 1066 A.D., and for hundreds of years in northern England, and then through two brothers who came to North America. Twice there was no male heir, and young men who married a daughter took her surname.

The Revolutionary War started a movement in Virginia to navigate westward into Kentucky to avoid military service, and about that time, either my Grandfather Conyers' father or his grandfather showed up in Kentucky and then kept moving west. My father was born in Kentucky, but the family eventually went to western Kansas. My father, John, left home probably as a teenager and drifted about the West, ending up as a prospector in Arizona. There he finally had some luck and hit a pocket that gave him a little capital, money that he didn't need to live on. He invested it in an ice cream parlor in Globe, a mining town about seventy miles east of Phoenix.

As he luxuriated in owning a business, he realized that he was lonely; Globe was not a town full of unattached young women. This boom town had sprung into existence to provide workers for the Old Dominion Mining Company, a deep copper mine. John knew what to do: he advertised. He had an answer from a young woman in Ohio. Letters were exchanged and then he got on a train, probably in Phoenix, and went to Ohio. Soon a bride and groom went west from Ohio.

Aimee Rayl Conyers, the bride, eventually took a train east to Marion to stay until she could bring her new baby back to Globe. At that time there were few doctors and no hospital in Globe. The baby was a little girl named Marion, after her mother's hometown. All was well until Marion, at age six, developed meningitis and died. Everyone was devastated but Aimee was soon pregnant again and, in due time, returned to Marion where I was born in 1915. Then Aimee took me back to Globe. In 1920, she went back to Marion for a visit with her parents and a sister who had also been in the west and who had, in fact, experienced the San Francisco earthquake and subsequent fire. She had been so frightened by the quake that she had quickly found a job in Spokane and worked there until her father asked her to come home to Ohio and help him in the business that he had started.

Jim Rayl was not a good businessman. He had been through a bankruptcy where he had lost the farmland he had inherited from his father. Apparently, he and his brothers all lacked a money-making – or keeping – gene. Jim was the oldest, and Tom was next. An alcoholic, Tom died as a paretic in the Ohio State Hospital in Columbus. He had a son who was also an alcoholic and ended up living in Globe. Tom's son had a son, who moved with his mother to Chicago and disappeared from the view of his father's family.

Another brother, Ed, died very young, after marrying Min, whom his family thought had a dubious reputation. She survived him by many years and had a kind of revival as of my daughter Louise: the imaginary playmate. This was a slightly eerie experience, as Louise had never seen her and probably had only heard her name mentioned casually, but Aunt Min was with us for several months in Louise's early years and then suddenly disappeared.

Another brother in my grandfather's generation was Will, who sold his land, went to Florida, and bought a small orange grove. He had two sons and a daughter. The older son, Hazen Rayl, went back to Marion and eventually married Erla Cheney and worked for the little company his Uncle Jim had started. Hazen had one son, whom I lost track of many years ago.

My Conyers grandfather settled down in Garden City, Kansas, the setting for Truman Capote's novel, *In Cold Blood*.

Dear Colin

Dear Colin:

This letter is from your great-grandfather Conyers, the father of your Grandmother Selanders. In all probability you will have no memory of ever seeing me because I was a rather old man when you were born and I will probably be dead before you are old enough to remember me, just as I don't remember my grandfather Rayl, your great-great-grandmother Conyers' father who died when I was five.

I am writing this because I have often wished that I had some record of the past of my family, and I hope to leave something that may answer some questions that occur to you as you grow up.

I will leave the letters with your mother, who will give them to you to read after you reach your twelfth birthday, which is about when your mind will expand and you will begin to think for yourself. This writing is to take the place of actually talking to you.

You will quickly learn that at the time you were born, I was in a pessimistic mood. The U.S. is involved in a senseless war in the Middle East, the administration has no sense of fiscal responsibility, and you are being saddled with a huge debt which may never actually be paid off. The pundits are predicting a return of the plagues, and Al Quaeda roams free.

Meanwhile, I get more rickety and disorganized every day, and my short-term memory suffers, but at least I don't have Alzheimer's.

You don't realize it, but you have lots of ancestors. You have two parents, four grandparents, eight great-grandparents.

I have never uttered one syllable of baby talk in my life, not even when your grandmother Selanders was born. I figure children really don't appreciate it and don't need it. If they mispronounce a word, they will soon correct it without prodding. When your mother was small, I remember that she had a problem with some letter combinations. When she guided your great-grandmother, instructing me to turn on "Geen" Road, I turned on Green – and long before she went to school, she had corrected it to "Green." Children learn a lot of grammar without it being taught to them.

It has been a struggle for the past few days to get started on my "letter from the past to the future" project. Normally, writing for me involves a period of germination that may last three to thirty days, but my mind has been blank all week. In the early spring of 2005, we had a lot of cool but nice days with no hints of planetary warming, and then the thermometer climbed to eighty-one degrees on Tuesday, and collapsed on Wednesday.

The political and economic news continues to be dire, and every pronouncement of George W's continues to be threatening, if it makes any sense at all. The headline news today is that he is being sued by various teacher unions over the lack of funding for the grandiosely named "No Child Left Behind" act. However, he has said that schools have plenty of money, and once he has made a pronouncement, that is the final revealed truth, and nothing will ever change it. Don't try to confuse him with facts. My hometown has announced that 10 percent of the total teaching and administrative staff will not be replaced next year as retirements and resignations take their toll. When I was a classroom teacher, classes had thirty-some students, but since then, class size has been slowly inching down to the mid-twenties. Here we go again.

In Lansing, a GM town if ever there was one, people are beginning to worry about the future of GM. In Iraq, the "insurgency" bubbles as fiercely as ever. Since gasoline seems to be dropping below $3 per gallon, I'm sure we will all stop worrying about fuel costs. I hope many of the situations that depress me will be alleviated by 2017. If not, your people are in big trouble.

Perhaps the problem that worries me most is our failure today to confront the many problems that we should face but actually turn our backs on. It seems to me that the "W" administration has encouraged a cold-blooded attitude that reminds me of the 1930s, when conservatives held views of FDR that were venomous, to say the least. Some people considered him to be the anti-Christ, or at least a "limb of Satan." Displays of this attitude vanished after Pearl Harbor, but I am sure that the vitriolic opinions persisted. Along with this, there was a tendency to ignore the many real problems we faced then. World War II then solved many of them, and many people came to venerate FDR.

Now I realize that I have been venting my frustration into your letter. This I had resolved not to do, but from time to time I may relapse into vituperation just to release my tensions. You should know that my political opinions were mined as I was growing up.

Dear
Colin II

Dear Colin:

Again I take up the chore of writing to you from the past, on a wet, cold day in May. I need to stay with this task, even though I fatigue easily and my hand is unsteady. I have previously told you a little about some of your dead relatives, having at least mentioned the people from my side of the family, many of whom I never saw when they were alive.

A powerful personality was your great-great-great-aunt Zona Rayl, who was born in 1875 and died in 1961. A small, rather thin woman with reddish brown hair, she did not so much walk as march. She did not climb stairs; she attacked them. I don't know if she frightened away possible husbands or simply was not interested, but she never married. Your great-great-grandmother, her sister, also showed little interest in men, but that was after she became a widow. When she was in her forties or early fifties, Zona's sister did go out with two or three men.

Zona left home some time around 1900 and obtained a job as an office worker in San Francisco. She was there for the earthquake, and she must have been badly frightened because she moved to a job in Spokane, Washington, within a few weeks. She was reluctant to talk about her West Coast experience, never volunteering any information and responding briefly to questions. I know that her father, Jim Rayl, asked her to come home to Marion at some point because his little business was getting out of hand.

I do not know whether he begged her help or commanded it. At that time, many fathers regarded their children, particularly daughters, as chattels. I will bring this up again when I get to your great-great-grandfather Gracely, the mother lode of horror stories about intra-family relationships and their abuse. Since Jim Rayl died when I was five, I just don't have much firsthand experience to call upon.

I know that he seemed to prefer to hire relatives. He hired his brother Tom, a notorious drinker, who was unreliable, and a cousin who stole from him. He did hire his nephew, Hazen Rayl, who was loyal and honest and a handyman to boot, but he certainly did not manage his own personal affairs very well. Like his uncle Tom, he died fairly young and quickly.

Now we can turn to your great-grandmother's family. She was born Mary Gracely to Harvey and Hattie Mae Wolford Gracely. Notice that her middle, or maiden, name was Wolford. Her father was John Wolford, a lawyer originally from Canada. He became the top lawyer in late nineteenth century Marion, representing the leading bank and the Marion Steam Shovel Company, which was expanding due to the effort to build the Panama Canal.

He also owned a farm and a business block in Marion, which still stands downtown although it is largely unused. It was the site of the Woolworth five-and-ten-cent store, a much-desired tenant in the late nineteenth and early twentieth century. Woolworth paid a good rent and took care of the maintenance of the building. But the building was a white elephant by the middle of the twentieth century. By a stroke of luck, I managed to sell it in such a way that it was a source of income for your mother and her siblings for many years, and its tax and insurance bill were off our hands. I did the same with the farm.

When you read something that you don't understand, ask your parents. I will give you a hand with "white elephant," however. The country now known as Thailand, called Siam up until World War II, looked at albino (white) elephants as sacred. The king would give them to noblemen he disliked, as the elephants' upkeep was very expensive and the donee could not give them away or sell them.

John Wolford died young, leaving behind a widow and a young daughter. The daughter was your great-grandmother, Hattie Mae. Her mother had paid little attention to financial matters and was overwhelmed as a new widow. As a child, Hattie Mae had paid attention and was soon in charge. She was an intelligent woman who was also a good cook but hired indifferent ones and ate what they cooked without complaining. She felt that the entire laundry should be ironed and hired two women to do the laundry, which included mangling the towels. The mangle is probably no longer in existence, but it was a device for ironing laundry which involved a heated roller and a sleeve that could be pushed against the roller. Laundry was air dried, which involved hanging it from a line either outdoors or in the basement on rainy days, which left the laundry a little stiff and wrinkled.

Hattie Mae married Harvey Gracely, the son of a German Methodist clergyman. There was a German Lutheran church in

Marion where services were conducted in German until World War I. Harvey went through high school in Marion, which was unusual for boys who were not college-bound at that time, and then immediately into the drafting room at Marion Steam Shovel. He was courting Hattie Mae at that time.

She intended to go to college and attended Lake Erie College for Women for one year. But she didn't like it and did not return. You will not find many people who have ever heard of Lake Erie College for Women; shortly after Hattie Mae left, it merged into Western Reserve University, which much later merged into Case Western Reserve University, which is still going strong in 2005.

Harvey wanted to marry right away, but Hattie Mae refused, saying that people would think she had left school early to marry. They waited three years to set the date. They had five children, one of whom was stillborn (dead at birth). Your great-grandmother produced Mary; your grandmother, Louise, who is still alive in Florida at this point; and John and William, both deceased. John died of a heart attack while driving. He did not hurt anyone and gently ran into a tree, not even damaging his car. William died earlier of cancer. Although he was the family member who took the best care of himself, he died an unpleasant death.

Mary was educated as a teacher and so was Louise, while John and William were educated by the U.S. Navy, at Case Western, as engineers. After he was discharged, William went to the University of Michigan Law School and practiced in Marion for a while with the firm his grandfather had started. Eventually he went to Florida, where he was in practice for himself until his death. John worked a short time for a manufacturing company in Hamilton, and then went to General Electric's Aircraft Engine plant in a nearby Cincinnati suburb.

Mary graduated at a time (the immediate post-Depression 1937) when teaching jobs were scarce and went to Stanford for a year to get an M.A. in history, a subject which she taught for only a year or two. Most high schools wanted to reserve teaching slots in history for coaches, a situation that has resulted in several generations of historically-illiterate Americans. Now, work-study programs are leading to the employment of some teachers who are actually prepared to teach history. Whether or not this will finally produce a public that understands history and civics remains to be seen.

A Significant Event

My daughter Louise had become very friendly with a teaching nurse from New Mexico, who is about her age and, like Louise, an Episcopalian and devotee of Florence Nightingale. They decided that the church should show more respect to Florence Nightingale, who actually has been slandered by some Church of England people. Between them, they prepared a resolution which they jointly presented to the General Assembly in 2001 in Philadelphia.

In the late summer of 2004, there was a celebratory service in acknowledgement of the long-overdue recognition, which simply placed Nightingale's name on the prayer calendar. As good Nightingaleans, they won over the dean of the Cathedral in Washington, who coached them after he came on board.

Louise and Barbara were invited to the service at the Cathedral of Saints Peter and Paul in Washington. Louise's husband Bill and I went along. We flew from Detroit to what was supposed to be Regan Airport in D.C. While we were waiting to board, the flight was cancelled and we were veered aboard another flight bound for Dulles. We landed close to the originally-scheduled time but soon a violent thunderstorm hit. In the midst of this, we set out for the city in a four-door Buick at the rush hour. It seemed like a slow trip at the time but under the circumstances and the traffic conditions, it was reasonably quick.

We ended at a Holiday Inn in Georgetown, where we ate and turned in early. The next morning we learned that our luggage had arrived during the night but that no one knew where it was. About 10:00 a.m., the bags showed up in our rooms. Louise was getting edgy and had Bill take her to the Cathedral, although the event was not scheduled to begin until 4:00 p.m.

In the middle of the afternoon, Bill and I drove to the Cathedral and staked out our positions. There was a steady stream of tourists going through, some in guided groups and others on their own. If you have ever visited the Cathedral, you will remember that the floor plan is traditionally cruciform, with the chancel containing space for a large choir loft just east of the crossing, which had been stripped of seating.

Chairs for the participants were placed there.

There are four immense Gothic pillars at the corners of the crossing. The huge pulpit is next to the one at the right of the audience. Vergers with staffs led a formal procession as the choir sang, which brought the participants into their places. The dean of the Cathedral introduced the participants, who included the surgeon general of the U.S., Dr. Satcher, Louise, Barbara Dossey (a woman who had written a poem about Florence Nightingale), and representatives of nursing education. Just before the formal program started, three uniformed nurses, who were part of the Surgeon General's staff, came in and took chairs immediately in front of us. They wore summer naval uniforms. All were tall and the chests of two of them were bedecked with ribbons.

Louise and Barbara spoke from the pulpit. When Louise spoke, she looked like a child – a tribute to her hair stylist. She sounded like a mature woman, however. That image will stay with me forever. The widow of a cousin of mine who lives in Washington also attended and joined us and friends of Louise and Bill for dinner together.

It was a weekend to remember.

Of Time
and Memory

Folk wisdom says that as one ages, time speeds up, and so it seems. However, it may be that as we grow older our perception of time seems to move at a speedier pace. I am content to leave theories of elastic time to the science fiction writers. Perhaps there should be some more reliable measurement than the rotations and revolutions of the earth and the moon. Astronomers expect that the moon's revolution about the earth will gradually decay, and that the moon presumably will crash into the earth in some distant future.

My perception is that time goes galloping by much faster than it did when I was younger and more able to keep up with it. But that brings us to the function of memory, which may be the key to the whole conundrum. It is memory that tells us that time contracts and expands; none of our sensory perception devices do that.

The word "memory" reminds me that my memory is not the trustworthy instrument it used to be. Sometimes it was a nagging presence that got me everywhere early, and I always remembered what I had had for lunch. This is no longer true, and I believe it is the reason I now perceive time as always fleeting. My altered short-term memory used to stuff itself with trivia all day long, which, in retrospect, made the days seem longer.

I used to perceive memory as being a large container or bin, into which my senses dropped items which could then be recovered with a minimum of stirring and effort. I now believe it is a small warehouse with storage racks, shelves, and bins. When my senses lob a memory in the door, the aged attendant, limping and distracted, may simply let it hit the floor, which is by now rather cluttered with forgotten memories. Memories from early life are still rather neatly stored on racks and shelves near the entrance. Some of them at times may be displaced by new memories and fall on the littered floor.

The Greeks assigned a muse, Mnemone, to memory, and another, Clio, to history; yet, history is much like my individual warehouse, on a gargantuan scale. We have little knowledge of peaceful, preliterate people and events. Yet, there are rather detailed accounts of the campaign of Alexander two-and-a-half millennia ago. It was fortunate for Alec that there were literate, articulate Greeks around to put some of it down on paper or lambskin or whatever. Clio has expanded her record-keeping capacities at a rate that is immeasurable in the centuries of the last half of the second millennium.

Since about 1980 I have lived under the shadow of a threat to my well-being that ranks with fear of death. It was about that time that I began to understand Alzheimer's as a threat to elderly people. A Marion, Ohio woman in her late fifties developed it, and quite early it became a very serious case. Her husband, about the same age, quit his job and stayed home with her. Ten years later he died, exhausted by his lonely struggle, exemplifying the words of a doctor acquaintance, "The families are the real victims of Alzheimer's."

When I retired, I began every morning by doing the Cleveland Plain Dealer crossword to reassure myself that I had not had a "strokelet" in the night. I did discover that there are differences from day to day.

A lifelong friend in Tucson died from Alzheimer's only six years after showing early signs of the disease. An older friend became semi-catatonic after a few years with Alzheimer's, and lived on, and on, and on . . .

Then, after the death of my wife Mary, and my removal to Michigan, my son-in-law's mother became part of the Upton Road family. Mildred was a small woman, about 4'10", with quick, bird-like movements. A sharp beak-like nose completed the whole picture. She was past ninety at that time and had been a widow for nearly thirty years. She had been an elementary school teacher and seemed somehow childish herself. She was a naïve person who could never tell that she was being kidded. When a joint grandchild was baptized in a Methodist Church in Marion, Mildred exulted that the baby had been baptized a Methodist and could not understand my comment that I thought she was baptized a Christian. Mildred really felt that Christ died for Epworth Methodist Church. I found her exasperating and felt guilty for letting it happen to me. The totally amnesiac Mildred, who could not remember her own house (where she had lived for nearly ninety years) and asked to "go home" when she was there, was a figure to be pitied. She did not mean to irritate me, but she did.

As time marched on, I became more comfortable, believing that I had passed the age when one is most susceptible to Alzheimer's, but then I began to hear of new Alzheimer's patients who were very senior, and finally broached the topic with my M.D., who laughed at me and finally gave a simple early-sign test and told me that I had aced it. That was some comfort, but there is still the problem of my temporary loss of recall for names. It is still with me, and I am sure it is not going to go away and leave in peace.

If memory worked perfectly, everyone would have "photographic" memory. One exposure would brand itself on one's mind totally and in perpetuity. One reading of War and Peace would mean that the reader could accurately reproduce the whole ball of wax a decade later, a most improbable feat. There are people who can memorize at a glance, but there may be quantitative controls that put limitation on this activity. Memorization, particularly of poetry, was much admired before the beginning of the twentieth century. Poetry should be easier than prose; the rhythm and the rhymes are helpful. Some people can hear a melody, and play or sing it back, a trait immensely useful to musicians and mystifying to those of us who lack it.

Besides reproductive memory there is recognition memory, or the ability to recognize a clue and dredge up a larger image, such as the clue which is one's own key for a large complex idea, or concept.

GIOVANNA LAMMERS

I was born in Bologna, Italy and grew up in a small farming community nearby during World War II. I attended the University in Bologna and graduated with a masters degree in Latin and Italian language and literature. I also trained as an opera singer and won a prestigious award the same year of my degree. Unfortunately I was not ready to take on the challenge the prize entailed. As a result I decided that that career was not for me, married an American studying in Italy, and landed in the U.S.A. I raised two children, Stefania and Gregory, taught Latin and French at East Lansing High School and Latin and Italian at M.S.U. I eventually returned to my singing for pleasure and sing periodically for family and friends. I love teaching and, after retiring from the high school, I now teach Italian to college students.

Don't Worry about Style or Polish in the First Draft

"*Vita mortuorum in memoria vivorum eat posita.*" Roughly translated: "The life of the dead continues in the memory of the living." These words written over 2000 years ago by Cicero have stuck in my mind since my school days.

As I settled down to write these life stories at the insistence of my children, I realized that, through my words, I was keeping alive the memory of people so dear and so important in my life. In doing so, I had an uplifting feeling of power as I had found a way of paying them homage and, at the same time, of giving my children and, I hope, their children, the gift of getting to know their grandparents and great-grandparents, dead too soon to be remembered.

Memories started streaming out of my mind from the moment I decided to put words on paper. The pleasure I found in reliving those stories turned what I started to do to please others into an incredibly enjoyable activity for me.

When I decide on a story, I sit at the computer and let it flow out of me without worrying too much about style or polish. I return to it after listening to the well-crafted stories I hear in class, and I make a few changes to eliminate words that do nothing to enliven the narration. Usually I like what came out of me the first time around, because it has the immediacy of telling what I remember and what I felt at the time.

La
Castiglia

Difficult to believe, but I was blessed with a happy, magical childhood as World War II was raging all around me. I could attribute my good fortune to my parents certainly, but they couldn't have done it without the wonderful people who worked, struggled, and loved in the Ghetto della Castiglia.

My mother was the midwife appointed by the town of Sala Bolognese, thirteen miles north of Bologna. She was required to live in Padulle, one of the four villages that made up the town, which was also the site of the city hall. When my newly married parents arrived in Padulle, they thought they would live in the apartment assigned to them as part of my mother's contract, but they soon discovered that it was occupied by the recent widow of a schoolteacher with three small children. They had no heart to enforce the contract and found a modest place in Padulle's Ghetto della Castiglia. The word "ghetto" elicits images of poor and crowded dwellings somewhat separated from the rest of the community. In origin it referred to the part of Venice called Borghetto, where the Jews lived, but it later acquired the current, more-general meaning.

My ghetto was roughly square-shaped with one side open to allow the entrance into a courtyard surrounded on three sides by thirteen human dwellings and on the fourth side by chicken coops, pig sties, and rabbit cages. There was also a stable for a mule. In the center was a well, since indoor plumbing was unknown in Padulle, and off the center in front of some of the animal shelters was a low, small building with a sign on top of the door in pretty gothic letters, "LATRINA." The well water was not potable, so one of my many daily chores, but a pleasant one, was to get water from a fountain in front of city hall, where women loved to gather to keep the local gossip alive.

Our neighbors were hardworking poor people who were making a meager living as day-workers in the fields, when needed, during the harvest. In the winter they kept busy in many other ways to add to their modest incomes. The women spun wool, wove cloth, and made and repaired clothes. Some of the men made and repaired tools; others made brooms and rakes. The mule owner offered his services to haul whatever stuff needed to change location.

My parents were outsiders and the subjects of great curiosity for the inhabitants of La Castiglia. Both were well-educated and held responsible jobs. My father worked for the city hall in Bologna as a building inspector, and he had recently returned from Algeria, where he had worked for a French company building roads and bridges. My mother had served as midwife in another region, which meant that to these people, born and raised in the same place for generations, she had traveled and seen the world. The few photos taken before I was born show a happy young couple full of hopes and expectation for my arrival. But difficult days were looming.

In December 1940, the river Reno flooded the area and Padulle was under more than three feet of water. My eight-months-pregnant mother was gingerly lowered from a window onto a boat and eventually went to live with her married sister in the city, where I was born on January 21, 1941. This little drama took place against a huge, ominous backdrop of war raging already on three continents. My father was drafted a week after my birth. Soon after, my mother returned with me to Padulle, where her neighbors, in spite of the dreadful future they were facing with sons, brothers, and husbands leaving every day to go fight the war, surrounded her in a huge embrace of love and support.

I became the youngest child of these thirteen families. There were always arms ready to hold me, cuddle me, and twirl me into the air. I slept in everybody's house. I ate at everybody's table as my mother was struggling to serve the needs of the population that was growing every day, as scared city dwellers sought refuge in the countryside from the perils of war.

My Father's Return

The tragedy that had been playing out in the fields and cities of Europe took a dramatic turn in Italy in the summer of 1943. The infamous alliance of Hitler and Mussolini, known as the Axis, was strained by the constant Allied attacks by air, the huge losses suffered by the Italian army, and by massive anti-government demonstrations in the large industrial cities of the North. The Axis came to an end with the fall of the Mussolini regime and Italy's signing of an armistice with the Allied Forces of Britain, France, and the United States on September 8. The Italian army was disbanded, and the Germans embarked on a fierce campaign of retribution against their disloyal allies. This was the backdrop to the events that led to my father's return.

The situation was so chaotic and dangerous that only prayers and waiting were left to the many families hoping to see their men come home. Rumors and reports of the lucky ones who returned soon after the signing of the armistice alternately brought hope and despair as the bombings became ever so frequent and ferocious as the days went by. My mother was in a state of great anxiety bordering on despair when, finally, two weeks after September 8, my father was carried home on a horse-drawn cart from the Bologna train station.

He was so weak that he could not stand. To avoid being sent to fight in Africa, in a war he did not believe in, he did what many others had done. He had his healthy bottom teeth pulled, while others chose to have one big toe cut off. These mutilations made them ineligible to be sent to the front line. Without teeth, he could not eat properly, especially the poor diet of an army in disarray. He contracted dysentery and became so sick that he was placed on a bed of straw in a cargo train.

Given the disastrous state of the railroad system, the frequent target of heavy bombardments, it took two weeks for the train to cover a distance that today would take only a few hours. During the long stops along the way, the locals ventured to look into the train and, when they discovered that it was full of sick and disabled soldiers, they brought them water and whatever little food they could spare. These acts of compassion kept them alive, but barely.

With his sunken cheeks, long hair, and beard, and so weak he could not stand, my father repulsed me, even after my mother had shaved him and given him a big bath where, she recalled, the top of the water was covered by lice. It pained her to see my reaction. She kept encouraging me to show joy for the return of my father, whom I had seen only a few times since my birth and who now craved the love and the embrace of his little daughter. For days I recoiled from his presence.

I have often felt great sorrow for my behavior, especially when he recounted the dangers and the horrors of those two weeks, when the thought of returning to his wife and daughter gave him the strength to endure and survive.

In the Shelter

The aerial bombardments became closer and more prolonged, and now the people of La Castiglia got together and dug for days to bury their meager but dear possessions. They also talked about the underground refuge they dug, and how we waited in trepidation and fear for our homes and our lives during the bombardments.

At the sound of the sirens, the adults called together the children while assembling a few things of value they didn't want to lose. My mother had a knack for grabbing the least valuable objects, like an old pot or my only stuffed animal, a little dog I called Biancolino, or, worse, a dusting cloth or a chipped cup.

Gino Bianchi was in the latrine when not a siren, but a low-flying plane everybody called *Pippo* flew, as he put it, right over his head. Everybody knew that after *Pippo* the bombs would start falling almost immediately. Gino ran out of the latrine without buttoning his pants. As he was running for the shelter, the pants fell lower and lower, impeding his flight, so he took them off and threw them away. When he arrived without pants in the shelter, his wife met him with some pointed and angry questions. He tried to explain his predicament but couldn't quite calm her down. At this point the council of the elders decided that a pair of pants, no matter how valuable in those days of great poverty and shortages, was not worth fighting for when any minute we may have to face Saint Peter. That settled it for the time being. Later, Gino and his wife joined in the laughter, and Gino would say that his wife made him pay dearly for his lost pants.

Many times the bombs exploded so near the entrance to the shelter that earth, debris, and shrapnel reached us inside. When this happened, Mariolina, a very mild-mannered and devout lady, exploded into imprecations to God and the saints in heaven. As soon as she realized what she had done, she fell on her knees and recited the act of contrition, only to repeat the same sequence until the explosions stopped.

For us children, the time spent in the shelter seemed like time stolen from our play and unbridled exploration of fields and ditches, where we loved to play hide-and-seek and other games. Our mothers tried to keep us entertained with stories and songs and little games of manual skill, since the space did not allow any other activity. This worked for awhile, but we sensed the tension and distractedness of the adults, who tried to fake a playful tone while their minds were heavy with worries and couldn't be as engaged as we wanted them to be. We then became restless and cranky and our complaints exasperated our parents who, at times, became angry to the point of spanking us, only to regret it bitterly later.

My mother came up with a good idea one day, especially for the younger ones. She dug up a good blob of clay, wrapped into a wet cloth, and encouraged us to shape it into little figurines of people, animals, houses, and other everyday objects. Once we thought our little creations were done, she gently placed them on a big pot cover, which she carried by the handle outside to dry the figurine in the sun, when it was safe.

When my mother was away tending to the birth of a child and I was in the shelter without her, I started to relate her absence to the possibility that the outside explosions might endanger her. Many of the women who were watching me later told me that I became very quiet and often prayed.

The older kids were more difficult to control than the little ones, especially because they felt the omnipotence and invulnerability of youth and wanted to go outside between bombs to report what had happened and what had been hit and, maybe, spot a fallen parachute, whose silk umbrella was a very coveted possession in those days. I remember two instances in which the abandoned parachutes appeared as attractive summer dresses on several young girls once the war was over.

One day, three or four of the older kids seemed strangely calm and kept looking at each other in a conspiratorial fashion. When the noise outside became very loud and threatening, they opened up the wine bottles they had been hiding. They had managed to collect several mice in the bottles. The poor little critters started running here and there in the small crowded space, over, under, and around us. The women, whose nerves were already frayed, started jumping and screaming, and soon it was chaos. To this day I feel a shiver of terror at the thought of that pandemonium, and I do believe that my phobia about mice started on that occasion. So powerful, in fact, was the effect it had on me that I removed myself from the presence of the adults whenever they started recounting the mice story.

Our German Guest

War must be the ultimate aberration devised by men because it forces them to deny the humanity of their enemies.

After my father's return, the German retaliation for Italy's betrayal as it left its alliance with Germany and switched its alignment to the Allies took on dangerous and systematic tactics. First there was a house-to-house search for all able-bodied men who were taken and sent to concentration camps in Germany.

As my father started to recover, thanks to the denture my mother was able to get from a dentist in exchange for the few, precious food items she was able to acquire from the local farmers, this new threat presented itself. My mother and Titta did not sit on their hands but found a place to hide my father and Pippo. There was a double soffit in our house, a place so small they could barely fit and where they were literally buried when word, passed from house to house, signaled that the Germans were about to reach La Castiglia. They removed the floor tiles quickly to allow the two men to enter. Then they replaced and covered them with a bag of chaff, making sure that they left a crack for a little air to get through. Usually they spent no more than half an hour there but when they were allowed to return to the light of day, they were as white as ghosts. After this threat ended and the Germans retreated more and more to the north for their last offensive against the Allies, every household was forced to give shelter to a German soldier. One was assigned to our house and, for lack of a better place, my parents set up a bed for him under the staircase. Because of mistrust and inability to communicate, our guest mostly kept to himself.

One evening, when it was very cold, my mother invited him to sit in front of the fireplace, the only source of heat in the house. He accepted.

I was almost three years old and I thought I could entertain our guest by asking my mother to show us the steps of a folk dance she had learned when she first started her career in the Marche region. We referred to this dance as the *danza marchigiana*. "Mamma," I said, "Show us how to dance *la danza partigiana*." A frigid silence fell in the room. My mother tried to explain that I had mispronounced the word and it was a *danza marchigiana* from the region where she had worked before she came to Padulle. The German was not swayed by her attempts and left the room in a huff. My parents were mortified and scared because in my young mind I had confused the word *marchigiana* with *partigiana*. The *Partigiani*, of whom I heard frequent mention in those days, were, in fact, the Italian guerrilla soldiers who greatly assisted the Allies in their fight against the Germans. Of course, our guest must have decided that, since only the truth comes from the mouth of babes, we must be in contact with the *Partigiani* by giving them aid and comfort. In some ways he was right.

My father had a primitive radio, which he kept and listened to under the bed to hide it from the Germans. At certain times of day he could receive Radio London, which broadcast the news about the war and the movements of the Allied troops through the mountains of central Italy. This news was precious for the local *Partigiani* in order to organize their activities in support of the Allies. My mother, given the relative freedom of movement allowed by her profession, was able to pass on this information to a place where it was needed. As a result of the slip of my tongue, for awhile our house was watched day and night.

In the spring and summer of 1944, the frenzied fight increased in virulence. As we spent more and more time in the air raid shelter, my mother decided that she would teach me a short poem that I would recite on Christmas Day in church in front of the crèche. This was a long-cherished tradition in Padulle, and in that year, after so much suffering, the event loomed in many peoples' hearts and minds as a respite from the daily ugliness. We hoped that the hostilities would stop for a few days, which, I believe, had been agreed upon by both sides. With the help of their parents and the nuns, children practiced for months, trying to memorize their lines and recite them with clarity and feeling.

On the afternoon of Christmas Day at Vespers, all men and women came in their best clothes to the church for this long-awaited event, one of the few in the social life of our village. There was great trepidation among the children who were afraid they would forget their lines, while their parents pleaded with them to stay calm and give a lively delivery, as if the family name and respectability depended on their performance.

My mother, who had a way with words, had written my poem, a

short prayer to the infant Jesus to look down on our bloodied world and restore the peace and understanding everyone so longed for. During the long hours spent in the shelter, she coached me and other children, and we had numerous opportunities for rehearsals in front of our companions. I was the youngest, but she was confident that I would hold my own. And I did! The reports I heard years afterwards were glowing. I spoke with so much feeling that I brought tears to many eyes.

Our German guest was also in church that day. At the exit he came toward my mother, who was holding me in her arms, and he was visibly moved. He smiled as if to congratulate me. My mother returned his smile. At that point he reached into his wallet and pulled out a photo of two young children. My mother looked at the picture as tears came to her eyes and took the man's hands into her own.

The Teacher Who Ate Her Pet

One of the saving graces for the people who lived in the countryside during the worst years of the war was the ability to keep a few animals as a source of food. Everybody had a few chickens, ducks, rabbits and, when possible, a pig. I say "when possible" because it wasn't so easy to find a farmer who had baby pigs to sell. My mother was a good source for this network because she went into many farmers' homes to deliver babies, some belonging to the farmers, of course, and some belonging to the refugees from the city who had taken shelter with many of the farmers. There was great excitement when she brought the news of a litter of piglets, and plans were made immediately to go and get them in exchange for various services, such as spinning wool, weaving, working the land (when possible), carpentry, tool repairs, and the like. The piglets were fed with chaff and other scraps. From this very poor diet they grew into wonderfully big animals who usually met their demise in the fall. For us children they brought a lot of excitement and companionship. They were our pets and we loved to help with the feeding. We played with them by scratching their backs with sticks, and we all had a name for them.

In the spring of 1945, Titta and my family shared a pig – a pink, round pig that looked promising for the fall. I had named him Cicciolino, "Little Fatty," and he was a wonderful companion. He knew when I brought him food and seemed to thank me with his grunts and the wiggling of his curly tail. The people of La Castiglia had a row of pig sties and chicken coops, where we children spent time observing their behavior and feeding and comparing them. They had become a part of our greater family, and somehow we had accepted the inevitable fate that was reserved for all of them. I am sure we were sad when one was chosen for supper, but we also knew that its death was a noble sacrifice for the enjoyment of the whole family. We learned very early to accept these facts of life.

In early spring of 1945, due to frequent bombardments and no advanced notice, the people of La Castiglia decided to move with few belongings to a big farm far from the center of the village. Almost a hundred people assembled there and lived for about two weeks in very crowded conditions. We slept on straw wherever there was some space, including in the stables with the animals. Of course, we had to leave our own animals behind, but for a while the men took turns returning at night to feed them. In the last few days before the liberation of Bologna and the surrounding areas, the fighting was practically nonstop. I still remember the night skies red with explosions and the continuous flight of airplanes. It became too dangerous for anyone to move, even during the night, so our poor animals were left unattended. Somebody daring to pass through town reported that the pigs were screaming from hunger.

Their noises must have attracted the attention of the German soldiers, who were becoming more and more desperate because of the disarray of their units and the difficulties of getting supplies. One night, as the pigs were letting out their complaints about the food they were not receiving, the retreating German soldiers took as many of them as they could. This was the night of April 20, 1945.

On April 21, the news spread like wildfire that the Allies had occupied the city, and the German Army – or what was left of it – had retreated. There was great jubilation. We returned from our hideout and met the Allied troops in their tanks in the streets. We were cheering them and throwing flowers picked in the fields, and they were throwing us candies. It was an unforgettable day.

After the first exciting moments, we returned to our homes to find out what had happened. Several buildings were damaged, but we had each other and the rest of our lives and we were elated. Soon our minds turned to the animals. Rumors were going around that the fleeing German soldiers had taken them and the silence that came from where they were kept confirmed our suspicions and fears. All coops were empty, all sties were empty except – surprise – the last one, where Cicciolino, too weak for any further complaints, was lying down in a state of exhaustion. We couldn't understand what had happened and why Cicciolino had been spared. Maybe the Germans ran out of space or were interrupted by bombs or other dangers and ran without emptying the last sty.

My parents and Titta felt an embarrassment of riches, but my mother was quick in declaring that Cicciolino belonged to the whole Castiglia and we would all share in his gifts. November came, and one day I was sent to the home of some friends away from my house. When I returned, Cicciolino was hanging upside down, and preparations were made for the cutting and sharing of his flesh. I had a shudder of horror and sadness for him, but I was soon caught up in the preparation for the banquet we would have after all the sausages were made and everybody had a share of meat to be salted and saved for the winter. There was enough meat left to be cooked on the grill and enjoyed that night. What excitement! There were makeshift tables set up in the courtyard with bottles of the new wine that the vines, neglected during the last few years, had nonetheless been generous enough to contribute to this feast that brought us all together in a thanksgiving for peace and life renewed.

Whenever I see a reproduction of a painting by Pieter Bruegel called *The Peasant Dance*, which portrays a village feast, I can't help but imagine myself and all the people of La Castiglia in the painting, because it captures magnificently the memories I have of that early November day.

Years later I told this story to my students at East Lansing High School. They were shocked to hear that I ate the animal that had been my companion. The news spread and young people who were not my students came between classes to ask me if it was true that I had eaten my pet. I tried to explain to them that necessity was at the root of it, but they would not accept it. For years I was known as "the teacher who ate her pet." This gave me food for thought.

What taught me at such a young age that I had to accept the death of a familiar animal as a necessary sacrifice for our survival? Do our young people think about the animals that were slaughtered for them to have hamburgers? Are the neatly cellophane-wrapped packages of meat they see in the supermarkets so removed from the reality of a slaughtered animal that they fail to see the connection? Living with chickens and ducks and pigs gave me a sense of a deterministic law that governs life and gives every creature a place and a purpose. Those animals kept us alive so that we could fulfill our own lives, and their sacrifice was looked upon with gratitude and as a great blessing.

JOYCE DYER

My mother said I was born singing and asking "why." An avid desire for learning led to academic and business training and a teaching diploma from Sherwood Music School in Chicago. World War II caused some dark days but also opened up doors in business from clerk to consultant in public health and social services. There I met and married a wonderful man and became mother to his five children. It was happiness I had never known. His death from a sudden heart attack brought darkness into my world, but his wonderful children brightened the journey of my tomorrows. I lost my sight at the age of eighty but with electronic equipment I have found new joy in writing. My world is bright with ever-broadening horizons.

Keep in Mind Those You Want to Reach

"Mom, why would you ever marry a man with five children?" It was the voice of my youngest stepdaughter, Kathy, coming over the phone from California, repeating a question I am often asked. I thought I would try to write something. I took up my pen and sat down to try to find a way to make the journey from my heart to those

I loved so much.

At first nothing happened, and I just sat and waited. Then I began to remember the children as I had seen them that first day we met, and the words just started to flow. "One Fine Day" was born. At 4:00 a.m. I folded up my work of love and sent it off to Kathy.

I joined a writing class but announced at the first session that I had nothing to read. I had spent the time writing a letter to my daughter trying to explain why I had married a man with five kids. Almost in a chorus came the words, "We'd like to know that!" I was puzzled at the quiet that met the reading. When it was finished, smiles broke out. Someone said, "Why, that's a love story." I was stunned. I had not anticipated this.

The ringing of my phone greeted me at home and the voices of Kathy and her older sister echoed the expressions of my class. The two excited people were saying "Oh, Mom, you've got to continue writing. That is a love story and we have always thought Daddy was the most romantic, noble man we knew." So I continued writing, and thus was born my love story.

My only suggestions to anyone who would write a story: Write from the heart; keep in mind those you want to reach; keep a sweet sense of humor.

I believe my best work comes when I write with an attitude of sharing, making my reader feel involved beyond just reading a story.

One
Fine Day

It was a holiday weekend. The quiet of my tiny second-floor apartment matched the unnatural quiet of the street below, the main street of the small city where I lived and worked. The stillness was broken by a knock on my door. I had been aware of the sound of footsteps in the stairway that led from the street to the corridor outside my apartment but had paid no attention. There were other apartments in the building, but everyone seemed to have gone to spend the holiday elsewhere. This day, Sunday, and recent events in my life had evolved in a way that left me at home alone, so I turned my thoughts and energies to attacking work that waited to be done for the company that employed me. There had been a disastrous fire that had destroyed the plant and offices. Since my job seemed to be involved in all aspects of the company life, my apartment became the center for administrative activity until other quarters could be established.

As I cautiously opened the door, I looked up into the face of a tall, lean man with dark, flashing eyes that were underscored by a broad grin. This man was no stranger to me but I was surprised that he would appear at my door. Eventually I became aware that, with an ever-broadening grin, he was holding out a stack of papers to me, apparently waiting to be asked to come in. Finally I recovered and, trying to hide my embarrassment, stepped back and allowed him that privilege. This man was not a member of the company but, through an arrangement with the owner, was using the plant facility and offices to develop and construct a project of his own.

Although I knew him only casually, I had been asked by the owner to provide him any assistance I could. Since I handled all things confidential and this project involved patents and a great amount of correspondence and contracts, it seemed logical that I would become closely involved. However, from a personal viewpoint, I had come to look upon him somewhat disdainfully and secretly categorized him as a cynical smart-talker. I had decided to keep a formal distance between us. Now here was this man standing in the middle of my little apartment, carefully explaining to me that it had been necessary for him to check on a part of his project located away from the plant, where it had been safe from the recent fire. The papers he was bringing required my attention so he had brought them in person, knowing I would be working at home. As he turned to leave, I saw him hesitate and glance around.

Looking back at me he asked, "Hey, what are you doing for the rest of the day?"

It was obvious that nothing exciting was going on. What could I say?

Then I heard him say, "Come on. Go back to Lansing with me. I don't know just what, but I do know the family has something planned. Nothing fancy. Just a picnic, cookout, or something. It's early in the day and I know they would be happy if you would join us."

As he spoke, I saw in him a person I had never seen before. Heard something in his voice I had never heard before. Gone was the cynicism. His eyes were still showing a hint of mischief, but there was an air of vulnerability about him that was different. I had heard bits of gossip being tossed about. Something about a marriage gone wrong. But battling recent problems with my own divorce had taken its toll, and tunnel vision made me oblivious to much of what was going on around me. How could I speak of all the work that was waiting to be done when he knew the crisis was under control and was insisting that his work could wait and that he would get me back home by evening?

I tripped down the twenty-four steps to the street, leaving the safety of my little escape nest. A man I hardly knew ushered me into a strange automobile, on my way to join a family I had never met, specific destination unknown, early on a Sunday morning. The drive was short and we soon stopped in front of a large white house on the bank of a lovely river. Doors flew open and people of all ages, shapes, and sizes came to greet us. We were completely surrounded, with the man accompanying me in charge lining everyone up and making introductions all around.

First, there was Kathy (Kathleen), a bright-eyed, preteen, all legs and arms, strong little body trembling with excitement, trying impatiently to follow orders to quiet down.

Next came Jill, a lovely, fragile, shy little blossom of a girl showing promise of the best of the ten years yet to come, trying to suppress giggles lying just under the surface of a demure smile.

Then there came Butch (Norman), not quite out of the "little boy" stature, with a captivating smile, exhibiting all the charm of his father, with a certain air about him giving promise of the strong yet gentle man he was to become.

Next I met Sue (Susan Mavaurneen, her father called her), already a young lady in her teens. She was soft and womanly, bright and loving, graceful of body. She was as pretty as the Irish lass her father likened her to, yet mature beyond her years with a certain elusiveness that seemed to set her apart.

Finally there was Bonnie (Bonita), now in her mid-teens. Beautiful and strong in mind and body, with features of loveliness and a maturity belying her young years, she was clearly the eldest. The weight of responsibility and dependability were very evident, but a bit of the little girl vulnerability came through.

With the introductions over and all these happy people reaching out to me, I was beginning to know something of what the term "family" meant, and I was a bit overcome. Everyone was jumping with excitement as they talked about the plan for the day, scolding and prodding "Daddy" to get going. I looked up into the proud smiling face of the man being called Dad, Daddy and, sometimes, Father. I began to realize I was seeing the real person behind the smart facade of the man I had avoided knowing. At that moment, hurried as it was, our eyes met and the joy I saw in his was almost overwhelming.

But there was more to come. I looked toward the house and there, seated in a chair on the front porch, quietly observing the scene, was a small elderly man wearing a hat and casually smoking a cigarette. The door behind him opened and a tall woman of regal bearing stepped from the house, joining the quiet man on the porch. She was dressed very casually and had a man's red print work handkerchief tied around her head. She was carrying a large box and, without looking toward the street, called out, "George. Where in the hell have you been?"

There was a scramble as the chattering little mob raced to aid this lady who was so clearly in charge. As the way cleared, the lady, whose elegant demeanor remained intact, saw me and, without a moment's hesitation, came forward to meet and welcome me.

I learned that "family" consisted of a devoted father, his five children, his father, and his mother. No more time to lose. We were off to celebrate the day. In a whirl of action, mysterious boxes, utensils, and all manner of things appeared and were quickly and efficiently stowed in the ample depths of the trunk of the car. I was directed to take a place in the center of the wide front seat. Kathy sat beside me, with her little arms locked around one of mine. George's mother, Cora, took her place in the space remaining. George's father, Clarence, sat with Bonnie. Sue, Butch, and Jill found places together in the rear seat, and George claimed the driver's seat. Off we went, all nine of us, in the big blue Ambassador.

No one had yet mentioned a destination – just that we had the makings of a picnic. As we drove, I began to recognize that we were following along the shore of Lake Michigan heading south toward Indiana. It was a route familiar to me from past trips to Chicago, where my sister and I had attended Sherwood Music School. We passed fruit stands and made a stop to pick up some of the local produce. Cora was especially eager to please her taste buds with some much-loved plums. She hastily acquired a box of the plump beautiful things, which everyone else promptly rejected with fervor; but I could not bear to see this lovely lady turned down, so I joined her and we had a great time by ourselves.

Soon after the stop for fruit, we crossed the state border into Indiana, where we found a rural park. As if by magic, boxes from the car trunk surrendered their contents – fried chicken, salads, hot coffee, cold lemonade. I was so unused to such activity that I hardly recall the details of food spread out on a tablecloth anchored to a large picnic table. It was almost more than I could take in.

I learned that Clarence had recently retired from the office of the Secretary of State. Cora was a deputy director of a division of a state department. The four of them had pooled their resources some years before and located the family together in the large home where I had just met them. Cora was a woman of great energy and very socially active. Clarence was bright, witty, and gifted. He was interested in all of life but seemed now to be content with less activity.

The day passed quickly. Cora and the young people seemed to find lots of exciting things to do, such as looking for all kinds of plant and animal life. I began to discover so much to admire in George and his family. I just relaxed and let time flow by. We drifted into a long stroll around the peaceful grounds. As we walked, we seemed to find so much to talk about – the project, its origin in a dream, George's hopes for its future. Rather than just a maze of letters and plans, the project began to take shape and come alive for me.

Clarence had found a place where he appeared content to observe the world of trees, spacious grounds, and the abundance of nature all around him, quietly enjoying the ever-present cigarette. We hesitated beside this gentle man for a time. George had grown very quiet. I looked up to see a shadow of sadness come over his strong tanned features and saw a film of tears dimming the flashing dark eyes. He caught my look of surprise as I tried quickly to look away. He regained his composure, but with a slight choke in his voice, he told me what had been coming to his mind.

He said, "I know I'm going to have to do it some day. I'm going to lose him, but I can't bear to think of that day."

The day was beginning to move into evening. Light shadows formed slowly and a slightly quieter family began to gather, still chattering and full of energy, but energy directed toward the trip home and the promise of the evening to come. We packed and took our places in the big car. Once again the car was in motion, northbound toward Michigan. The twilight was beautiful. The songs became quieter and the car games less energetic. Kathy, her little arms again holding on one of mine, looked up at me, leaned her head against my arm, and slowly closed her dark eyes, so like her father's, and slowly drifted off to sleep.

The day was drawing to a close and with mixed feeling I found myself wanting it never to end. But we returned to the front of the big white house. Sleepy people slowly stirred and made their way up the steps to the front door of home. "Good nights" were said, tired legs climbed stairs to bed, and picnic spoils were unloaded to be dealt with in the kitchen. All was at peace in the big white house, and it was time for George to keep his promise to get me home.

After a short drive we were back at my door, where the day had begun. We took a quick look around the apartment to see if all was as it should be and then went back to the door. George hesitated a moment and we exchanged a long look. He quietly closed the door and I listened to his slow footsteps going down to the waiting car. I stood, alone again, wishing those footsteps were coming up instead of going down. The quiet was softly broken by the whirr of the car motor slowly fading into silence, and the day was over.

I could not know it then, but that day was the beginning of the most wonderful years of my life, a life I had only dreamed of, a family I could never have imagined.

Ever
After

I was back in my apartment. The quiet of the street below matched the silence filling the room as I slowly surveyed the efforts I had made to put my life together after my divorce. I told myself to get busy and organize for the day ahead, but reflections of the day's events kept creeping in, taking away all ability to concentrate. Finally, I went to bed, still trying to get my thoughts together.

Surprisingly, sleep came quickly and I was startled to be awakened by the ringing of the phone. I revived when I saw by the bedside clock that it was after midnight. Darkness filled the room. Who would be calling me at this hour? More than a little apprehensive, I crept to the phone located near the entrance of the apartment.

Cautiously I said, "Hello," and was shocked to hear the voice that responded. It was George. I knew he would be away, hopping by plane from place to place, following his project as it was demonstrated all over the country. He was calling from San Francisco. I realized it was early evening out there. He had talked with the family, and he repeated what I often had heard him say, "No matter how luxurious, a hotel room is only four walls when you're away from home."

Then he went on, "The family asked about you and wondered when they were going to see you again. Mother was really impressed with you and wants me to bring you to dinner as soon as I get back to town." He then talked about the reception he had received and how exciting the day had been. "I'm sorry about the late hour, but I wanted to talk and thought you wouldn't mind." He was right. I didn't mind at all. When we said good night, he said he would let me know how things were going.

True to his word, nightly calls began to fill my days with expectation. Problems at my job were coming under control. Reorganization at work was going more smoothly all the time. Even my personal life seemed to come into focus, and there seemed to be light at the end of the tunnel.

Another day was coming to a close. I was hurrying to finish with last-minute details. My back to the office door, I looked up from my typewriter directly into the smiling face of George, who was perched on the windowsill, grinning broadly. He said he had just gotten in and was home from his travels, at least for a while. He had orders from his mother and the family to bring me home to have dinner with them, and they would not take no for an answer. So what could I do? Before I could think of anything to say, we were on our way and were soon greeted with bright smiling faces and lively chatter.

We were ushered quickly to the dining room and were seated around an oval-shaped table sparkling with china and silver spread on a white tablecloth. George was seated in the middle of the table, with his mother to his left, then his father, then five eager children, then me, an arrangement that left me seated next to George. A stack of plates had been placed in front of George. They were encircled by serving bowls and platters of food, from which George filled a plate for each person. With this quickly accomplished, conversation began to pick up as the food was consumed. There was much catching up to do. They talked of school activities. Everyone was involved. Bonnie had cheerleading and Butch had wrestling. They talked about studies, teachers, and other kids who were all known to George and the family.

When dinner was over, everyone joined in the clearing and kitchen chores. There was some scattering of the family as evening came, but most of the action centered on just chatting. George's mother, Cora, his father, Clarence, and George eagerly exchanged news and the latest gossip about state government and new people and activities in the political scene.

Soon the evening was waning, and George was getting prepared to take me home to St. Johns when Cora mentioned a new shopping center opening in the Detroit area. It was called Northland. A number of downtown shops were opening branches offering attractive merchandise. She was eager to visit the new stores and asked if I had been shopping there. When she learned I had not, she quickly suggested that we plan a trip together. She said George could go with us, and we could make a day of it. The pre-holiday season was just ahead, and she wanted to see what was new in fashions. She urged me to join in the fun. We agreed to go on the first Saturday that George was finished with his rail car tours.

We parted, saying "good night," and George and I were out in the night, heading off for St. Johns. It had been a lovely evening and, again, I found myself wishing it was just beginning instead of ending.

Back in my apartment, George seemed reluctant to leave, so I asked if he would like a cup of coffee. He quickly said "yes" so I got out the percolator, and soon we were sipping coffee and talking about the plans for rebuilding the plant and offices.

It was getting late when we walked to the door to say good night. With his hand holding the door, he turned and looked down at me and, with a quizzical smile, said, "I wonder . . ." With that he bent down and put his lips on mine. Before I realized what had happened, he went quickly through the door and down the stairs to the street. I heard the sound of the motor as he drove his car away into the night. The nightly telephone calls continued, but nothing was mentioned of the surprise good night.

Then, one evening, there was George, grinning down at me and enjoying the disbelief on my face. I had expected he would still be on tour but now the coffeepot was on and he was telling me he was home to stay. He had accepted an offer from the owner of the company and had been placed in charge of rebuilding the plant and offices, essentially as the chief executive officer of the company. The family wanted to celebrate. He'd come after me to join in the celebration.

So there we were, back at the big white house with even more excitement than before. The house rang with plans now that Daddy was back to participate. Finally it was good-night time for George and me back in my tiny apartment. The coffeepot had served up its contents and, hand in hand, we made our way to the door. At the door, turning to look down at me and taking both my hands, he asked, "Could I have a good-night kiss?"

I stood motionless, unable to speak. He raised my face to look deep into my eyes. Bending low, he slowly pressed his lips over mine as I closed my eyes. This was no little-boy-steal-a-kiss-and-run moment. It was deep and real and seemed the most natural thing to do. As I opened my eyes, still unable to move, I saw him drifting slowly through the door and away into the night.

The days began to fly by. The site was being cleared for the new plant, and two women had been rehired for the offices. George was more deeply involved in responsibility every day but managed well and kept time free to enjoy his homecoming. I had dinner with George and the family almost nightly. Every day seemed to require my company: school activities, meeting all the young friends, athletic events, open houses, hockey games with George, shopping with Cora. George escorted us and seemed to enjoy it all. Then came pre-holiday parties and large affairs – the Charity Ball, the Pink Ball (the big St. Lawrence Hospital charity), and then the inaugural ball for Governor

Williams, where Bonnie and Sue cleared the floor with their jitterbugging. What events they were!

Now evenings with the family extended into weekends, with Butch letting me stay in his room. I rushed from St. Johns with the gown I was to wear. The girls hurried me up the stairs to their room to help me dress, curled my eyelashes, and raided their grandmother's dressing table for just the right perfume, making sure I had a sufficient number of crinolines under my short cocktail gown.

These days and nights were not all partying. There were fall festivals, and at one of them I rode my first Ferris wheel and, seated between Butch and George, had the thrill of rocking atop the wheel when it stopped to let passengers on or off. Then there were early 5:00 a.m. risings on Sunday morning to join Butch and George in delivering *The Detroit Free Press* and *Lansing State Journal*, not by automobile, but from large canvas bags on a coaster wagon.

This was followed by breakfast and services at the neighborhood Presbyterian Church. We must have looked like a Norman Rockwell illustration, with Cora seated beside me and George and the five remaining members filling the pew to the end. The minister placed my hand in George's and shook our hands together as we said good-bye.

One day as Cora and I stood together watching George and the kids working in the yard, she put her arm around me and said, "I have never seen George so happy." As I turned to look at her, she said, "One more thing I want you to know. You are the first person I have ever thought I could give the children up to."

I couldn't say a thing. I was so moved by her words. We just stood holding each other. I had not realized how deep our love had grown. No words were needed. The rush of everyone surrounding us as they returned to the house interrupted our moment, their enthusiasm filling the kitchen with laughter.

Later, at home alone, I began to recall other occasions that made me think more clearly. It seemed as though suddenly I realized how naïve I had been. Coasting along in this happy world, I was willingly overlooking the serious consequences. I began to think that everyone looked on me as already being a member of this wonderful family.

Neither George nor I had openly mentioned marriage. Then, one day Bonnie enlisted my help in carrying armloads of supplies for a party being given to cheerleaders at her high school. As we gave up our burdens, she began introducing me to those I had not met, announcing to the world that I was going to be her new mother. This set up a party by itself, as the coaches and girls gathered with cheering applause.

As we were on our way to St. Johns one night after spending time with the family, George took a small box from his pocket and pressed it into my hand. He often brought me small gifts, so I was not surprised. I opened the box and found a lovely pearl ring. When I looked up, he gave me one of his typical broad grins.

After I found my voice, I asked, "What is this?"

He answered, "Anything you want to make of it."

Not knowing what else to do, I placed it on my right hand. After all, it was just a ring. But when he said good night, he moved the ring to my left hand and said, "That is where I would like it to be. I know it is not a diamond, but if it's all right with you, the diamond will come later."

After a kiss good night, he was gone, leaving me to accept this as his proposal. It was his way of asking me to be his wife and become a mother to his children.

It seemed this was no secret. The whole world knew except me. I had not allowed myself to believe. So what could I do?

At church with my mom, George's mother and dad, my three sisters, their husbands and children, our dearest friends, George's (soon to be our) five children, George and I promised to become as one, each cherishing the other always.

We began to live the dreams that we dared to dream. The day was Saturday, April 16, 1955.

REBECCA STIMSON

My earliest memories are about books that were read to me or given to me. My personal library was co-founded by Mary Poppins and Winnie the Pooh. Long trips to Michigan's upper peninsula – or anywhere the family traveled – meant hours of entertainment listening to my mother read aloud. I had heard *The Agony and The Ecstasy*, *Ring of Bright Water*, *Bells on their Toes*, and *20,000 Leagues Under the Sea* by the time I was eight years old, which is when I started writing my first book.

All my work life has been about language. I worked for eighteen years for Lansing Community College, sharing my love of words through teaching reading and writing. I was the director of Michigan Literacy, Inc. for several years, and worked in three independent bookstores. I am currently the manager of Archives Book Shop, write for Sparrow Health System, and am working on two mysteries and a screenplay.

Just Write, and then Write Some More

I have only one sibling, an older brother who lives on the east coast. The girlfriends I write about in "Maine Stay" and "Adding Amy" have been like sisters to me for decades. After my parents died, these girlfriends became even more my family. We have been through a lot together. We aren't always happy with each other, but we always take each other in. Just like family. We have been separated by time and circumstance and geography, but there is so much that keeps us connected. I tell these stories to share the beauty of these women whose companionship and support mean the world to me.

I use the stream-of-consciousness method for getting started with my writing and for maintaining momentum. Eventually, the stream carries me away and I can't stop. I advise you to write. Just write. Then write some more. Don't allow the critical voices in your head to interfere. Just keep writing.

Then read and revise. The process is like surveying your garden and then weeding it. Remove the extra foliage that's covering up or choking out what you've worked so hard to grow. Once you've cleared the space a little, you can see where you need to fertilize or plant some more.

I find it thrilling to type, or write, as fast as I can think. But it is also exciting to read and polish the written piece, especially when I hear what works or I make something work better. The most satisfying experience is hearing my friends and family – the ones who know the stories and the ones who don't – laugh or cry in the right places. It's a great feeling.

Adding Amy

Every day, I look into a mirror that is framed with photographs of my best friends from high school and me. The four of us – Deri, Candy, Julie, and I — have been friends for thirty-six years. The pictures remind me of conversations, celebrations, and disappointments. What draws us together? What pulls us apart? What brings us back?

We spent most of our high school life together, but we didn't see much of each other the year after graduation. Julie and I went to different colleges in Kalamazoo. Candy and Deri got really good jobs at Michigan State University. But Deri and Candy used to barrel down to see us in D's old blue Biscayne, so we didn't feel disconnected. I left Kalamazoo after the first year to go to MSU; Julie returned home the second year. Once we were all back in Lansing, I actually saw less of them for a while.

In February 1976, Candy told me Julie had given birth to a little girl. Our Amy. The first time I saw her, her eyes hadn't started focusing yet. Julie thought only her world had been lit with the brightest sun imaginable, but the rays would touch us all.

Amy was three years old when I returned home from graduate school. I babysat for her once then. She was a thin, tall sprite with a halo of soft brown curls, big brown eyes, a pert little nose, long slender fingers with tiny, perfect nails, and creamy, tawny skin. We played some board games, and I read to her from *My Tall Book of Make Believe*. She loved the stories and pictures, as I had at that age. By mid-afternoon, I was hoping she would give me a rest while she napped. But she was too excited. I think she was still talking when her mother came to get her late that night. I've never been so tired.

Shortly after this adventure, I moved with Deri into a house several blocks down the street from Amy and Julie, so we saw much more of each other. I'd sit at the dining room table smoking cigarettes with Julie and her housemate Cyndi, who'd tell stories about the regulars at the place where they waitressed while I talked about the characters who came into the downtown bookstore where I worked.

We also tried to talk about Amy without her knowing it.

Sometimes she would be in her room off the kitchen, and we'd think we were safe; but then she would call out to us to stop talking about her. Even then, we did as she commanded. Sometimes she'd be outside orchestrating some play among the kids who'd gathered around. She'd charge into the house, screen door slamming behind her, and flounce dramatically over to the table. She might flop into a chair or stand next to her mother, hip on the arm of the chair, her curls almost as high as the top of her mother's head, her long fingers picking at Julie's sleeve. The kids would stare through the screen at us, asking her what they were going to do next.

Amy loved getting dressed and sometimes changed clothes several times a day to suit her mood or purpose. There were two laundry baskets in her room: one for Clothes Worn and one for those To Be Worn. Anything she'd had on – however briefly – would go into the Worn basket.

To this day, Amy is a meticulous dresser and scrutinizes her mother's clothing for imperfections. When shopping with our friend Candy, she provides running commentary and inquiry about Candy's choices:

"That is too old-lady."

"You don't really like that color, do you?"

"Too many buttons."

"Plaid? Are you serious?"

Sometimes we remind her about her Under Roo period.

When Julie married and they moved to Holt, years passed without our seeing each other. In 1994, Candy and I went to Amy's winter homecoming. We sat in our cross-town rival's gym, admiring our little Amy on the homecoming court in her green satin formal, handsome date on one side and proud mother on the other. We went to her graduation and open house a few months later. I finally got to meet her best friend Catherine. But it made me sad.

Later, I lamented to her mother, "I missed her growing up. I really regret I wasn't a part of her life for so many years."

"It's not your fault. We were living different lives. What's important is we're spending time together now," she said with maternal wisdom.

It was a death that brought us together for that conversation. Julie called to read me the obituary for the younger brother of our dear friend, Rick. We reminisced about Rick, who had died of AIDS ten years previously, and mourned the self-destruction of his brother. We went to the funeral home together – a trip I would not have made on my own.

Although we called each other a little more regularly, we still didn't get together much until my father died. Then Julie and Amy phoned me every week to see how I was doing and ask after my mother. Julie said to me once, "You call me if you need anything. Anything."

Of course, I said what people usually say: "Thank you. I really appreciate your support. It means a lot to me." But in my heart I felt there wasn't anything anyone could do.

However, Julie didn't stop there. "I mean it, Becky!" I heard the maternal tone. "I know what it's like. When my dad died, I just shut down. I didn't talk to anybody about it, and I didn't want anyone to know."

"What do you mean? How could people not know?"

"I felt bad. It was the worst thing that had ever happened to me. I didn't want anyone asking me about it. I just went to school and kind of avoided people."

That's exactly how I felt. "When did he die?"

"Right after school started. Our sophomore year."

"Jeez. I never knew."

"I didn't want you to. So I know how you can just close up. Don't do that. You call me."

Well, I didn't call, but neither did I forget her words.

For the next two and a half years, my brother and I dealt with the guilt, anxiety, and relief of placing my mother in assisted living. She had dementia and could not be left alone. For years before his death, my father had been covering for her for years, caring for her the way a person cares for the love of his life, as he called her, a pattern of protection and support firmly rooted in fifty-four years of devoted family life. But that's another story.

Julie and Amy kept up their regular contact. After my mother died, they invited me to every holiday meal. Most touching was the first Mother's Day without my mother. Amy left me a voice mail message: "I am calling to invite you because you are one of my mothers, and I want you to go to dinner with us. I know you're going to say it's Sunday, your day of rest, and you want to stay home with the dogs, but you come to dinner. Grandma will be there, and she wants to see you. We're going to a yummy buffet, and we'd like you to go to church with us. Julie can pick you up at 10:00. Come on. You know your mother would want you to." When she's right, she's right.

With both my parents gone, I struggled to decide whether I wanted to move into the family home. Either way, the sorting through and removal of fifty years of accumulation fell to my brother and me – mostly me, since he lives on the East Coast. But Deri and Candy made several trips from Traverse City to help, and Amy always joined us.

Candy reported to me during one such visit, "You know you're Amy's new project."

"Really? Hmm. I wonder what that means."

"She thinks you might get buried under some pileage." Her eyebrows raised, Candy looked at me hard.

We knew that Amy's involvement meant relentless pressure to complete the task. Actually, I benefited most when I couldn't see the forest for the trees. Sometimes she'd help me figure out what had to be done just because I didn't want to do what she thought was next.

For months, Amy was with me almost every weekend, going through drawers and boxes, packing stuff up, hauling bags of clothes to Goodwill, moving furniture and rugs and boxes, finding mouse nests, dusting and vacuuming, picking up sandwiches, and just generally helping me stay focused. I simply couldn't have done it without her.

Since then, if we haven't spoken for a few days, she will call: "Everything OK, B? It's been a while. You call me." If I don't call back soon enough, she'll call again: "Where are you? Are you at yoga? Are you outside with the dogs? You aren't broken are you?" she'll ask. It's reassuring to know that she's keeping track of me.

It was Amy who made the mirror I look into every morning. For Christmas two years ago, the five of us were in my dining room helping me settle into my new life. Amy presented each of us a large package. Simultaneously we unwrapped four mirrors framed by scores of carefully overlapped images of us, glued together in perpetuity. There we are. Through the ages. Examining each frame took a long time, as the four of us rotated around the family table. There were quiet moments of remembering or laughing and teasing: "Look at those glasses!" "Why don't you cut your hair like that again?" "When was that taken?" We clamored, "Amy . . . how . . . when . . ." She beamed. My voice caught and my eyes filled with tears as I thanked her. I held the mirror up and saw Amy's face framed by the history of her four mothers.

For her mother's birthday a couple of years ago, she scheduled time with a professional photographer for the five of us. Of course, our favorite photos are the ones with Amy at the center. Yet she gave us a gift that puts us at the center every day, surrounded by the friends who will always be part of who we are.

Maine Stay

Several years ago, when my friend Candy's sister turned fifty, there was much angst over the planning of her birthday party. Fortunately, I was just a sounding board. But I started worrying. I didn't want to fret over who was being left out and who had to be invited to the celebration of my fiftieth. I didn't want to think about what restaurant would be affordable and meet everyone's dietary needs. I didn't want too much noise and a bad cake. I knew at least one of my three best friends shared some of my concerns.

"How about we go somewhere together?" I asked as we all sat drinking beer on my porch four summers ago.

"Sure. After dinner? Remember, I go to sleep early," Julie answered first, always up for an adventure as long as it wasn't after 8:00 p.m. since she had to be at her job at 0-dark-thirty.

"No, I mean a trip. To celebrate our birthdays. Our fiftieth birthdays."

"I'm game," said Julie, first again. "I got plenty of time to plan."

"Like where?" asked Deri, the practical one.

"I don't know. I just don't want to deal with other people thinking I need something done for me," I looked at Candy. She rolled her eyes. "I'd like to be pampered," I went on. "Like a spa weekend. Somewhere I could get a massage, a facial — "

"A mud bath," Julie burst out. "Yeah! I'd like that."

"Hmm," said Deri.

"I'm for that if I can get some botox. Maybe a face lift?" Candy pulled the skin at her forehead back toward her ears.

"No!" we all shouted. We've heard this plea for plastic surgery from her before.

"So are we interested?" I asked.

"Yeah!"

"Okay."

"I guess."

The wheels were set in motion. We decided wherever we were going, we would go in the off-season. Two of us live in Lansing, and two in Traverse City. When any of us got together, we'd talk about where we might go and what we wanted to do when we got there. One of us, a single mother with one child living at home, courted the new experience. One of us, a self-employed grant writer, willing to go into debt for a good vacation. One of us has a shopping addiction matched only by a desire to get away. One of us wanted to go anywhere that we'd be happy together, seeing this milestone year from a new perspective.

As we mulled it over this first time, the choices ranged from three weeks at a villa in Italy to a long weekend in San Diego. There wasn't any urgency because we had three years to plan.

We continued to discuss, and we developed guidelines: it had to be within a six-hour plane ride; it couldn't be a place Candy had been with her ex-husband; it had to be near shopping, good food, and nature; and it had to include lodging with a fully equipped kitchen so we could cook.

Months passed without planning progress. Two of us could frequently be heard uttering, "This is never going to happen." But two of us believed.

All of a sudden, it was July 2003, and we all acknowledged that we needed to make reservations. Sitting around Candy's dining room table, having cocktails, wearing the new we're-almost-fifty tiaras presented to us by Candy and Julie's daughter, Amy, we got out the atlas.

We looked at Florida. "It's too hot," we agreed.

We considered New Orleans. "It's too damp and moldy."

We mentioned Texas. "I'm not going where George Bush is King!"

In the end, we agreed on Maine. We zeroed in on the Camden/ Rockport area because it is Wyeth country, and we all wanted to be on the ocean. We chose the week after Columbus Day for the trip, because rental rates and airfare would be significantly reduced.

"We're taking our chances with the weather that late in the year," Deri said. "The color will be gone. It'll be rainy."

"It'll be cold, too," Candy added.

These comments elicited my usual Pollyanna-like response. "So it's cold. Sounds like Michigan. Maybe there'll still be color. We never know when the leaves will change here."

"Won't bother me," Julie agreed.

"I'll just have to mail a box of clothes, so I can dress in layers," Candy said with finality.

More time passed and more discouraging words were spoken, but some of us still believed that we would, in fact, take this landmark trip.

Meanwhile, we all took action. By Christmas 2003, we had gathered web sites, travel guides, clippings, and maps. Deri sent us e-mail links for a variety of places she'd found to rent, from an eight-bedroom 200-year-old house on a salt farm to a two-bedroom walk-up overseeing a yacht club. We discussed the options via group e-mail and phone calls and decided on a newish house on Rackcliff Island near Rockland. After we made the deposit, the owners sent Deri more pictures. In front of the house were smooth, flat rocks the size of Volkswagens. I would spend hours sitting on them – in wind and sun, morning and evening, smelling the water and listening to it slipping up and over.

We arrived in Portland late in the afternoon. It was rainy and cold. Julie and I wondered if we'd ever hear the end of it.

The next morning, the wind chased big puffy white clouds around while we ate wild Maine blueberry pancakes in a tiny diner. With very little time before we had to pick up our rental car, Julie and Candy hit the first of many stops on the gift-shop circuit. Deri and I went in search of a used bookstore. We were drawn to a narrow façade with bright round objects in the windows: The Queen of Hats. We had to investigate.

Deri started trying on wool felt berets. I wandered over to the window and a whimsical display of fairies and wands . . . and crowns. Made by a local artist using suede-cloth, Velcro, "jewels," and a glitter gun, they were the perfect substitutes for the rhinestone versions we couldn't pack.

"Deri, look! Travel tiaras!" We chose ones we thought suited Julie and Candy.

"Perfect," she agreed. "I want the one with the ivy."

Soon we were picking up the car, crowns under cover. Before we left the parking lot, I made an announcement. "Deri and I found something to help us celebrate and remind us how special we are. Pick one and pass it on." I handed the bag to Candy.

Candy mused over the two purple ones. Here, Jully," she said. "This has to be yours because it has the most glitter on it." She kept the one with subtle glitter threads and oval 'gems'.

"Cool!" Julie exclaimed as she took the glitterful purple band with heart-shaped "stones."

"The green is good for you, B," Candy said, handing the one I wanted back to me: square "emeralds" and glitter swirls.

"And I have the one with nature on it," our wood nymph, Deri, said as she modeled her crown of ivy and small green "gems."

We adjusted our crowns and hit the highway. Right away we found an oldies station. I drove, Candy co-piloted, and everybody sang. In a few short hours, we arrived at Rackcliff Island, sun shining and wind blowing, sending the biggest waves of our fortnight splashing over the rocks.

The interior was all wood and windows with an open floor plan and a wood stove to take the chill off. Deri and I shared a twin room in the loft; Candy, the light sleeper, took the room next door, well away from our sawing logs and the symphony Julie led from her room on the ground floor. There was a bathroom up and one down. The kitchen was well equipped. By that I mean we had pots to cook the lobsters, all the tools you needed to eat them, and a dishwasher.

Every morning we sat with our coffee and tea and watched the tide come or go, sun glinting off the water, singing and dancing to music on the oldies station.

Julie would be the first one up, her habit of rising at 5:30 a.m. a hard one to break. We had agreed to let each other get up at our own time, keeping quiet until 9:00 a.m. One morning, Julie couldn't resist doing the hand dish washing left over from the previous night.

I, often the latest riser, had heard Deri pull our door shut as she left the room. I was vaguely aware of the sounds of water running and the low hum of voices. I dozed, pillow over my head, then the sound of plates clacking and cupboard doors bouncing shut reached me.

I heard Deri say, "Julie, you know sound really carries upstairs." Silverware jangled. My teeth clenched. I breathed deeply and tried to relax, sure the noise would cease soon. Then came the clanging of lobster pots and lids against each other and the stainless steel sink. My mood was stormy. I sprang out of bed, yanked jeans and sweatshirt and socks on, and pounded down the stairs. I saw Deri looking at me over her glasses as I flew past, straight to Julie.

Bless her heart, Julie looked up at me and said, "You're up early."

"Yes," I hissed in her ear. "I heard the alarm!" She looked genuinely surprised. I spun away from her, shoved my feet into my shoes and stomped out the door. It took me about a quarter of a mile to calm down. Fortunately it was a bright, cool morning. I inhaled the damp fresh air and exhaled my frustration and irritation. When I returned about twenty minutes later, Candy was fixing her cereal, Julie was watching *The Today Show*, and Deri was at the table working on our jigsaw puzzle. I made my tea and sat down next to her. We looked at each other.

"I told her," Deri said quietly.

"I know. I heard you once. Oh, well."

An hour passed. We'd all had breakfast, and Julie and Candy had gotten dressed. I was outside, appreciating the water and the sky. Julie came up to me and said, "Sorry, Beck. I didn't mean to wake you up. I just wanted to contribute. Candy and Deri made dinner, and you loaded the dishwasher. I went to bed early, so I couldn't do the rest of the dishes til this morning."

"I know, Jewels. It was just such a rude awakening."

"I'm sorry." She put her arm around me.

"I needed the walk. It was really nice once I calmed down. But next time, wait, OK?"

"OK, Honey," she said, and pinched my cheek.

One night, Candy gave us presents. "All right, girls," she called, emerging from Julie's room, where she had assembled our gift bags from the "extra layers" box she had mailed. "Here we are. All the little do-dads we need to get dolled up for our night out."

"Ooh, sparkly." Deri pulled the long silver one-size-fits-all gloves on.

"Jewelry!" I put on the little square zircon earrings. "And a 'B' necklace."

"We have to have bling bling," Candy declared.

"Mine says 'Julie'." Julie showed her necklace. "And sheesh, a pack of Chuckles."

"Gotta have a little sugah," Candy reminded us.

We put on our gloves and bling bling, straightened our tiaras, and set the timer on the camera.

Every day we drove our rental car around, making trips to Christina's World, Rockland, Rockport, Port Clyde, the Thomaston Prison Store, Camden, and numerous points in between. Oh, and we wore our tiaras practically the whole time. They felt like a headband, and we got used to seeing them on each other, so we forgot we were wearing them – until an outsider would ask, "Is it someone's birthday?"

One of us would answer, "It's all our birthdays. Our fiftieth birthdays." Or "We're just special, and these remind us of that." There's nothing like wearing a crown to make you feel like a queen.

Especially at the prison store.

I was buying window props, curved, notched sticks that hold a window open at different levels. The blue-eyed, rosy-cheeked inmate behind the counter said to me, looking at my tiara and Julie's. "Those are pretty nice."

I told him our story, mentioning of course that we were all fifty.

"Oh, no. I'm sure you can't be more than thirty."

My what a charming smile he had. "Uh huh. Not for a while, but thanks!" I'm sure our lively dispositions and jewels were dazzling him, too.

As he bagged my window props he asked, "You gonna use these to beat away the men?"

"Oh yeah, that's a good idea," I laughed. I was flirting with an inmate.

Julie and I went and sat on sleek wooden stools at the front of the store to wait for Candy and Deri. Candy got into a conversation with the same young man:

"This is our second time here this week. We love this place. We'll probably have to come back some day. But by then we'll be buying those walking sticks."

"We'll be here." He handed her her bag.

"It might not be for a while," she answered.

"We'll still be here," he said matter-of-factly.

"Why? What are you in for?" She laughed nervously. The people in line behind her looked uncomfortable. The inmate didn't answer. Our eyes popped, but we made it outside before we all started hooting.

The Thomaston Prison Store wasn't the only place we shopped. Candy and I had to ship boxes back because we indulged our need for mementos a little too much. I got books and yarn and t-shirts. She wouldn't want me to say what she sent home. In fact, she made me swear I wouldn't. Her box was so heavy the UPS guys didn't believe her when she told them what was in it.

"I'll bet you've never had anyone ship anything that strange before," she challenged.

"Someone sent birch logs back to New Mexico once. That was probably the weirdest thing we ever shipped," the clerk answered.

"Well, how bout if I told you it's my ex-husband? That'd be pretty weird!" We laughed heartily. The men behind the counter just stared at us. Maybe it was the tiaras.

The miracle of the trip is that four fifty-year-old women who live alone lived in the same house for ten days, spent hours in the car together every day, shared two bathrooms, and coordinated their expectations and interests. The few tense moments passed without hair pulling or name-calling. We loved each other before we left, and we love each other still. In fact, every once in awhile we talk about where we're going next.

HELEN E. HARGER

Writing for our high school newspaper, I decided I wanted to be a reporter, especially after participating in a press conference with high school journalists. We were invited to interview Eleanor Roosevelt. That was memorable!

I graduated with a degree in journalism from the University of Wisconsin–Madison in 1945. After three years of reporting for two newspapers, it was time to start a family.

With three daughters to support, I gave up the reporting idea, and finally settled into a teaching position with DeWitt Middle School in Michigan, retiring in 1987.

Two years ago, celebrating my eightieth birthday, a longtime wish of mine was fulfilled: I had my first ride on a Harley-Davidson motorcycle.

Set Aside a Specific Time for Your Memories to Become Stories

My prelude to writing my memoirs really began in 1980, with a telephone call from Florida.

"Hello, Helen. I'm Bill Harger of Winter Park. Are we related?" After delving into family history/genealogy, what do you do with the information filling many notebooks?

I needed a disciplined approach to writing the stories I had accumulated over a period of eighty-plus years, for unless a specific time is set aside for memoirs, often they do not get written.

Because I had a few years' experience in journalism, my stories tend to be reporting rather than author-ing. (When a reporter starts getting fancy with the words, his fellow reporters jokingly accuse him of trying to be an author.)

After the births of my three daughters, then getting them into school, I considered going back to journalism, but reporting is not an eight-to-five job. I needed structure, so I finally ended up in the classroom. Because I had not had writing assignments in high school, I made sure my eighth grade students did plenty of writing. Again, discipline comes into the picture, because in order to write, one has to think.

My approach to writing life stories was rather haphazard, until I got underway. One idea worked its way into other ideas/stories: my travels with grandson Dorsey, the characters of my mother and father, my friends, my childhood, my three daughters . . . and on and on. Often my ideas were born from humorous events in my life, and one idea reminded me of another. I wrote in no particular order, but I'm now getting my book put together for my daughters, a niece, and two nephews, beginning with my genealogical searches, dating back to my immigrant families in the 1600s.

In the words of Julia Childs, *Bon Appetit!*

Forgive Us Our Press Passes

A few plusses go along for the family of a reporter on a state's major newspaper, in our case The Detroit News.

There were passes to events at the Michigan State University auditorium, passes for the family to attend Ford Motor Company's annual Christmas press party at the Ford Rotunda, and, of course, passes to the MSU football games.

My husband, Don, called late one Saturday morning to say he was working on a story for the News and wouldn't be home in time to take in the MSU football game. Since I had the tickets available, I called my next door neighbor, Naurine Sloane, to see if she would like to attend with me. She was delighted.

"I'll make a thermos of coffee for us, since it's chilly out and we might want to warm up," I explained.

It was a boring game. I believe we were playing a Kansas team, and MSU was at least thirty points ahead late in the first half. Time for a sip or two of java. Suddenly, BOOM, at my feet. There was dead silence in the stands, until I shouted, "Good grief! My coffee's exploded!"

There was great laughter in the stands. Frank Hand, a Lansing State Journal reporter, was sitting ahead of us and to the left, and said, "Helen, it wasn't your coffee," as he pointed to the hip pocket of the man directly in front of me.

It took me a few seconds to get the message, especially as the man started taking pieces of glass out of his pocket. The glass had a whiskey label. Whiskey!

Whiskey all over my shoes. Naurine and I continued to laugh, and when we had finally settled down, one of us would giggle. Then we'd be off again, until those sitting around us were becoming a trifle annoyed. It was a runaway game for State, and we were still giggling, so in the third quarter I said to Naurine, "Want to go?"

That's the world of press passes. So is it any wonder that one day right after church, my daughter Sue, a third grader then, excitedly exclaimed that if she knew the Lord's Prayer by next Sunday, she'd get a surprise. She insisted that I hear her, even though I insisted that she already knew it.

"But I have to be sure I've got it right," she begged.

"Okay," I agreed.

Is it any wonder that she said, ". . . forgive us our press passes, as we forgive those who press pass against us?"

Travels with Dorsey

Toward the end of the school year my students became restless. Multiply that by ten, and you'll get eighth graders who are about to say good-bye to middle school and hello to high school. It's an exciting time for both students and teachers.

Martha was a sweet, happy, agreeable blonde who was particularly atwitter one day at the end of the semester; "unusually hyper" is putting it mildly.

"Martha, I never have seen you so excited. What's the matter?" I asked.

"Nothing's the matter, Ms. Harger. It's the end of the school year, and every year my grandmother takes my younger sister and me on a trip."

"Where are you going this year?" I queried.

"I don't know. It's always a big secret until we are on our way!"

What a great idea, I thought, just the thing for Dorsey. My grandson was eleven years old at that time and was due for something special.

"How would you like to go to Pontiac to see where I lived as a girl?" I asked him.

"Great, Grandma! When can we go?"

Right then I set a date, just a few days away, and said we'd ask his mother and dad if that would be OK.

"There's only one rule, Dorsey," I said. "You must wear clean socks." He was going through the stage of seeing how many days he could wear the same pair of white socks.

Aha, I thought. I'll just throw in a little genealogy by taking him to the cemeteries in Pontiac where my ancestors are buried.

When I picked him up at his home at ten o'clock, I zapped him with two more rules: he could not swear, nor could he burp.

"Grandma, what about 'the other'?" he asked.

"Strange that you should ask, Dorsey. Last week in The Detroit News I read in the doctor's advice column a question asked by a woman who wanted to know if it was normal to have to pass gas. The doctor replied that it's thought that the average person has to pass gas thirteen times a day. Now I picked you up at ten o'clock, so I assume you've had time for the first six times. I'll have you home by three o'clock, so you'll have time to do the other seven after that."

"OK," he agreed.

Our first stop was at a small Waterford Center Township Cemetery just west of Pontiac. There I showed him the graves of his great-great-great grandparents, which were beside his great-great-grandparents. He didn't act appropriately interested in this lesson, but as soon as I completed the story, he exclaimed excitedly, "Grandma, there's Dan Quayle's tombstone!" He was pointing to the trash can. Oh, well! I'll humor him by laughing. Big mistake! Every trash can we encountered after that, the same reaction, Dan Quayle's tombstone!

Next I showed him where the hospital I had been born in used to stand. That hospital had been torn down to make way for a larger, more modern structure.

On to my childhood home at 99 Franklin Boulevard. Along the way, I pointed out the homes of father and son who owned the buggy manufacturing company, before buggies became extinct. He feigned interest.

On to the church, First Presbyterian, where his grandfather and I were married, not far from Oakhill Cemetery, where the Hargers are buried. By then, I wasn't too disappointed at his lack of interest. "Ah," I thought, "he'll love to see our lake home north of Pontiac." We parked in front, and walked to the back of the house, the lake side, where I took him to the top of the hill to look down at what used to be a boathouse. A young man there looked up with a quizzical stare.

"Do you mind if I show my grandson where I grew up?" I asked.

The man ran up the hill and said, "I just knew this house had a history! Tell me about it. What are those pipes in the lake?" I explained that they were part of our lawn sprinkling system. He had many more questions and then insisted that we go into the house to see how it had been remodeled.

We entered through a rear entrance of about ten by four feet, where there was once a long shelf on which Mother often left her pies to cool, pickles in a crock, and my favorite crock of her homemade mincemeat. We kids often lifted the lid on the crock and dipped in our curved fingers to get a big taste of mincemeat. I think she added the spirits just before baking the pies, but it was good anyway. The pantry just off the kitchen had been made into a two-piece bathroom.

The owner had made two apartments out of the house, so our

spacious dining room, which easily seated twenty people, was now a bedroom. Of course, I noticed the bed was unmade. My beloved sunroom also was now a bedroom housing another unmade bed.

The ceiling of the sunroom/bedroom had stains, showing that someone had not taken care of roof leaks. Our home had a slate roof. Apparently, when slates fell off, repairs were too costly to make.

Fortunately, the upstairs tenant was not home, so the young man could not take us upstairs. The staircase had been partitioned off with a doorway. When we were kids, we sneaked down the stairway very early Christmas morning to see if Santa had left us the toys we had asked for. When I say early, it was early, about 3:00 a.m. When I was four years old I had pneumonia; I managed to get up and descend three or four steps, but then asked Bob to see if Santa had come.

After that house tour, all I could think was, "I'm glad Mother wasn't here to see that house. During World War II, while we were living in Pontiac, Mom had rented the house out to a man and his father. They didn't pay the rent, and Mom couldn't have them evicted because it was against the law during the war. When Mom eventually got them out, she went into the house to check the condition, and looking at it, she started to cry. She had to have the entire house re-plastered.

The younger renter had been nasty to Mother every time she asked him for the rent. One such time, he complained about the two-car garage being too small. "What's the largest car you ever put in that garage?" he asked.

Mother replied, "A Lincoln!"

Later, telling the story, she said, "But I didn't tell him that the Lincoln didn't fit either, so we had to sell the car."

Once outside again, the only thing Dorsey showed any interest in was a boat on a trailer in the driveway. He was only eleven years old. What did I expect? At least I enjoyed what was to become an annual event: Travels with Dorsey.

And I got him home by three o'clock, as I promised.

Travels with Dorsey II

My grandson Dorsey and I had taken a one-day trip to my hometown, Pontiac. We graduated from auto to train. When he was twelve, we went to Washington D.C. We traveled to Denver by train when Dorsey was thirteen, and again when he was fourteen. All were great trips with the usual rules: clean socks every day, no swearing, and no burping.

We had to skip a trip when he was fifteen, but when he got his driver's license at sixteen, times changed; he could help with the driving. I suggested a destination I always had wanted to reach: Yellowstone National Park.

My greatest worry when he was younger was letting him go into the men's rooms alone. I had heard about shenanigans in men's rooms and had always told him that I'd be outside by the door. If he needed help, he was to call me. I'd have been mortified if he had called.

However, at sixteen he was about 5'11" and weighed at least 225. He was a lineman on his high school football team and could handle any emergency, I thought.

Off we went, eight days after his sixteenth birthday and eight days after he passed his driving test, with temporary license in his pocket. When we first talked about going to Yellowstone, he announced, "Grandma, I'm not going to drive through Chicago!"

"That's OK, Dorsey; I hadn't planned to let you."

We bypassed Chicago, driving south of the Windy City.

When we went into Iowa, I turned north to visit the Field of Dreams. It looked just like the movie setting, except for two souvenir booths. The corn was beautiful, tall and green, and I half-expected "Shoeless" Joe Jackson to emerge from that cornfield.

As we toured through Iowa and South Dakota on the second day of our trip, Dorsey announced that he didn't want to drive in the mountains. "Don't worry, Dorsey, I had planned to drive in the mountains," I assured him.

About every hour or two, or every two rest areas, Dorsey took his turn driving, and I was completely at ease. I had ridden with him previously. We were traveling in his father's van, because that was the vehicle Dorsey had learned on.

He pulled into a rest area in Iowa, and we each headed for our sides of the restroom. When I returned to the van, it was my turn to take the wheel.

Soon Dorsey slid into the passenger's seat, heaved a big sign of relief, and said, "Grandma, I just saw the worst thing in the men's room!"

Uh oh! My worst fear of sexual predators had arrived, and we had no cell phone.

I thought I'd probably have to call the highway patrol, so I told Dorsey we weren't moving until he told me what it was. I didn't express my fear to him.

"It was so awful, I just can't tell you," he said.

"I'm not starting this car until you do tell me," I replied.

We sat. No action. He finally caught on that I wasn't going to start the engine, so after what seemed like fifteen minutes, he said, "Do you know what a man was doing in there?"

"No, just tell me."

Silence.

"I just can't tell you, Grandma, it was so awful!"

"Dorsey, I'm not moving until you tell me."

Another time of silence.

Finally, he started, mumbling, "He was . . . I can't say it."

Another time of silence.

Again he started, "That man was . . . brushing . . . his . . . false teeth in the washbowl!"

Whew! I could relax.

On to the Badlands, visiting Mt. Rushmore and the Crazy Horse sculpture, and before I knew it, Dorsey said, "Grandma, can I drive in the mountains? But when I look down, it might make me sick."

"Dorsey, when you're driving in the mountains, your eyes hopefully will be on the road."

He was a big help when I was driving in the mountains, for he told me when to shift into low. "Where did you learn that?" I asked.

"My dad told me."

About ten miles east of the entrance to Yellowstone, we decided it was time to find a motel. It was a rustic cabin in the mountain area, and Dorsey's first comment was, "Where's the TV?"

The camp had permission to build a huge campfire, where guests relaxed and told stories of travels.

After our travels through Yellowstone National Park, we were ready to leave.

We went south through Wyoming to I-80, east to Cheyenne, and south on I-25, headed for Greeley, Colorado, to visit my daughter, Sue, son-in-law Steve, and their two children, Nathan and Maya.

Once we were en route home, I asked Dorsey what his favorite place was, and his reply surprised me. "That cabin in the mountains. It was so peaceful."

The following year, we took one more trip together: to Colorado by auto.

The next year at graduation, I asked him what he'd like for a present. He said, "A train trip to Colorado . . . all by myself."

On
Education

"No child shall be left behind" is a federal law, so now the schools are graded. Teachers also are taking flack for students' failures.

"Schools are failing our children," headlines have read.

"Hogwash!" I say. Parents are failing their children, but too many people are not daring to utter those words. The problem is politics.

Schools are expected to educate children, but they cannot raise a child's IQ!

As an eighth grade English and journalism teacher for over seventeen years, I'm at sea as to how to raise a child's IQ, or how to get a child to learn when that child doesn't want to learn. Yet, that's what is expected of teachers.

At a parent-teacher conference, a father claimed that I wasn't motivating his son. He was an educator himself, and he could make no comment when I declared, "Cut it out! You know as well as I do that motivation begins in the cradle."

Another mother claimed that I was telling people that her daughter planned to drop out of school at age sixteen and get married. The girl herself had told some friends her plans during a science class, then blamed me when her mother heard that tale.

After denying having passed on the information, I said, "While you're here, I'd like to talk to you about your daughter's absences from school. This year she was absent forty-nine days in one semester, forty-nine out of eighty."

"Last year she was in a Christian school and never had any problems," Mother replied.

"No problems?" I countered. "Her records show that she was absent forty-nine days in one semester last year, too."

"Well," the mother said, "if you were a Christian, you'd understand."

"Oh, but I am a Christian, and I believe that God wants that girl to be educated. However, she doesn't have a chance if she's not in school forty-nine days out of eighty." The daughter had to repeat eighth grade. I never did learn what kept her daughter out of school so often.

Another mother did her son's homework assignment one day. The good penmanship gave it away. When questioned by his teacher, the mother said, "Well, it got done, didn't it?"

Some parents just do not have a clue. Schools cannot raise a child's IQ!

I never have forgotten the words of my science professor, teaching genetics at the University of Wisconsin, as he pounded on the podium, declaring, "Every one of you must have at least four children!" In 1942, he predicted a "dumbing down of America (my words)."

The answer is not giving schools the A-B-C-D-E grades; it's to educate parents to help, not hinder, their children's education. It's easy to blame teachers; they don't dare speak up.

I propose classes for expectant parents, with records kept on which parents attended those classes. Then give a grade to parents.

Some of my suggestions to parents also include:

· Hug your children often and tell them you love them and expect them to do their best work in school, so that they will be happier as adults.

· Read to your children, beginning at a very early age — well before kindergarten.

· Talk to the young ones and get them to talk to you. It's amazing how often a teacher has a student who cannot express him- or herself.

And here's a controversial opinion:

· If you had a hard time learning, you might consider limiting the size of your family. Heredity might be a factor.

· If your child excuses himself for not doing his lessons by saying, "The teacher doesn't like me," don't take his word for it. Quickly call the school to make an appointment to talk to the teacher. You might be surprised.

At the beginning of each school year, I asked the students to write on a three-by-five-inch card both the mother's and father's home and office telephone numbers.

"Why do you want my dad's number?" they'd ask.

"So if you don't cooperate after a call to Mom, I'll call Dad."

I had to call only one father, because their son's disruptive behavior was way out of control. I can't reveal how angry his mother was because I had called the boy's father, but it worked.

Perhaps this seems that I did not enjoy teaching eighth graders.

Those kids are going through a difficult age: puberty with its boy/girl problems, many blended families, parents going through divorce, time for driver education, and many other changes. I did enjoy the students! They were without guile, often using words not appropriate for eighth graders, but totally innocent and delightful.

Before teaching, I was a theme reader for two Detroit public schools: Central and Wilbur Wright. I assigned many writing opportunities for my eighth grade students. There were a number of them who wrote nothing. Most of my students expressed themselves very well in writing. After all, to write, one has to think. Do I get an E for teaching those who did not do their assignments? Would my school be penalized? Give the parents the E!

One of my students shared with me a keen interest in the witchcraft trials in Colonial America, so we had many personal discussions on the subject. It wasn't until much later that I learned that one of my ancestral grandmothers had been hanged for witchcraft in 1658, in Hartford Square, Connecticut. I was eager to relate that tale to the student several years after she had graduated, but she was killed in an auto accident in Alaska. I never failed to mention to my students on their first days in my class that my g-g-g-g-g-grandmother had been hanged for witchcraft. They got the message.

Eighth grade was the year our students had "sex ed," as we teachers called the unit on reproduction when we discussed it among ourselves.

One day a boy sitting in the rear of the classroom, looking out the window, shouted, "Hey! There are two frogs out there mating!"

As a body, the entire class arose from their seats, intending to witness that act.

"Whoa!" I said. "Please sit down."

One boy shouted, "She wants to check it out for herself."

Yes, I headed for the window, looked out, and said, "Yes, he's right."

Then another student said, "They can't be frogs, because frogs have to mate in the water." I guessed they were toads. That event occurred during the last five minutes of the day. Within two minutes after the class was excused, two of the male teachers entered the classroom to check it out. Such news travels fast!

I loved teaching eighth graders! I was pretty good at controlling disruptive students in my English classes, and journalism class was very casual. One day I eavesdropped on a conversation between four or five girls sitting near my desk. They were complaining about a teacher who had pets. I said, "Do I have pets?"

"Heck no!" one girl exclaimed. "You're mean to everyone!" Great laughter. That girl was the daughter of a school board member.

Every spring our eighth graders went on a field trip to Greenfield Village in Dearborn, with our eighth grade teachers as chaperones. The students signed up for a particular teacher. One year I had a group of ten girls. That was the least exciting group I ever had. The girls were intent on taking each other's pictures the whole day.

The next year it was a group of ten boys who were poor students and real cut-ups. I was razzed unmercifully by the other teachers, but that was best group I ever had. They were afraid of getting lost, so they stayed by my side. They even asked if I'd take their friend Luis, too. I had a little chat with Luis about the behavior I expected, so my group became eleven.

In 1987, the year I retired, I was honored by the art class with a mural and a small replica of that mural. I was so surprised and pleased.

ELEANOR CLAPP SMITH

I grew up in the small town of Galesburg, Michigan (population 1200), about nine miles from Kalamazoo. My family were pioneers of Kalamazoo County. We have nine land grant deeds from the government. While in high school I was the Kalamazoo County Woman's Singles Tennis Championship three times. Besides playing in the school band I played with the first jazz band. I graduated in 1939.

Today I am still playing tennis and have completed twenty-seven years in the "Second Time Around Ladies Band" in Lansing, Michigan. In 1986, we performed on *The Today Show* with Willard Scott. On April 30, 2004, we were invited to play when the last Oldsmobile rolled off the assembly line! I play tenor sax, soprano sax, clarinet, and the "bones"—the oldest known instrument. The first bones came from the ribs of animals!

I graduated from Sparrow Hospital School of Nursing in Lansing, Michigan in 1943. While in training, the Japanese bombed Pearl Harbor. After graduation I served in the Navy Nurse Corps from 1944-1946, at Philadelphia Naval Hospital and Parris Island Naval Hospital, a Marine Corps Base. After World War II, I was a visiting nurse in Baltimore and Washington, D.C. I served on the Sparrow Hospital Women's Board of Managers for over twenty-five years. I am currently writing the History of Nursing at Sparrow. I am proud to be a participant of the Harvard Nurses Health Study, for over twenty-eight years. It is the longest most comprehensive study ever done on women. Their findings will impact women of the world. I have had a very exciting life!

Now that I am eighty-four years old, it is a joy to write about my experiences. It is the "stuff" life is made of. I wouldn't have missed this opportunity!

Write as if You Are Telling the Story to a Friend

I woke up one morning and the "The Unexpected" came into my mind very clearly. It was one of my favorite experiences in my career as a visiting nurse. The recollection was so vivid that I was able to sit down and write it in one sitting. Usually when I write, I record a sequence of events, then I go back and change the wording. Often, after I have sketched an outline, I start the story again from a different point of view.

I am older now and events from the past pop up into my mind, triggered by some other situation that happens. I have more ideas that come to mind, and I know I'll never get them all written. I have had such an exciting life. I always write in longhand so I can cross out a sentence or rewrite the story. The computer is too cumbersome for me.

My writing has changed since I first began my memoirs. Our teacher said, "Write as if you are telling another person your story." This has helped me so much. That is my suggestion to someone who might like to write his or her memoirs. Write as if you are telling the story to a friend; get it down on paper, especially family stories. They are the "stuff" life is made of.

The
Unexpected

I was a navy nurse in World War II. When I returned to civilian life in 1946, I became a visiting nurse in Baltimore. I loved my work. The patients were my friends. I was assigned to a walking district, where I walked from house to house instead of riding the streetcar or driving a Visiting Nurse car.

One day I was sent to care for a patient in another nurse's district. This was a poor neighborhood where the houses were separate, unlike the ghetto where families lived in a single room in one big building. There was no bell. I knocked on the door. No answer. I knocked harder, several times. No answer. I stood looking around for someone to ask about Mrs. B.

Just then, I heard a window open above me. From the second floor a key was being lowered down to me on a string about ten feet long. I didn't see anyone. No one spoke. I took the key and unlocked the door. It looked like the door led into the house, but actually it led to a narrow, dark flight of stairs to the second floor.

Mrs. B was there to greet me. I gave her back her key. She appeared to be a pleasant woman. My instructions were to give her a tub bath. In those days, the Metropolitan Insurance Company gave its members six free visits a year. This must have been the case here.

The second floor was one rectangular room. It looked like an attic, with a pitched roof, no ceiling, and just boards on the ends and sides of the room. At one end was a table with three chairs, a stove, and a refrigerator. On one side there was a bathtub and a toilet. There were no partitions.

Mrs. B and I talked a bit while I laid down my nurse's bag, took my jacket off, and washed my hands. I filled the tub with warm water and gave her a nice bath. She told me that her son was in the army. She was hoping he would come home safely and that it was hard for her to get along without him. She missed him. My heart went out to her. She was very easy to talk with. She didn't complain about her circumstances, although the living arrangements looked barren and bleak to me.

When I finished her bath, she just sat in the tub and did not say anything. I was disturbed because I thought maybe I hadn't done something her regular nurse usually did. Then she turned to me and said, "That felt so good. Could you just give me another bath all over again?"

It was a pleasure. She was so sweet I wished I could have taken her home with me rather than leave her in this barren room.

About three years later I was sent to an address in a middle-class neighborhood. The houses were on plots of land with grass and shrubbery. I knocked on the door. A young man opened it. I introduced myself. He said, "I know you have come to give my mother a bath."

Just then, Mrs. B came into the room. We both recognized each other. We hugged. I had tears in my eyes. She didn't cry at all. She had lived in three years of bliss, reunited with her son.

While I gave her a bath, she told me her son had come home from the army safely. He had gotten a GI loan and bought this house for them to live in. She just smiled and was her pleasant self. She was happy to be living back with her son in such nice circumstances.

As a visiting nurse, I learned early that I hadn't lived enough of life yet to understand what my help truly meant to people who lived in circumstances very different from my own. I had no idea of the conditions people coped with. Poor people are wise people. They learn how to survive in their situation. I remember wondering that if I had been born in the ghetto, how would I have known there was a better life? If I did find out, how would I get out of the ghetto on my own? There are so many children born into poverty. I kept wanting to take patients home with me, but I never did.

A Mother Dies, a Baby Lives

I was a third-year nursing student at Sparrow Hospital in Lansing, Michigan. The year was 1943. I was twenty years old. (At present I am eighty-four.) As a senior nurse, I was on night duty, alone on a floor for probably ten-plus patients. Sparrow was a small, 150-bed hospital. Night duty can be scary, but if you need help you call the night supervisor.

This night, a young woman in her thirties was admitted to our four-bed ward. She was about eight months pregnant and very sick; she was not talking or reacting. Dr. Dunn ordered blood tests. In a very short time, he determined she had meningitis. Immediately the doctor ordered her to be moved to a private room. Meningitis is contagious. The other patients in the ward were at risk of contamination. Dr. Dunn helped me move the patient.

We barely got her situated when she expired. Dr. Dunn brought a sterile pack of instruments into the room. I assisted him while he calmly made the long abdominal incision required to save the baby's life. Then carefully, very gently, he lifted the live baby from the lifeless body of the mother. He methodically severed and tied the umbilical cord. The night supervisor took the baby to the nursery. Dr. Dunn instructed me to go to the nurses' home and change my uniform, which I did. I then went back on duty. This was necessary to prevent contamination of my patients and myself.

You can imagine how much I had to tell my nursing friends the next day. We discussed the whole situation thoroughly. We all thought Dr. Dunn was a hero. (He was a favorite doctor among the nurses.) We felt so sad for the mother. In later years, I would pass Dr. Dunn on the street or see him at the hospital. Whenever I saw him, I thought about the events of this story. Dr. Mansel Dunn has passed on.

After this many years, the baby girl would be about sixty years old. I wonder . . . did she live to grow up? Did she know how she was born? I would love to meet her.

Our Gorgeous Nest

The windows behind our TV are covered with a network of vines, leafed out at this time of year. My husband and I noticed two birds fluttering their wings and turning their heads constantly among the vines. Then in an instant they would zoom away. My husband said he thought they were building a nest.

We could see the architecture of a nest taking place as the days passed. The birds would flutter around as if they were consulting with each other about how the nest would be situated. We couldn't tell the "he" from the "she." One would zoom down, pick up a small, slender twig about two inches long, put it in place in the nest, then sit on it, just as humans would sit in a chair to try it out for comfort. One flew up with a piece of clear plastic about an inch square. The bird dropped it at least three times, then carefully placed it next to our window. It resembled a shield to keep us from looking into the nest, we thought. Or maybe the bird family wanted a lovely bay window. It was remarkable to see the mother and father plan their house architecturally, to be a safe, warm place for their family.

The nest rests on the only two vines that cross each other, providing a solid base that won't move. The vines are strong. The leaves protect the nest from rainfall, direct sunlight, and prying eyes.

This is a gorgeous nest, built to perfect specification.

I wonder, do birds have a brain?

Zoom! There they go after a dinner of worms. We can't wait for the eggs and babies.

Molly

While I served as a navy nurse in World War II, I was transferred from Philadelphia Naval Hospital to the naval hospital on Parris Island, South Carolina, a marine corps base. Scuttlebutt (rumor) labeled it the "end of the world." It was a terrible place. Recruits tried to escape by swimming away or committing suicide. The drill instructors had complete charge of a recruit's life. They could injure them at will with a swagger stick. Recruits learned to march in sand in over 100-degree heat. When they dropped, we took care of them in the hospital.

Being commissioned officers, the nurses lived in houses on the base instead of in barracks. Each night, two black maids prepared and served our evening meal. We were dressed in duty uniform and seated according to rank. The chief nurse sat at the head of the table, with the j.g.s (junior grade lieutenants). The rest of us ensigns sat at other tables. My friend Molly sat at the head table. She said it wasn't much fun, the conversation so-so. She would turn around and wink at us while we had more fun.

Molly grew up in Kimball, Minnesota, the twelfth of fourteen children. She trained at the Sisters of Mercy nursing school in Devil's Lake, North Dakota. Molly and I hit it off right away because we both liked to play tennis.

All too soon she was transferred to the Navy Medical Center in Bethesda, Maryland. While there, she cared for Carl Vinson's wife, Mary, who had severe rheumatoid arthritis. Carl Vinson, a Democrat from Milledgeville, Georgia, was chairman of the powerful Armed Forces Committee in Congress. Mrs. Vinson and Molly became great friends. Mrs. Vinson suggested that Molly meet Mr. Vinson's aide, Tillman Snead II. They were married in 1946. Molly resigned her commission and nursed Mary Vinson until her death in 1950.

Mr. Vinson invited Till and Molly to live with him in his Chevy Chase, Maryland, home. The Sneads eventually had two sons, Tillman III and Carl. Chairman Vinson was "Grandpa". Mr. Vinson retired from Congress in 1964. The Sneads lived with him in Milledgeville until he died.

Molly and I always kept in touch. After the war, I lived in Hyattsville, Maryland. One time we met in Washington, D.C. to go shopping, taking little Tillman with us. He was darling, hiding from us among the clothes.

Molly invited me to visit several times. Mr. Vinson was like a friend, very easy to talk with. I learned that Mr. Vinson went to Washington as a young congressman in 1914, at age thirty-one, the youngest member of the Sixty-third Congress. His public service extended over fifty years, longer than any other congressman in history. When he took a seat on the Naval Affairs Committee in 1917 he became a national figure through his political philosophy, "military preparedness," which took the United States through two world wars. Mr. Vinson completed twenty-five terms of office. No man served in the House of Representatives longer. In October 1964, Mr. Vinson was presented with the highest civilian award in the Unites States, the Presidential Medal of Freedom. He had served with nine presidents.

On October 11, 1975, Molly invited me to attend the ceremony of the keel-laying of the U.S.S. Carl Vinson, the world's most powerful nuclear-powered aircraft carrier, in honor of Mr. Vinson, at Newport News, Virginia.

Molly was asked to christen the ship. This may sound like an easy task, but Molly told me over the phone that the champagne bottle is very thick and hard to break over the bow of the ship. She had been practicing on a tree in her backyard. Young Tillman had gotten into drinking some of the champagne.

We both were excited about being together again. On the day of the christening, Molly wore a stunning red suit. She sat on the platform with Mr. Vinson and other dignitaries. She knew where we were sitting and waved to us. Afterwards she asked me how I liked the band playing "Anchors Aweigh." I loved it!

There was an elaborate reception after the christening. It was wonderful to see Molly, although our private time together was brief.

It takes six years to build a ship. In 1982, Molly invited me to Norfolk for the commissioning of the ship. Mr. Vinson had passed on. The ceremony was held in the hanger of the ship. The airplanes had been put out on the flight deck. Molly made brief comments about Mr. Vinson. She looked wonderful and spoke well. I was very proud to know her.

All guests were taken on a tour of the ship. It is like a floating city with living quarters for 6,000 personnel. My friend's generosity was overwhelming.

Once more Molly invited me to a special event. This time it was Tillman Snead III's wedding in Milledgeville. We really went wild. It was an extravagant, lovely wedding. That was the last time I saw Molly. We kept in touch by phone for awhile. We've lost contact, but my memories are still vivid. I had read in the paper that the U.S.S. Carl Vinson was anchored in the Atlantic near Boston.

One of my classmates at Sparrow in Lansing had a son, Mike Riordan, who was retiring from the navy. He was captain of a submarine stationed in Bremerton, Washington, on Puget Sound. I was invited to the retirement ceremony. As we were walking up the steps to a beautiful, huge white house provided for captains, Mike said, "Eleanor, the U.S.S. Carl Vinson is parked in my front yard." There it was, floating peacefully out on Puget Sound. The scene brought back all the wonderful memories of my friend Molly.

Edward Wheeler Sparrow Hospital

In August 1940, my parents drove me from Galesburg, Michigan to Lansing, Michigan, where I entered Sparrow Nursing School. That night as I laid my head on my pillow, I thought: "These three years of training will be the best days of my life!" From then on, Sparrow was in my heart forever.

The hospital was founded by a woman in 1896. In 1912, through a generous gift of $100,000 by Edward Sparrow, a modern forty-four-bed hospital was constructed on Michigan Avenue. The hospital was managed by dual boards. The men on the Board of Trustees were responsible for maintenance of the building and the staff of doctors. The Women's Board of Trustees was responsible for the housekeeping and nursing staff. The hospital still has dual boards. I am proud to say that today, Sparrow is one of the best one hundred hospitals in the nation.

From the beginning of my love for Sparrow, I could never have dreamed of the stories I would learn about the amazing history of Sparrow.

Bath Disaster

On May 18, 1927, in Bath, a small town outside of Lansing, Mr. Kehoe, a demented former janitor at the local school, planted 500 pounds of dynamite in the school. Forty-five children were killed, and many others were seriously injured. After the explosion, Mr. Kehoe went home, where he had wired his farm, and blew up his house, killing his wife, who had just come home from the hospital following surgery. He destroyed the barn, with the animals inside, and planted mines in the fields so no one could work the land. He drove back to the school, parked his car in front of the school, and blew himself up. This disaster was considered the worst of its kind in the United States until the Oklahoma bombing of the Murrah Federal Building.
The following quotes and notes are from nursing school graduates who worked at the hospital on the day of the disaster. Their remarks

are from the book, *Sparrow Tales.*

Marie Fenner, 1924, said "At the hospital, parents wanted to know whether their children were in the wreckage or in the hospital. Is he or she alive?"

Bonnie Vowler Smith, 1924, heard the SOS on the radio asking all Sparrow nurses to report to the hospital. "I got my neighbor to look after my kids and went right to the hospital. There were screaming children and parents trying to find each other. It was heartbreaking."

Florence Lechlitner Alexander, 1927, said the phones at the hospital rang at about 10:00 a.m., informing the nurses to be ready to help the victims of the explosion either in emergency or in the Operating Room. "We heard the sirens coming, but we surely were not prepared for the sights we were to remember for a long time. The doors opened, the children were wheeled in, all ages, teachers. Soon we had them waiting in stretchers on both sides of the hall. We gave a lot of hypos for pain and shock. A lot of parents came crowding in trying to locate their children. One teacher died on the stretcher. She was really blown apart. For a week in my sleep I could see and hear these poor kids cry."

Ione Inglis Week, 1928, said, "There was a strange, quiet atmosphere over the whole hospital broken by a sobbing parent, who finally found her child, a scream now and then. Everyone was saying prayers. My roommate was in charge of the morgue, where there were bodies on bodies. For a long time after we could not get to sleep at night, so we would huddle in one room and talk the night away trying to find the answer as to why a man would wire the school house to do such a deed."

Helen Miller Perrine, 1929, said, "School children began arriving by car and ambulance. They were all ages with brick, cement, dust, rubble through their hair, clothing, all embedded in their wounds, lacerations, fractures, multiple bruises and fright. Several were in shock, some with skull fractures, matted hair from hemorrhage and rubble, foreign objects in wounds and eyes."

Ninth grader Perry Hart had a small piece of steel embedded in his ankle. Following surgery, he developed osteomyelitis in his ankle. Idiform gauze packing dressings had to be replaced three times daily, decreasing as he improved from this very painful procedure. He used to play the harmonica to cheer up the ward patients and the nurses as well as himself.

One little girl who was pulled from the rubble unhurt, went home to bed, pulled the covers over her head, and stayed there a week. There are twenty living survivors of the "Bath Disaster." They have a reunion every year.

World-Famous Quadruplets Are Born

On May 19, 1930, quadruplets were born at Sparrow, to Carl and Sadie Marlok. We believe they were the only identical quadruplets in the world at that time, all coming from the same human egg cell. Nursing graduate Eloise Graham Harding, 1931, said, "Agnes Gilmore, 1919, was O.B. Supervisor. Dr. Howard Haynes delivered them. He was a general practitioner and did not anticipate a multiple delivery. Dr. Haynes handed one baby to her, then another, and another. When he said there is one more, she thought he was not serious, so it was a few seconds before she turned around to receive the fourth baby. Sparrow made the national news that day."

Sparrow nurses were famous because the little girls were born at Sparrow. We have a precious picture of the "quads" being held by Nurses Duncan, Morley, Jessep, and Raven Severns. The *Lansing State Journal* printed a coupon for readers to send in girls' names. The response was 3,107 pieces of mail with 9,000 sets of names. Sadie Marlok selected their names to begin with E,W,S,H, and named them in order of birth: Edna, Wilma, Sarah, and Helen. The winner of the contest was submitted by thirteen-year-old Nancy Haynes, daughter of the doctor who delivered the babies. Reams of information have been recorded about their childhood, growth, and development.

Sarah explains about growing up that they were asked to report to the National Institute of Health, in Washington, D.C.: "The doctors wanted to study us. They gave us all kinds of tests and hooked us up to all kinds of machines. They watched us work and asked about our dreams. We had to stay there five years." There are many pictures of them in Miss Simmons Dancing School. They performed professionally. Sarah was the only one to marry. She had two sons, David and William. William died. David now has three young sons. Wilma died several years ago. Helen died last year. Edna and Sarah live in an apartment building. Sarah is giving some of her memorabilia to Sparrow archives, so we see her frequently. Edna and Sarah are still the oldest living quads in the world.

Polio Tissue Isolated in Autopsy at Sparrow

In 1937, a nineteen-year-old man died at Sparrow Hospital, the victim of the dreaded disease of polio. Sparrow doctors sent tissue from the autopsy to the University of Michigan, in Ann Arbor. From there the tissue went to the National Institute of Health, where the infecting agent was identified as a new strain of polio. From this Lansing strain came exhaustive research nationwide and, ultimately, the vaccine created by Dr. Jonas Salk in the 1950s. This was the first effective preventative of polio. By the year 2000, health officials were close to the goal of ridding the world of polio. The tragic death of the Lansing man and the work of Sparrow doctors helped make this possible.

Fifty-six Sparrow Nurses Served in World War II; Thirteen in World War I

During World War II, a large plaque with the names of the fifty-six Sparrow nurses who had served the military was hung in the lobby of Sparrow Hospital. The plaque has been placed in our newly formed archives. We have pictures and the names of all thirteen World War I nurses. One of those army nurses was Irene McDonald Braman. She graduated from Sparrow in 1914, and graduated from Boston Floating Hospital in 1917. Nurses cared for children whose parents put them on the ship during the influenza epidemic of 1918. She was sent to Italy for five weeks, to Greece for three weeks, and to Serbia for seven months. She received a medal from the Serbian Red Cross. I knew Irene and think she is one of our star nurses. I was in second-year training when the Japanese bombed Pearl Harbor. About half of my class served in the army or navy nurse corps.

My plan was to be a missionary nurse, but I later decided to become a navy nurse and served in the naval hospital in Philadelphia and the marine corps base on Parris Island, South Carolina. Three of my classmates, Marge Madole Riordan, Mary Helen Richardson, and Helen Bouck Adams, served on the same hospital train in England and France. It is unbelievable that they served together. The names of all the Sparrow nurses who served in the military have been recorded in the Women's Memorial in Washington, D.C. Our book,

Sparrow Tales, has been placed in the libraries of Sparrow Hospital and the State of Michigan, as well as in the Women's History Archives, Schlessinger Library, Radcliff College Library in Cambridge, Massachusetts, the Library of Congress, and the Army War College Library in Carlisle, Pennsylvania.

My oldest sister, Charlotte Hazen, lived in Lansing. Her son, Paul, was born at Sparrow just before Pearl Harbor. My classmates reported every day to me how he was. Because I didn't work in the nursery, I couldn't see him. Paul became CEO of Wells Fargo. When my niece, Susan, was born, I was working in O.B. Dr. Wadley could not get there for the delivery. The intern, Dr. Trecott, delivered her. I was the scrub nurse. That was exciting for me and the family. Years went by. I lived in the East after the war. I returned to Lansing in 1956, when my younger sister Mary Louise died of breast cancer. Her three children, Brad, Maurice, and Marcia, were all born at Sparrow. I was asked to serve on the Women's Board at Sparrow, which I did for twenty-seven years. I learned so much more about Sparrow apart from a student's view. The Women's Board decided to sponsor the Breast Self-Examination Clinic. As I was the only nurse on the board, they asked me to be the coordinator. My job lasted twenty years! I wanted to do it. My sister was gone, and self-examination could save a woman's life.

Many changes have taken place at Sparrow: the new professional building, the skywalk, new treatments, heart catheterizations, by-passes. It seems to me that miracles are happening all the time, compared with how we functioned as nurses in the 1940s.

For the past twenty years, I was caretaker for my husband, who had emphysema, an aortic aneurysm, six by-passes, and operations on both carotids. He has been in E.R. at least twenty times. He was on oxygen for six years. Each day, I was thankful for Sparrow Hospital's expertise. He needed and used all its facilities. He died on December 11, 2004, in hospice on the St. Lawrence campus. Sparrow Hospital met all our needs. Even the new hospice is gorgeous.

Now you can understand why I have come to love Sparrow.

ELEANOR MARAZITA

Curiosity, love of learning, giving, receiving and nurturing have been a part of the tapestry of my life. For me, each day is a gift! The next person or experience may be the most exciting yet.

My childhood took place in the farmlands of Indiana and Indianapolis, the Capitol. After age ten, we moved to Michigan. My formal education was in Cheboygan Schools, Central Michigan University, and Michigan State University. Over the years my political concerns have evolved from very conservative to moderate. My curiosity about people and their stories motivated me to see other cultures and to study their history. Travel throughout the world is my avocation. Reading, drama, music, and storytelling have enlarged my life.

Community involvement in numerous organizations, at all levels, has given me an opportunity to serve and learn. I spent seventy years as a student, thirty years as a teacher, and fifty years as a wife. My husband and I parented seven fantastic children through adulthood and they have presented us with fifteen wonderful grandchildren. We have hosted exchange students from nine countries. These experiences have supported and nurtured me as a person.

When I asked a friend to define me in five words, they were: curious, energetic, organized, flexible and tenacious to the end. I am eternally a student with a thirst for knowledge.

For the First Draft, Write as Fast as You Can

My choice to participate in a writing class gave me a scheduled time to write. Putting words on paper isn't easy for me. Memories are my markers and measurements. I started by making a brief sentence list of situations I remembered, or had been told about, of my infant and preschool years in Indiana.

Putting the first brief headline on paper primed my recall of more details. Then I decided what could or should be left out, so the story wouldn't have too much detail for the reader.

Before I sit down to write, I allow myself a block of time, usually an hour, before I need to leave for class. Then I write as fast as I can until the timer rings. Before class starts, I read what I have written to myself and make any obvious corrections. This first draft just flows. I revised to make technical corrections that allowed me to stay true to my story. My limited time and lack of disciplined procedures and seventy years of great potential stories have been frustrating for me.

I have written in longhand, as I'm not skilled on the computer. I am distracted when making corrections. My writing flows along with my thinking. I try to listen to my inner dialogue.

A friend has typed my handwritten notes, and used grammar- and spell- check features. This process is especially helpful when making changes and corrections.

On the Ledge of the School Window

When fall came, it was time for all my friends to go to school. The square brick and stone elementary school was close to our house. We could run through that same empty lot where we played hide-and-seek. There was a path that led right to the school. On the first day of school, I learned that I wasn't going to go because I was too young. Now that wasn't fair. I could read the headlines and words on the newspaper placed under the food on my wooden high chair tray.

I watched the neighbors leave. It was too quiet, and my little brother was too small to play with me. Outdoors alone, I decided to go and see what the other kids were doing. I crawled up on the wide ledge of the school window. The cement was dusty and scratched my knees, but I could see into the room. I tapped on the window and waved at a neighbor boy when he turned around (with the rest of the class) to see what was happening. I watched and waved while the teacher talked to the class and then to my neighbor. He came out of the room, out to the window, and grabbed my hand. He was mad! He walked me back to the house.

I repeated those trips for three days, and then the teacher found out my name and sent a note to my parents. We didn't have a phone. My folks were proud of my love for reading and wanting to be at school, but they didn't want me to be a nuisance. Their solution was to make a chest harness with an attached five-foot leash. They fastened me by the leash to the metal clothesline that was stretched between our clothes poles. The poles were about twenty feet apart. I wore quite a path running back and forth, waiting for my friends to come home after school.

Schools continue to represent learning and fun for me.

Photo Scraps

The night my parents were married in 1933, they ate their celebration dinner at a Greek restaurant in Elwood, Indiana. The radio was on and the voice of Franklin D. Roosevelt said, "The banks are closed!" The only money my parents had was $320 in the now-closed bank. My dad was twenty and had been driving a truck at night and finishing high school during the day. My mother had just graduated at eighteen and was living on her family's farm.

Although my parents' life was harsh, I was never aware of any of their struggles. My earliest memory is of hanging by my knees on the porch rail with my skirt hanging over my head. I kept pushing it out of the way so I could see what was going on. There was a car hooked up to a flatbed trailer, and my family was moving furniture onto it.

My grandmother was helping my mother. Although I wondered what was going on, the sunshine and dust were more interesting. Many years later my grandmother told me I couldn't possibly remember that move because I was only two years old.

We lived in a house on a corner lot on a dirt road that led to a large cemetery. My dad added a pantry and a partition to a larger room, so my brother and I could each have a room of our own. My bed was against the new wall, and I could hear critters scratching there at night. Our outhouse had a half-moon carved in the door. I was too short to look in or out and had to rattle the handle to find out if it was in use.

There were several houses like ours on our dirt road. I loved to run and play with the other children. One favorite activity was to grab hands to make a human chain, and then run into the cemetery to a low-branched elderberry tree. When berries dropped to the ground, we would make a circle and start moving faster, stamping berries til they spattered our legs. Then we'd all fall down and roll in the mashed berries.

My mother and dad worked long hours and had a young girl stay with my brother and me during the day. One Sunday there was a loud knock at the door. My mother answered it. The man at the door said he was taking pictures of children and thought we would be good models. My mother told him that she didn't have any money. He said he'd take the pictures anyway and we could pay for them next week. My mother said she wouldn't have any money then, either. He convinced her to put a pretty dress on me and posed me sitting on an end table.

The next Sunday he was back with a manila envelope. We sat around our kitchen table while he took the four pictures out, one at a time, and arranged them. He wanted only twenty-five cents each. My mother never cried, but I could see tears starting to form.

She said again, "I don't have any money."

His face started to flush, "Look, lady, the film costs money and I can't give these pictures away. Don't you have something you can trade?"

Now my mother's face flushed, and she said, "No."

He pushed the wooden chair back, and it teetered as he left the room. He slammed the door and started across the back lot. We rushed to the front window and watched him. The weeds were waist high, and I could see burrs catching on his pants. The wind was blowing, and he was making slow progress. He finally stopped, took out the envelope, and looked at it in disgust. He pulled out the four pictures and, one at a time, tore them and threw the pieces in the air. He brushed his hands together, dropped his head, turned, and walked out of the field. We never saw him again.

After he was out of sight, we went out to the lot and carefully picked up the little scraps of pictures. We spread them out on the kitchen table and fitted them together like jigsaw puzzles. I still have them.

4-H
with Heart

"I pledge my head to clearer thinking, my hands to greater service, my heart to greater loyalty, and my health to better living."

This pledge for 4-H-ers was a mantra for me as a 4-H Club project member. For my first project, I pulled a thread to straighten the coarse fabric, and measured and folded the hem at both ends of a towel. I painfully pinned, with straight pins exactly at right angles, and then basted with regular half-inch stitches. The next step was to practice neat overhand stitches for the finished hem. The now grubby, much-handled towel was washed, then line dried, pressed, labeled, and finally turned in to be displayed at the local project exhibit in a school gym in Indianapolis. My project was given a blue ribbon. The great fun I remember in 4-H was underway.

My family moved from the agricultural area of central Indiana to northern lower Michigan. For the next seven years, 4-H continued to be my main extracurricular activity in Cheboygan, a town of 10,000 people. The main project work for girls was sewing, cooking, canning, and gardening. Both boys and girls could raise and show a variety of livestock, including chickens, rabbits, cows, sheep, and pigs. Project work was judged at a county level by volunteer leaders. The blue ribbon winners progressed to the state level and finally to the national level, where a few students who qualified were treated to a week in Chicago.

I continued my interest in club projects at the Extension Office in Cheboygan, the county seat. The number of projects available continued to increase. I was recognized for several kinds of projects, including furniture refinishing, knitting, sewing, canning, baking, and public speaking. My first trip outside Cheboygan, except to visit relatives, was to Michigan State University for state-level competition in the summer of 1948. We stayed in corrugated metal Quonset huts. These had been constructed to provide classroom space for the onslaught of World War II veterans taking advantage of the GI Bill. Even though the huts were hot in the summer, cold in the winter, and always dusty and noisy, I was thrilled to be there on a college campus with other kids who had similar interests.

I was awarded trips to MSU for the next four summers and met many friends. I loved to watch the presentations of different projects, including my favorite: the animal showings. Both the animals and the 4-H-ers were being judged. The animals were housed under the bleachers at the football stadium. The area was closely policed, and the only smell was when you were in close contact with the animals. These were clean, warm animal smells. Each cow or pig had been raised as a special project. They reached the state level because they looked good and behaved well. All of the animals were groomed within an inch of their lives. They were curried and fine- brushed. Talc powder was used on white hair, and oil on darker hair. The hooves were waxed and buffed – they were real works of art. At the close of the season, the animals were auctioned to restaurants or animal breeders.

My friend, Paul, asked me to come and watch him show his litter of pigs. The showing required seven pigs and a show person. The idea was to keep the pigs in order by guiding them with a board. A piece of plywood larger than the pigs was allowed. The pigs seemed to flow along together with a change of direction caused by just a slight motion of Paul with his board. It was almost like watching a sheep dog control its herd. I'd never watched pigs before.

Although this litter of white Poland pigs was small, it was a few months old. The pigs had been selected for their shape, alertness, and agility. Paul told me about their personalities and how they behaved. He had one male runt that was very smart and quick, and its tail stood up with a double curl. His tail straightened as a warning that he was going to take off. They'd be moving along as a group, and then the pig's tail would start to straighten and away he'd go. Paul was good, but that pig was a thinker. I still laugh when I think about that pig and his tail.

During my senior year in high school, I became a club leader. My younger brother, Bill, was a member. No tea towel for him. He made a short-sleeved shirt. He did a good job of following directions and using a sewing machine for the first time. The judge brought it to my attention that I had goofed: I had told my brother to put the buttonholes and buttons on the wrong side for male clothing.

In my last year as an active member, my sewing project was a red, lined coat, cut from a blanket. I also made a two-piece tweed fitted suit with piping in the seams, self-covered buttons, and bound button holes. This was a pretty complex project. I was chosen to be in the state style show at Michigan State University. My folks came down to see me. I was one of the top ten selected to go to the Michigan State Fair to model.

My final honor was going to the 4-H Club Congress in Chicago. There were 4,000 students there. The Michigan delegation stayed at the Palmer House Hotel. Each delegation brought something to exchange with the other 4-H delegates. The most impressive delegates were from Texas and wore cowboy hats, vests, and cowboy boots. Their trade items were live horned toads. Michigan delegates brought Petoskey stones.

The final night we had an elegant sit-down dinner. The entrée was a cut of rare roast beef and twice-baked potatoes. Our group was sitting on a balcony overlooking the main floor. I could see the other delegates on the floor. They were a panorama of movement and trading.

The waiters were busy returning the untouched plates of beef that was too rare and the fancy potatoes to the kitchen. My farm-bred mother would have sent hers back, too. However, I had learned to enjoy rare beef along with my dad, who had grown up with town habits.

After completing college, I was a 4-H leader for fifteen years, and our children participated in available projects. My memories of the 4-H pledge and my sharing with the other members are still a steady glow for me, sixty years later.

Main Street

When we moved to Cheboygan I was ten years old, and it wasn't unusual to hear people speaking Polish and French. They had come as immigrants looking for lumbering and farmland. People would stop me on the street and ask me to talk because I had a Hoosier accent and sounded funny.

Saturday night in Cheboygan had a feeling of expectation. I worked in a dairy bar, where we served ice cream in sundaes, shakes, splits, sodas, and malts. Each worker was expected to do whatever needed to be done. That included scooping ice cream and getting it ready to be delivered to the booths. When the customers left, the dirty dishes were bussed. Counter tops covered with used ice cream dishes had to be washed by hand and the counters polished. I developed a skin allergy on my hands from the detergent that summer, but I still had to wash dishes and help clean up. My shift started at 3:00 p.m. and lasted until the store closed at 9:00 p.m. It usually took an hour to scrape down the grill and have everything clean and shipshape.

I can still taste the hamburgers from that grill. First, we scooped the hamburger in a level scoop, patted it into a patty, and put it on the hot grill. While the burger was sizzling, we cut the bun in half, brushed the top with butter and grilled it, and put the bottom half on top of the meat. That was flipped over onto a plate and covered with the grilled top. Pickles, ketchup, and mustard were added to taste.

We had a screen door on the front of the store. I can still feel the handle and hear the slap of the door closing. A perfect Saturday evening began on a balmy night. The walk across the Cheboygan River Bridge, with a pause to check out the lights on the icebreaker, was a pleasant two miles to the center of town. By 10:00 p.m. the stores were closed, except for the thirteen bars. Young people parked their cars at the curb and rolled down the windows. They were checking out the people who were walking the street to see and be seen. Adding to the fun were two lanes of cars passing each other and driving very slowly down the street looking for anything interesting. By 10:00 p.m., almost every unmarried person had chosen a driver in a car to ride with. The parade left town and headed to Mackinaw City. The route was a lovely road with thick pine trees on both sides and an occasional glimpse of the water of the Straits. The parade of cars headed directly for a large wooden building called The Barn. The dirt parking area was always packed, and the lights and music vibrated in the summer evening. For the four years of my life in high school, I went to The Barn every Saturday night.

The music was live, loud, and repetitious. The polkas sounded just like the waltzes, but they were fun to dance to anyway. We did Grange-style square dancing, which consisted of four partners forming the sides of the squares. The caller sang the calls and the first partner led the call. The other three followed the lead. If you weren't sure of the call, you'd head for the fourth-couple position so you could watch and learn the pattern. There hasn't been another period of my life where this kind of dancing was possible.

When I went to 4-H Club Congress in Chicago, the 4,000 delegates had the use of a two-story dance hall. The upstairs was for round dancing and the downstairs was for square dancing. Eight of us formed a square and found out that we were all from different states, but we all knew how to square dance. The caller hollered out, "Anyone who doesn't know how to square dance?" We all said, "No." When the dance started, we found that some of us had different movements for the same calls. The first do-si-do had us twisted between straight handshake style and gripped hands with the girl turned half around before she was released to go on to her next partner. Many were accustomed to the Western style, where each set has four separate calls, and you don't get a chance to correct yourself. That was a hot, sweaty, wonderful night of fun and turned out to be my final square dance.

I was seventeen and had never really traveled outside of Michigan except to visit family in Indiana. I had been selected to be a delegate to represent Michigan in my skill areas at the national congress in Chicago. We were supervised, of course, but it was in a huge city with thousands of other people my age who had been selected as I had. That trip reinforced my desire to meet interesting people and to travel.

The next Saturday night, when I got back to Cheboygan, the parade and mating ritual continued on Main Street. I've never been part of that kind of scene since I graduated from high school in my small town.

Expanding
Horizons

My dream of travel began when I was six years old. My fascination prompted me to write to a travel agency and ask for information on a trip to Europe. Agents came to call on my parents, who were surprised at their sales pitch and just laughed at the possibility of overseas travel that I had requested. Until I was an adult, there was never money enough for my family to travel distances by car or plane and, in my family, girls weren't permitted to hitchhike.

In college, I met and married my husband, Phil. Twelve years later we had our seventh child. Traveling was still not a financial possibility.

Phil said he wasn't interested in traveling abroad until he had seen the USA. So, three years later, I started teaching full time with a goal to travel. I wanted to celebrate finishing my master's degree by taking camping trips with our family in the USA. A few days after I graduated, we started out on a five-week, 8,000-mile trip of the western states.

During the summers for the next four years, we rented a pop-up camper and took our kids to every state in the continental U.S. The travel bug was mine, and the only way we could travel was on a shoestring. Phil and kids really would rather have stayed at home. During the school year I researched places of interest and mapped the routes. We also planned menus to keep our costs within our tight budget, and organized the storage of food, clothing, etc., in our camper. As the older kids got into high school and had jobs with conflicting schedules, the number of summer travelers began to dwindle.

When we traveled, I was the navigator. Phil drove, and two kids were assigned to read the travel books and find a camping site with running water, flush toilets, and electricity. Have you ever tried to back up a pop-up trailer without outside mirrors? The mirrors were missing on our first trip, so another requirement was a pull-through slot at a campground.

One year, our car died the week before our planned departure, so we started out in a new nine-passenger station wagon. It was a beautiful navy blue station wagon with fake wood panels. Every two hours, we had a rest stop and rotated seating positions in the car. Have you ever tried to sit with two other people in facing pop-up seats in the back of a car? We had carefully planned our meals and had all the food packed for the trip. On the road, we would buy milk and bread, but that was it. For the next five weeks, we slept on fold-down beds, with two or three people per bed, head to foot. The kids' memories of that trip are different from mine.

Our first stop was in Hannibal, Missouri. I was excited to see the Mississippi River and decided to go to see the Mark Twain memorials the first morning before breakfast. When we got to the park area, I got out the nine plastic cereal bowls, filled them with cereal, poured milk and nine glasses of Tang, and turned around to call the kids. They had disappeared, along with my husband. A tour bus had just pulled up and the tourists were getting out. My husband led the kids in retreat with, "Who's that crazy lady up there?"

Our second night in Kansas, we were in a very flat camping area. I went promptly to sleep while Phil and the kids hung on for dear life as high winds hit our camper and rocked it most of the night. The kids said later they figured we would be blown away like Dorothy in *The Wizard of Oz*.

We drove three hundred miles each day. In each state, we stopped at the state capitol and took a tour of the building. Our oldest daughter read *The Lord of the Rings* to us while we drove. When we arrived at a destination, the family insisted she keep on reading until she finished the chapter. Then we would set up camp, relax, and go on to see anything of interest (to me) in the area. I had never seen a mountain until we came from the flat plains of Kansas to the outskirts of Estes Park. We arrived at sunset and hurried to set up camp. Afterwards, we drove the Peak-to-Peak Drive. It was perfect. The sun was setting and cast a beautiful light on the mountain scenery. There were the trees, mountains, bubbling springs, and the smell of pine. Just before we turned off to return to camp, I looked back and saw a rainbow and a cowboy lassoing a cow in the plains at the foothill. It was the first time I had seen a real cowboy.

I did get my first solo trip to Europe in 1975 and went on to become a world traveler. In the years since our first United States travels, my dream of international exploration has led me to circle the globe in one seventy-three-day trip, walk in all twenty-four time zones, travel in over 115 countries, and visit all seven continents.

Evelyn Taylor

Born in Brooklyn, New York, I lived there for one month before
moving to Malverne, a mile square community on Long Island,
nineteen miles east of Manhattan. At eighteen, I enrolled at Hartwick
College, in Oneonta, New York where I met my soul mate, Bill, first
day freshman year. From here the journey wound through West
Virginia, Arizona, Missouri, and, finally, Michigan, which we've called
home for the last twenty-five years.

Let Your Writing Open a Window into Your Psyche

In January 1998, I enrolled in a writing class. My daughter,
Lauren, contracted terminal adolescence, and I searched for sparks of
the little girl hidden under the "gangster" garb. The stories I wrote
about her childhood buoyed her self-esteem and strengthened our
relationship, which had been frayed by the challenges of suburban
teenage life.

Lauren survived adolescence to branch out and set roots in
Kalamazoo, an hour and a half away. Suddenly, I found myself
searching for my mother. I missed experiencing Mom as a woman. She

took ill and died at the age of sixty-five, before I had lost the perspective of a child.

I cannot ignore the void left by Mom's disappearance. For twenty-seven years she served as my lifeline. Twenty-seven years ago the line snapped. Maybe that's why Mom is surfacing. Today's her ninety-third birthday and the beginning of the end of my life, when I'll have lived without her longer than I felt her warmth, her arms around my shoulders, and her kisses on my cheek. Mom never met her grandchildren, held them close, rocked them as babies, or relished their accomplishments.

I reach the crux of the matter. What started as a search for my daughter and my mother metamorphosed into a search for myself. I write to open a window into my adult self, a portal for my children to peer into after I'm gone.

I entered class with a blank tablet and immediately grappled with the mechanics of writing. I learned by example, listening to my classmates and popping books on tape into the car stereo. I learned by writing and reading the product to my class, husband, children, and family pets.

For me, what to write can be a problem. I've led an average existence. I grew up in the same house, with the same parents, with the same relatives close by. Even the cat I adopted at seven lived until the month before I married.

My existence reeks of stability, not of intrigue. Each time I power the laptop, I wrestle with transforming ordinary experience into absorbing tales, ones worthy of a good read. The quest continues; the challenge omnipresent.

The Mother Who Loved Me

Unbidden thoughts wake me at 3:00 a.m. I pull the pillow over my head and try to suffocate unwanted memories. I work to regain sleep, but it's no use. One memory invites another, and I succumb.

What is the trigger? I search the events of the preceding afternoon, and the voice of Harold Kushner on National Public Radio returns. One phrase stands out: "A strength built upon the rock of the memory of that love." Why is she appearing now? No matter. She is, and I must go with the flow.

Mom has returned before. She was at Kyle's birth, ten months after her death. When Kyle was four, I perched on the front stairs, bent in two. I could hear Kyle stamping across the room above. Mom's image appeared. She tapped her foot and pointed her finger at me, admonishing, "You be nice to my grandson."

Tears welled in my eyes, and I picked up the copy of *Growing Child* that arrived in the morning mail. I studied the developmental milestones of the four-year-old. I climbed the stairs, entered Kyle's room, and read *Green Eggs and Ham* to him.

In July 1999, as Dad was dying, Mom filled his room. Mom, captured in watercolors at Bear Mountain, hung on the wall. Across the room, her photo guarded Dad's bed. As he lay tossing and turning, she joined the vigil. Time passed slowly, and my eyes locked onto her photo. I silently begged, "Mom, help. Release Dad from his pain!"

Reeling from lack of sleep, I join Kyle for lunch. Kyle, twenty-three, leans back against the booth. I sip tea. Kyle reaches for the salt and takes a bite of his cheese omelet. "I always assumed your mother was a homemaker, that she stayed home all the time and kept house." The statement came out of the blue. We hadn't been discussing my mother.

"No." I shake my head. "No, I mean yes." I pause, not sure what I mean. "My mom enjoyed being a housewife. She did not stay home. She kept busy."

"I never knew your mom. You need to write a story about her." I smile. Mom thinks so, too.

We finish lunch and leave the restaurant. I head home, snaking through Michigan State University farms. Patches of gold, rust, and burnt umber dot the landscape. The air smells of newly mowed hay. Meadows surrounded by wire fences roll past. Cows congregate by feeding troughs. Serenity induces reflection, and Mom occupies my thoughts.

Mom's descriptions of her youth were pencil sketches waiting for color. She didn't mention teachers, schools, or friends. On trips to my aunt's house, she'd point out the family home. We walked past it to reach the beach.

I'd stop on the sidewalk and squint, trying to see through the curtained windows. "Where's the kitchen?"

Mom pointed towards the back of the house. "My mother cooked large meals. She had to feed the boarders, so she kept chickens in the backyard. Once, we had a hen we named Mollie. I'll never forget the day my mother served Mollie for dinner." Mom smiled. "No one ate."

I stared at the enclosed veranda. I smelled the saltwater four blocks away. White sand crunched between my toes. The wail of a lone gull broke the calm. I could almost see Mom playing dolls on the porch.

"Come on, we have to get to the beach." Mom headed down the street. My arms bowed under the weight of the beach blanket, as the odor of salt increased. Seagulls swooped and soared, their cries intermingled with the sound of pounding surf. We trudged across the sand and staked our spot. I ran into the foaming water and jumped a wave. Mom hugged the shore.

"How come you never learned to swim when you lived so close to the water?" I asked. It seemed an obvious question.

"It's hard to swim in the ocean," she responded, an equally plausible answer.

It wasn't until last year that my cousin solved the puzzle. "Our grandmother complained that her daughters pressured her to move to Rockaway. The minute they moved, your mother married and ran back to Astoria."

The light dawned. The family left Astoria, a stones throw from Manhattan and the Bronx and settled in Rockaway Beach, twenty miles south but still part of Queens, when Mom was nearly grown. My mother was never a child by the beach. She was a child of the city.

I became aware of Mom's first marriage, when I was fifteen. She called me into the living room. I leaned on the television. "I have something to tell you." She stood near the front window. She clasped her hands and shifted her weight from foot to foot.

"I was married before. I wanted to tell you before you heard it from someone else." A million questions popped into my head. I let out a long breath.

"How long were you married?"

Dim light filtered through the curtains, and the mantle clock ticked loudly.

"Twelve years. His name was Harry." A tear rolled down Mom's cheek.

"Did you have any children?"

"No. I had a baby who died at birth."

"My mother with another husband? No way!" I kept my thoughts to myself. "Then, this doesn't change anything." We did not bring up the subject again, nor did anyone else.

After Mom's death, I cornered Dad, digging for information. Dad worked with Mom's brother-in-law at the Federal Reserve Bank in Manhattan. When Mom's parents hosted a party, Dad tagged along. "Your mother was there with Harry. Harry hated family parties and they left early," Dad explained. My eyes grew large. "We didn't date until they separated."

I knew the rest of the story. In June 1943, Mom boarded a train alone for Jacksonville, Florida as divorce was not recognized in New York. This was a feat, as Mom did not travel easily. A weekend away threw her into a frenzy. She obtained the legal decree and returned home.

Dad picked Mom up at the station. They did not marry right away. Actually, Dad shied from commitment, and Mom ended the relationship. Dad attracted women, but when they mentioned marriage, he bolted. This relationship proved to be different. "I knew I had to do something or be alone the rest of my life," Dad told me. Dad contacted the Fed's medical department, which referred him to a psychiatrist. With help, he tried again, and Mom agreed to see him.

"I'll never forget the day I proposed. I had no idea how to get engaged. We took a subway to Central Park. While there, I reached down and picked up a gingko leaf. As I rose, I asked your mother to marry me. She accepted. I bought her a corsage of roses and tickets to *Jeannie, The Gang's All Here, Government Girl* with Michael Redgrave. I had reservations for dinner at Longchamps Restaurant. During dinner, I pulled out the ring."

"What did she say?"

Dad laughed. "She said, 'Don't be so obvious. Everyone is staring.' They were."

Fifty-five years later, Dad reached into his drawer and handed me a bundle. "I still have the pressed leaf from Central Park, the rose petal from her corsage, the restaurant ad, and the movie program." The date, "February 22, 1944" and a hand-drawn heart encircling the initials E.B.-J.G. were scribbled on the movie program.

I looked at Dad, and my eyes watered. "For someone who didn't know how to propose, you did a good job!"

On March 4, 1945, Mom and Dad wed in Fairlawn, New Jersey, as divorcees could not remarry in New York. The next day, they boarded a southbound train. Mom returned to Florida under happier circumstances. The clouds lifted, and a new life was launched.

I finally arrive home. Memories of Mom swim in my head. I unlock the front door and throw my coat on the banister. I run to the family room and flip the computer switch. I organize my thoughts, determined to catch Mom before the memory fades. I drum my fingers on the table and repeatedly click the mouse. Finally, the cursor appears, but my fingers falter on the keys. I relax, and my shoulders sag. There is no rush. Mom never left. She lives within the recesses of my soul.

Most times her influence is subtle. Her presence surfaces in everyday occurrences. Whenever I bake apple pie, she's my coach. When I walk through Kroger, she urges that I choose Gravy Master or Wondra flour. When I brush past an Entenmann crumb cake or stare at Boarshead ham in the deli case, she reminds me they are my husband's favorite. When Perry Como flows from the car radio, I hear her sing. Her words escape my mouth. "God helps those that help themselves," we pause, "but don't get caught."

Lately, Mom's presence is tangible. She's heavy on my mind. The fountain gushes and images rise to the surface. It is time to mine forgotten memories, to share Mom with her grandchildren. It is time to flesh out the mother I love, the mother who loved me.

Normal
Didn't Stare Back

I drop into the armchair, leaning back against the cushion. I close my eyes, letting my mind go numb. I begin to drift off. A thought hiding just below the surface nags me awake. I try to remain blank, hoping it will materialize. I visualize the medical chart that I reviewed that day, and I recall "Bell's Palsy," written in small letters, under "Past History." Earlier in the week, Lauren mentioned that a friend was struck twice with the disease in separate incidents, first on one side of his face, then on the other. I've been there, so long ago it seems like a stranger's life.

The second time was no big deal, at least for my parents. No reason to panic. I walked into the kitchen and pointed to my face. I knew what Mom was thinking. We spent the preceding weekend in Hope, New Jersey. Leaves blazed with fall colors. The air was crisp and frosty for October. I washed my hair and didn't give it time to dry, as everyone was impatient to get going. Personally, I blamed it on an earlier weekend, when my friends and I camped at a Girl Scout camp in the Hudson River valley. I shivered from Friday night to Sunday afternoon, counting the minutes until I could head home.

Mom bundled me up and drove to Dr. Eisen's office. Treatment changed in the intervening seven and a half years, a virus replacing cold as the culprit. "Go about life as normal." Easy for Dr. Eisen to say! He wasn't sixteen and in his junior year of high school. Now, when I wanted to skip school, I couldn't. I stared into the mirror. Normal didn't stare back. My face was frozen flat, with my right eye partly open. If I didn't talk, maybe no one would notice.

My mind wanders. I travel farther into the past. Late afternoon on Long Island, the street lights glow, and a dusting of snow covers the front lawn. I sit crossed legged on the floor. The doors of the TV cabinet hang open. Dishes clatter in the background, and the odor of onion oozes from the kitchen. Perry Como's newest hit, *Begin the Beguine*, flows from the radio perched on the refrigerator. "This is WNEW," William B. Williams announces.

Mommy enters the living room. She hands me a peeled carrot. I stick it in the right side of my mouth. The left side of my face stays contorted. My right eye remains fixed on the Mouseketeers. "I'll be right back," says Mommy, slipping into her coat. It must be 5:45 p.m. Mommy drops Daddy off at the station every morning at 6:10 and picks him up in the afternoon at 5:50. The trip to Manhattan spans one hour, including a subway connection in Brooklyn. The Long Island Railroad runs on time.

The back door creaks. I flip off the TV. Running, I slide across the kitchen into Daddy's arms. I chatter.

"Whoa, you're talking so fast, I can't understand you." Daddy heads toward his bedroom, unloosening his tie as he walks. The hall light reflects off the top of his head.

Mommy herds me into the kitchen. "Let Daddy change his clothes."

Mommy pulls the table into the middle of the kitchen. I wedge behind the table, the wall and the short white refrigerator. She piles polish bologna, boiled potatoes, onions, and carrots into a bowl. She reaches for the milk bottle and fills my glass. Daddy slides into his chair.

"How was your day?" Daddy glances in my direction.

I stop chewing, glad to rest my jaw. "Thea got off the bus at our house." I emphasize each word, hoping to be understood. "We played dolls. She brought a bag of get-well cards."

Mommy reached for a few potatoes. "Miss Kelly sent a stack of work."

Daddy smiles. "We'll tackle that after dinner."

"I get to leave the house tomorrow. Mommy's taking me to see Dr. E." My eyes glow in anticipation. "Since we'll already be out, we're going to have tea and bowties with Mrs. Brackenstein." I bounce in my seat. "Did you see my new scarf? It's Corona's colors – blue and white. It's so big it goes around my face three times." My feet hit the floor.

"Slow down! You can model it for Daddy after supper." Mommy leans across the table. "Mae finished it this afternoon. She figured it would keep Evie's face warm." Mommy changes the subject. "The Girl Scout cookies are in."

Daddy groans, mentally calculating the number of hours needed to deliver one hundred boxes of Thin Mints. He shakes his head. "We'll deliver them on Saturday." Mommy begins to clear the table.

"I'm sorry. I didn't mean to get sick," I say. Daddy laughs and pats my head.

"I have a Home Bureau meeting," says Mommy as she runs hot water into the sink.

Daddy relaxes against his chair. "After helping Evie with her homework, I'll head to the basement and work on scrapbooks."

Basement! Daddy caught my attention. "Can I, can I, ride my bike?"

Mommy grabs a dish towel. "After your exercises!"

I run down the hall, fling open the coat closet, and stare into the full-length mirror. Mommy sets the timer for five minutes. I sing "cheese," relax, and sing "cheese" again. The left side of my face remains fixed in a rigid grin, the eye barely open.

Our dog, Huxley, interrupts my memory, when he butts my hand as if to say, "Enough of that, I need attention." I laugh and nuzzle my face into his cheek. I return from March 1959. "It must have been scary," I said, my voice barely a whisper. Huxley listens intently. I remember Dad's words. "When you woke up and couldn't open your left eye, we were beside ourselves. Your face was twisted. We thought you had a stroke."

Huxley moans. I shudder. Now a mother, I understand the panic. "It must have been hard on Mom." Huxley rolls over. "She was housebound for ten weeks with an almost nine-year-old." Huxley springs, heading for the kitchen. I pull myself up and shuffle along behind him. Maggie wags her tail in the doorway.

"I know, I know, it's time for dinner."

I scoop their meal into their bowls and begin cooking ours.

Trading Betty Ford for John F. Kennedy

"I'll die on September ninth." Sun filtered through the shades in Hope's hospital room. Outside, the late July sun torched the desert below. "It's my son's birthday. People in my family die on a relative's birthday." Hope rested against her pillow, as the air conditioner droned. Hope's breathing was labored. Those few words devoured her reserve.

Each time that Hope, thirty-eight, gained enough strength to be discharged home, the cancer reared its silent head, and she reclaimed her bed at Maricopa County General Hospital on Thirty-Second Street in Phoenix, Arizona. Hope returned to my floor. I was the medical social worker.

The day after our conversation, Hope lapsed into a coma. I hesitantly mentioned her prediction to her oncologist. "No way!" the oncologist countered. "She can't survive six weeks." At 7:00 a.m., September 9, Hope succumbed.

Weeks later, the telephone rang, and my cousin's voice raced across country. "You must come. Your mom looks terrible. Her lungs are full of fluid. Every breath is an effort."

My legs gave out and I slid down the wall. The room swam as I worked to control my voice. I must have carried on a conversation, but no details registered. "Uh, thank you." The connection went dead.

I contacted her doctor. "She's not that bad, but . . ." His indecision radiated through the phone. "It's not an emergency." He paused. "You might as well come."

Dad feared my visit would scare Mom into thinking she was close to death. "I could use your company," he finally said. My bags were already packed.

I entered the hospital room, plastering a grin on my face. Mom looked up and smiled. She had entered South Nassau General three weeks earlier. I watched her chest quietly rise and fall. Her lungs no longer strained to catch air, since they were drained of excess fluid.

The week passed quickly. My hospital visits were mixed with dinners out. On entering the house, Dad and I threw on the lights to hide the emptiness. It didn't work. I lay in my bed listening for familiar sounds. They failed to materialize. No smell of bacon hit my nose in the morning. No hum of the radio playing WNEW reached my ears. Dad hid behind his routine – brewing coffee, making toast and running to the village for *The New York Times*. Mom's lungs continued to improve.

If I had known it was the last time I would be with Mom, I would have hugged her longer and tried to and memorize every inch of her face. But I didn't know. It was a routine good-bye. She was scheduled to leave the hospital to begin the next step in her two years of treatment. I needed to return to my husband, Bill. For one more week, Mom, Dad, and I huddled together, a family once again.

The plane trip lasted three hours. Except for periodic announcements by a stewardess or pilot, the trip was silent and uneventful. It didn't take long to order a Tab or eat the tasteless airplane dinner. I opened a novel. After reading the same two pages three times, I stowed the book. I stitched Christmas motifs on needlepoint fabric. I studied my efforts. One angel sprouted three wings. I ditched this project, too. The overhead lights dimmed, and I leaned back and closed my eyes but could not sleep.

Uninvited thoughts pounced, grabbing my attention. I pushed them away, trying to capture happier images. I concentrated on Arizona and our house, purchased three months earlier. The September desert landscape still blazed under one-hundred-degree temperatures. Red fruit on the pomegranate tree in the backyard wrinkled, and the roses withered months ago.

I recalled cooler times – times that reminded me of Mom and Dad's visits. During one of these times, Christmas 1975, Mom discovered the breast cancer. I shuddered, opened my eyes, and stared toward the back of the plane. Passengers appeared to be sleeping. I rose and asked the stewardess for a glass of water. Returning to my seat, I admitted defeat and allowed my thoughts to roam freely.

That Christmas, Mom noticed her left breast's disfigurement but kept mum, refusing to spoil our holiday. She visited her doctor when she returned home. A biopsy led to a mastectomy with twenty-seven lymph nodes testing positive for cancer. The time between the two procedures felt like months, although it really was only a couple of weeks – still too long for my liking. I wanted to shake her doctor: "Don't you know that's my mother!"

Mom and Dad returned to Arizona. Mom drew me into the spare bedroom. "Would you like a look?"

"Look?" I knew that wasn't the right answer. This felt like a test, and I wasn't passing. Mom's eyes locked on my face, and her hand trembled. "Sure!" I sounded confidant but my stomach churned. Oozing sores pierced her flesh. "That's raw!"

Mom sighed. "It's not healing well." She buttoned her blouse. "I'm in a research program. The one Betty Ford is in." I heard the pride in her voice. Mom and Betty Ford broke new ground together. Mom became an experiment.

The pilot interrupted my reverie. I glanced out the window in time to catch snow on the Rockies. A stewardess placed another Tab on my tray. I joined the line for the lavatory. I reclaimed my seat and rested against the window, tracing the outline of cloud formations. My sight slid inward.

Earlier that year, one of my patients, Calvin, took me aside. A stocky African American, he examined his fingers. "I won't make it to next year." He glanced at my face, and I must have shown surprise. "No, I'll die before the end of the year." He sounded adamant. I knew enough not to contradict him.

The year before, Elizabeth Kubler-Ross addressed an audience in Tucson, Arizona. Words tumbled from her mouth as she paced. Passion energized every gesture. The longer she lectured, the lower I slumped into the upholstered auditorium chair. Thankful I attended the session alone, I scurried out of the building, hiding my tear-stained face.

Doubts quietly seeped in, slowly at first, and then growing into a dark fog that threatened to pull me under. My emotions flared at odd moments. The home health nurse roused my anger, when she complained about caring for her aging mother. The nurse, in her fifties and a grandmother, dared to have a mother. Instead of mouthing sympathy, I bit my lip and slid unnoticed from the room. Tears welled as I silently screamed, "This can't be happening. I'm only twenty-seven. I'm too young to lose Mom."

The sound of wheels emerging from the lower regions of the plane offered escape from my thoughts. A "fasten your seat belt" sign flashed overhead. I pushed my baggage underneath the seat, relieved to be back in the desert.

On Sunday, November 20, the phone rang. "Happy Birthday!" Mom and Dad sang, shortening the miles that separated the East from the West.

"Thanks!" said Bill. "How are you feeling?" he asked my mother.

On the extension, I heard her giggle. "I feel good."

The giggling continued. "I start chemotherapy Tuesday. I'll have to get a wig." The giggling deepened into laughter. If I had known it was the last time I would hear Mom's voice, I would have memorized every word.

On November 22, my supervisor sounded an alarm. "You have to call the E.R. in New York."

"Huh?" It took a while for me to comprehend the request, then I understood too well. I reached for the phone and started to dial. My hand shook, and I replaced the receiver. Finally, I placed the call.

A nurse explained that Mom couldn't tolerate the chemotherapy treatment, and her doctor had called an ambulance. "Your mother died before reaching the emergency room." The last phrase sunk in. Mom died. She traded Betty Ford for John F. Kennedy, dying on the fourteenth anniversary of his death.

The room grew dark. Not a sound broke the stillness. The walls closed in, and the air felt heavy. I struggled to catch my breath. The office looked alien. I lifted the phone and dialed Bill's number. His "hello" broke through the haze. "Mom died." I said, and began to sob.

That night, I lay in bed courting sleep. It refused to be coaxed. I rolled into Bill. He looped his arm over my shoulder and pulled me close. His breathing deepened. "I can't handle this. You have to help!" I mouthed this phrase over and over. Tears streamed down my cheeks and rage began to build. I silently screamed, shaking my fists. Bill stirred and I froze, arms hovering in mid-air. He turned over.

I stared at the overhead light, not daring to move a muscle. I could just make it out in the dark, its familiar shape vaguely reassuring. Suddenly, I felt lighter; a weight lifted off my shoulders. The worst that could happen did. The wait was over. I sighed.

"Are you all right?" Bill hugged me, and I slipped into slumber.

On Wednesday evening, we entered the funeral home. Chairs stood in rows in the middle of a large room. At first, the room appeared empty. I swung around and froze. A casket with its lid propped open hugged the far wall. Mom lay still, not one gray hair out of place.

"Doesn't she look beautiful?" said someone behind me. I turned to find myself face to face with the first group of mourners.

"Beautiful?" I almost spoke aloud.

"Oh, Evelyn, I'm so sorry . . ."

Faces floated in and out murmuring kind words. I felt hands

grasping my hand and shoulders. I kept my back to the casket. "How nice to see you again! How's your family? Thank you for coming!" Bill and Dad looked as tired as I felt.

Saturday morning dawned chilly and wet. Gray clouds covered the sky, and hinted at snow. Wind whipped my navy jacket, as I entered the funeral home. I froze on the threshold. Aunts, uncles, cousins, friends, and strangers mingled. The funeral director greeted and ushered guests to their seats. Bill squeezed my hand, and I squared my shoulders. We followed Dad to the family row. I steeled my emotions, struggling to keep my mind blank.

Sod squished underfoot, as we trekked through Pinelawn Cemetery. Mom's casket rested on rollers adjacent to a large black hole. I shuddered, wrapping my coat about myself as tightly as possible. The reverend uttered a few final blessings.

We entered our friends' basement. They skipped the burial to arrange a feast. Festive conversation, soft lights, and the smell of food filled the room with warmth.

An old friend pulled me aside. "Guess who made that cheesecake?"

I stared at the dessert table. A cake smothered with crushed pineapple claimed the place of honor. My eyes grew wide, and I slowly shook my head. "Noooo!"

"Yup," he grinned. "They found it in your freezer. They didn't think your mother would mind."

A smile spread across my face. Mom would have been flattered. It took years to master the recipe cut from *The New York Times*, years for it to become Mom's signature dessert. Finally, I laughed.

Dad, Bill, and I returned to Arizona. Convincing Dad to return with us proved easy, too easy. Bill and I flopped on the couch, oblivious of the trials of the next four months. Dad slowly unpacked, forcing his baggage into the closet.

Shortly after I returned to work, a co-worker approached my desk. "Calvin died," she told me. I remembered our conversation seven months earlier. Calvin waited to December to fulfill his prophecy.

I shuddered. "He was so sure. How did he know?"

My co-worker opened his mouth and then changed his mind. I ached to push death aside and concentrate on living. We both pulled out our notebooks and shared caseloads.

SUNNY WILKINSON

I am a full-time professor at Michigan State University and full-time jazz singer and mother. I have sung with The Count Basie Band, Rob McConnell and the Boss Brass, Mark Murphy, Milt Hinton, Clark Terry, Curtis Fuller, and Edgar Winter, among others. My latest CD release is with big-band on Chartmaker Jazz, called Sunny Wilkinson "High Wire." My other CDs are Alegria, on the Hibrite label, and Sunny Wilkinson, on the Positive Music label. I perform regularly at jazz festivals and clubs across the country and am the professor of jazz voice at MSU. I am the past president of the Michigan chapter of the International Association of Jazz Educators and the past chairperson for IAJE's Women's Caucus. I co-founded IAJE's "Sisters in Jazz" mentoring program.

Think of Yourself as a Writer

As much as I would love it, I have never written on a schedule. I write in the cracks. I write if I am inspired, or I write as an assignment for class. A deadline is great incentive. I find that the more I write, the freer my creative energy. It's as if the world expands and my vocabulary increases, as does my ease in writing.

I see things to write about wherever I go. If, however, a period of time goes by and I do not write, beginning again is tough. Words come more slowly and ideas take longer to form. I have spoken to many composers and painters about this. They all speak of a similar process. It takes awhile to get into the creative groove or flow. Once you are in it, it's heaven.

Be patient with yourself while you are finding your way in your creative process. If you are in a down period, make sure you write anyway. It is the writing itself that will free you up. During this coping period, your writing may or may not be good. But don't judge it while you are trying to hit your stride. Leave it alone and come back to it when you are in a good writing space. You may be surprised at how good the writing is.

When I started writing, I wanted to make sure I sounded educated and intelligent. As a consequence, the writing was stilted and adjective-laden and really didn't have my personality in it. Finally I began to trust myself and not censor or filter my words. Then my stories began to ring true. Your voice and your own words are of value. Let them flow. They are the only vehicles that you have to truthfully tell your own story.

You will be influenced by the world around you: where you go, what you see and hear. Great writers will also influence you. I have found that if I am reading a particularly good book, I will start writing in the author's rhythm. It's freeing and fun. It stretches you. Purposefully be observant. Notice everything in your environment with a writer's eye and ear. Take it all in. There is a great story around every corner.

Think of yourself as a writer. If you are writing, you are a writer. Keep a cool head to help you edit or expand your work objectively, and a warm heart to help you access the depth of your emotions and express them without restraint. The two are good working companions, and they will help you balance your writing.

Above all, have fun. Keep your sense of humor. Be a kid riding on a merry-go-round for the first time. Enjoy the ride!

Dust
Motes

I have decided that if I am to be a writer, I must write about dust motes. In my reading this week, two authors have used them to enhance their descriptions of setting. Erica Jong in *Any Woman's Blues* says, "We fall to the floor of the foyer (wide oaken planks, a hooked rug, a few dustballs chasing each other around as if they were tumbleweeds in the wake of our stampeding horses)." In the essay "Going Home," in *Slouching Toward Bethlehem*, Joan Didian writes, "Questions trail off, answers are abandoned, the baby plays with the dust motes in a shaft of afternoon sun."

I doubt if men notice dust motes, let alone use them in their writing or bother with their significance.

I've just finished reading Jack Kerouac's *On the Road*. What a satisfying experience to read its lush cadences. It's the rhythm of the words, not so much the words themselves, that is significant in Kerouac's writing. What is jazz if not time? "It don't mean a thing if it ain't got that swing."

Torpor, beat culture, lack of culture, booze, drugs, and on-the-edge sexual adventures dull by comparison to the rhythm of his lines. Dig this and the undulating swing groove of his writing. It refreshes me, opens up vistas, wrenches off the tightly held lid to enthusiasm. Hurrah, I'm alive!

Sha-ba-do-n-de-dot. I am zipped up on coffee and zipped up on life. What you listen to and hear, you become. Writing in the rhythm of Jack Kerouac. Hell, my life is written in the rhythm of Jack Kerouac, one long lyrical jazz solo interrupted by surprising jazz rhythms, riffs of the night and of life. I breathe in his rhythm and exhale, perhaps a smoother L.A.-influenced beat, but beat all the same.

Sometimes I wonder why I am the only mother at the Williamston park who whoops and hollers, clambering on the jungle gyms, pushing my fifty-year-old energy into my seven-year-old's space. We play tag and climb under one-foot-tall platforms with spiders and rotting mulch to hide, for seeking purposes only. And then, I break into what I do best . . . sha-ba-da-n-doo-we . . . free improv . . . listening to the chord changes around me and creating with them. That is it. That is why I do what I do and live like I live.

Even in my ad-libbed, whacked-out jazz solo of a life, I observe dust motes. Women do. For whatever else we are, we are keepers of the hearth and home. I suspect that Jack Kerouac never wrote about dust motes. I doubt that he ever noticed them.

Dust balls, dust bunnies, dust motes are the ephemeral swirlings of a woman's world. We notice them. We agonize over them. We clean them. We shove them under beds. We hold them up to the light for closer examination. They glitter and, in the light, disintegrate in our hands.

Sunny
in Chrisland

"Mama, look at this." A furry yellow and black caterpillar with a lion-like mane is crossing the trail. "Ooh, Mom, come here and see this fungus." Oyster-shell-colored mushrooms shaped like dinner plates and just as large stick out of the side of an old oak.

"Look, Mama, an orange seed. Isn't it beautiful? Oh, I just love being out here like this. And, Mama, I love you so much. You are amazing. Don't ever forget how much I love you." My heart swells. First we hug with me standing, the top of his head hitting my breastbone. Then dipping to one knee with my head halfway up his seven-year-old torso, I am allowed a thirty-second snuggle. Quickly disentangling, Chris is off to explore more mysteries. "Wow, this fungus looks like 1,000 pancakes stacked on top of each other. And that one looks like a string of tiny rotten bananas."

Last week the temperature was in the forties, a premature portent of winter. Today, however, it's in the high sixties and Chris expresses it best when he says, "Mama, the sky looks like Wyoming." The sun is graciously filtering through the trees in its own dappled world, picking out its favorites by illuminating them in highlight. Fall has just begun to impress us with a smattering of red and gold amidst the green, pointillistic offerings of Mother Nature.

Chris picks up a curved five-foot-long stick. "Look, Mom, I'm a praying mantis." Wide sweeping gestures of flailing arms. Stick moves up to forehead. "Mom, look at my long eyeball." Stick turns into a weapon to fight the boss. The boss is the main opponent from the Mario Brothers video game, which he has superimposed into Chrisland, the land of Chris, his own invention. Chris talks incessantly, inventing strategies for beating the boss. I acknowledge him each time he pauses for a breath, but I am only hearing the sound of his voice floating around me.

Distancing myself from the immediacy of being Mommy, I myself float, in Sunnyland, savoring the drone of the crickets in the fecund swamp to my left. For a moment I fall in love with Michigan again and move out of my internal universe to see the expanse of her beauty, the giant oaks hung with wild vines, the maples horning in on their territory.

Chris jumps into Sunnyland and says, "Mom, check this out. A red mushroom." There amidst tiny, delicate fern-like trappings are magenta mushrooms about half an inch in diameter. They capture my son's attention. He captures my heart with his ability to see beauty in the tiny things. We make no headway on our hike; so much to see and savor.

"Oh, Mom, a snake trail!" With my adult vision I see that someone has dragged a stick along the trail. I do not interject this into our childlike day. We follow the track, eyes peeled for motion in the brush.

Little blue-black berries hang heavy on a bush with purple stems. Chris twists off a branch and it becomes an umbrella with ammunition on the ends of each spoke. "Okay! The boss flings poison berries into the robots' mouths to put them out of commission. Bang! Zippo! They're history." Chrisland again, the world of his own making. A grin erupts from Chris, a goofy Chinaman grin, his buckteeth, zooming in different directions, and amazingly cute. He begins to stalk me with his purple berries of doom. Berries are flung in my hair and down my shirt. I pretend to eat one. I dodge. I skip. Chris plants his body in front of mine as I swerve around him. He leaps in front of me again, a barrier of Chrisland proportions.

Caught off guard, I trip, yanking the muscle fibers of my hamstring. Afraid that I had reinjured my leg, I try to regain my balance. I flinch. Anger stomps out of my throat and I fling it at Chris. "How could you trip me like that? You know I have a hurt leg. Now look, I've injured it again."

I immediately regret my outburst. Collapsing in a puddle of tears, Chris cries, "Oh, Mommy, I'm so sorry. I didn't mean to hurt you." Ashamed of my storm, I sit on the trail still damp from rain and scoop him up. "I know, Sweetheart. It wasn't your fault. I'm so sorry that I yelled at you." We cuddle a bit closer, wet bottoms on both pairs of jeans, and recover our humor. I gingerly stand and realize that I'm not badly hurt. He wipes his nose on my shirt and gives me his Chinaman grin, and we are off to discover more treasure.

All of a sudden, Chris dives off the path, all hands and arms, lunging in the direction of a six-inch-long garter snake. In a blink he has it captured. It writhes and wraps itself around his wrist. Chris coos, "It's alright. Calm down, little snaky." As if the snake understands, it settles, entranced by Chris' gentle stroking down its body. After several minutes, he quietly places the snake on the trail and we watch it disappear under some brush.

As the sun begins its descent, the air around us cools and we know it's time to start for home. Hand-in-hand, arm-in-arm, we head back to the car, full of our day's adventures and full of joy in each other's company.

On a Weather-Worn Bench

I sit on a weather-worn bench, toward the back of the garden, with a colorful Mexican blanket draped behind me and pick at the uneven threads riddled with Peyote Birds that streak through the loose-woven fabric. My friend is warming up her voice, swooping soprano sounds up and down the scale. Twisting an orange from its branch, I peel it and pop a fresh slice into my mouth and feel the sweetness explode at the back of my throat.

Sitting here in my friend's backyard, I relish every movement of air and the constancy of the California winter sun, feeling as plump and as juicy as the orange I just savored. Winter is a relative term. At home in Michigan, it's twenty degrees and gray, everything dormant, waiting for spring. Here, life is ever-constant, fecund. Winter's dormancy is a subtle motion, shifts in shades of green. Here, there is every kind of fruit tree imaginable. Rosemary grows in pots, spilling over to the ground.

When I lived in L.A., lemon trees ran amok in my yard. In spring, the sweet and tangy fragrance overwhelmed the neighborhood and beckoned to all the local bees. Seemingly year-round lemons hung on the trees: lemons for the taking, for fish and lemonade and rubbing into cuticles; lemons to feed the neighborhood; lemons to waste, lemons to rot on the trees. When I first moved to Michigan, I couldn't bear to buy a lemon. It was outrageous to pay fifty cents for an old dead thing when I was used to fresh plucked.

Two different kinds of avocado trees dropped their fruit with a crack that invariably woke me up in the middle of the night, huge ripe avocados for the taking, always good for lunch, good with shrimp, good to smear as a facial mask. I rarely buy them now. They are small, black, and shriveled, beaten up by travel and time.

Now a visitor in L.A., safe from intrusion in my friend's backyard, I put my book down and pull my t-shirt over my head to feel the sun on my body. Luxuriating in the warmth, I look down at my fifty-year-old body blossoming under the kindness of the sun and release the tension I had been holding in my shoulders.

Several years back, when I had stopped breast-feeding

Christopher, I would routinely squeeze my breasts to make sure that I still had milk. Several ducts always produced a creamy substance, not milk really, more like a pre-milk, colostrum, which is rich and full of nutrients for the newborn. I liked knowing that I still had life's potential within my body.

I recall the sensations, the delicious intimacy of nursing my boy, his smell and the sweetness of his skin. Chris would gaze at me, full of wonder, smile, and then shyly bury himself in my chest. I remember the feeling of "let down" in my breasts when he would begin to nurse. An ache of complete connection washed over me. When he was through, exhaustion would momentarily overtake me, depleting me utterly. This was followed by the sweetest peace, a woman's private peace.

It has been several years since I checked for milk. When my doctor told me the squeezing was most likely disturbing the duct and causing it to bleed, I stopped. But today, with the L.A. sun so warm and everything bursting with life, I feel compelled to try. Perhaps I am still as fertile as the ground around me. I gently squeeze my breast, applying pressure in the manner of a young mother pumping her milk for her infant. There it is, a tiny droplet of white liquid, a residual bit of life's milk still fighting for survival in my fifty-year-old body. Suddenly the milky white substance turns black: a spot, a drop of black liquid demanding me to stop. No longer will I search for milk in my aging body. Farewell to my childbearing years. Hello to the wisdom of the crone, the new ride. I stop the pressure. I stop.

With a gaze around the yard, I relax back into the poetry of my book and savor the beauty surrounding me, both of which will sustain my inner life in years to come. I relish the sun on my body and the effortless tones of my friend's soprano voice. I feel my skin browning in the sun and know that I'm ready to face the next part of my journey. I am ready. I am content.

Looking in the Mirror

Looking in the mirror I see my daddy's face staring back at me: his mouth mostly, pencil-line lips with a catty-whampus smile, slightly crooked on one side. I like this idea, seeing Daddy's face in my own. If I touch my lips, I half expect to feel the black soot lump that Daddy carried in his lower lip. He was a long jumper in high school. One day, an ungainly start sent him ass over teakettle and he landed face first in the gritty black sand pit, ripping open his lip and embedding in it his lifelong trophy. It was there, even at the end, when his skin was paper-thin, luminous, translucent. His wrinkles smoothed out and his skin glowed, except for his lip, blackened in that small spot where he still bore the mark of his early athleticism.

We got the call from my brother David on July 1. "Sarah, you should know that we are putting Dad in hospice tomorrow morning. Oh, Sarah, he's so ready to go. He's incontinent, wearing diapers, he can't see to read, and he can't hear or hold a pen. He has pneumonia again." Then my brother chuckled and said, "I asked Dad if it was time to go into hospice and he bellowed out angrily, 'I will not go back there!' Again, with the resonance only a preacher can muster, 'I will NOT go to that horrid place!'"

"But, Dad, I thought that this was what you wanted."

"I will not go back to that hospital."

"I said hospice, Dad."

Dad let out an enormous sigh, relaxed his shoulders, and softly said "Oh yes, yes. Thank you. Thank you."

There was a pause. Then David said, "Sarah, it's time for you to come."

Ron, my husband, Chris, my ten-year-old son, and I packed quickly and booked a flight to Tucson, where Daddy was living in an assisted care facility.

By the time we arrived, Dad had not eaten for four days. It would be fourteen more before he passed.

Walking into Daddy's room, everything seemed the same – his treasures around him; pictures of his family; myriad sculptures and paintings of Jesus, some smiling, some suffering, some dark, some light. Daddy, so gaunt, with big globes for knees sticking out from under the sheets, was the anomaly. He had diminished and was ashen and devoid of the vigor that once animated him so brightly. An oxygen tank was whirring away in the corner, supplying pure air to his drowning lungs. He roused and smiled. Through his film-clouded eyes I could feel his warmth shining through. He patted the side of the bed. My sister, Debbie, and I each took a side, molding our bodies to his.

"Thank you, thank you, thank you," he said. "Love, love, love." This took great effort to say, with gasps in between each word. But the air in the room became rarified, richer with us all being together.

I grew up in a family that sang together. We sang in church, we sang on hiking trails and around campfires, we sang at home with records blaring as accompaniment. Harmony was just another form of communication in our family.

On one of our visits early in the week, we sang together. It started softly, almost a chant. Debbie was on one side of the bed. I was on the other. The chant turned into "Fairest Lord Jesus." Daddy responded with a smile and began mouthing the words to his favorite hymn. That gave us all the encouragement we needed. We began singing every beloved family song we could think of: "Now Let Us Sing" and "Our Paddle's Clean and Bright," two-part songs that melded our voices into the warm beauty that is always present when Debbie and I sing together.

After one more chorus of "The Northern Trail," Daddy doing his best to throw his head back and let his beautiful tenor voice rip, he signaled by a tap on the bed that he had enough. He was exhausted for the day.

Mostly Debbie and I would just lie with him, one on either side, cuddled up close. He would rest and sleep; we would bend our bodies around his bony shape. At every visit, Daddy would thank us for being such wonderful daughters and send us away with blessings of love, love, love and thank you, thank you, thank you, always in threes, like the trinity.

My son, Chris, insisted on bringing the video of his most recent piano recital to Tucson so that his grandpa could see it. I hesitated mentioning it to Dad, as the TV was in the next room. He was so weak that I couldn't imagine he could get out of bed. But Chris plunged right in, saying, "Grandpa, I could show you the video of my last performance right now if you'd like."

Without a moment's pause, my father nodded his head emphatically. "Absolutely," he said. "I must see that tape."

Two nurses supported him on either side and swiveled him upright into the wheelchair. Barely able to stay erect, Dad was rolled gently into the room where the TV was housed. With immense effort Daddy roused and engaged his full attention to the tape; he listened, absorbed in the sounds of my ten-year-old son playing piano in concert. He managed a smile and a trio of thank yous and then waved to be taken back to bed. This would be his last time out of bed.

Several months after Daddy died, I got a call from my sister Debbie. She had just returned from Phoenix, going out of her way to visit Daddy's last church, Asbury Methodist. "It was the perfect place to spread the last of Daddy's ashes," Debbie said.

Momentarily, I strayed to the heavy plastic bag filled with my portion of Daddy's remains, which lay in my bureau drawer at home. I am having difficulty confronting the idea of spreading those ashes. Somehow while they are still in my drawer, Daddy is within reach, still tangible. For me, this is the most difficult part of his death: his absolute absence. That dear part of my life is gone irretrievably. The ashes in my drawer somehow defy death, all the while confirming it.

While I still have impulses to call him to discuss genealogy or just to hear his voice, those ashes will stay put in my bureau drawer. Perhaps later I'll confront spreading them to the wind.

Debbie recaptured my attention by saying "Do you remember our scrawny Charlie Brown Christmas tree we planted at the church in 1969?"

"Of course," I said. "We would watch it grow each year, stronger and taller until it became the biggest tree on the property."

"Sunny, you should see it now. It's huge and unwieldy, branches going every which direction. What a perfect place to put the ashes, don't you think?"

"Absolutely." I agreed.

"It was kind of funny, though," she said. "When I walked out back, there was a bum sitting on the steps with a half-empty bottle of whiskey. At first I was upset that he was there to watch me, but then I remembered how Daddy used to always seek out the local drunks and invite them to church. Do you remember that?"

"I had forgotten," I said.

I flashed back to being nine years old in Fairmont, Minnesota. A man named Jack lived with us for a while. I found out later that he was a sober alcoholic, just out of prison, trying to reclaim some value in his life. Dad believed in him and opened our home. I felt proud of my daddy at that moment, realizing that he was one of the guys who really tried to live as he preached.

"Anyway," said Debbie, "I spread them under that tree, no ceremony. But somehow it was just right."

We said good-bye and I found myself drifting back to our last day with Daddy.

After spending the morning with Dad, we decided we needed a little fresh air. As we left the building, the monsoon season erupted. Raindrops the size of dimes plopped out of the sky onto the desert floor. We all ran out into the parking lot and raised our faces to the sky, trying to eat as many as we could catch in our open mouths. Later, as if to celebrate our time together, a clear full double rainbow, stretching valley-width across the Tucson basin, heralded my daddy's time on earth and his passing.

Debbie's Mountain

Cloistered, safe in my window seat, I peer down from 20,000 feet in the air. The landscape around Las Vegas is dead and unredeemed. The azure waters of Lake Powell, carved out by underwater roadways, look eerie from the sky. Nothing lives around it; turquoise waters starkly contrast the surrounding brown of the desert.

Patches of green emerge. The dull brown drifts to a vague pink. Hues intensify: rose mingles with burgundy as the Grand Canyon gashes the landscape, an interloper on the scene.

In the distance is Humphrey's Peak, a promontory that draws the focus to Flagstaff, Arizona, home to my sister Debbie and her family.

Almost on top of the mountain now, I am pulled into Debbie's living room, into the sway of her family's easy intimacy. Fibers emanate from my solar plexus, leap out of the airplane and attach themselves to Humphrey's Peak in an attempt to linger a moment longer. I can almost see the mountain bend in the direction of the plane, pulled by my intention.

James, Sean, and Ryan have just finished mopping up the homemade gravy that drips down the sides of the biscuits that James concocts every Sunday morning. Perfect gravy every time, savory and thick. With the TV on *International Soccer*, the boys lounge with their plates atop their laps, feet splayed in every direction across the coffee table.

At the foot of Humphrey's Peak, Debbie, dressed in a long, gathered skirt, is conducting the Unity Church choir. On Sundays, she breaks her open-air policy, covering her legs with a pair of suntan panty hose that are full of little tags and catches from wear. Her mascara, hastily applied, slightly smudges her lower lid. Her lipstick is a hint of color. Debbie's exuberance is drenching her choir. As it pours over them, they sing better than they are able.

Debbie's family drifts out of my mind's eye as Humphrey's Peak wanes from view. I strain to recapture the image of my sister's arms waving in a conductor's pattern. A miracle, there it is again, distant, snow-capped, a beacon to my heart's treasure. Then it disappears.

With a sigh, I settle back and slip open my book for a good read.

TRISH LACKEY

Some babies insist on rushing into life and continue rushing head on thereafter, as in the story of my life. I was born premature on a military base in 1947, delivered by a drunken doctor who had been out celebrating a little too much before being called in for an early morning delivery. It was one of the few times in my life when I could be described as "small." I went home in a shoe box used for a car seat. A small dresser drawer was my bassinet.

I grew up refining the destiny of rushing into life's adventures while surviving numerous foolish adolescent escapades, many which provided the basis of my memoirs. Extensive travels as a military brat opened my world to acceptance for alternative views on the foundation of beliefs, ways of living, and people in general. My teenage years engulfed the rich experiences of living in Germany and Morocco during the 1960s.

Having never developed roots as a child, I continued traveling all my adult life, never living any one place for more than a few years. Being under the influence of Aquarius, I have peppered my travels with a spiritual searching and a deep sense of connection with God, attributing to Him the success of my survival today and the blessings of my daughter, Sara, and granddaughter, Dakota.

The combination of travel and the necessity of making a living produced a kaleidoscope of occupations including cleaning horse stalls and being a lifeguard, as well as working in property management, accounting, insurance, real estate, and financial counseling. Eventually, I climbed the corporate ladder of a multi-billion dollar conglomerate.

Write from the Heart

I have approached writing my memoirs as a series of stories taken from my life. I have no fixed agenda or order dictating my approach. I have made numerous draft lists of exciting and interesting events that have happened to me that I would like to share with others some day. As a memory pops into my head, I jot down a note on the "draft list" of words that rekindle the memory.

Basically, I get a sudden urge or desire to write about a particular moment in my life and, as the mood strikes, I get pen and paper ready. Finding a quiet chair, I curl up, close my eyes and let my mind drift back in time and watch the events unfold. I write in ink on a lined tablet, scribbling barely legible words as visions float about my head. I feel and taste the moment, then try to put down the words that recreate what is going on in my head. My tablets look like a disaster zone as I scribble, cross out, and rewrite. Reconnecting thoughts bounce all over the pages as I jump back and forth in time between thoughts and scenes. I feel much like a painter, dabbling here and there until I finally find the right combination that paints a scene that, hopefully, a reader will feel part of.

Once the rough handwritten draft is to a point where I know what I'm trying to do, I go to the computer to bring order and clarity to the chaotic scribbles. I first concentrate on deciphering my hand writing, relying heavily on spell- and grammar-check to correct hastily typed thoughts. After the written draft is transferred to typed, I then read it over and over; go away; come back and read it again, all the while polishing the piece until I am satisfied the story is conveyed to the best of my ability.

My advice to anyone who it thinking of writing is to "just do it." Don't be afraid or judgmental of your efforts, write from the heart, and share your writing with family and friends when you feel comfortable. Let your memories, imagination, and creativity flourish.

Moroccan
Horse Ride

The tall bay gelding, Allegro, was testy as usual on this bright Moroccan morning. Evading the groom's attempt to saddle him up, the two engaged in a slow motion ballet, humorous to watch despite the big bay's insistent stabs at the groom's back, with snapping teeth chomping on air. The groom, Allegro's cautious caretaker for years, skillfully avoided the sharp teeth and occasional swift kick with a casual indifference to the aggressive bay's advances. Eventually, Allegro was tacked up, full of vim and vinegar, ready for the day's adventure.

The crisp early morning air invigorated everyone, horse and human alike. We had planned this outing all week. Our goal was to ride out from the stables, pass by the large open-air markets, take a short cut through the King's Forest, and come out across town by the rolling dunes behind our homes in time for lunch. Allegro's familiar antics promised a thrilling ride. Coco, a docile chestnut gelding, stood patiently as his rider mounted and gathered the reins, prodding the gentle steed toward the open stable gate and out into the large field running alongside the stable yard.

I eagerly approached Allegro, who was prancing at the end of the groom's hand clamped firmly on his bridle. Struggling to keep up with the antsy bay, I managed to swing up into the saddle; my weight, settling upon his back, had a calming effect. We trotted out of the gate to catch up with the other rider. Passing Coco, Allegro took his place as leader of the expedition. We were two naive American teenage girls in 1964, riding unescorted into the Moroccan countryside outside of Kenitra.

Just outside the gates, past the open field, we melted into the dusty hustle and bustle of the Moroccan medina, a large open-air farmers market. Weaving through the maze of merchant stalls, throngs of haggling shoppers, market mongrels, sheep, goats, and camels, we finally made our way to the edge of the King's Forest, an old magnificent garden of unkempt towering trees and winding paths hugging the ancient city.

The pounding rays of the Moroccan sun on our backs lost their power among the dappled shade of looming giants. Shaking off the dust of civilization, we galloped into the forested caverns of by-gone days, enjoying the rush of cooler air. Allegro, snorting at invisible monsters, led the cruise along familiar paths until we broke into an open clearing. Out of breath from the exhilarating run, we slowed to a walk, meandering across the cheerful meadow.

"Do you think we'll run into them again?"

"Them" was a wandering hostile Bedouin tribe that we constantly ran into while riding. No matter which direction we rode to try to avoid them, we always seemed to get in their way and they always prevented our success in reaching home. This expedition was another attempt to avoid "them" and ride from the stables to our homes on the opposite side of town.

"I don't think so. They had just set up camp when we ran into them last weekend. If we stay more to the northwest this time we'll miss them," I confidently assured her.

Re-entering the shadows of the forest, we strolled along the northern path toward home. Teenage gossip of school events dominated the lazy conversations, our chattering the only disturbance in the stillness of the silent domain.

Leaving the majestic forest behind, we embarked upon the rolling grassy dunes bordering the far edge of town. Coco, feeling the anticipation of reaching our destination, crowded Allegro for the lead. Overconfident from getting this close, we started giggling as we remembered our prior attempts to get this far.

Reaching the top of a large knoll, our jovial mood was shattered by the sight of the dreaded Bedouin tribe camped below us. Our abrupt arrival, announced by barking dogs followed by shouting children, was greeted in the traditional onslaught by a pack of attacking dogs accustomed to the two silly American girls on horseback screaming and fleeing in terror.

"I'm not running away this time," I bravely declared.

Foolishly jabbing Allegro in the ribs, we shot headlong to meet the wave of dogs racing toward us. Dropping the reins and holding onto the saddle, I encouraged the powerful bay to be "all that he could be." The mighty gelding dove into the pack of dogs with the hateful vengeance of an enraged bear. His muscles rippling, every fiber of his being intent on killing dogs, he began a ballet of death. Powerful teeth tossed what wary dogs he could catch, as front hooves crashed among the tangling canine retreat. Punching rear hooves rolled stragglers like leaves in the wind. The watching throng of villagers, realizing the immense turn of events, raced toward the battlefield of confusion, shouting for the rescue of their trusted companions.

From the safety of the knoll, pleas for our usual hasty retreat floated down as the drama unfolded. Torn between the desire to flee and his willing obedience to stay, Coco paced the crest in agitation. As the crowd of women and children engulfed the scene rescuing their dogs, men shouted for a truce. Allegro stood as a mighty titan, quivering with anticipation. Surrounded by excited villagers, I gathered the reins, unsure what to do next, as an elderly man took charge, chastised the unruly dogs for their inhospitable behavior, and invited us into his tent for tea, restoring peace to the balmy day. We had earned their respect.

From that day forward we no longer dreaded running into the wandering Bedouin tribe. As the legend of the two foolish American girls and their brave warrior steed spread, we became honored guests on many occasions and among numerous Bedouin tribes, who always invited us in for tea. Everyone wanted to meet the famous fighting horse and hear stories of Allegro's love of confrontation.

You Gotta Listen

The day had been long and frustrating – one of those bad days at work when Murphy's Law takes over and, like dominoes gone awry, everything cascades in the wrong direction. Now, home from work, I thought I would try to add a cheerful highlight to the day by cooking something special for dinner. John, my husband, was out puttering in the backyard. I had the tranquil kitchen to myself. All I needed was a cookbook. But, alas, they were still packed. We had moved into the house several months ago, but my demanding work schedule left little time to unpack the non-essential boxes now stacked in the spare bedroom.

Standing in the doorway, trying to remember which kitchen box the cookbooks were in, I surveyed the mountain of boxes scattered throughout the room. I was puzzled; it actually seemed like the piles had grown. "Oh, well," I thought. The only way to find the books was to open boxes and look inside. Moving aside the more obvious "not-this-one" boxes, I opened the first best guess. It held only linens and knickknacks. The second box contained more linens and towels. Tackling the third box, I paused in surprise. What's this? Underneath a covering of crumpled newspapers, the box was filled with empty beer bottles. "Very strange and perplexing," I thought. The next box revealed the same: a stash of empty beer bottles hidden underneath crumpled newspapers.

Suspicion began to creep into my mind. I methodically attacked each closed box. An assembly line of boxes, overflowing with empty beer bottles, piled up behind me. Crumpled newspapers littered the floor. Finding the cookbooks did little to ease the anger slowly boiling within. I had exposed dozens of boxes filled with the disgusting bottles and deceptive newspapers. John's solution to AA meetings was to hide the evidence of his failure and claim the program a success. Closing the door behind me to conceal the damaging evidence, I went looking for John. Opening the screen door to the back yard, I stepped out onto the small patio and spied him tinkering with the garden sprinkler.

"Hey, John," I hailed. "Can you com'ere a minute?" Not waiting for a response or giving him any chance for questions, I ducked back into the house. Once again at the closed bedroom door, I stood waiting, guarding the hidden battleground and the awful secret it held.

"What's up?" he inquired, approaching me and the barred door, wiping his damp hands on his pant legs.

Silently I turned the cold door knob. Watching his face intently, I gently nudged the door open, revealing the chaotic room. John recognized the bottles immediately, his bemused smile slowly replaced by the fear of a trapped animal as he realized what I had discovered.

The ensuing argument heated up quickly. Accusations of disappointment and deceit flew furiously, swirling around repeated pleas for just one more chance and promises of reform. The verbal onslaught of angry, hurtful words heaved back and forth alarmed our dog, Holly. The large golden retriever began barking and anxiously leaping about the room, adding to the chaos.

"I can't take it any more, I'm leaving you!" I flung at him as I fled from the room, heading for the front door as I cut through our bedroom to grab my purse. Holly raced before me and jumped up on our bed, her excited barking reverberating off the walls.

Closely on my heels, my tormentor followed in hot pursuit. He caught up with me by the foot of our bed and grabbed my arm, yanking me around to face him. Firmly clasping both of my shoulders, his steel fingers tightened, digging into my arms. His pleas hardened into demands.

"You gotta listen to me," he commanded loudly, shaking my body violently for emphatic punctuation. Alarmed by the intimate aggression, Holly jumped from the bed and began anxiously tugging at my clothes, trying to pull me away from him.

"No!" I foolishly shot back, struggling to be released. "I'm leaving you! It's over!" I spat with finality.

"But you gotta listen," he persisted, maintaining his vise-like grip on me but slowly losing his hold on sanity. "I promise I'll do better. I'll stop drinking," he pleaded, frustration quivering in his voice as he continued to accent each word with an emphatic shaking of my shoulders, causing my head to flop like a rag doll. Steel fingers suddenly clamped around my throat before I could respond. "Don't leave me," he cried, the final remnants of sanity slipping away.

Staring into his cold blue eyes, searching for the gentle man I knew, I couldn't find any humanity left to bargain with. Temporary insanity clouded over reason, obscuring his ability to recognize the peril he was putting me in. Choking me, he continued shaking my head, spitting out his rambling pleas in a desperate attempt to hold onto our marriage.

I couldn't breathe and my lungs burned from the failed effort. My struggles only intensified his violent grip on my neck, and he slowly strangled away any resistance. My anger turned to fear. No longer able to defend myself, I became completely helpless. A surreal haze clouded my vision, dulling all my senses. His voice became faint, drifting off into the distance.

Holly, trying to rescue me, kept leaping upon my back, repeatedly grabbing mouthfuls of hair and pulling, yanking out hunks of long strands in her efforts to pull me from his death grip. Blackness swirled around my head as I slipped into unconsciousness.

I later awoke disoriented, discarded in a heap on the hardwood floor, unaware of how much time had passed. Alone, ruffled and dazed, I wobbled to my feet and headed for the sanctuary of the bathroom. Muffled sounds behind its closed door stopped me from entering. Staggering past the closed door, using the narrow hall walls for support, I made my way to the kitchen door, paused then stumbled across the vinyl floor to the sink. Hunching over the porcelain basin, eyes closed, I waited for strength to return, dimly aware of Holly's frantic scratching at the back door. John must have put her outside, I thought. Then, turning on the faucet, I splashed the cold, reviving water over my swollen face.

Refreshed, I was filled with a renewed determination to make sure he had a clear understanding that I was walking out of his life. I returned to the closed bathroom door, knowing I would find John on the other side. I flung open the door without knocking, its crash against the wall startling him, preventing him from completing his lethal task. Surprise turned to disbelief at seeing me standing there. Shock stung my senses as awareness of the gruesome scene unfolded before me. The sickly sweet smell of fresh blood assaulted my nostrils. We both realized what was happening at the same time. Thinking he had killed me, John had retreated to the bathroom sink, floundering in the darkest depths of despair and depression. Filled with remorse, and with insanity still dictating his actions, he had savagely slit his left wrist halfway to the elbow, exposing taut tendons and loose veins. Glistening red blood spurted with his every heart beat, splattering the walls, covering the small sink, and spilling into puddles at his feet.

"Oh, my God," was all he could mumble.

Grabbing towels, I frantically wrapped his gushing arm. John was once again meek and mild-mannered, although humbled by facing the reality of his own struggle for survival. Mumbled apologies and shame accompanied our head-on rush to the emergency room.

Oblivious to the stares and whispers my appearance created in the crowded alcove, I paced the hospital emergency room for over eight hours while waiting for John to come out of surgery. My disheveled clothing was splattered with blood, clumps of hair clung to my torn sweater, my face was pale and puffy, my eyes swollen. Perfect black and blue hand prints encircled my swollen, bruised neck.

"Are you all right, Miss?" an approaching police officer inquired.

"Yes, I'm fine," I assured him. "I'm waiting for my husband. He's an artist and hurt his wrist when he tripped and fell on his palette knife." I fabricated an alibi for John and thus the charade of a perfect marriage continued.

The Baby Who Couldn't Cry

For a brief moment the sterile pre-delivery room was once again shrouded in an eerie quiet. In labor, lying on the narrow gurney-turned-bed, I had been staring at the pristine ceiling for hours. A light blanket covering my tummy chased away the chill from the electronic monitors jelled to my pregnant belly. Surrounded by hospital white, I glanced around, catching a glimpse of the young woman and her husband behind the curtained partition next to me. Together she and I had endured hours of silent labor, with soft moans the only evidence of our efforts.

Down the hall, a primordial scream once again pierced the night. Its agonizing intensity vibrated the hospital walls, intruding into every tiny waiting room and agitating the other expecting mothers-to-be who were fighting their own demons of pain. Each screamer's outcries had triggered my own bouts of labor, causing a wave of hot pain to slowly spread across the small of my back. Pulsating tension infused every muscle with an instinct to push the new life into this world until silence once again took over and the contractions fled, followed by a flood of relief. Thus the screamer and I dueled through the night till early dawn, minutes imitating hours.

"I wish she would shut up," I complained to the nurse entering the room.

"They just wheeled her down to delivery," she comforted me. "Let's check and see how you're coming along." After fussing with the baby monitors, she did a quick check for dilation and then abruptly fled from the room. Within minutes the flustered nurse returned, ushering in a team of colleagues. Amidst their mutterings, fidgeting with dials, and repeated dilation checks, I once again plunged into labor pains.

"Try not to push," commanded the doctor. "You're not dilated enough," he informed me.

"The baby's in gross distress and you need an immediate C-section. The nurse will get you ready while I schedule a surgery room." Attempting a reassuring smile, he patted my hand, turned, and hurried from the room.

The ominous words failed to register as I clung to the reassurance and comfort provided by the nurse who was rearranging my sheets and pillow. With a quick call, she confirmed the location of the surgery room arranged by the doctor. The nurse was joined by a co-worker, and with the hospital gurney ready, the efficient pair whisked me through the maze of corridors till we burst through the double doors of the operating room. The room, already abuzz with preparations, intimidated me with glaring bright lights and glistening stainless steel. Centering the gurney under the huge operating spotlight, I was outfitted with a small green pup tent which jutted from my shoulders and peaked above my chest, successfully shielding the delivery activity from my view. Rolling my head, I strained to see and understand what was happening around me. All I could make out were distorted reflections flickering in the curves of the polished steel shade of the brilliant spot light suspended above the crowd of attending physicians clustered just beyond my sheltered view.

"I'm going to start your anesthesia now," an attendant softly whispered in my left ear. "I'm giving you just enough so you'll not feel anything, but I want you to stay awake." After adjusting dials, he settled in a chair by my shoulder. Leaning closer to monitor my progress, he tried carrying on trivial chit-chat meant to keep me mentally alert and distracted. All I could do was mumble polite responses, pre-occupied with the unfolding drama. The dull, prickly sensation spreading across my abdomen brought to my mind images of me being split open. I listened intently for the first wailing cries of my newborn.

A sudden flurry of activity intensified my concentration. Out of the corner of my eye I spied a swarm of white-shrouded shadows scurry past and surround the other operating table in the room. I listened to silence marred only by scuffling feet; no baby cries invaded the busy room.

"There's no heart beat," the baby doctor whispered. Time stood still under the burden of silence filling the room.

"GOD DAMN IT!" he shouted, "I said, there's no heart beat!"

His anger electrified the attendants. Just beyond my view, I heard their gallant efforts. Like a swarm of aroused wasps, the attendants buzzed around the hapless infant. Machinery wheeled past. A faint gurgling could be heard as a nurse suctioned fluids from the stillborn's mouth. A rhythmic CPR thumping replaced the baby's absent heartbeat. The attendants muttered and gave no clue of the success or failure of their efforts.

"Clear!" yelled the doctor, defibrillator paddles poised above the tiny form.

"ZAP." I heard no newborn cries.

"ZAP." Still no cries.

Amidst silence, the doctors and attendants fussed around the motionless baby. Suddenly, moving as if in a choreographed ballet, they surrounded the infant's gurney and wheeled it out of the operating room, double doors clanging behind them. And still, no newborn cries.

For days, my baby Sara roller-coasted in a life-or-death fight for survival. Every major organ failed or threatened failure at different times, making transport to a better-equipped trauma center impossible – until day thirteen. Then God looked down and blessed her with resilient spirit, giving her strength and a zealous will for life. I hadn't heard my newborn baby cry because the umbilical cord had wrapped around her neck, and looped under a wrist and back around her neck, binding an arm to her throat with a deadly necktie. Labor had caused a slow strangulation. It was six months before Sara, with healthy lungs, belted out an infant's wailing protest.

MARGARITA SANCHEZ

Forty-four years ago, I was uprooted from a comfortable (some might say privileged) existence in Cuba to an orphanage in Philadelphia. I ended as a Cuban refugee in Miami Beach. After high school, I enrolled in Miami Dade Community College because I failed to get a secretarial job. I went on to earn a Bachelor's of Art degree in sociology at Florida Atlantic University and a Master's degree in social work at Florida State University. I've been a medical social worker for most of my professional career. I'm currently a manager in the patient support services department at Sparrow Hospital in Lansing, Michigan.

Four years ago, I started writing as a hobby. I write personal vignettes, usually infused with humor. Publishing my work was never a goal, but I can't deny my excitement at the opportunity to self-publish this story. This experience forced me to look at my writing more critically. With one story in print, I hope to publish more in the future.

A Deadline Will Motivate You like Nothing Else

My father's death was my wake-up call to write. At eighty, he was the last of his generation. When he died, there was no one left to tell the stories. I had no interest in the family history before, but now I had so many unanswered questions. I write for my son in case he ever wonders why I left Cuba, just like I wonder why my grandmother left Spain.

Writing does not come easy for me. I procrastinate and write only when I have a deadline. Before I start to write, I jot down anything that I want to include in the story. When I wrote about leaving Cuba, I jotted: goodbye at the airport, decision to go to Philadelphia, one and a half years at Cabrini, our reunion. I mull over these events to recall every detail. I discovered that some of my best thinking is done in the shower and while I am driving.

Next, I rehearse in my head ways to tie these memories together into a story. Two or three nights before the deadline, I sit down to write. I compose at the computer, where formatting and correcting are so easy. I use spell-check and the thesaurus tools in the PC, but I also reference a college dictionary and an unabridged Spanish-English dictionary.

When I can't think of an opening, I start writing the middle of the story, then go back and fill in the beginning and the end. I proof and edit from a hard copy. I concentrate on improving the verbs and removing whatever is superfluous. My class is a constant source of inspiration and support. I've begun to experiment with dialogue and I plan to learn how to describe my story settings in exquisite detail.

Fleeing Cuba

Good Bye

"*Fidel Castro es un comunista.*" That's what my father said when the adults gathered after dinner. I lived with my extended family, and every night after coffee, all conversation focused on Fidel. The laws implemented by his revolutionary government disturbed them deeply. They speculated about Cuba's future and hoped for American intervention to derail Fidel.

The fervor of the Revolution continued to escalate. People showed support by dressing in military garb. The televised public trials and daily executions of those accused of crimes against the Revolution transmitted a clear message: dissidence will be brutally crushed. Fidel demanded allegiance: "Make a choice – are you with me or against me?" My family was against Fidel and that made us *gusanos*, worms, the label used for those not supporting the government.

Fearing interference with parental rights, my mother and father decided to get my brother and me out of Cuba. Tia Tessie, my mom's older sister, and her husband, Tio Ernesto, were contemplating a similar fate for my cousins Ernesto and Carlos Erdmann. Empty seats were evident in my classroom. Normally my teacher would tell the class when someone was sick, but these absences were permanent and not discussed. I was warned not to tell anyone of our plan, since we did not know whom to trust. My brother and I had no say in this decision. My parents believed that getting us out of Cuba was necessary, and we would do as we were told.

To this day I do not quite understand how the arrangements were made. The U.S. State Department, the diplomatic core, school administrators in Cuba, airline executives, and Miami's Catholic Welfare collaboratively devised a plan to evacuate Cuban minors. Parents wishing to get their children out of Cuba contacted dissident Cuban educators, who passed the requests to diplomats. Under diplomatic immunity, the names were safely carried to Father Bryan Walsh in the Archdiocese of Miami. Father Walsh was authorized by the U.S. State Department to waive the visa requirement as long as a certified social agency assumed full responsibility for the well-being of the children in the United States. Catholic Welfare, the Protestant Service Bureau, and the Jewish Welfare for Families and Children agencies agreed to take the children into custody. The names of children approved for visa waivers were returned to Cuba and given to the airline executives, who scheduled their flights. This came to be known as Operation Peter Pan. Between 1960 and 1962, thousands of unaccompanied Cuban children were sent to the United States.

On January 27, 1961, my parents took my brother and me to Boyeros Airport to board a Pan-American KLM flight to Jamaica, with a stop in Miami. My cousins, Erne and Carlos, were going with us. Our instructions were to get off in Miami. They didn't say who would be waiting for us in Florida or where we were going to live. I don't think they knew.

I don't remember crying when my parents hugged and kissed me good-bye. I wanted to be brave. I was twelve years old, and my parents had just told me that they did not know if or when we would see each other again. I was on my way to a foreign country with my eleven-year-old brother and my cousins, who were twelve and thirteen. I was the only one who spoke English, and I felt totally responsible for getting us to Miami. I was terrified.

Reluctant as sheep, we approached the plane. There were many other unaccompanied children on board. Upon arrival at Miami, the stewardesses steered our flock through customs and registration. All four of us registered with Catholic Welfare. That's when I spotted Tia Rochy, my mother's younger sister and my only adult relative in Miami. She was in the next room among a sea of strangers, waving her arms wildly, trying to get our attention. I did not feel so alone. I was allowed to stay in her tiny, one-bedroom apartment. The boys had to sleep nearby in St. Joseph Orphanage.

The next few days were strangely satisfying. I had not seen my aunt for several months. She had lost a lot of weight and now smoked continuously. It was great to be with her and my cousins Maita, age six, and Lourdes, age three, again. But where was Tio Picky? He was the first one in the family to go into exile. Picky was a pilot for Cuba Aeropostal. When his best friend began conspiring against Fidel, Tia Rochy and Tio Picky were perceived to be guilty by association and were followed everywhere by government agents. Tio Picky did not feel safe, and on his next scheduled flight to Miami he requested political asylum. Tia Rochy was not volunteering any information, and I sensed it was best not to pry.

Months later I found out that Tio Picky was in Nicaragua training for the Bay of Pigs invasion. El Frente, the CIA-backed organization that recruited him, provided Tia Rochy a $280 monthly stipend. This was the entire family income, and there was never enough to cover expenses. Tia Rochy was an emotional wreck. On the one hand, the uncertainty of Tio Picky's whereabouts compounded by the responsibilities of being a single parent was more than she could bear. On the other hand, she had many new friends, most of them Cuban refugees, who were very supportive. These new friends picked up the boys every day and brought them to Tia Rochy's apartment. There was a steady stream of visitors, so to make myself useful I learned to make Cuban coffee. A *cafécito* was the only amenity shared with anyone who dropped in.

During the next week, the Catholic Welfare determined our fate. The three boys were going to Philadelphia, but I was given the choice to stay with Tia Rochy. I chose to go to Philadelphia, naïvely believing that my brother and I were going to be together. Our flight departed on February 6, 1961. With us on the plane were two of my cousins' cousins, Batty and Yoyi, twelve and thirteen years old. We were greeted at the airport by representatives from the Catholic Resettlement Council of the Archdiocese of Philadelphia. Without explanations or much of a good-bye, the boys were taken to St. John's Orphan Asylum. Then Batty, Yoyi, and I were dropped off at St. Frances Xavier Cabrini Home, an orphanage. I felt betrayed.

Life at Cabrini

Mother Xavier and the Mother Superior welcomed us to our new home. Mother Xavier supervised the kids at the orphanage, and Mother Superior was in charge of everything. They were kind. I don't remember what was said, but they served us tea with cream and sugar and a piece of apple pie. It was the first time I had tasted tea and did not really care for it, but the apple pie was delicious. We must have arrived during school hours because there were no children around. After the snack, we were allowed to go outside and play in the snow. This was a first for all of us. We put on our wool coats and gingerly stepped from the path onto the snow. As we gained confidence, we walked down a slope until we sank knee deep in the snow. We had to march our way out. Snow got inside our shoes, our socks, and the bottoms of our coats. When we went inside, we were wet and very, very cold .

Cabrini Home was a modern, three-story, tan brick building located on a hill. Half of the building contained the orphanage; the other half was the nunnery. The chapel, library, kitchen, and laundry facilities were shared. The nuns dressed all in black, and we addressed them as "Mother." Our dormitory rooms were spartan but spacious. My room, on the third floor, had linoleum floors and four beds neatly made. I don't remember pictures on the walls, but there were curtains on the windows. Next to my bed was a nightstand, and I had a small closet by the door. All girls on the floor shared a large communal bathroom down the hall and a lounge where we did our homework, read, ate snacks and, if allowed, watched TV.

We unpacked our belongings, and Mother Xavier issued each of us a school uniform. What did not fit in our closet was stored in a locked hallway closet. At suppertime we finally got to see all the other girls who lived there. The youngest was three and the oldest, Angeline, must have been around eighteen. Most girls were between first and eighth grades and attended St. Donato's Parochial School located a few blocks away.

The older girls at the Home were assigned daily and weekly chores. Chores were rotated every month so that no one was stuck washing mountains of dirty dishes in the kitchen. Four girls were needed for dish duty. One washed, one rinsed, and two dried and put away the dishes. Washing dishes was the most disgusting chore. The stainless steel sink was so deep that when it was my turn to do dishes, I had to stand on a stool to reach its bottom. As I washed the plates, the warm, sudsy water turned murky, greasy, and cold, with food scraps floating all over. I hated how that dirty water felt on my hands and arms and the stench of my wet blouse after I finished the dishes.

Life at Cabrini was predictable. Each weekday started with mass at 6:00 a.m., then breakfast, a walk to school, home for lunch, and back to school. After school we had a snack. I looked forward to the afternoons when cold leftover pizza was sent to our floor on the dumbwaiter. We could eat as much as we wanted. We did homework or chores until supper, and we had some free time before bedtime.

On weekends, we had mass, then breakfast, chores, lunch,

playtime or an occasional field trip in summer, and supper and watched about one hour of TV before bedtime. On Sundays we always watched *Bonanza*. Our daily routine was not much different than that of the nuns, except that instead of going to school, they taught school, and they prayed a lot more.

I settled in, accepted my new life, and made the best of it. Because I spoke English, I was enrolled in the seventh grade, the same grade I was in when I left Cuba. I got all As and Bs. I think my name may have been hard to pronounce because the nuns started calling me Margaret Sancheis. They also thought I spoke too loudly and gestured too much, so they always encouraged me to lower my voice and not to use my hands when I spoke.

At Cabrini I learned all kinds of new and very useful skills that I am certain I would never have learned in Cuba. Within a very short time, I could wash and iron clothes, make my bed hospital-style, sweep and mop floors with the best of them, set the tables, wash a million dishes, and help with food preparation in the kitchen. I especially liked to clean the chapel. The main responsibilities were to dust everything and mop and wax the floors. The first time I used the polisher, it jerked me down the center aisle. The machine controlled me. The harder I pulled, the more wildly it thrashed from side to side. I crashed it against every pew. I was very proud of myself when I mastered the operation of that heavy machine. My favorite place in the Home was the library. It had an extensive collection of young adult books that I was free to borrow anytime. I read dozens during my tenure at Cabrini. I missed my family, but in an orphanage everyone is in the same boat and dwelling on your feelings did not get you an ounce of sympathy.

Batty and Yoyi did not adjust well. They must have been pampered in Cuba because they did not know how to do anything for themselves. They could barely comb their hair. English was a major barrier. It was humiliating to be turned back to the fourth grade in school. They were isolated because they could not communicate. They cried a lot and lamented their fate. I felt sorry for them and tried helping them as much as I could. I was glad their parents came to get them after a couple of months. After they left, there was no one with whom I could speak Spanish.

Getting in touch with my brother and cousins was next to impossible. Telephone calls were difficult to schedule. I just gave up trying; my inquiries were brokered through the nuns. Most news about them came in letters from Cuba. I was able to visit them at St. John's just one time. We were so happy to see each other. They showed me around. Their home was much older and darker. All the windows on the first floor had security bars, and the bathroom toilets flushed on their own every few minutes. I had never seen self-flushing toilets before.

All letters I sent to my family in Cuba were positive. I concentrated on my progress in school. I did not dare question my parents about their plans or efforts to come to the U.S. The government regularly intercepted correspondence, and anyone wanting to leave Cuba was de facto a *contrarevolucionario*. I could not put them at risk and did not want them worrying about me. They had enough to contend with.

Turmoil Back Home

Back in Cuba, everyday life was becoming more difficult. My parents, aunts, uncles, and grandparents debated the wisdom of leaving Cuba every night. For my parents, going to the United States meant reuniting with us kids, democracy, and freedom. But leaving Cuba also meant walking away from everyone and everything they had ever known and loved. Family, friends, home, and livelihood all had to be left behind to start life over again. No one believed that the United States would tolerate a Communist enclave just ninety miles away. With us children safely away, they hoped to weather the storm in Cuba, certain that U.S. military intervention was imminent.

The 1960 revolutionary initiatives to confiscate land and nationalize private property were already implemented. The Agrarian Reform Law limited the number of acres that an individual could own. Anything above the limit was confiscated. My mom's uncle lost his cattle ranch in eastern Cuba. The Nationalization of Property law targeted American-owned industries. The electricity suppliers, telephone companies, oil refineries, and sugar processing plants were all nationalized.

Fidel proceeded to curtail diplomatic relations with the United States. Right after we left, in January 1961, he expelled all American citizens. Only eleven U.S. diplomats were allowed to remain in Cuba. Eleven was the same number of Cuban diplomats certified to work in Washington D.C. Americans were given forty-eight hours to leave the country.

Urban reform came next. With this initiative, all rental properties were appropriated. Anyone who had rented and lived in a dwelling for thirty or more years was declared the owner of said property. These new owners could trade their property with someone else, but they could not sell it outright. Anyone renting a dwelling for fewer than thirty years now paid rent to the government. My dad's sisters had invested their inheritance in real estate. They lost all income from rental properties.

In the spring of 1961, all schools were closed from the sixth grade through high school. Students unable to attend school were expected to volunteer to teach reading and writing in rural areas. Peer pressure was used most effectively to get volunteers. Once away from parental supervision, these teen volunteers were easily influenced to support the government. The books issued to teach reading praised the Revolution's accomplishments. Inadvertently, the student volunteers spread Fidel's gospel and, in the process, indoctrinated themselves. This new ideology disengaged children from their parents. This was what my father feared. That's why we were sent to the United States.

Neighborhood watch committees were then instituted to be the eyes and ears for the government. Every street block had a neighborhood watch committee. The job of the members was to keep an eye on everyone and everything and be government informants. They organized volunteers for governmental programs such as cutting sugarcane, educating rural children, and making neighborhood improvements. Anyone who did not support government initiatives or participate in the "voluntary" efforts was suspect. Even going to church was looked at unfavorably. In his frequent marathon speeches, Fidel legitimized neighborhood watch committees and urged all Cubans to be vigilant of their friends, families, and neighbors. These committees felt empowered to harass and intimidate individuals and their families into compliance.

This was the repressive climate endured by my family in Cuba. My father's predictions had come true. The exodus of Cuba's upper and middle class was now steady, despite the fact that property and assets of anyone leaving the country were immediately confiscated by the state. Almost everyone leaving believed that their departure was temporary, three to six months at most. They were certain that U.S. military intervention was imminent.

The Bay of Pigs invasion, on April 17, 1961, was that long-awaited attempt to overthrow Fidel Castro. By air, the Nicaraguan-trained, exiled Cuban pilots aimed to disable the military runways so that the Cuban planes could not take off. The ground troops landing at Playa Giron struggled to establish a beachhead that they hoped the U.S. would recognize and support as the site of a legitimate Cuban government. Even though this invasion was a covert CIA operation, the U.S. failed to back up the Cuban fighters. The promised American air support never came, and in less than twenty-four hours, most of the Playa Giron invaders were captured and sent to prison. Fidel crowed about his decisive victory against the *Yanquis*. Tio Picky did not participate in the Playa Giron invasion. He was on leave in Miami tending to Tia Rochy, who was on the verge of a nervous breakdown.

To avoid further uprisings, the homes and businesses of suspected dissidents were searched. If weapons, U.S. or old Cuban currency, or anti-government propaganda (e.g. literature from the Catholic Youth Organization) was found, the head of the household was taken to jail or to a detention center without any judicial process. Any remaining doubts my father might have had about leaving Cuba vanished the night of Playa Giron. Armed soldiers picked up my father in the middle of the night and accused him of hiding firearms in his hardware store. At gunpoint, they searched the whole place and found nothing. He was taken to the police precinct with other suspected dissidents. He was released the next day, but he understood that the neighborhood watch committees were tracking his every move and would not miss an opportunity to harass him. After Playa Giron, Fidel finished consolidating his power. He expelled all foreign priests from Cuba, effectively eliminating the influence of the Catholic Church on the population. Not enough priests were left to nurture religious beliefs or to challenge governmental actions from the pulpit.

On May 1, 1961, Fidel declared Cuba to be a socialist republic, and my parents decided it was time to leave.

Getting to Miami

From Miami, Tia Rochy wrote to the State Department in Washington, D.C., to request a visa waiver for my mom, her sister. She explained that my mother, an executive secretary in the Cuban Ministry of Labor since 1946, was subjected to threats and intimidation because she refused to join the Communist Party and carry a rifle to perform guard duty. Quitting her job would be tantamount to declaring herself a dissident, which would further jeopardize her situation. She feared that Castro would soon prohibit the departure of Cuban citizens to the U.S. and that if a visa was not granted, my brother and I would remain orphans indefinitely. She finalized her letter by pledging financial support for my mom so she would not become a burden on the welfare system.

From Philadelphia, I also wrote to the State Department requesting a waiver of passport and visa requirements for my parents. On July 20, 1961, both were granted visa waivers. My mom purchased a one-way ticket on the last ferry to leave Habana, and on August 3, she arrived in Port Everglades, Florida. My aunts tell me that my mom brought the maximum allowed, packed in the biggest duffel bags they had ever seen. She even packed a dress to wear to my graduation.

My dad continued going to work every day as if nothing was happening. On September 19, he pulled down the three metal garage-size doors to close the family business for the last time. He gazed around the only workplace he'd ever known, the hardware store purchased by his father when he was still a young man and later astutely managed by his mother into a profitable business. He grew up in this store, delivered its goods on his bicycle as a young man, and took over the business when Grandma started to slow down. He went to the office for one final look. Then he closed the door behind him and walked away. He never looked back. The next morning, he boarded a plane for Miami, leaving everything behind.

Tia Rochy and Tio Picky welcomed my parents into their home. It was a typical Cuban refugee household. Four families (eight adults and five kids) lived in a three-bedroom, one-bathroom home. Since they were last to arrive, my parents slept in the garage. Their bed was next to the washing machine. They received public assistance ($100) for two months, until my father got a job cutting sheet metal for $1 an hour. They could not support us, so we remained in Philadelphia.

Cabrini Girls

During my first six months in Philadelphia I went through puberty, gained more than thirty pounds, and cut my hair short. Having outgrown all the clothes I brought from Cuba, I wore clothes donated to the orphanage, the same as the other girls did. In addition to my school uniform, I had three dresses, one pair of black shoes for school, and a pair of play shoes. When I came home from school I changed into one of the two well-worn, drab-looking dresses and put on my play shoes. The third, fancier dress was for church on Sundays and was kept in Mother Xavier's hall closet. My physical appearance had completely changed and with it my identity. I was a Cabrini girl.

Everyday life was still predictable, but there were special events that all of us looked forward to. In summer, a carnival was held on the grounds of Cabrini Home. This was a community fund-raising event benefiting the home. Cabrini bustled with preparation activities the week before the carnival. From our bedroom windows we watched men build many booths and transform our playground. The whole neighborhood turned out to play chance games and enjoy fabulous Italian food. We were allowed to mingle freely in the festivities well into the night.

At Christmas time, the nuns placed all Cabrini girls with families. Two of us were placed with the same family. I thought it was sad and strange that both of us had parents, yet neither of us could be with them. We were picked up on Christmas Eve and got to their apartment in time to finish trimming the tree. This helped break the ice and get us all in the spirit.

That night we went to their neighbor's party. There were lots of people having fun dancing the "twist." That apartment had an artificial silver Christmas tree illuminated by a floor light that changed colors. The tree's silver branches turned to the color of the light shining on it. I had never seen anything like it. I remembered my last Christmas in Cuba, feasting with the whole family on pork, black beans, and rice. I felt out of place and homesick.

The next morning there were gifts under the tree, but the only present that mattered was a Brownie camera from my mom and dad. I was not expecting any gifts. I had not seen my mom and dad for almost a year, but they loved me and that camera proved it.

I don't know how my brother spent Christmas, but on February 9, 1962, he was placed in a foster home. Apparently he had not adjusted to life at St. John's Orphanage. According to my parents, he threatened to stay outside in the snow until he froze to death. His foster parents, Mr. and Mrs. Hubert O'Reilly, lived in the suburbs. They brought me to their home for a visit. The O'Reilly's home was magazine beautiful. They had three children of their own and two

Cuban foster children, my brother and a teenage girl. They treated my brother as one of their own. This was a sharp contrast to the institutional atmosphere at the orphanage.

On Easter Sunday everyone at Cabrini went to mass at the parish church. Cabrini girls always got a new Sunday dress for this occasion. We went to the retail store, where we were fitted with frilly, lily-white dresses, gloves, shoes, and hats. The little ones may have looked cute in their Easter outfits, but we teenagers looked like lampshades. When we marched down the central aisle of St. Donato's Church to occupy our place of honor in the front pews, we were definitely lampshades on parade. Everybody in church gawked at the Cabrini girls. We looked so different from other girls our age. These outfits perhaps were meant to highlight our innocence, but instead they accentuated our outcast place in the community.

Our Reunion

Back in Miami, my father found a second job managing two apartment buildings in Miami Beach. Free rent and utilities were provided in lieu of wages. They moved from Tia Rochy's house to live in a furnished one-bedroom apartment on Miami Beach. With their own place and a small income they were now able to support us. On May 21, 1962, they wrote to the Catholic Charities of the Archdiocese of Philadelphia to request our return.

The plan was to fly to Miami on June 13, right after schools closed for summer vacation. I came down with the mumps just after I received the news. I was really worried, almost in panic. Would I be allowed to travel if I was sick? The nuns did not give me any reassurance. They were treating my symptoms with conventional medicine, but I wanted an immediate cure. I pleaded for divine intervention. On my knees, I prayed and made all sorts of promises to every saint I could think of, and every morning after mass I washed my cheeks and neck with the Chapel's holy water. It worked because my swelling went down.

Reunion day was bittersweet. The nuns hugged and blessed me. We had smiles on our lips and tears in our eyes. I did not develop close friendships with any of the girls, but my departure from the orphanage was stressful for some. My story had a happy ending; theirs was still dubious. At the airport, I hugged and kissed my brother and my two cousins, Erne and Carlos. We were giddy with anticipation. All of us were dressed in our finest outfits. I wore the lampshade dress. Like me, my cousins had grown quite a bit, but my brother looked about the same. After a year and half of speaking only English, my Spanish was a bit rusty; nonetheless, we could not stop talking.

Our entire family was waiting at the Miami airport. Everyone hugged, kissed, laughed, and cried all at the same time. We could not stop touching each other, almost afraid to let go. We could hardly believe we were a family again. We went to Tia Rochy's house, where family friends were waiting to see us. It was a grand, loud party that spilled into the front and back yards and ran into the night. Tia Tessie teased me about my American accent. Tia Rochy was amazed about how much we had grown. Eventually, my parents, my brother, and I left for our new home in Miami Beach. My cousins took over my parents' bedroom in Tia Rochy's garage.

KATHLEEN W. SEIM

I was born and raised in Superior, Wisconsin as a Wisconsin dairy farmer's daughter. I currently live in Lansing, Michigan. I'm a Michigan state police security officer assigned to the governor's security unit. I also work for the Dewitt Township fire department as a firefighter and emergency medical technician. I'm a first aid instructor for the Michigan state police and I teach first aid classes at the American Red Cross.

My son, Jeff, and his wife, Nikki, who live in Mulliken, Michigan are expecting their first child in October. It's a girl! I have two step-children and three step-grandchildren, all of whom live in Michigan.

I enjoy drawing and painting and I decorate my home and yard with my own original creations. Going to the extreme at Halloween, I scare the treat-or-treaters away.

I especially love loading my big, hairy dog, Wooly Bully Bear, in my vehicle, and driving to Wisconsin to spend vacation time with my family. I guess it's true – you can take the girl out of the country, but you can't take the country out of the girl.

Choose One Main Idea to Convey to a Reader

When I write, I think about the past, and the story is there. It has been developing for years in my head. I want to write the story so I'll never forget it.

I find a place to write that feels comfortable to me. Sometimes I enjoy sitting in the corner of a restaurant, drinking coffee and scribbling as fast as I can. The thoughts flow and I can't write fast enough to keep up. I write steadily for a paragraph or two or maybe a page or two. Then I stop and re-read what I wrote. I write alternative word choices and sentence structure in the area above and below several of the sentences that I have just written. I continue to write, following this same pattern. When I'm mentally exhausted or my hand hurts, I put it all down.

Later that day, or the next day, I will pick it back up and re-read what I have written. I evaluate the different options surrounding the sentences and choose the one I think is best. If I still can't decide, I ask for opinions from different friends.

When I write, there is usually one main idea I want to convey to the reader. Everything else in the story leads up to, explains, or shows how that idea affected someone or something. I want this idea to reach the readers' minds and have them become emotionally involved in the story.

My submission of "Barn Boards and Memories" is a shortened version of the original story. However, it offers up a taste of the country flavor and the events in our everyday lives.

I wrote the majority of "Barn Boards and Memories" while I was visiting my family in Wisconsin. I shut myself in a bedroom and wrote and wrote and wrote. The conditions were perfect since I had my family available to answer questions about forgotten dates or types of farm machinery used. With those blanks filled in, my mind was free to release the memories.

Everyone has an amazing story to tell. So pick up a pen. We want to hear yours.

Barn Boards
and Memories

When the House Burned Down

How much of our youth can we remember? I think it depends on the impact of an experience. I was five years old when our farmhouse burned down.

The cold, blistery winters of Wisconsin meant full-rolling fires in the old wood and coal stoves. In the early 1950s, it was difficult obtaining and maintaining the fuel necessary to provide heat and guard against the frigid, penetrating winds. To be safe and warm was the priority during those below-zero temperatures. Outdated, faulty stoves, improper fuel sources, and creosote build-up in the chimneys sparked many fires throughout the countryside.

It was a few days before Christmas and we had a strong fire going. A roaring sound, like a loud tornado, whirled in our chimney, indicating a fire had developed. The walls ignited and our house was on fire. Mom called the fire department and then rushed me and my brother Dave to the barn. I remember her saying to me, "Stay inside, don't open the door, and keep an eye on your brother." Then she was gone.

Dave was only a toddler, running around half-dressed. Watching him was the last thing on my mind. I opened the barn door a crack and peeked outside. The house was filled with flames. People were running everywhere. I got jealous when I saw my older brother, Bobby, standing with some adults. I closed the door. Losing track of time, I busied myself playing in the barn.

The fire department put out the fire and left. Nothing could be saved. Partial walls, bricks, and ash were all that remained. I'm sure it all looked hopeless to Mom. It was then that she saw Dave. He was sitting in the gutter, covered with cow manure. No place to clean up, no clothes to change into, and no place to call home.

With the addition of a wood stove, we turned the old garage into our new home.

Once, while we lived in the garage, a movement at the foot of my bed awakened me. I peeked from my covers and locked eyes with a rat. He stared back for a few moments, then ambled away, probably wondering about this strange creature inhabiting his domain.

It was several years before my dad and uncles finished building the new house. It was constructed adjacent to where our old home had been. The new house was 672 square feet with three bedrooms, a kitchen, and a living room. My two brothers, Bobby and Dave, shared a bedroom. I was lucky. Since I was the only girl, I got my own room. We had no running water or bathroom. Living without running water and no indoor toilet was nothing new to us. We hadn't had those conveniences in the past. We could never have afforded those privileges.

Well Water

Our water source was a well, located under the pump house. A motor triggered the pump's arms, which moved up and down in a rhythmic motion every time the motor was turned on. This would work the water from the cool depths to the surface. The pump house also held a water-filled cow tank. The milk produced by our dairy cows was put into large cans that were lifted into the tank for storage until the milk truck arrived and pick them up. The milk needed to be delivered daily to the creamery. Another cow tank, which was outside, was kept constantly full: this was the one the cows drank from.

We kept a large crock full of water in the house. A dipper was used to get a drink. It was the best water I ever tasted, so cold and fresh. As the crock emptied, we'd carry a filled bucket from the pump house and dump the water into the crock.

Once or sometimes twice a week, we would use an old metal tub filled with hot water to take baths. Between bath times, a washcloth was used for a quick refresher.

Mom used an old wringer washer to do the family laundry. A large, water-filled tub was set over an open fire outdoors. When the water got hot, it was dumped into the washer. The clothes were washed, wrung out, and pinned to the line to dry.

Mom was alone one day when the artificial inseminator man came to take care of the cows. She was standing in the pump house talking to him. He headed to the barn. Mom had a piece of twine hanging from her hand. When she turned the pump on, it got caught in the pulley of the pump jack. As her hand was being drawn into the belt, she reached up with her free hand, grabbed one of the rotating pump arms, and stopped the action. She yelled for help. The man ran back and shut the pump down. Her hand was severely bruised. She wore the splints and bandages the doctor applied for several days. Still, she would milk cows by hand twice a day.

The Outhouse

The outhouse on the farm was a small wooden structure located about twenty yards from the house. Unlike the more deluxe models, it was a one-holer. I remember sitting in it and seeing a mouse scurry across the floor. Next thing you know, I'm singing to myself, "There's a mouse in the outhouse."

Once when my brother opened the outhouse door, a porcupine surprised him. With its head wedged in the hole and its rear poking out, Dave thought it was stuck. By the time he rounded up the rest of us to see it, the porcupine had found its way out and was waddling away. My Lord, it was big as a washtub!

Use of an outhouse was an accepted yet difficult part of life. It sure was inconvenient during those forty-below Wisconsin winters. In the early days, we used Sears catalogs and old newspapers. We gradually advanced to toilet paper. Progress. Isn't it wonderful?

Dairy Cows

As little kids, we sat on cows while Mom and Dad milked. The stanchion limited cows' movement, so we were fairly safe. Mom and Dad would fill a big bowl with fresh milk, and the cats would come a-runnin'. Mom and Dad milked by hand for many years, and then the milking machine entered the picture.

Occasionally after I got home from school, I'd spot Mom coming from the fields carrying a newborn calf, still wet from birth, weak, and unable to stand. A concerned momma cow would be at Mom's heels. A new baby was coming home.

The country's rendition of an old wives tale literally includes a "tail." As the story goes, when the cows are turned into the woods after the night milking, bears find their amusement. They chase the cows and pull off their tails. Some swear by this; others scoff at the idea. Spotting a shortened tail after a night filled with fearful cow bellowing, I relinquished my doubts. After all, I was witness to the "bear" facts of the matter.

The Tractor

I was about seven years old when Dad introduced me to the family tractor. I was sitting on his lap, steering. A big mistake. The combination of our driving skills proved to be disastrous as we went crashing into the garage. Climbing off the tractor and walking away, we pretended nothing happened. Dad calmly straightened the mess up later by replacing a few boards.

We had an Allis Chalmers tractor. While Dave was moving it one day – crosswise, on an incline – it rolled. One of the tractor's big tires landed on Dave's back. Bobby and Cousin Allen were in the area. They ran to help. The combined adrenalin of two strong country boys allowed them to lift the tire slightly. Dave squeezed free from entrapment. Miraculously, he suffered no permanent injuries.

The electric start didn't always work on the Allis Chalmers. Many times, Bobby had to crank the tractor manually to get it going. Once, when he was fourteen years old, he gave it a powerful spin. His wrist broke cleanly, with the top of his hand facing the top of his forearm. Arm settled in a bucket of cold water, he was off to the doctor's office. Amazingly, he suffered no permanent repercussions from the break. Shortly thereafter, the Allis Chalmers was replaced with a John Deere.

Dad's Outside Job

Setbacks such as cattle loss, machinery failure, and unexpected medical costs made it impossible to survive solely on the farm's income. Dad took a job at the creosote plant, where railroad ties were coated with an oily preservative. Dad's job was climbing the piles of ties and impounding identification numbers on them. How he did smell when he came home from work with his clothes blackened from the creosote! My brothers and I would fight to get his metal lunch box because once in a while we would find a candy bar in it.

After a short stint with the creosote plant, Dad took a job working for the Soo Line railroad as a section hand. The section crew careened along the rails in a small motorized car, commonly known as "putt-

putt." They did repair work to the tracks. My Dad loved working for the railroad. The job, however, took a toll on his health. The noise of the train yard diminished his hearing. Then, one cold winter morning, his section crew dropped him off at a remote piece of tracks to do some repair work. They didn't come back to get him. Attempting to return by following the tracks, he was alone for hours. Eventually, his employer sent a crew to retrieve him. Dad was hospitalized with frostbite. He lost the majority of strength in his hands, yet continued to work for the railroad until his retirement. Asked why he didn't sue, he responded with a common assumption of the times, "If I do anything, I will lose my job. Then where would I be?"

Dad also worked the farm. We were all in the fields on afternoons and weekends. Dad's specialty was keeping the fence line fixed so that the cows wouldn't get out. The fence line routinely needed to be inspected. A wire stretcher would be used to set the barbed wire in place against the fence post to which it would be secured. Every so often, the posts would need replacement, too.

Haying Season

Once haying season began, it consumed our lives. When we were little, we would sit for hours on the back of the baler as Mom baled. For entertainment, we watched the rectangular bales drop one by one to the ground. Sometimes we played with our toys in the dirt on the road. Thus, Mom could keep track of us until we were old enough to help, which was decided by our ability to lift a forty- to fifty- pound bale.

During the day, Mom would cut, rake, or bale accordingly to provide the final product: hay. Sometimes, Bobby or Dave cut or raked to prepare for the next day while the rest of us loaded the hay wagon. Each load held 100-125 bales. Each afternoon we would get one to three loads of hay in. Each load was usually four tiers high, with bales stacked side-by-side. The load would be bound by crisscrossing bales of the fifth layer. Standing on the ground, the boys could throw bales up to the fourth tier on the wagon. I never knew anyone could be so strong.

By the time I was about eleven, I was driving the tractor. Occasionally, I would pull the hay wagon, keeping a slow, controlled speed, pushing in the clutch for a momentary halt, so bales could be hoisted on. Mom or Bobby would usually stack. Dave threw bales or drove. Dad would fill in wherever needed.

When the load was full, we would head back to the elevator, which leaned against the barn. After all the hard work, we'd sit up high on the top tier for the ride home. The relaxing breeze cooled our faces, and we challenged the trees by grabbing their leaves as we passed by.

Then it was time to unload the bales. We would dig a hook into each bale individually and toss it onto the elevator. The elevator had a chain link pulley system operated by a motor. The belt would carry the bales to the top, where they would drop through a hole in the wall of the barn into the area commonly known as the hay barn. Safe from any threatening weather, the bales would be stacked when time permitted.

The elevator could be dangerous, as is true of all farm equipment. Curiosity almost cost Dave a finger when he was a little child. While poking around examining the operation of the elevator, his finger caught between the gear and chain and was severely lacerated.

After work in the fields each day, I would do my homework, set my hair, and sleep on the curlers. Some mornings came too early and my hair would still be wet.

Pets

Over the years, we had many pets. While playing in the barn, I once counted twenty-nine cats. I also had rabbits. While in town one day, I spotted a starving rabbit in a cage in someone's yard. Although it was against my upbringing, I broke into the cage, hid the rabbit in my coat, and brought him home. I named him Famine, and he became the largest, most striking rabbit of them all. We always had lots of collie pups around. They were purebred but not AKC-registered. We would sell the males for $25 and the females for $15. Bobby tried to raise mallard ducks. The dogs got through the fencing and killed them. There was my pet Jet, a pig. We ended up eating him. Most amusing was Dave's goat, Chocolate. He jumped on car hoods, followed you like a shadow, and was a general nuisance.

I had my pinto pony, Little Joe. He wanted to break me as much as I wanted to break him. That horse could open any door or gate. He was quite the entertainer, however. I would touch his leg and he would paw the ground with each touch. Portraying a mathematical genius, he would pound out answers to simple addition and subtraction problems. As I left the school bus, Little Joe would be waiting at the fence. I'd greet him. He'd bite my purse, steal it, and run. The kids on the bus loved this. Eventually, he had to be sold. He wasn't a benefit to the farm.

There was no reason to keep our Shetland pony, either, but he was ever so cute. He was short and bulky with shaggy, mottled, red-brown hair. We called him Chimp. We didn't ride him. We just loved him. While petting Chimp one day, I noticed he stood motionless, had a blank look to his eyes, and was frothing at the mouth. The vet came and discovered a nail imbedded in Chimp's back. Chimp was diagnosed with lockjaw, and the vet put him down.

My favorite pet, by far, was my Spitz-mix mutt dog, Snowball. I got Snowball while we were out selling eggs. At one stop, I spotted a medium-sized white dog running amongst a pile of junk. I reached my hand to her and she growled. After some coaxing, she came out. Eventually, I was holding her in my arms. The owner claimed that Snowball was mean, but she offered the dog to me. I talked Mom and Dad into keeping her.

Snowball was my best friend. We walked, worked, and slept together. She was a one-person dog and I was that person. With knees to floor, crouching on elbows, I would do my homework while Snowball lay on my back. When you come in from freezing winter weather, your feet, hands, and rear end pinch as they thaw. I would sit on the wood stove to "get the chill out." Snowball would bounce up about three-quarters of the way. I'd reach down, capture her, and cuddle her on my lap. We loved sitting on the stove.

She had pups once. During the night, I awoke to little puppy cries. The pups were born elsewhere, but she had carried each individually and dropped it on my head. Years later, when I began to drive, she would lie in the back window. I took her along whenever possible. A friend to the end, she lived to be seventeen years old.

Fall

In the fall, the wood had to be cut. Dad, Bobby, and Dave cut down smaller-sized, hard, dry trees with saws. They were loaded on our wagon, an old truck frame with a single axle underneath. Long stakes pointing upward were placed at the corners of the wagon as supports to keep the trees contained. The trees were taken back to the farm. When the pile held approximately 500 trees, it was time to set up the equipment. A saw rig was mounted to the front of the F-12 Farmall tractor. A pulley belt enabled the tractor to operate the rig.

Dad would hand a tree to Bobby, who would maneuver it into the saw blade. As each piece was severed from the tree, Mom caught it and threw it aside. The blade screamed as it sliced through tree after tree. When time permitted, we would all pile wood into the shed. Throughout winter, armfuls of the wood were carried into the house and placed into a cardboard box.

Fall also meant apple time. We had numerous apple trees and each produced abundantly. Picking apples was fun. A couple of us climbed in the bucket on front of the tractor, and someone else operated the tractor. Swinging the bucket in and around the branches, we might hit a trip lever. We'd be dumped, apples and all.

Apple pie, apple crisp, applesauce, baked apples, canning and freezing apples – you name it, we had it. We had so many we would stop strangers out for a Sunday drive or people lost down our road. They wouldn't leave without a gunnysack or two full of apples.

Fall was also harvest time for our fabulous gardens. We had at least two huge ones. Mom had the green thumb and did most of the gardening. I was the official vegetable picker and cleaner. None could do it better: I was quick, thorough, and did no sneak munching.

Food

Throughout the summer, we enjoyed fresh beans, peas, squash, tomatoes, onions, carrots, beets, and pumpkins so big that just one would fill a wheelbarrow. Cabbage heads were ten inches across. When shredded, one would fill a seven-quart canister.

Our farm provided the majority of our food supply. If we wanted chicken for supper, we'd get one from the coop, kill it, clean it, cook it, and eat it. Chicken was also used many times for holiday meals. The big difference at holidays was that the chicken got stuffed.

In the fall, we also butchered and froze a winter supply of chicken. We'd form an assembly line. Mom would cut off the chickens' heads. After the headless birds flopped around for a while, they would be dunked into a scalding bath. This would release the feathers for easy plucking. This was the job I preferred, since the next step was gutting. I liked to leave that job for the boys. Usually it was a toss-up which of the two jobs I got. I didn't argue. At least I didn't have to cut off their heads.

We picked wild strawberries, June berries, raspberries, blackberries, grapes, currents, and chokecherries. Yum! Picking berries was another of my designated duties. Once again, I refrained from taste-testing. Not an easy task. Tying an empty plastic ice cream pail to my waist with a piece of twine, I would plop down in the field. I simply picked the wild strawberries in a circle around myself. Then up and on to a new spot. Picking berries took hours, and I rarely left before my bucket was full. Grandma would come with us to pick berries, and the entire family would drive to more sandy areas, where blueberries were more abundant. It became a big family outing. We also canned jam and jelly.

The fields are absent of wild strawberries now. Grasshoppers are also sparse. How they would fly up, frightening me with every step I took! Sadly, frog eggs are also gone. Ditches holding water used to be speckled with frog eggs. Gathering them in Mason jars, watching their transformation into tadpoles was a science lesson in itself.

How We Amused Ourselves on the Farm

Behind our old weathered barn stood an enormous manure pile. It was created by load after load of manure transported by wheelbarrow from the barn gutter. Sometimes our Black Angus bull would stand on the hay wagon and eat loose hay. It would take a talented bull to jump so high, but he had a secret. The hay wagon was by the manure pile. He'd climb the pile and step onto the wagon.

My brother, Allen, and I used to play a game called "eenie, ienie, over." We would stand on opposite sides of the pump house. We tossed a ball back and forth over the top of the building as we shouted, "eenie, ienie, over!" There were no warning words, however, the day not a ball but a brick flew over and smacked me alongside the head. Picking up the brick, I ran to their side of the pump house. But they were all gone. Cowards.

We always enjoyed visits from the out-of-state cousins. They became the recipients of country-kid torture. One of our favorite games was called "po-po sticks." First, find a long fallen branch, dip the end in fresh cow pie, then CHASE. The goal: to land a glob on the enemy – I mean, the cousin. But since this was not a contact sport, hitting with the stick was prohibited. Wow, how the cousins would run! Wildly flying through a barbed wire fence, a certain cousin from Minnesota cut her stomach and still carries the scar today. After a mighty chase, treeing the cousins in the barnyard willow meant certain success. Surrounded with an overpowering supply of fresh ammunition, victory was ours.

The boys, in particular, enjoyed playing "war" when the cousins came to visit. A couple of relic military helmets found at Grandma's were distributed. Sticks, broken chair legs, or any miscellaneous metal rods magically transformed into weapons of destruction. Joining in a game or two, I was witness to the brutality of war. Oh, the inhumanity. War included diving, jumping, rolling, and the ever-popular surprise pounce. But beware the grenades. Mushy tomatoes and partly rotten oranges served best for this purpose. Considering the strength of the forces, there was never a casualty of war.

Allen got hold of a couple of used Polaris snowmobiles. It was common knowledge that if you went for a ride on them, you would return walking. Whether stuck in the snow or stranded from a perpetual belt problem, the snowmobiles made the walk inevitable. Traversing and digging through the fields on foot seemed endless. Just as you gained support on the snow, it would cave in, leaving you buried to the thigh. A high step out, false support, and a crunch – once again you'd sink through the icy top layer. Arriving home and acquiring assistance, you were off again to save the sled.

We had a blast when field snow conditions were perfect for snowmobiling. It was smooth sailing. We placed a chair on a toboggan and then tied the toboggan to the snowmobile. Riding the chair through field after field, I'd wave and smile to every passing motorist. I felt like a queen on her throne.

We never had a snowblower. We had Mom. I would have to say that she shoveled the most until we acquired a plow for the tractor. We had to keep our fifty-yard driveway up to the railroad tracks cleared. The county snowplow took over from there and opened the rest of the road. Once, to save Mom from shoveling the area to the tracks, I parked my car in snowplow territory. The snowplow driver buried my car in a mountain of snow. With the help of my brothers, we dug it free. Under the hood, we discovered the engine was completely compacted with snow. We used our hands and cleared what we could. It wouldn't start. My brothers pushed and I popped the clutch. I roared off to work.

Because of finances and obligations to the farm, we never took a vacation. Visiting relatives once in a while was the closest we came. Every other year or so, the entire family would climb in the car and Dad would drive the forty-five minutes to visit Grandpa John and Great-grandpa Ole, who offered us a small bowl of vanilla ice cream with fresh strawberries.

From there, we'd travel down the road to visit Uncle Einar at his strawberry farm. With a thick Norwegian accent, he called out the greeting, "By golly, look who's here," as we stepped from the car. Because the cows back home would need milking again soon, it was a short visit. We would head out, loaded with boxes of big luscious strawberries, courtesy of good ol' Uncle Einar.

Leaving the Farm

Mom and Dad watched over us carefully. This was a difficult task indeed, considering their workload. They trusted us to be responsible for ourselves. Centering our lives on the farm, we worked together as a family. It was the best: a balanced life of hard work with freedom to explore, learn, and grow.

Time passed. The Vietnam War came and Bobby was drafted. When he left, work transferred to the four of us. I left to start a life of my own, and work passed along to Mom, Dad, and Dave. As Dave was making his plans to leave, bulk farming was taking over, which replaced the transportation of milk from cans to bulk tanks on trucks. The process caused the demise of many small dairy farms, including our own. Only the larger farms had the funds to make the transition. Dad retired and sadly passed away a few years later. Mom moved to Grandma's to help care for her.

Now the farm stands alone. The house is gone, as is the barn, garage, pump house, and all the out buildings. But the land remains, vast and desolate. It silently whispers the vibrant haunts of activity past. The wind tells our stories: hardships, struggle, and strife, the lessons of life. Broken barn boards grace the ground, sporadically intertwining with the new brush growth. In the structural sense, nothing remains. But what's meaningful does – the memories.

The Proposal

As I opened the door, he stood with his hat off, nervously fingering the brim. "May I come in?" he asked.

He wore overalls and a simple plaid shirt. Although I didn't know him, his demeanor was non-threatening. I waved him in.

In a shy way, he set about his business. With head tipped, he explained that he was brother-in-law to my Mennonite landlord. He was looking for a wife. His brother-in-law had mentioned that I was single, hard-working, from a farming background, and paid my rent on time. He stated that it would honor him if I became his wife. His proposal made me feel proud. He had a farm, and according to him, the girls nowadays just didn't want to work the farm.

All that hard work had been the reason I left the farm. However, I also had to consider all those wonderful years with acres on which to run, laugh, and be free without judgment.

Recently, I had become engaged to a man whose young wife had died. This had left him with two small children to raise alone. So under the circumstances, I courteously thanked the gentleman for his consideration. I wished him luck on his quest.

With a sad expression, he nodded and started toward the door. Then he turned and looked with sincerity into my eyes. He spoke as deeply with his eyes as he did with his words as he reaffirmed that his offer would hold. His final words were, "Will you please contact me should your engagement break?"

Catching my breath, I whispered, "I will."

RITA LIBERACKI LUKS

I grew up in Unionville, Michigan, graduated from Michigan State University, and taught elementary school in Iowa, Unionville, and then for thirty years in Okemos, MI. After my first retirement I worked with elementary intern teachers at Michigan State University for ten years.

Having time to devote to writing is a treasure. I listened to my father, mother, and her sisters, tell stories for so many years, awed by their talents to paint pictures with words. With my new found time I have begun to write and record my stories for family and others. Many times I've struggled through situations and muttered, "Someday it will make a good story." Someday has arrived.

Since my second retirement I spend my time pursuing whatever I choose to do. Much of it is shared with my supportive husband, John, our seven children, thirteen grandchildren and one great grandchild.

If Something Doesn't Add to the Story, Let It Go

My mind plays with stories, taking bits and pieces from life and fitting them together in many different ways. "Germans" is an example of a story I wrote in my mind long before it ever ended up on paper. I composed different versions of the story depending on where my emphasis was placed. The story changed when I thought about Daddy, where my values related to discrimination came from, the neighborhood and people who surrounded me as I was growing up, or recollections of the way World War II affected me as a child. The story stayed with me, changing form over the years, and resurfacing as I have written it when I combed through my memory for a story to begin writing my life stories.

It would seem that after working a story in my mind for so many years it would easily flow when I sat down to write it, but it never works that way. After writing it down, I go back and fiddle with words in an attempt to choose the exact ones that will convey my ideas. Reading the work aloud helps me feel the flow of the words, and composing on the computer makes them easy to change. When I lay the piece aside and go back to it later, it isn't unusual to have a few words that need to be changed jump out at me. It surprises me how obvious this becomes when I go back to the story with a fresh mind.

I list the points I want to include before actually sitting down to compose a story. How discouraging it is to complete the story and have ideas that haven't been incorporated! It seems like such a waste of something good. Realizing that some words won't add to the story and letting them go is sometimes difficult, but necessary. I tell myself to keep those thoughts in mind, and maybe they will fit in a different story another time. Perhaps it will be the beginning of a new one.

Germans

Sometimes it was frightening just to get home from school. What if the Germans or the Japs were hiding behind the hedge just past McCoy's garden and were waiting to ambush you just before you got to Burgess's driveway? No matter how hard you tried to see through the solid branches of the tall cedars, you didn't know what was on the other side before you got there. You could run to get past there faster, but then you might step on a stone or something else that was booby-trapped and just blow yourself up. At least if you walked, you could avoid such a tragic end and, at the same time, you could step on cracks and help win the war. It worked best if you stepped on the exact center of the crack and chanted loudly in just the right rhythm, "Step on a crack and break a German's back." Or, if it was a day you decided to fight the Japs, it worked just as well to "step on a crack and break a Jap's back!" It was also possible to alternate the enemy from crack to crack and help fight both wars at the same time. That sure gave a lot of power to someone who was just a kid.

I needed to get home. My family needed to be informed of what I had learned at school – that all Germans are bad people.

Henny Penny never had a more urgent message to tell the king. This was life and death. I needed to tell Daddy and make sure the rest of the family knew about it, too.

The supper table was the place to get to everyone at the same time. They'd all be there. We always were. Mother was at the head, with Daddy to her left and Me-Too-Bruce in his high chair next to him. I was on Mother's right, scrunched in by the stove behind me. Andy sat next to me. Judy was at the other end where us younger kids could keep an eye on her to see what she ate, so we'd know what we liked to eat. Then we'd wait to see if she decided the milk was sweet or sour, so we'd know if we should drink it.

That was where I made my announcement about the Germans. The information was all over school, and now my family knew about it, too.

Daddy, who really was wise enough to be king because he knew everything, asked if I knew any Germans. Of course, I didn't.

Germany was way overseas. How would I know any Germans?

He said we knew lots of Germans. Grandma Singer, who lived across the street and grew beautiful flowers that she lovingly overcrowded into the vases she placed on the altar for Sunday mass, was from Germany. Grandma Koreck, who lived just the other side of Aunt Mary and Uncle John next door and also grew beautiful flowers, even though hers were never in church, was also from Germany. If Grandma Singer carried homemade bread across the street to our front door, you could count on Grandma Koreck to reach the back door at almost the same time with fresh-baked strudel. These two wonderful grandmas who tried to outdo each other in keeping our family in baked goods were Germans?

And what about Gaeths, who lived just past Korecks? Did I think they were bad? We ran down the street and stood on the edge of their lawn to watch the train, hoping the engineer and caboose man would wave to us. Ruth Gaeth was so blond and beautiful, and Rollie was the tallest person in the world. Eleanor always talked with me. Their parents usually weren't outside, but they must be nice if their teenagers were. Germans? Really?

Lots of people, like the Hertzlers that went to our church, were Germans. It didn't make sense that bad people would be in church. From that point on, a lot of things didn't make sense. It didn't make sense to say that Germans are bad people when I personally knew that wasn't true. Maybe some Germans, but not all of them, are bad. It made sense not to say, "All Germans are bad people." "All" isn't a very good word to use when you are talking about people.

It was very confusing when Daddy drove us past Hertzler's farm to see German prisoners of war working in the sugar beet fields while soldiers with guns were guarding them.

Maybe Daddy knew how the Germans felt because when he asked my grandpa if he could marry my mother, Grandpa said it was fine with him, but that he should keep this in mind: "There are two things the people in this town hate: Polaks and Catholics."

Disillusions

I got out of the car and walked from Georgia to Alabama. Aunt Mary and Uncle Jack insisted that I walk across the state lines when we crossed from Michigan into Ohio, and they had been ordering me out of the car at every state line from there on.

"Think of it as a great adventure," they said. "How many people do you know of who can honestly say they walked from state to state all the way from Michigan to Georgia?"

A few steps over the border, I climbed back into the car, and we continued on to Demopolis, where we'd meet up with Uncle Jack's sister, who was coming from Texas to return their boxer, which she had been dog sitting for months. I must have shared the back seat all the way back to Fort Benning with that giant dog beside me, yet I don't have a single recollection of the return trip.

I do remember Vera. She worked for the lady we all stayed with in Demopolis. I was reading a book on the sun porch early one morning while waiting for someone else to wake up and keep me company when she came into the room carrying a mop. She was startled when she saw me and started to back out. I told her my name, prattled on about what I was doing there, and offered her a piece of Dentyne gum, which she refused by saying, "I shouldn't take it."

That seemed like a strange reply. Why shouldn't she take it? When I asked her a direct question, she answered me, and I had a lot of direct and very nosy questions. I found out her name was Vera and discovered we were both fifteen that summer of 1953. I asked about her school, but she didn't have one. She had to quit school to go to work and help her family. She had to get up early to walk to the place where she caught a ride on the back of a truck that took her into town, where she worked from seven to four, six days a week. I worked, too, in my dad's restaurant, but only on one or two days after school for a few hours and a shift on Saturday or Sunday. Sometimes, if the Snack Bar was really busy, Daddy would ask me to come in and help. Then I would go in and work through the rush time. If something special was going on at school or with my friends, I didn't have to work at all. And getting to work was much simpler. I could walk, but usually I'd just call and Daddy would come pick me up.

The lady we were staying with paid Vera one dollar a day. Vera paid the truck driver fifty cents a day for her ride. The other fifty cents she gave to her mother to help out the family. I got paid forty cents an hour during the week and sixty cents an hour on the weekend. The money I earned was mine, and I decided how to spend the money myself. I had just saved enough to buy my plane ticket from Atlanta to Detroit and several new outfits to pack in my suitcase. Vera was wearing a faded, old lady dress.

Vera said she couldn't talk anymore. She'd get into trouble for not working and lose her job. All this was just not right for a fifteen-year-old like me. I would get things changed for Vera. That shouldn't be difficult.

I brought up the subject over black bottom pie and sweetened ice tea when our hostess took me out to lunch. "Vera needs a raise." My hostess listened to me explain how Vera really only made fifty cents a day because she paid half of her wages for a ride. She worked hard for nine hours every day and only got to keep fifty cents. A dollar a day wasn't even a fair wage.

Without hesitation, she agreed with me. She said it wasn't right and shouldn't be like that. She told me people always took advantage of Negroes. She wanted to do something about it but she couldn't. That's what other people paid their maids and if she paid Vera more, it would cause a lot of problems. Vera would tell others and they would want more money, too. Then all the people in town would be upset with her for getting something started. No, it would not be right to cause such a problem. My fifteen-year-old mind didn't agree with her reasoning. It wasn't right to cheat Vera just because other people cheated their maids.

My experience was limited. Vera was the only black person I ever had a conversation with, but I knew she'd be better off in Unionville. Thank goodness I didn't live around people who thought like that. Thank goodness my parents weren't that kind of people.

Later that summer, something happened that never had happened before. I was working with Daddy one afternoon when a Negro man, his wife, and a the third person – his wife's mother, I think – parked on the main street right in front of the Snack Bar and came inside. They sat down at the table to the left of the door, right in front of the window. Negroes were in Detroit and down south, not in Unionville.

I looked at them and then at Daddy and said, "What should I do?"

This amused my father. He said, "Go wait on them!"

The man was very polite and ordered for all three of them. I wrote it on my little green pad. One half-chicken, one quarter-chicken (dark meat), one fish and chips, and three coffees with cream. It was like waiting on anyone else. I felt it was a special honor that they chose to come into our restaurant. I kept their water glasses and coffee cups full. If they liked the food and the service, they'd probably come back again. No one else came in while they were there, so I had lots time to give them excellent service.

When the man paid the bill, Daddy started a conversation and walked outside with him. This was one of his favorite things about the restaurant, talking with the customers. When he came back inside, he told me he had just done something that was one of the hardest things he'd ever done in his life. He asked the man to never come back again. He told me that as much as he hated to do that, he didn't have any other choice. The Snack Bar was our livelihood, and if Negroes started coming there, the local people would stay away. The merchants in town wouldn't even sell him the supplies he needed, and he would soon be put out of business. He had to think about his family. My fifteen-year-old mind didn't want to believe any of this happened. There must have been some other choice. Why did he even have to tell me?

Liar

Kids shouldn't be worrying about death, especially one that wasn't going to happen. My challenge as big sister was to help Bruce understand that Father Cahill wasn't going to die. I told him he might have heard someone say that, but just because they said so didn't make it true.

"They don't know what they are talking about. Maybe they just don't know that sometimes people don't die from cancer. Especially priests. Practically everybody in town is saying that Father Cahill is really a saint because he's such a good person. He even likes people who aren't Catholics. He's the chaplain for the fire department. If you want to listen to other people, that's the kind of thing you should listen to. If enough people pray for Father, God will listen to their prayers and let him live. I know people who are Lutherans, Methodists, and Moravians who are praying for him besides all the Catholics who are praying for him. He isn't going to die."

"You lie. You told me the same thing when Sport died."

That happened years before, when our dog ate poisoned meat that a man in town said he put out to kill a wild animal that was hanging around his place. Sport was lying beside the furnace down in the basement, stretched out on his side with his four legs straight out in front of him. The veterinarian said there wasn't anything he could do for him. Bruce was crying, but he calmed down when I told him Sport would be fine, and we knelt together beside our dog, stroking his shiny coat. Besides, I really thought he might get better. He was just lying there, sleeping so calmly. I didn't lie. Why would he even think that and how could he compare a dog to our priest?

Father Cahill died. I really didn't believe he would. I didn't think about what Bruce said about my being a liar for a long time. Not until Daddy died.

Mother and I were doing dishes together on Christmas Eve, and I told her I was glad Daddy was getting better and looking so good since his heart attack. She told me he really wasn't getting better. He was getting worse. His health was extremely bad. The next few days, I was very angry with her for saying such a terrible thing. Four days later, he was dead. I realized that Mother tried to protect me with her honesty. That's when I thought again about what Bruce said.

Years after Daddy died, one of my third grade students was in a tragic automobile accident. He was on the critical list for weeks. Every day my students asked, "Is Matt going to live?" and I told them that the doctors and nurses were doing everything they could to help him get better, but they didn't know yet if he was going to live. Parents began to call me at home demanding that I tell their children he was going to be just fine. I realized it would be wrong to do that. Wanting something to be a certain way wouldn't make it so. Matt lost sight in one eye, but eventually recovered enough to come back to school. I knew I had handled the situation with honesty.

Twenty years later, Bruce asked me if I thought he should have heart by-pass surgery. I was ready, as usual, with my big sister advice. "Go for it! This is your chance for a long lifetime. Just think how different things would have been if that kind of surgery had been available for Daddy. This is your chance to be here for your kids and Sherry. It is absolutely the best thing that could happen for you."

While Bruce was in the hospital, Sherry and Chad stayed at our house. Sherry spent many hours at the hospital, and Chad spent many hours running around with Aunt Rita looking at carpet samples. I knew he was worried about his dad, so I tried to keep him busy. As we were pulling into the Sears parking lot, he was wishing out loud that he were old enough to go visit his dad at the hospital. Next he was telling me that he didn't want his dad to die. Bruce had come through the surgery with no difficulty and would be home ahead of schedule, in a couple days. This time I had my facts straight and didn't just let my heart speak for me. I reassured him that his dad would be home soon and he didn't need to worry about him dying.

Chad spent the next afternoon printing note cards with his cousin Beth. That same evening, his dad died.

Using one of his handmade cards, Chad wrote a note to Bruce and slipped it into his pocket at the funeral home. I never read the note, but I'm sure an eight-year-old would have written, "I LOVE YOU, DAD. LOVE, CHAD." In my worst nightmare, he wrote, "AUNT RITA LIED TO BOTH OF US."

The Candy
Cane

It was there before I even had a chance to think about it. I sat up,
rubbed the sleep from eyes, looked, and looked over the porch railing
at the church across the street – that's when it happened. My hand
reached under the cot, pulled the candy cane I'd been sucking on the
night before out of my shoe, and popped it into my mouth. The
second it touched my tongue, my brain remembered what day this
was. I licked the sweetness off my tongue onto the pillow. Without
swallowing, I ran into the kitchen to get some water. I wiped the candy
off my tongue and then gargled. It shouldn't count the same way as
eating something would. Then I brushed my teeth extra hard. But I
still wasn't really sure. The nuns said you had to fast from midnight
until after you went to communion. God didn't want to get into a
stomach that had food in it. I guess He needed a lot of space when He
jumped out of that tiny white host.

This was my First Communion Day, so I wasn't sure what
happened when God got inside you. I knew you had to fast, and then
when you went to communion, you never chewed the host. It should
just slide down your throat. Chewing it would be like eating God. If it
got stuck to the roof of your mouth, you couldn't put your finger in to
get it off, and it shouldn't touch your teeth at all. You should just keep
on trying to get spit to the roof of your mouth until He got down from
there and went down your throat. I wondered why they called not
eating "fasting." Why didn't they call it going hungry? And why
midnight? Kids don't stay up until midnight. I didn't really
understand it, but going to communion was going to make me very
holy, and this would be a very special day.

You could make your first communion if you didn't eat anything
after midnight and if you didn't do any more sinning after going to
confession. I didn't do any more sinning, but I was worried about that
candy cane going right into my mouth and messing up my fasting.
Sinning was easy not to do. I had been to confession already. I
confessed all my sins. I couldn't really remember just exactly how
many times I disobeyed my mother and father in my whole life, so I
said ten times. That sounded like a number God would believe. I was

a pretty good kid and usually did what my parents told me to do. I didn't think I should make up any more numbers because God might not like it, so for my second sin, I just said that sometimes I fought with my brothers and sister. I didn't think God expected any more sins than that from a seven-year-old kid. They were all just the venial kind. I hoped it was OK with God that I didn't tell any mortal ones, but it would have been another venial kind if I made up a lie about having any mortal ones. I never killed anyone so I didn't have any mortal sins. I studied everyone ahead of me in the line to go to confession, and I didn't think they did any mortal ones either. The nuns acted like we had both kinds to tell the priest about. I figured they couldn't have any kids of their own, so they probably didn't know much about us. I also thought it was strange that they were all married to God. But that didn't have anything to do with this problem.

There were other things they didn't really understand either. They told us that babies that aren't baptized couldn't get into heaven. I had a baby brother who died. He was baptized, so he was in heaven, but I knew God wouldn't just send other babies who weren't to a limbo place. Big people who sinned could go to purgatory and someday get to heaven, but a baby who never did anything wrong couldn't ever get into heaven. Who would really believe that?

They said lots of people never went to heaven. Only Catholics could go to heaven. Other people went where the dead babies were. It wasn't their fault that they didn't know they had to be Catholic. I believed God took all good people to heaven, but I didn't tell the nuns that. If they believed God was good and kind and loving, they would figure that out for themselves. We were Catholic, but Grandpa and Grandma Wilcox weren't. They went to a Methodist church, and they planned on going to heaven. Mother and Daddy never said some people couldn't go to heaven. Just the nuns told us that in catechism class.

They said some other things, too. They said that when we went to confession, the priest couldn't really see who he was talking to because there was a piece of black screen hiding the person going to confession. The priest was supposed to be God's messenger on earth, and he could give people some penance. Like he'd tell them to say three or five Hell Marys and three or five Our Fathers, and the sins went away. The nuns said he couldn't see who was talking to him, but he really could. I have proof of it. I know he could see me because when I saw Father John after I went to confession, he put my hands together and told me the next time I went to confession I should remember to hold my hands like that. He also told my parents that I said Hell Mary and not Hail Mary. I heard them laughing.

Maybe they were also wrong about your stomach having to be so empty. I really didn't think any candy taste got down there; but just in case it did, it would be good to know they were wrong again. I didn't tell Mother and Daddy about the nuns being wrong about other things, so I didn't want to tell them about the candy. Maybe they would say the nuns were right about it, and they wouldn't let me put on my new white dress and fancy veil and make my first communion.

I'd decide for myself.

Just Talking

This was truly a Shit! Damn! Hell! situation if there ever was one. Few occasions arose that evoked my newly acquired complete college cursing vocabulary. It was going to get nasty, and I had brought it on myself. Kind of. If they just automatically stuck money in my checking account ahead of time, I never would have had to call home and say I wrote out a check for $14 to the court and it needed to be covered. No questions, and this would never be happening to me.

When I gazed out the window and saw *both* of them standing there, I knew I was in trouble. Daddy was never comfortable leaving the Snack Bar at this busy time of day, and Mother didn't need any help to find her way to the Bay City bus station. And there they stood. Together. This wasn't the typical, "I'm glad you're home. Do you want to go shopping while we're here in Bay City?" kind of day like Mother and I often spent together.

To make a bad situation worse, they just acted like everything was normal. Ever since I could remember, they would say, "You know what will happen if you do that," and I never had the nerve to go ahead and do what I may have been contemplating because I didn't have a clue as to what would happen. I certainly wasn't brave enough or foolish enough to find out. It must be really terrible, but because nothing terrible ever happened to me, I couldn't imagine what it could possibly be. They went on chatting about my brothers, Mother's school, and the snack bar. I went on thinking about their taking me out of MSU, and what it was going be like just living at home and working in the snack bar.

Maybe they didn't believe what I told them. It was really very simple. My boyfriend and I went out for coffee. Then we went for a drive and pulled off the road just to talk. A deputy sheriff knocked on the car window and said we were trespassing and gave us a summons to appear in court. We agreed to share the cost of the ticket, and that's why I had to write out the $14 check. All this was exactly true.

If they could get so upset by something so simple, it was a good thing I didn't give them the details about cutting classes to go for coffee and an early morning drive and then being forced to cut classes again to go to court. There was no need for them to hear about how frightened we were when we heard someone pounding on the window. My friend cleared a circle on the steamed-up window, and there stood a deputy, who asked what we were doing in there.

"Talking," we said.

"Talking?" he replied.

"Yes, just talking."

He commented that it must have been some conversation if we didn't even see the flashing lights on his car that was parked right at our back bumper. The property owner had called and complained, so he said he'd have to issue us a ticket for trespassing. I about died of embarrassment when the judge said we should rent a motel room if we wanted to talk. Next he ordered us to pay a $28 fine. We *weren't* doing what he thought!

We got as far as Quanacasee, and they both became silent. I braced myself. I saw my parents nudge each other. They were looking straight ahead, so I couldn't even read their faces. "I put the money in your checking account to cover the check you wrote to the court. Your mother and I have spent a lot of time talking about it."

This was going to be even worse than I imagined. They'd had a week and a half to mull it over and decide what to do. It was quiet again. Mother moved a bit closer to Daddy in the front seat, but no one turned to look at me. They were in no hurry to divulge whatever it was they were going to say. By now we were going through Wisner, and they nudged each other again.

Mother broke the silence. "When we were in college, we drove out to the country for a picnic. When we came back out of the woods, someone had built a fence around the car. We couldn't figure out how to get the car out."

"So I took down a section of the fence and we got out of there!" Daddy added.

This story was disgusting. These were *my parents*. It takes all day to build a fence. I didn't do anything that bad. There was one thing I had to know even though I didn't want to hear the answer. "What were you doing in the woods for so long?" I asked.

"Just talking," came the reply.

Mother scooted over closer Daddy. He put his arm around her shoulders, and they laughed the rest of the way home about how they knew I'd be worried because I was always so responsible. The memories it brought back for them were worth a lot more than $14.

Need more copies?

Need more copies? Want your own copy? Looking for a resource of 636 writing prompts to jump start your memoirs?

❏ The Teacher Who Ate Her Pet
  and Other True Stories by 32 People Like You
  Price: $16.95*
  Quantity: _____   Total: $ _____

❏ Something that Happened at Night:
  A Workbook to Begin Your Memoirs or End Writer's Block
  Price: $11.95*
  Quantity: _____   Total: $ _____

For orders shipped to Michigan, please add 6% tax _____

Shipping:
  $4 for the first book, $2 for each additional book _____

Check or money order
Payable to Talk Pretty Press for   TOTAL: _____

Name _____

Position _____

Institution name _____

Address _____

City _____ State _____ Zip _____

Phone _____ FAX _____

Email _____

Please mail to:
102 Sheridan Drive
Monroe MI 48162

Call 517.775.2636 to order NOW
Or e-mail nancyseubert@aol.com

* price subject to change without notice.

Need more copies?

Need more copies? Want your own copy? Looking for a resource of 636 writing prompts to jump start your memoirs?

❑ The Teacher Who Ate Her Pet
and Other True Stories by 32 People Like You
Price: $16.95*
Quantity: _____   Total: $ _____

❑ Something that Happened at Night:
A Workbook to Begin Your Memoirs or End Writer's Block
Price: $11.95*
Quantity: _____   Total: $ _____

For orders shipped to Michigan, please add 6% tax _____

Shipping:
$4 for the first book, $2 for each additional book _____

Check or money order
Payable to Talk Pretty Press for   TOTAL: _____

Name _____

Position _____

Institution name _____

Address _____

City _____ State _____ Zip _____

Phone _____ FAX _____

Email _____

Please mail to:
102 Sheridan Drive
Monroe MI 48162

Call 517.775.2636 to order NOW
Or e-mail nancyseubert@aol.com

* price subject to change without notice.